BUILDING
A
SPEECH

BUILDING A SPEECH

SECOND EDITION

Sheldon Metcalfe

Catonsville Community College

THE HARCOURT PRESS

Harcourt Brace College Publishers

Fort Worth Philadelphia San Diego New York Orlando Austin San Antoni
Toronto Montreal London Sydney Tokyo

Publisher	Ted Buchholz
Acquisitions Editor	Carol Wada
Developmental Editor	Laurie Runion
Senior Project Editor	Cliff Crouch
Senior Production Manager	Tad Gaither
Art Director	Priscilla Mingus
Electronic Publishing Coordinator	Barbara McGinnis

Library of Congress Catalog Card Number: 93-81244

International Standard Book Number: 0-15-501128-6

Address for editorial correspondence: Harcourt Brace College Publishers
301 Commerce Street, Suite 3700
Fort Worth, Texas 76102

Address for orders: Harcourt Brace, Inc.
6277 Sea Harbor Drive
Orlando, Florida, 32887

Phone: 800 / 782-4479, or
(*in Florida only*) 800 / 433-0001

Printed in the United States of America

5 6 7 8 9 0 1 2 3 4   067   9 8 7 6 5 4

To my mother,
who gave me the values,
and my father, who gave me the vision
to write this book

Contents in Brief

Quick Topic Reference Guide

Contents

Preface: To the Instructor

Public speaking is a building process, wherein students gradually acquire skills in speech research, organization, and delivery. Students learn these skills step by step from their own experiences, by observing the presentations of others, through peer criticism, and from the guidance of effective instructors. This textbook presents five units that organize skills in a sequence that is meaningful and understandable to students.

PLAN OF THE BOOK

Unit I, "Surveying the Territory," presents the classical origins of public speaking as well as the modern theories of communication. In addition, it considers audience analysis, listening, ethics, and apprehension; and it introduces students to their first speaking assignment.

Unit II, "Preparing the Foundation," describes how to select topics, write purpose statements, conduct research, and choose supporting materials for speeches.

Unit III, "Creating the Structure," discusses outlining and speech introductions and conclusions.

Unit IV, "Refining the Appearance," describes the refinements necessary to complete speech construction. It helps students build skills in delivery and language, and it explains the use of visual aids to support a topic.

Unit V, "Considering Different Types of Structures," describes informative, descriptive, and demonstration speeches; persuasive speaking, with sample convincing and actuating speeches; presentations for special occasions, including the after-dinner speech; and speaking in group situations.

FEATURES OF THE SECOND EDITION

Building a Speech, Second Edition, retains all of the successful features of the initial book. It is written in a conversational style that appeals to students, and it presents a flexible arrangement adaptable to a variety of instructional approaches. It continues to offer guidelines for major speaking assignments, present information about recent technologies in research and audiovisual aids, and provide interesting sample speeches. This edition also includes updated examples and illustrations, additional theory in the audience analysis chapter, and amended exercises and bibliographies throughout. It retains the early speaking chapter, the popular chapter on apprehension, and the helpful presentation of alternative introductions and conclusions. In addition, *Building a Speech* now includes some important new features.

New Chapter on Ethics

As a result of scandalous or questionable ethical behavior, leaders in government, private industry, sports, and religion have in recent decades been monitored more closely than ever before by the public and media. It is therefore appropriate for a public speaking textbook to present material that describes the historical significance of ethics, helps students to evaluate ethical speaking behavior, and recommends alternatives to students making difficult choices in speech development. Chapter 6, "Considering the Ethics of Public Speaking," focuses on each of these areas and includes a speech—"The Right Way: A Matter of Principle," by James E. Perrella—that raises some important ethical issues.

New Informative and Persuasive Speaking Chapters

Informative speaking is now presented in two chapters. Chapter 15, "Speaking to Inform," examines the difference between information and persuasion, considers several categories of informative speeches, and concentrates on the descriptive speech. It provides guidelines for descriptive presentations, and presents a sample descriptive speech entitled "The Computer Virus: Disease of the Computer Age." Several alternative introductions and conclusions are included to help students recognize a single speech can begin and end with a variety of creative strategies. Chapter 16, "Informative Speaking: Demonstrating Procedures," focuses on the process speech. It provides guidelines to help students develop presentations employing audiovisual aids. A student demonstration speech, "Having a Heart," includes visual aids to help with discussion and analysis.

Persuasion is also presented in two chapters. Chapter 17, "Speaking to Persuade," describes the nature of persuasion, identifies types of persuasive appeals, and discusses persuasive organization. It includes guidelines for the speech to convince and presents a new student speech, "Let's Stop Auto Repair Rip-Offs!" The sample convincing speech presents two speech bodies to help students understand different organizational techniques. A speech body using the reasons sequence is presented in Chapter 17, and a speech body using the problem–cause–solution approach is included in Appendix A. Chapter 18, "Speaking to Persuade: Motivating Audiences," identifies strategies for motivating audiences, describes Monroe's motivated sequence, and offers guidelines for constructing the persuasive speech to actuate. A new actuating speech, "Ignorance Is Not Bliss," is included to help students apply the steps of the motivated sequence.

New Critical Thinking Section

Many college and university speech courses present units on critical thinking to help students examine research and evaluate data more comprehensively. Chapter 2, "Building Your First Speech," includes a new section on critical thinking to encourage students to test information, structure their thoughts logically, listen to different perspectives, and think independently. Several exercises are presented to give students practical experience in thinking critically.

Expanded Research Chapter

Chapter 8, "Conducting Research," includes comprehensive lists of library references, and provides descriptions of general references and substantive sources that will help students understand the differences among principal investigative tools. It also lists major software versions of periodical indexes that can be found in many college and university library computer systems.

Revised Gender and Culture Sections in Audience Analysis Chapter

Chapter 3, "Analyzing Your Audience," includes a revised section that presents conclusions from several studies supporting differences in psychological perspective that arise from gender. In addition, it contains an expanded section on cultural and ethnic origins designed to provide students with a greater awareness of the challenges facing public speakers in an ethnically sensitive society.

New Speeches

The second edition contains four new speeches. In addition to speeches by Garry Trudeau and Jesse Jackson, Appendix A now includes "Remarks" presented to the Republican National Convention by AIDS sufferer Mary Fisher. James E. Perella's speech "The Right Way: A Matter of Principle" appears in Chapter 6. Complementing existing informative speeches developed by students are two new student-prepared persuasive speeches. The convincing speech, "Let's Stop Auto Repair Rip-Offs!" is presented in Chapter 17, and an actuating speech, "Ignorance Is Not Bliss," appears in Chapter 18.

ANCILLARY PACKAGE

The ancillary package for *Building a Speech*, Second Edition, contains an instructor's manual complete with learning activities, a test bank, transparency masters, and a videotape which includes both professional and student speeches.

Acknowledgments

A writing project of this scope cannot be accomplished without the assistance of many individuals. My thanks goes to the reviewers whose comments helped in the revision of the second edition: Christopher Bates, University of Maine; Gary Eckles, Thomas Nelson Community College; John LaHoud, Ulster County Community College; Jim Moody, South Suburban College; Gary Shaffer, Ambassador College; and Marlene Taber, College of the Sequoias.

I also want to acknowledge the Harcourt Brace team for this new edition: Laurie Runion, developmental editor; Clifford Crouch, senior project editor; Priscilla Mingus, art director; Tad Gaither, senior production manager; and Barbara McGinnis, electronic publishing coordinator.

Kathryn Lang, developmental editor for the first edition, continues to provide friendly encouragement and interest. I am also indebted to many outstanding colleagues at Catonsville Community College, including a superb library staff who were important resources for numerous areas of the book. And my wonderful public speaking students deserve special praise for their continued help, creative examples, and energetic suggestions. Finally, Howard and Betty Metcalfe have always provided encouragement and support throughout this time-consuming process.

Introduction: To the Student

Building a Speech, Second Edition, is designed to help you become a success-ful public speaker. It is grounded in the philosophy that you, like most under-graduate students, can master the steps of speech construction if provided with a caring environment, clear blueprints, and creative examples.

This book establishes a caring environment through a conversational style that aims to both interest and motivate you. It conveys encouragement by including topics, such as apprehension and listening, that will help you to real-ize that you are not alone in your struggles. This book gives you direction by providing detailed blueprints for major speaking assignments, and by includ-ing specific principles for audience analysis, speech outlining, use of audiovi-sual aids, and delivery. Finally, since students learn best through examples, *Building a Speech* includes numerous illustrations, instances, and examples taken from the presentations of basic speech students who have successfully applied textbook theory.

It is my hope that by reading this book and by actively participating in your speech course, you will be able to achieve your full potential as a suc-cessful speaker in all aspects of your life.

UNIT OUTLINE

Chapter One

INTRODUCING THE STUDY OF PUBLIC SPEAKING

Chapter Outline

Key Terms and Names

Aristotle
Channel
Cicero
Communication model
Corax
Decoding
Encoding
Ethos
Feedback
Gorgias
Logos
Message
Noise
Pathos
Plato
Quintilian
Receiver
Rhetoric
Sender
Setting
Shannon and Weaver
Sophists
Sophistry
Source
Symbol

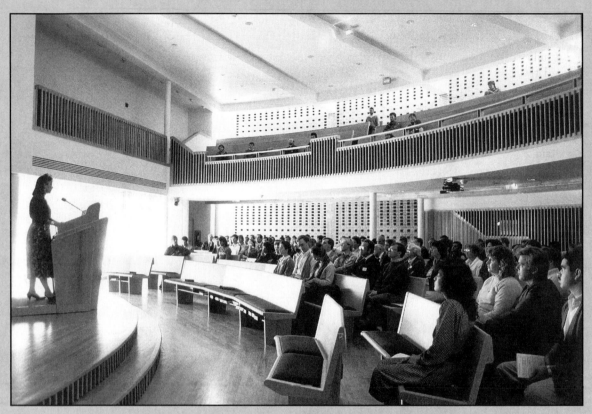

Janice Fullman Photography/
Picture Cube

"The right to be heard does not include
the right to be taken seriously. The latter
depends on what is being said."
—HUBERT HUMPHREY

*D*uring the recession of the early 1990s, college graduates have found themselves facing a declining job market. Studies conducted at Northwestern and Michigan State Universities concluded that almost one-third of the jobs for recent graduates had been eliminated because of the poor economy. In fact, the *Chronicle of Higher Education* referred to the process of job-seeking as a "fight."[1]

In difficult economic times, effective communication is more important than ever. Successful communication helps us to compete for new positions or to maintain present ones. Active listening enables us to acquire additional job skills or to build networks with colleagues. Clear organization allows us to convey our ideas logically. Understanding techniques of delivery gives us the ability to adapt our messages to different listeners and settings. While the application of communication skills cannot guarantee us a job or a career, a knowledge of these building blocks can at least help us to compete, giving us a "fighting" chance.

Chapter 1 considers the importance of communication in today's world and presents historical perspectives about communication. In addition, it describes a contemporary communication model and applies its components to public speaking.

COMMUNICATION IN THE MODERN WORLD

Imagine that you have lined up two job interviews. The morning interview is for a position as a computer programmer with a nationally known company; the afternoon interview, for a similar post at a smaller firm. You are a little nervous, but you feel confident that you will make an impression.

On arriving at the mirrored office complex on the twenty-first floor, you are ushered through a maze of work modules into a conference room, where twelve people are seated in swivel chairs around a long table. At the opposite end is someone named Frank, who stands and introduces himself as the division director. He asks you to take about five minutes to describe your education, work experience, and pertinent skills. You begin:

> Well, I, uh, uh, I, uh, I've heard a lot about this company, and I wanted to tell you about my experience. I had another job with a company—I was a computer programmer with UNISYS, but uh, uh…Oh, wait! Before I talk about that, I wanted to show you some stuff I brought. Uh, uh, I have it right here—it's got to be here somewhere—I had it this morning. Oh, well. . .

The interview is terminated quickly. You are crushed. You had not expected the interviewer to ask you to give a five-minute presentation about yourself. You did make an impression: You were disorganized and unprepared.

You recover from the morning disaster and regroup for the afternoon appointment. You grab lunch and jot down four principal areas you want to emphasize about yourself. After writing an outline, you practice your speech, discarding irrelevant points and mentally weeding out verbal distractions such as "uh, uh."

Arriving at the small computer business, you are welcomed into the outer office. "Barbara" introduces herself and invites you into a lounge area, where you begin your presentation:

> I'm really glad to meet all of you. You appear to have a growing business here. As I came in, I noticed that people seemed to have enthusiasm and energy, but I also noticed that they appeared relaxed. Those are qualities in a prospective working environment that I think are important. I also noticed that you have a lot of IBM-compatible equipment. I've trained on IBM hardware and software systems, and I've also had experience working with many other computer systems and software packages. So what I'd like to do, if it's okay with you, is to describe my education, job experience, and some special skills I possess which I think could be helpful to your organization.

Although the preceding examples are hypothetical, they are realistic life situations which may remind you of similar experiences of your own. In the first interview, the applicant rambled and hesitated due to lack of preparation; in the second, the prospective employee presented introductory remarks with clarity and precision. We can't categorically state that the disorganized interview destroyed the applicant's chances, nor can we say that the well-prepared interview produced immediate success. But a well-organized applicant has a much better chance of making a positive impression and of achieving successful results.

While a job interview is one type of speaking situation we all must face, effective communication skills are needed in many additional situations. Consider:

Giving a friend some simple street directions to a party

Proposing a toast at a wedding

Watching a bank teller demonstrate how to use the 24-hour money machine

Hearing a doctor describe a surgical procedure he must perform on a family member

Expressing sympathy to a colleague over the loss of a close friend or family member

Motivating a church group to donate canned food and clothing to the needy at Thanksgiving

Persuading an IRS tax auditor that a deduction was a legitimate business expense

Listening to the boss explain reasons for not granting a promotion

Convincing a police officer not to write a parking ticket

The above list includes speeches that provide information, reinforce feelings, and demonstrate a process. It also includes speeches of action and speeches of conviction. Each situation requires effective speaking and listening skills.

We are also affected by communication beyond our own territory. We are touched when ex-basketball star Ervin "Magic" Johnson comforts a little girl who is infected with AIDS. We send clothing and medical help when we see thousands of Americans who have lost their homes because of a flood. We donate food when we hear the pleas of starving families in Somalia. We feel angry when we see the followers of Saddam Hussein chanting "Death to America." We examine our living standard when a presidential candidate asks "How are you doing?" We weigh the arguments as United States senators debate the pros and cons of a nomination to the Supreme Court. We laugh when we hear comedian Dana Carvey do an impression of Ross Perot. We fall silent when an ex-soldier reads names on the wall of the Vietnam Memorial.

Every day of our lives, we apply principles of communication. We inform, we shape, and we move others; we are equally informed, molded, and moved by others. Our success in these everyday situations often depends upon how effectively we speak and how carefully we listen.

Success will take some energy on your part. But, if you are willing to spend the time, you can improve your speaking skills and be more successful in each situation you encounter. Remember that your goal is not to be Arsenio Hall, Liza Minelli, Tom Cruise, Hillary Clinton, Whoopi Goldberg, or Ronald Reagan. Your goal is to be you: a more confident and effective you.

THE CLASSICAL ORIGINS OF SPEAKING

In ancient times, public speaking was called rhetoric, which means "the art of the orator."[2] Classical rhetoric specifically dealt with skill in persuasive oratory, or the ability to convince and move an audience to a specific point of view.

Corax is considered to be one of the founders of rhetoric. In the fifth century B.C., a tyrant subjugated the citizens of Sicily and confiscated their property. When the dictator was overthrown and democracy restored to the island, the courts were jammed with people trying to reclaim their lands. Corax influenced judicial oratory by developing a method of speaking that helped the common people argue their court cases more successfully.

Gorgias (483–376 B.C.) was a brilliant speechmaker and a highly influential teacher in Athens. He tended to emphasize an ornate style, figures of speech, and emotionalism. Those such as Gorgias who taught oratory and charged a fee to their students were called *sophists*. At first sophists were respected teachers, but later a number of con artists took over the schools and exploited students solely for financial profit. The word sophistry came to have negative connotations, implying the use of deceitful methods and faulty reasoning.

Isocrates (436–338 B.C.) was a rhetorician even more influential in Athenian society than Gorgias. In addition to teaching many Greek orators, Isocrates wrote a number of manuscripts and an autobiography describing his ideas. He believed that a speaker should be well educated in the liberal arts and of good moral character, and he emphasized that a speaker must possess freedom and independence, yet demonstrate self-control. He adapted the ornate style of Gorgias into a more fluid prose style of writing and speaking.

Plato (428–348 B.C.) had little regard for rhetoricians such as Gorgias and Isocrates. He described his concepts in "dialogues," which were stories written in play form. In his dialogue entitled *Gorgias*, Plato attacks the methods of the sophists and claims that rhetoric is not a useful pursuit. In his dialogue *Phaedrus*, Plato charges that sophists corrupt young people and that rhetoricians are more interested in dishonesty, style, and opinion than in truth. While he conceded that rhetoric could deal with truth, he continued to insist that rhetoric was "not a true art."

Plato's famous student Aristotle (384–322 B.C.) wrote *The Rhetoric* and challenged many of Plato's negative opinions about oratory. To Plato's charge that rhetoric lacks truth, Aristotle responds that objective truth exists only in science and mathematics. Plato wrote that rhetoric is flawed because men base their reasoning on opinions and beliefs; Aristotle replied that belief is the highest degree of certainty in the world of human beings. Aristotle introduced what he called three methods of proofs: *ethos*, the ethical appeal; *pathos*, the emotional appeal; and *logos*, the appeal to logic and reason. Aristotle's work helped to elevate public speaking to a respected place and has influenced thinkers and speakers to the present day.

Among those influenced by Aristotle were Cicero and Quintilian, two Roman orators who also added to the literature of rhetoric. Cicero (106–43 B.C.) was a skillful orator and a respected teacher who thought that the speaker should be educated in the liberal arts.[3] In his book *De Oratore*, he discusses topics such as writing, audience analysis, anxiety, evidence, and argument. Quintilian (35–95 A.D.) was a famous Roman lawyer who stressed that the "true orator must be, above all, a good man . . . skilled in speaking."[4] In his book *The Institutes of Oratory*, he describes the speaker's purpose when he writes: "There are also three objects which an orator must accomplish: to inform, to move, to please."[5]

Classical rhetoric involved real human beings who persuaded, who moved, and who influenced nations and civilizations. The writings of Aristotle, Cicero, and Quintilian were read by thinkers during the Renaissance, by reformers in England, and by revolutionaries in colonial America. Men such as Patrick Henry, Thomas Paine, Thomas Jefferson, and James Madison applied many of Aristotle's speaking techniques and energized the spirit of a new nation. Throughout our history speakers such as Abraham Lincoln, Sojourner Truth, Susan B. Anthony, Theodore Roosevelt, Franklin D. Roosevelt, John F. Kennedy, and the Reverend Martin Luther King, Jr. have applied ancient speaking principles to move an often reluctant nation into a more ethical course of action.

The classical Greeks and Romans influence *our* communication as well. When you arrange a speech into an introduction, body, and conclusion, you are applying Aristotle. When you research your topic, Cicero smiles. When you practice the delivery, Quintilian nods knowingly. When you apply moral principles, Isocrates sheds a joyful tear. We are indebted to these individuals for their contributions, and we continue to employ their speaking principles in our contemporary lives.

THE COMMUNICATION PROCESS

When we speak in any given situation, most of us take communication for granted; sometimes we succeed and sometimes we fail. But communication is not merely a haphazard, trial-and-error occurrence. Often there are very good reasons for our success or failure. The more we understand about the process of communication, the more we can improve our skills.

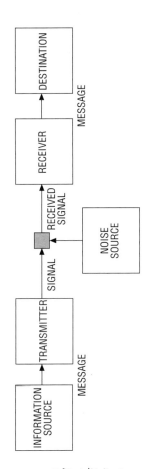

FIGURE 1.1

Claude Shannon and Warren Weaver, *The Mathematical Theory of Communication*, copyright 1949 by the University of Illinois Press. Used by permission.

A great many experts have written about communication and have developed theories called "communication models." In the 1940s, Claude Shannon, an engineer at the Bell Telephone Company, and Warren Weaver, a mathematician, wrote *The Mathematical Theory of Communication*,[6] which became a classic in the field. Shannon and Weaver stated that in order for communication to take place, there must be a *source*, a *message*, a *channel*, and a *receiver*.

While this model was helpful in understanding communication, it was later criticized for its lack of flexibility. This communication model was often illustrated as a flat line with a source at one end, the message and channel in the middle, and the receiver at the other end. The model tended to give the inaccurate impression that communication is a static activity which does not change or develop. The model may accurately simulate mechanical transmission of signals over a telephone line, but it does not describe the fluid interaction of human beings.

More recent theories have emphasized the idea that communication is dynamic: It is always changing, growing, and developing.[7] These communication models can be illustrated by a circle rather than a line. Senders can receive messages as they are sending them; receivers can likewise send and receive at the same time. Human communication can be adjusted to new feedback and influenced by the environment. Communication changes and unfolds on the basis of ever-changing human experiences.

A Communication Model

It is helpful to establish a model to understand the dynamic process of communication. We will consider seven aspects: sender, message, channel, receiver, feedback, setting, and noise. And to explain each part of the model, we will use a simple example: a job interview between two people.

The Sender: Encoding Ideas into Symbols   The *sender* is the originator of communication. Within the sender are the ideas, thoughts, feelings, and intentions which begin the process of communication. Suppose, for example, that you are the sender in a two-way conversation. The idea–thought–feeling

FIGURE 1.2

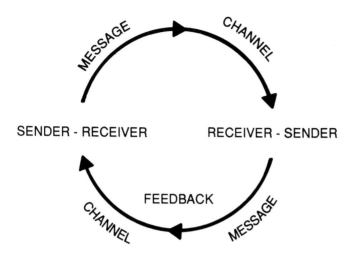

"employment" has just popped into your brain. You reflect upon the idea for awhile until you encode it. *Encoding* is simply the thought process and motor skill of the sender that changes an idea–thought–feeling into an understandable symbol. *Symbols* are verbal and non-verbal expressions or actions which have meaning. In this case, words such as *job* and *applying* symbolize the verbal meanings, and a handshake and an application form would symbolize the non-verbal meanings.

The Message   Even though symbols have meaning, they must be arranged in some kind of logical structure. If you said "job, applying..." there would be meaning, but the verbal symbols would lack organization and might be confusing. If you smiled and said the word "I..." the non-verbal coupled with the word symbol would still be incomplete. You must have a *message*, which is a set of structured symbols. So you decide to encode your ideas into the message "I'm applying for the job..." You, the sender, have now taken the idea–thought–feeling from inside your brain, encoded or changed the idea–thought–feeling into a set of word symbols (*applying, job, I'm*), and arranged these symbols into an organized structure called a message: "I'm applying for the job..." Your message is clear, precise, and understandable: It has meaning to you, and potentially to someone else. But while you have organized the appropriate message, you have not yet been able to communicate to the other person.

The Channel   The next step in the communication process is the selection of a channel. A *channel* is the means of transporting the message. The channels we use to transmit messages are sensory: We convey our messages through sight, sound, smell, taste, and touch. To communicate, you must now choose one or more of these sensory channels to convey the message, "I'm applying for the job..." You could simply state the message. You could present a résumé, you could shake the interviewer's hand, or you could smile. You could even wear a stylish suit and apply some appropriate cologne or perfume before the interview. Each decision presents you with a different combination of sensory channels. You therefore make the decision to use all or some of these techniques to employ as many senses as are desirable.

The Receiver: Decoding Symbols into Ideas   At this point in the process there is a sender (encoding the ideas into symbols), a message, and several channels. However, communication is still incomplete because no connection has been made to the receiver. The receiver is the destination, the goal of communication. When you come face to face with your interviewer, you now have the potential for communication since you have a destination for the message. You verbally state, "I'm applying for the job. . ." Non-verbally, you smile, shake the individual's hand, and present your résumé.

Immediately, the process that occurred to generate communication within the sender now occurs in reverse within the receiver. The receiver *decodes*, or changes the symbols in your organized message into ideas–thoughts–feelings that the receiver can use to give meaning to the message. While we now have a receiver and decoding to add to the communication model, we still need a response to complete the communication circle.

Feedback   *Feedback* is a verbal or non-verbal response. Feedback can tell you whether communication has occurred, how it has been received, and whether it has been understood. Feedback is a reaction from the receiver to the sender: It can be positive and negative, verbal and non-verbal. Feedback provides dimension and transforms communication from a one-way into a two-way process.

The most obvious feedback is from the receiver. Having gone to all the trouble you just took to send your multi-channel message, you hope for positive feedback, such as, "I'm happy to accept your application. You have a good chance for the job." You could also receive additional sensory feedback, such as a pat on the back or an invitation to lunch. We hate to mention this, but negative feedback can occur as well. The interviewer could conceivably respond by throwing your résumé on the floor, pointing to the door, and stalking out of the room.

But the wonderful thing about feedback is that it can transform senders into receivers, and receivers into senders; we can send and receive messages simultaneously and alter our messages based upon the responses that occur. As you send your "employment" message, you become aware that your interviewer is smiling. Upon receiving this information you modify your message. You return the smile, move toward the interviewer, and say "I really like this company—everyone seems so friendly." Messages continue to change on the

FIGURE 1.3

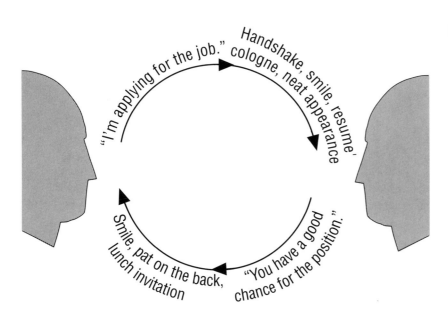

basis of new information sent and received. Feedback circularizes communication, provides dimension, and allows us to adapt to new circumstances.

Setting   The communication process does not exist in a vacuum. Instead, it occurs in a *setting*, which includes occasion, environment, space, and time. A speaker must consider how the occasion influences the message. The physical and psychological conditions differ for a business meeting, an anniversary, a marriage proposal, a birthday, or a Christmas party. When the occasion is clearly understood beforehand, the speaker selects an environment that will be appropriate for the delivery of message.

An administrator arranging a job interview could imitate the opening example of this chapter and choose a formal conference room with a long table. This intimidating environment could be designed to convey rigidity and control to the prospective employee. On the other hand, an interviewer might use the second approach and select a lounge area with comfortable chairs and background music to convey informality and cooperation. The employer might consider spatial factors by seating individuals at a round table near a bright window ornamented with hanging plants. The interview could be scheduled for the lunch hour, when messages could be communicated in a relaxed and unhurried manner.

You can see the importance of setting in supporting the communication process. When thinking through any speaking situation, consider the aspects of occasion, environment, space, and time so that the setting will support your communication successfully.

Noise We have established that for communication to take place there must be a sender, message, channel, receiver, feedback, and a setting. Noise, however, is a factor that can cause disruption or disturb the flow of communication. *Noise* is a distortion or a distraction to communication: It interferes with the process and reduces the effectiveness of communication. There are three types of noise: external, internal, and semantic.

External noise External noise is any interference that can be perceived by the senses in the speech setting. It is important to emphasize that the word *noise* does not always refer to sound. If you try to deliver your employment message and your interviewer suddenly glimpses the arrival of specially ordered equipment, chances are that your message won't be completely communicated. If the inter-

FIGURE 1.4

Cartoon by George Goebel

viewer is interrupted by the intercom buzzer every five seconds, your message is not likely to be received clearly. Or the location of the interview may be so chilly that your potential employer is concentrating on shivering rather than listening to you. If the external noise is too great, communication will be lost. For communication to occur, either the interference must be eliminated or the sender must adapt to the situation. If the room is too cold, you can diplomatically suggest that the heat be turned up or that the meeting move to another room. If there are numerous interruptions in the conversation, you can try to condense your presentation or make a comment or a joke about the situation.

Internal noise While you can usually sense the source of external noise, you cannot always perceive the cause of internal noise. Internal noise is any interference or disruption to communication that occurs within the receiver. You may have just said "I'm applying for the job and I have a résumé and a portfolio for you to see" and you discover that your interviewer isn't listening at all. In fact, the facial expression of your prospective employer reflects tension. There may be any number of internal distractions acting as barriers to you. The individual may be ill, worrying about a personal problem, or combating distress from a confrontation with an employee. As a speaker you cannot always know what internal problems are causing distractions within listeners, but unless the distractions are removed little communication can occur.

Finding the source of the negative feedback is sometimes a way to understand the disruption and restore communication. If you are sensitive to the tense facial expression of the interviewer, you might carefully ask, "Have I come at a bad time?" or "Is there something wrong?" and begin to explore the reasons for the disruption. Once you have worked through the problem, you can try your message again.

Semantic noise One other type of noise that creates a barrier to communication is semantic noise. Semantic noise is any barrier to word or other symbol meanings arising from different environments, nationalities, pronunciations, values, or experiences. If your interviewer is Japanese and speaks little English, you can see the obvious language barrier to communication. If the interviewer is a Boston native and tells you, "I'm sorry I'm late for the appointment—I had to 'paahk' the 'caah,'" the accent might create a semantic barrier. If the interviewer asks, "Can I get you a soda?" the word *soda* could mean anything from "soft drink" to an ice cream-and-syrup concoction. Saying "I'm applying for the job" could bring a stern reprimand from your interviewer: "Don't use the word 'job'—This isn't a 'job'—You are applying for a *professional position*." You would immediately become aware that perception, values, and occupational experiences have caused the interviewer to view the word *job* with negative meanings. You would need to refrain from mentioning the word and adjust to the new situation.

Semantic noise interferes with communication. To be a more effective communicator, you must become aware of these disruptions and begin to adapt to the semantic noise that exists between sender and receiver.

The Communication Model Applied to Public Speaking

You employ the communication model automatically in your daily life; now it is important that you apply the process successfully to public speaking situations as well. The following graduation speech demonstrates some of the pitfalls of communication.

The ceremony was held in a huge gymnasium where about a thousand graduates, parents, faculty, and administrators had assembled on a hot day in June. Since the auditorium was not air-conditioned, students and faculty sweltered in their black academic gowns. Every speaker's voice echoed because of poor acoustics. Moreover, planes taking off from a nearby airport passed directly over the gym. In this environment, the speaker began:

> Distinguished administrators, members of the faculty, platform dignitaries, parents and relatives, honored guests and friends, and members of the class of 1994:
> Today we gather within these sacred halls of learning to acknowledge the rite of passage—for all graduations can be considered rites of passage—we gather here to honor those of you who have aspired to higher goals, higher dreams, and higher hopes. And so we are proud to honor you today at this very special time. All of you have had the advantages of an education. And all of you are on the way to achieving your dreams. But there are many who have had higher dreams and higher goals who did not enjoy the advantages of an education at a university. They learned from the university of life. So I'd like to spend considerable time this afternoon talking to you about some of those people who succeeded in spite of their circumstances.

The speaker went on and on. Members of the audience became noisy and fidgety. Some graduates, dripping with perspiration, unzipped their academic gowns and used their commencement programs as fans. Every now and then, a low-flying jet would drown out the speaker's voice. A few faculty members dozed off in their chairs.

The speech was a disaster. The speaker falsely assumed that he would deliver his address to a receptive audience under ideal conditions. When faced with the difficulties of the speech setting, he did nothing to adapt his speech. He simply plodded along with his intended material as if nothing were wrong.

The speaker should have considered all aspects of the communication process. Audience members sent clear verbal and non-verbal feedback that they were hot, tired, and inattentive. The speaker paid no attention to the external noise of the jets, the heat, the audience chatter, or the internal noise of audience exhaustion and fatigue. Had the speaker researched the setting, he could have discovered the problems in the environment. To make matters worse, the speaker created further problems for himself when he told listeners that he would spend "considerable time" developing his points. This phrase implied that the speaker was immune to the heat, insensitive to the audience, and would do nothing to shorten his speech or otherwise adapt to the situation. Therefore, the audience became equally insensitive to the speaker.

You might think that this situation provides so many communication problems that even the best speaker would have difficulty handling it successfully. The situation is certainly bad but not impossible. Notice how *this* speaker has adjusted to the problems:

> Good afternoon, ladies and gentlemen. It's almost hotter than purgatory in here, isn't it? I wonder if we could have the ushers open up a few doors, so we could get some kind of cross-ventilation. Good. Okay. Thanks. Now I just want to tell you that I had prepared some remarks of celebration which I believed were appropriate to this event. But I've shortened my speech so we all can go somewhere else to recover from the heat and humidity. Let me just briefly tell you about some dreams, goals, and achievements—and one or two people who achieved those dreams against great odds.

This speaker has acknowledged the problems of the setting, attempted to make audience members more comfortable, and emphasized his intention to be brief. If you were a member of this audience, you would make the effort to listen simply because the speaker communicated that he was sensitive to the situation, cared about you, and was willing to modify his plans. The speaker has also done himself a big favor. Even though he has discarded some of his speech, the speaker knows that the audience will be more receptive to what remains.

Applying the Communication Model to Everyday Life

To build successful speaking skills, you should apply the communication process in daily speaking experiences. As a sender, you should be aware of your own strengths and weaknesses. You must be able to send and receive messages effectively, and you must realize that much of the responsibility for success in speaking rests with you. If a friend asks you to give an entertaining speech at a bachelor party, think of a topic that not only interests and challenges you but involves your audience. If you must speak at a zoning-board meeting in opposition to new high-rise construction, prepare a message with a clear purpose, thorough research, and logical organization. If your employer asks you to present a detailed financial report, be aware of the various channels of communication. Create interest by employing verbal channels (such as vocal inflection, volume, and emphasis), as well as non-verbal channels (such as facial expression, gesture, dramatic pauses, and visual aids).

Gear your message to the audience. Will bachelors enjoy the humorous topic? Are most of the zoning-board members for or against new construction? Do your fellow employees understand the financial data? Be able to accurately interpret and effectively adapt to audience feedback. Are the listeners on the back row yawning because of your speech or simply because they are tired? Do perplexed faces indicate confusion about your ideas? Do you need to alter any portion of your speech based upon audience response?

In addition, you may need to acknowledge the noise created by a disruptive late-comer, the incessant sneezer, or the distracting lawnmower so that you can regain attention. You may need to define terms where semantic experiences of speaker and audience differ. You may need to check out in advance the location of the speech to determine the available resources. Is there an electrical outlet, chalk, or easel? Is there a speaking lectern, microphone, or table? Is the room adequately ventilated, lit, or heated? Does the setting contain any elements that could create problems for your speech?

OBJECTIVES

You now find yourself in a course where you will be required to present speeches to an audience. This experience is important to your growth and development as a communicator. Learning from your classroom successes and failures should help you in other communication situations beyond the course. While we will discuss many concepts and principles, there are three overall objectives we want you to achieve: (1) You should be able to critically evaluate speaking situations; (2) you should be able to plan, prepare, and organize several types of speeches; and (3) you should be able to deliver speeches in front of an audience with ease.

1. *Critically evaluating speaking situations*   Be able to understand and to evaluate the speaking situation. What makes a "good" speaker? What constitutes a "good" speech? What are some aspects of the audience you need to consider when preparing a speech? What are some factors of the occasion you should know before making a presentation? When you can survey the territory and answer some of these questions about any speaking situation, you are well on your way to delivering successful speeches.
2. *Planning, preparing, and organizing speeches*   To speak effectively, you must prepare effectively. An architect draws a set of blueprints with clear specifications before a builder can erect a house. And while it may seem time consuming, a speaker must structure ideas into a coherent plan before

presenting a speech to an audience. While effective planning takes effort, the process is not necessarily difficult. In fact, if you have put sufficient time into researching and outlining your speech, you may find that speechmaking is a lot easier than you thought.

3. *Delivering speeches in front of an audience* How well do you communicate your ideas in public? Do you appear confident, knowledgeable, and enthusiastic about your topic? Are you able to deliver different types of speeches in different speaking situations? Are you able to progress logically from one idea to another? When you look at members of the audience, do you actually see them? Do you concentrate on what you are speaking about at a given moment, or does your mind wander? Do you employ gestures and facial expressions, or do you have nervous mannerisms? Do you rehearse the speech before presenting it to the audience?

Build your speaking ability block by block. Survey the territory, prepare the foundation, create a skeletal structure, refine the appearance, and finally, develop different types of structures. Learn from your mistakes, profit from your achievements, and effectively communicate to benefit yourself and others. When you develop the speech step by step, block by block, you will build a functional, pleasing structure.

SUMMARY

Public speaking, so important in our society, is grounded in the rhetoric and oratory of ancient times. Modern theories include the classic communication model of Shannon and Weaver, as well as a more recent communication model comprised of seven components: sender, message, channel, receiver, feedback, setting, and noise. You must understand the communication process and apply the process to speaking situations. Three objectives of this course are to help you: (1) evaluate speech situations; (2) plan, prepare, and organize speeches; and (3) effectively deliver speeches in front of an audience.

EXERCISES

1. How effectively do you communicate? Write down some of your strengths and weaknesses. Decide upon areas you'd like to target for improvement.

2. Think back on some of your own communication experiences. Which experiences do you feel were successful, and which ones would you characterize as unsuccessful? What elements in your communication caused success, and what elements caused failure?

3. If you were the speaker in the graduation ceremony cited earlier in this chapter, what different decisions would you have made about the problem of noise? Could you have created a more interesting and meaningful speech? Are graduation speeches inherently boring, or can they be rewarding experiences for everyone involved? Can you think of any graduation speeches you have heard that will be remembered by the audience? Explain your answer.

4. In your class, set up a variety of role-playing situations and have the class and your instructor judge how effectively you communicate your purpose. Here are some simple role-playing situations:

   a. A foreigner who can barely speak English has asked you to explain the best route to the airport. Give the individual directions that are clear and simple.

   b. You are in the process of a tax audit and an IRS agent is questioning several costly items under "business lunches" which you have taken as a deduction. Explain why these are justifiable expenses.

   c. In asking your boss for a raise, you are trying to provide as many reasons as possible to support your objective.

   d. You are standing at a traffic light and trying to get motorists who are stopped for only a few seconds to donate money to the American Cancer Society.

   e. You have been asked at a wedding reception to propose a toast to the bride and groom.

   f. You have smashed the front-end of the family car. Explain the problem as calmly as possible to a member of the family.

NOTES

[1] Susan Dodge, "For Some Graduating Seniors, Job Offers Abound; for Most, the Outloook Is Gloomy," *The Chronicle of Higher Education*, May 20, 1992, p. A28.

[2] Edward P. J. Corbett, *Classical Rhetoric for the Modern Student* (New York: Oxford University Press, 1971), p. 31.

[3] Lester Thonssen, ed., *Selected Readings in Rhetoric and Public Speaking* (New York: H. W. Wilson, 1952), p. 65.

[4] Thonssen, p. 156.

[5] Thonssen, p. 102.

[6] Claude E. Shannon and Warren Weaver, *The Mathematical Theory of Communication* (Urbana: The University of Illinois Press, 1949).

[7] C. David Mortensen, *Communication: The Study of Human Interaction* (New York: McGraw-Hill, 1972), p. 14.

READINGS

Corbett, Edward P. J. *Classical Rhetoric for the Modern Student.* New York: Oxford University Press, 1971. Corbett's excellent chapter "A Survey of Rhetoric" provided the basis for this chapter's discussion of classical public speaking. Included in this volume are a large number of readings from historical figures such as Benjamin Franklin, James Madison, Henry David Thoreau, Edmund Burke, and Malcolm X. This is an interesting and readable book for those who want a comprehensive discussion of classical rhetorical principles and criticism of speech literature.

Littlejohn, Stephen W. *Theories of Human Communication*, 4th ed. Belmont, Calif.: Wadsworth, 1992. In this scholarly work on the nature and theory of communication, the author identifies important terminology and describes numerous communication models. The definitions given on page 7 of the communication components are helpful to the basic speech student.

Mortensen, C. David. *Communication: The Study of Human Interaction.* New York: McGraw-Hill, 1972. While somewhat advanced, this text provides even beginners with a helpful explanation and analysis of the important classical and contemporary communication models. Part I, "Foundations," provides an interesting overview of communication and compares the linear communication model of Shannon and Weaver with the more circular model developed subsequently. This section is a good unit if you want an introduction with some enjoyable examples.

Mortensen, C. David, ed. *Basic Readings in Communication Theory.* New York: Harper and Row, 1973. This little book provides beginning students with readings about both the communication process and interpersonal communication. The articles, written by communication experts, are interesting and easy to understand. Three units especially helpful to your speech course are Part I, "Perspectives"; Part II, "Messages"; and Part III, "Channels."

Chapter Two

BUILDING YOUR FIRST SPEECH

Chapter Outline

Key Terms

Body
Conclusion
Critical thinking
Extemporaneous
Ethics
General purpose
Impromptu
Introduction
Manuscript
Memorized
Occasion
Specific purpose
Thesis statement
Topic

Walter Silver/Picture Cube

"As a vessel is known by the sound, whether it be cracked or not; so men are proved by their speeches, whether they be wise or foolish."
—DEMOSTHENES

*K*athleen DeSantis was a student at Catonsville Community College who successfully completed the basic course in public speaking several years ago. Her speeches were challenging and creative, and listeners always looked forward to hearing what she had to say. We asked Kathleen how she chose her topics and what she did to prepare for her speeches. She offered her blueprint.

First of all, I think about a topic a lot. I ask people questions. I get feedback from everybody I know, and I try to get an idea of what they'd be interested in—something different, something relevant—not the same old subject they've heard again and again.

When I have a topic, I ask knowledgeable people where to get material. For example, when I researched my persuasive speech on literacy, I talked to my parents, who are both educators. My mom teaches at the Maryland House of Corrections in Jessup, Maryland, and she spoke to one of the tutors at the Reading Academy, who gave her a poster and a newspaper article that I used in the speech. I also did a telephone interview with Janet Dent, in the office of Adult Education, who told me about the VIP—the Volunteers in Partnership—Program.

I wanted to get the audience to sign up and volunteer for literacy, and I remembered seeing a 1–800 number on TV where they could get more information about "Project Literacy"—so I copied it down and used that in my speech too.

I do more research when I go to the library. What I find most valuable is the magazine index on computer—it's called "Info Trac." You just type in the subject and it gives you the titles of magazine articles that deal with the subject.

Then I gather everything from the library and sort through all of it, throwing out the things that are irrelevant or don't support what I'm trying to say. I write a specific purpose so I don't go off on a tangent. And from there I do the speech in my mind. I try to see myself in front of the class. I work on an outline, always referring back to my specific purpose. Then I type it, I go back, re-edit, and change my mind. I get large note cards and write down my outline. I write key words—I use a lot of red ink and different colors to underline or make notes to myself.

And then I go back and practice, and practice, and practice, and practice; then I do it one more time on the morning of the speech—then, I'm ready. If you don't do something a lot, it's hard; but the more you do it, the easier it gets.[1]

Kathleen was a hard worker who followed the basic steps of speech preparation. This chapter provides you with nine general guidelines to help you build your first speech. It also presents a plan for thinking critically about speech construction. If you are willing to work, you can be just as successful as Kathleen.

PRELIMINARY SURVEYING

Think back to the last time someone asked you to prepare and deliver a speech. It may have been in relation to a job activity, community gathering, social organization, or church group. What was your response? Did you hesitate, and finally say, "No, I'm sorry—I'm not very good in front of a lot of people"? Or did you mutter a reluctant "yes," and then worry that you didn't have enough experience to be really effective?

If you have ever felt insecure about presenting speeches, you now have an opportunity to change. Public speaking is a rewarding experience which can contribute to your development as a person. It can help you improve your skills in organization and research, refine your abilities in delivery, and increase your sensitivity toward others.

You will be interested to know that many people are nervous when they deliver speeches. As a matter of fact, speech apprehension ranks among the top fears of most Americans. While you may never be able to eliminate your apprehension completely, you can learn to cope with your anxiety in order to deliver a speech successfully.

You are about to construct your first speaking assignment. You may still feel somewhat hesitant, but you've got to start somewhere. Try not to think about the structure as a whole. Rather, build the speech, piece by piece, carefully considering each principle and clearly understanding each step in the process. Before you know it, you will have completed construction and mastered the art of speaking in public. Remember Kathleen's last piece of advice: "If you don't do something a lot, it's hard; but the more you do it, the easier it gets."

CREATING A BLUEPRINT

To assist you in building your first assignment, nine guidelines are provided here as a blueprint for speech construction. Although these guidelines are presented in a sequence, not all speeches will follow this arrangement. In some presentations the steps may overlap, or even reverse. You might select and narrow a topic while you are conducting library research, or you might analyze the audience before you write the specific purpose. The process is similar to constructing a building; some steps—such as preparing the foundation and erecting the walls—occur in a prescribed order. Other steps, however, are more flexible. The guidelines are presented as a suggested sequence for you to follow.

Nine Guidelines to Speech Construction

Choose an Interesting, Well-Defined Topic The first step in building your speech is to choose a *topic* that is interesting to you, has potential interest to your audience, and is limited in scope. As you think about the topic, examine some of your past experiences and present concerns—areas which challenge you and stimulate your enthusiasm. Review your life experience, professional expertise, practical knowledge, or unique interests. Your chosen topic should also challenge your listeners and relate to their needs or curiosities. Audience members tend to be motivated by issues that involve their personal survival or their physical and emotional well-being. Finally, *narrow* the topic to a specific area which you can develop in detail within your allotted time limit.

Understand the General Purpose   Once you have chosen your topic, you must clearly understand the general purpose of the speech. A *general purpose* represents the direction of the material presented: General purposes are either informative, persuasive, or entertaining. *Informative* speeches enlighten and educate audiences. These speeches can define concepts, demonstrate procedures, or describe people, events, and experiences. *Persuasive* speeches influence and alter the beliefs, feelings, or behavior of listeners. In persuasive presentations, speakers seek to convince audiences to change beliefs, move people to action, or intensify listeners' feelings. The goal of the *entertaining* speaker is to gain a humorous response by poking fun at people, places, or events. While entertaining speeches may contain biting satire or convey serious underlying messages, the material itself should be lighthearted and enjoyable rather than persuasive or seriously informative.

Conduct Extensive Research   Your next step is to find interesting factual materials to support the topic and to establish your credibility as a speaker. Thorough research involves finding books and periodicals in the library that contain testimonies, examples, and statistics relating to the topic. Your research may also require you to conduct interviews with experts on the topic, or to gather information from institutions, businesses, or specialized organizations. The research process helps you to gain the respect and trust of your listeners; audiences tend to believe speakers who are knowledgeable about their topics and back up their ideas with facts or documented evidence.

Write Specific Purpose and Thesis Statements   When you have researched the topic, you need to determine the specific purpose and thesis statements of the speech. The *specific purpose* represents the main objective which joins all ideas to one common theme and enables the speaker to keep on target. The specific purpose statement includes the general purpose (or its paraphrase) and one topic idea stated in clear and concise language.

> *Specific purpose:* To inform listeners about my interest in parachute jumping

The *thesis statement*, often called the central idea or the central objective, expands the specific purpose and tells the audience exactly what main points the speech will develop.

Thesis statement: I'll tell you how I became interested, what happened on my first fearful jump, and why parachute jumping is an enjoyable hobby.

This thesis clearly indicates that the speech is organized around three major headings.

Write a Comprehensive Outline   Once you have determined your purpose and thesis, structure your thoughts by writing a *logical outline.* The outline will help to keep you on track throughout the presentation and still maintain contact with the audience. A speech has three basic parts: an introduction, a body, and a conclusion.

The *body* is the longest portion of the speech and contains the main headings which were identified in the thesis statement. For example, the speech about parachute jumping identifies the following three headings:

Body
  I. How I became interested
 II. My first fearful jump
III. Parachute jumping as an enjoyable hobby

Each numeral is then reinforced by subordinate points containing any examples, testimonies, and statistics you collected in your research. Your time limit will often dictate the number of main points which the body should develop. Generally, the shorter the speech, the fewer the main points. A one- to two-minute speech would probably contain no more than two or three main points, while a speech of six to seven minutes could expand upon as many as four headings.

Although the introduction and conclusion are much shorter than the body, they must also be carefully organized. The *introduction* should get attention and promote curiosity, as well as prepare the audience for the topic and thesis statement. You can generate listener curiosity by beginning with a catchy quotation, shocking statement, thoughtful case study, or stimulating question which relates to the issue. The *conclusion* resolves the ideas you have presented in the speech. You can summarize the main points, appeal to the emotions, cite a quotation, or use an illustration. What is important is that your audience senses a finality and a resolution to the topic.

Be Sensitive to Audience Members   As you organize the speech, consider carefully the needs and feelings of your audience. Present the topic at their intellectual level without talking over their heads or beneath them. Use language that they understand, and define any terms that may be unfamiliar. Be sensitive to the diverse backgrounds and experiences of your listeners, and be aware of the values and ideals that motivate them. Avoid examples that stereotype individuals, and stay away from offensive language. Let the audience know that you are genuinely interested in them and concerned about their welfare.

Understand Your Ethical Responsibilities Whenever you present a speech, you are claiming to have knowledge about a topic that could benefit the audience. At the same time, you have an ethical responsibility to convey this knowledge fairly and accurately without misleading your listeners.

Speakers who plagiarize or steal information without giving proper credit, withhold or distort facts, engage in name-calling, or advocate harm are employing unethical practices designed to deceive or manipulate their audiences. These tactics demonstrate a lack of respect for individuals and will eventually destroy the speaker's credibility.

As an ethical speaker, you want to gain the confidence of your listeners; be reliable and fair when you report information, and avoid deceptive practices. You will earn the respect and trust of your audience if you are honest and respectful.

Practice the Speech Success in presenting a speech requires practice. Transfer your outline to speaking notes and double or triple space between lines for easy scanning. Good notes will allow you to maintain eye contact with your audience and still proceed logically through your material. As Kathleen DeSantis suggested (at the start of this chapter), go over the speech a number of times so you are confident with the order and placement of ideas. If you can, rehearse in the setting where you will deliver the presentation. Work to eliminate distractions such as fidgety mannerisms, standing on one foot, or vocalized pauses like "uh, uh, um." Convey words and sentences so listeners can hear and understand you easily. Be accurate and descriptive in your use of language and know how to pronounce difficult terminology. Let gestures and facial expressions flow spontaneously from your natural enthusiasm. If circumstances do not allow you to rehearse in the speech setting, look over your speaking outline and conduct a mental review of your presentation. Remember that your goal in speech rehearsal is to unite all of your research and organization into a coherent, unified construction.

Be Confident and Prepared On the day of the presentation, arrive at the speech location early enough to avoid any last-minute scramble. Look through your notes to see if they are in the proper order. Relax, and take a few deep breaths as you wait for your turn. When it is time for your speech, walk calmly to the speaker's stand, placing your notes securely in front of you. Don't start the speech while you are still on the way to the lectern or while you are arranging your material. Take your time, and don't rush. Make certain that you are ready to begin. Look at the audience, and then state the first line of your speech with conviction.

Project confidence when you speak. Avoid making excuses or apologizing for mistakes. Speak clearly and distinctly. Try to make eye contact with all segments of your audience between brief glances at your notes. Stand up straight, and show the audience that you are prepared and ready to make the presentation. When you finish, don't pack up your notes while you are still talking or walk off in the middle of a concluding line. Wait until you have completed every part of the conclusion. When the last line of the speech is over, collect your notes, and walk calmly to your seat.

SELECTING A STYLE OF DELIVERY

Whenever you make a speech, you will need to choose a style of delivery which is appropriate to the speech setting. The *style of delivery* refers to your method of presenting the material—that is, whether the speech is manuscript, impromptu, memorized, or extemporaneous.

In situations where precision and detail are extremely important, speakers often choose to read word-for-word *manuscripts* to audiences. A scientist reporting on the results of fusion research at a convention, or a physician describing new treatments for AIDS victims to medical professionals, would write out the entire speech in advance. President Bill Clinton employs manuscript delivery because his words are analyzed and interpreted by millions of people around the world.

You may already have had to present an *impromptu*, or "surprise," speech without any notes or prior preparation. If your supervisor requested you to "say a few words" about your current work project at a division meeting, or a friend asked you to propose a toast at a birthday party, you were required to organize your thoughts and ideas on the spur of the moment. An impromptu speech is good to experience occasionally and helps you to develop the ability to think on your feet.

In situations where constant eye contact and accurate timing are necessary, speakers frequently use *memorized* delivery. Tour guides, stand-up comics, after-dinner speakers, and individuals presenting or receiving awards are often more effective if they memorize their material. In a Jay Leno-style monologue, for instance, the speaker wants to convey the punch line smoothly without distractions from notes. In this setting, memorization can help a speaker to respond quickly to audience feedback and to judge the right moment to deliver the humorous line.

While these approaches can be effective in a number of speaking situations, they have some clear disadvantages. In manuscript delivery, speakers often use their notes as a crutch and forget to look at the audience. These speakers may also tend to sound mechanical, forced, or monotonous when they read material which is written out word for word. Audiences rarely like speakers to read to them; they enjoy being acknowledged with eye contact in a spontaneous and conversational manner.

Speakers often use memorized delivery to promote the secure feeling that they have it all down in their heads. In practice, however, memorization causes speakers to spend large amounts of time concentrating on word, phrase, and

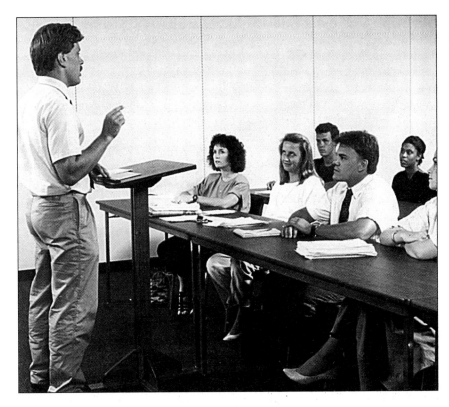

AN EXTEMPORANEOUS
DELIVERY ALLOWS A
SPEAKER TO COMBINE
SPONTANEITY WITH
CAREFUL RESEARCH AND
CLEAR ORGANIZATION.

Hal Rummel Photography

sentence order rather than on ideas. This style of delivery can even contribute
to fear and insecurity about forgetting some crucial portion of the speech.

While an impromptu speech works in a surprise setting, it is not advisable
to create this type of speech when the situation requires a carefully researched
and structured presentation. You can't make up a speech as you go along when
you must show research and preparation.

As you build your first presentation, you will find that the *extemporaneous*
type of delivery is the most helpful to you. An individual using this style
researches a topic, prepares an outline, and employs speaking notes—the
method we suggest in this chapter and describe throughout the text.
Extemporaneous delivery allows the speaker to develop eye contact with the
audience, adapt to feedback, and concentrate on the sequence of ideas rather
than on word or sentence order. Speakers in business and industry select
this approach to help them project confidence and credibility to their listeners. An accountant presenting a quarterly report to corporate executives or an
office manager training new employees wants the freedom to look at listeners, yet the security of a clear, well-organized outline. With an extemporaneous delivery, these speakers can be relaxed, spontaneous, and well
prepared.

THINKING CRITICALLY ABOUT SPEECH CONSTRUCTION

Unfortunately, when we hear the word *criticism*, we often think in negative terms, such as tearing down the ideas or arguments of others. Critical thinking should not be destructive; rather, it should be a constructive process in which we examine and evaluate facts and ideas so as to make more rational decisions and improve our understanding.[2] As you progress through the guidelines to speech construction, you can think critically by testing information, being organized, listening to different perspectives, and thinking for yourself.

Be Willing to Test Information

Critical thinking implies asking relevant questions. When you are researching a topic or choosing supporting materials, evaluate the information carefully. If you find a shocking statement or startling statistic, cross-check the material with other sources for reliability. If you are conducting an interview, don't be afraid to ask questions or ask for concrete verification of information. If you are listening to a speaker describing a new cure for a disease, examine the evidence presented and analyze the quality of the research. One speaker presented "constructive thought therapy" as a cure for cancer. While the topic was interesting, listeners were skeptical as the speaker expressed her opinions on the issue. One audience member commented, "I've heard of this kind of therapy, but I mistrusted the speech—there seemed to be no evidence." The speaker did not test the information and was too willing to rely on her own opinions and upon the hearsay of others. You can avoid this kind of difficulty by conducting a thorough analysis of your data and research materials.

Be Organized

Critical thinking is organized thinking. When you encounter difficulties in the process of building a speech, view them as challenges to be overcome rather than as obstacles to be avoided. Think of logical strategies for attacking problems. Define and understand the problem, seek solutions to the challenge, and then select a clear plan of action. If you discover that your audience disagrees with your controversial persuasive topic, find creative methods of appealing to their interests and needs. If you can't find material on your topic in the library, develop alternative resources by asking individuals, experts, or other institutions for information. If you have difficulty presenting the speech in front of an audience, analyze your problems and make changes by being more prepared, engaging in additional speech rehearsal, or requesting more feedback from your class and instructor. Identify problems, develop strategies, and be systematic in your approach to the speech process.

View Ideas from Different Perspectives

When we think critically, we learn from the experiences of others as well as from our own. As a speaker, remember that your point of view is not the only perspective on an issue. Be open to other ideas and be willing to learn from different viewpoints. If you find that facts do not support your idea, don't hang on to it, stubbornly refusing to give in. One student enjoyed the songs of the late Jim Morrison (of the Doors) and collected the rock singer's music on compact disc. For his informative speech, the student wanted to describe and play samples of Morrison's music for his audience— older, part-time students with families. The instructor suggested that he choose a more suitable topic for audience members. Feeling insulted, the student rigidly insisted that he could make the topic interesting to anyone. Unfortunately, the student learned the hard way. After hearing the music samples and little evidence, listeners repeated the suggestion made earlier by the instructor.

In a speaking situation, the composition of the audience requires that a speaker listen carefully to others. A speaker making a presentation to an audience of different races, religions, genders, or ages needs to demonstrate sensitivity and skill in responding to diverse opinions. A sign of maturity is profiting from the experiences of others, and growing as a result of other views.

DOONESBURY copyright 1988 G.B. Trudeau. Reprinted with permission of Universal Press Syndicate. All rights reserved.

Think for Yourself

Thinking critically means coming to your own conclusions after weighing the evidence. It does *not* mean believing everything that is handed to you. It is easy for us today to point accusing fingers at those German people who blindly accepted Nazi propaganda and helped to perpetuate state-sponsored crimes in World War II. But ask yourself how many times you have accepted and believed someone else's opinion without question. For instance, imagine that you are on your way to class the first day of the new term and a friend sees you going into the lecture hall. She stops you at the door and insists, "Try to get out of this class; the professor *never* gives A's or B's." Do you immediately drop the class, ignore the comment, or proceed with caution? This situation calls for critical thinking. Perhaps your friend is a chronic alarmist or is having difficulty in all of her courses. Possibly your fellow student had some kind of conflict with the instructor and holds a biased viewpoint about the situation. It is also possible that your friend is entirely credible and is giving you helpful advice. Whatever the case, the situation probably calls for investigation and more information before you make a decision.[3]

Although it is often necessary to ask for help, it is equally important to arrive at your own conclusions. Don't let advertisers, salespeople, or indifferent parties tell you what to think by quoting ambiguous "facts" or unsupported opinions. Examine the evidence yourself and arrive at a systematic conclusion.

SUMMARY

Nine general guidelines may serve to assist you in constructing your first speech.

1. Select a topic that is interesting to you and to your audience, and is sufficiently limited in scope.
2. Be aware of the three general purposes or directions of a speech:
   a. the *informative* enlightens the audience;
   b. the *persuasive* alters the beliefs, feelings, or behavior of listeners;
   c. the *entertaining* gains a humorous response.
3. Conduct research into your topic to obtain appropriate testimonies, statistics, and examples that support your ideas.
4. Write a clear, specific purpose or speech objective, followed by a thesis statement which states the two, three, or four main points the speech will include.
5. Write a comprehensive outline of the introduction, body, and conclusion to develop your ideas in a logical sequence.
6. As you construct the speech, be sensitive to the needs and motivations of your audience.
7. Be ethical and credible when speaking.

8. Transfer your outline to speaking notes, and practice the speech to develop a conversational, extemporaneous delivery.
9. Project confidence in yourself and in the material when you deliver the speech.

There are four styles of delivery: manuscript, impromptu, memorized, and extemporaneous. One of the most effective styles is extemporaneous delivery, which requires research and organization but enables a speaker to use a brief outline and maintain eye contact and spontaneity.

Think critically as you construct your first speech by testing information, being organized, listening to different perspectives, and thinking for yourself.

EXERCISES

1. Following the guidelines provided in this chapter, prepare a one- to two-minute informative speech introducing yourself to the class. Select a topic from the following areas:
   a. unique interest or experience
   b. career objective
   c. personal ambition
   d. brief autobiography
2. Divide your class into groups of two and exchange biographical information. Once you have learned some interesting facts about one another, develop a short (two-minute maximum) speech introducing your colleague to the class.
3. From a list of topics provided by your class or your instructor, select one topic for a one-to two-minute impromptu speech to inform.
4. Identify a problem you have recently solved. Evaluate your effectiveness in making the decision.[4] Describe the process you used to:
   a. define the problem
   b. research and understand the problem
   c. seek possible solutions
   d. choose a solution
   e. implement a plan of action.
5. Analyze two recently released movies you have watched. Describe one that stimulated your critical thinking. How did the movie contribute to your analysis and thought? Describe another movie which did not stimulate your thinking. Why wasn't this movie successful in developing your skills in critical thinking?
6. Read two editorials in the newspaper and carefully analyze the following:
   a. What claims are made?
   b. What evidence is used to support the claims?
   c. What do the editorials ask readers to believe?
   d. What is your analysis of the claims, arguments, and evidence?

7. Describe examples from your experience in which you made uncritical decisions fitting the following situations. Describe the consequences of your decision-making. Describe why the decision lacked examination and analysis. For example:
   a. You were disorganized.
   b. You failed to test information.
   c. You didn't listen to different viewpoints.
   d. You failed to think for yourself.[5]

NOTES

[1] Interview with Kathleen DeSantis, Catonsville Community College, Catonsville, Md., May 18, 1989.

[2] Based on a definition used in John Chaffee, *Thinking Critically*, 3rd ed., (Boston: Houghton Mifflin, 1990), p. 37. Much of this discussion of critical thinking is based upon Chapter 2 of Chaffee's book and Chapter 1 of Richard D. Rieke, and Malcolm O. Sillars, *Argumentation and Critical Decision-Making* (New York: HarperCollins, 1993), pp. 1–16.

[3] Chaffee, p. 55.

[4] Chaffee, p. 6.

[5] Exercises 6 and 7 are based upon Rieke and Sillars, p. 16.

READINGS

Chaffee, John. *Thinking Critically*, 3rd ed. Boston: Houghton Mifflin, 1990. Excellent for a thorough discussion of the nature and process of critical thinking. We recommend Chapter 2, "Thinking Critically"; Chapter 4, "Perceiving"; and Chapter 6, "Language as a System."

Hugenberg, Lawrence, and Yoder, Donald. *Speaking in the Modern Organization.* Glenview, Ill.: Scott, Foresman, 1985. Relates public speaking to organizations. A subheading of Chapter 3 entitled "Preparing the Message" includes four of the steps discussed in this chapter. Chapters 4, 5, and 6 expand and amplify each step in greater detail.

Rieke, Richard D., and Sillars, Malcolm O. *Argumentation and Critical Decision-Making.* 3rd ed. New York: HarperCollins, 1993. Helps students to apply critical thinking when developing arguments for persuasive speeches. We suggest Chapter 1, which contains a section entitled "Thinking and Being Critical."

Thomas, David A., and Fryar, Maridell. *Successful Business Speaking.* Skokie, Ill.: National Textbook, 1981. This little book is especially helpful to students who are specializing in business-related career studies. Includes an overview of principles provided in this chapter, and an application of these principles to business situations. In Chapter 3, the authors have included discussions of "the report" and "the briefing"—speeches frequently used in business organizations.

Chapter Three

ANALYZING YOUR AUDIENCE

Chapter Outline

Key Terms

Attitudes
Beliefs
Demographic analysis
Opinions
Stereotypes
Targeting
Values

Bob Daemmrich/Image Works

"The public is like a piano.
You have to know what keys to poke."
—AL CAPP

*O*ne evening on the NBC television show "Saturday Night Live," pop singer Sinéad O'Connor was appearing as guest artist. At the end of a musical number, O'Connor departed from the script and suddenly tore up a picture of Pope John Paul II. As she shredded the photograph, the singer shouted, "Fight the real enemy." The shocked studio audience was silent as the director quickly cut to a commercial. NBC switchboards were jammed with angry calls from hundreds of viewers complaining about O'Connor's behavior. Later, when a *Time* magazine reporter asked the singer why she didn't use other, less offensive ways of getting her message across, O'Connor responded: "The fact is that people are asleep. They need a short, sharp shock. They need that to make them stand up and listen. . ."[1]

Sinéad O'Connor may have succeeded in shocking viewers, but she violated an important principle of audience analysis repeated by Abraham Lincoln more than one hundred years ago:

> It is an old and a true maxim that a "drop of honey catches more flies than a gallon of gall." So with men. If you would win a man to your cause, *first* convince him that you are his sincere friend. Therein is a drop of honey that catches his heart."[2]

Our objective in this chapter is to help you analyze your audience in a speech setting. We want you to build strategies that encourage listeners to receive your messages favorably.

THE IMPORTANCE OF AUDIENCE ANALYSIS

When individuals or companies decide to invest millions of dollars developing new products or services, they conduct a *market analysis* to determine consumers' characteristics, their buying habits and motives, and their receptivity to new products.[3]

A developer, for instance, who intends to build a high-rise condominium must determine the nature of potential buyers and what they want in housing. Will homeowners be older individuals who can afford spacious living environments with cathedral ceilings, Jacuzzis, and wrap-around balconies? Or will prospective buyers be young professionals who want housing that is inexpensive, convenient, and practical?

We see the results of successful market research all around us. Auto makers introduce new mini-vans or reinstate large luxury models. Food companies produce dietetic and low-cholesterol products for health-conscious consumers. Political campaigns sway voting blocs such as senior citizens, farmers, and minorities with special-interest advertising.

Like the investor, you must analyze your particular "market"—your audience. *Audience analysis* refers to the speaker's examination of audience characteristis to determine the most appropriate means of motivating them to share or participate in the speaker's concerns.[4] You need to understand your listeners' needs, their environment, and their perceptions of you as a speaker. If you understand at least some of these characteristics, you will be able to adapt your speech to gain the most favorable hearing. Knowledge of the audience helps you to choose topics that are interesting, select supporting evidence that contributes to clarity and vividness, and use language that is appropriate. Audience analysis does *not* mean that you must compromise your values, or tell your listeners what they want to hear . The point is to adapt and adjust your presentation. The audience is your most valuable asset in the speech setting— it is the listener whom you ultimately want to inform, persuade, or entertain.

Audience analysis involves understanding five principal factors that can significantly influence listeners' reactions to a speech:

1. their perception of the speaker
2. their perception of the topic
3. their needs and motivations
4. social groups to which they belong, and
5. the occasion.

Audience Perception of the Speaker

Audiences develop very clear perceptions of speakers. They like or dislike speakers based upon the content of their presentations or reputations created through past speeches or actions. We return to the same doctor, hairdresser, insurance agent, or accountant because of the favorable perceptions and positive relationships we have built with them over time.

Your audience will likewise develop a perception of you as a speaker. They will evaluate what they hear in your presentations, and they will form attitudes about your choice of topics and your manner of delivery. If your speeches are usually interesting and prepared well, the audience will anticipate those qualities even before you speak—they will be receptive unless you prove them wrong. At the same time, speakers who are poorly prepared, illogical, or use unethical methods will create negative expectations that will be hard to overcome.

A student presented a speech demonstrating shoplifting. He wore a long trenchcoat with large inside pockets, and proceeded to tell his audience in great detail how to stuff various sizes of merchandise into the garment. He explained how to avoid discovery by store detectives and by mechanical devices. Some members of the class giggled nervously during the speech; others sat in frozen silence. After his conclusion the speaker added, "Oh, this was only a joke; I didn't really mean it. I don't believe in shoplifting." But it was too late; the speaker had severely damaged his reputation. When he delivered his next classroom speech, his negative image still influenced listeners. It took several presentations for the speaker to earn back his credibility with the audience.

Audience perceptions are not necessarily etched in stone; they can be changed or even reversed over time. During the 1992 Democratic presidential primaries, Governor Bill Clinton of Arkansas waged an uphill battle. The media asked questions about his avoidance of military service. Tabloids ran stories about Clinton's marital infidelities and experimentation with marijuana. Opponents questioned his character and integrity, and columnists frequently referred to him as "Slick Willie." As a result of voter skepticism, Clinton did poorly in early primaries. In New Hampshire, Clinton received only 26% of the vote, while former senator Paul E. Tsongas won with 35%. In Connecticut, Clinton lost to former California governor Jerry Brown by one percent. At the end of these primaries, Clinton as well as Tsongas were seen as "flawed candidates."[5]

But Clinton fought back. He appeared on interview programs, radio talk shows, and MTV. He ignored the attacks and addressed major foreign-policy issues, seeking presidential stature. Declaring himself "the Comeback Kid," Clinton won important primaries in New York, Wisconsin, and Kansas, and went on to become the Democratic presidential nominee. In the general election campaign, President Bush tried to revive concerns about Clinton's character, but voters—fearful about the deficit and the economy—narrowly elected Clinton to the presidency. To effect this shift in perception took considerable time and effort over a period of many months; voter attitudes did not change quickly.

An audience may be unfamiliar with a speaker and feel hesitant about accepting the speaker's ideas or viewpoints. An expert in fire safety who informs listeners how to protect their homes may project interest and concern, but if the audience has never heard of the "expert," the speaker may need to increase believability by describing his or her professional qualifications and experience.

Positive audience attitudes work to your advantage in a speech. If you have developed a favorable reputation, listeners won't be resistant to your influence. If listeners believe your ideas are supported by solid evidence and sound reasoning, they will be more open to you. If you appear confident and relaxed in your delivery, the audience will relax and listen to you. The attitudes the audience forms about you play an important role in your ability to educate and influence them.

Audience Perception of the Topic

If a large company hired a computer consultant to lecture on "Innovations in Computer Technologies" to a hundred secretaries and clerks, the speaker might assume the entire audience was computer-literate. That assumption might be erroneous, however. Secretaries, like people in many skilled occupations, have become highly specialized professionals. In many companies, certain secretaries known as "information specialists" have received advanced computer training and supervise the computer and data area of an office. Other personnel, such as receptionists or clerks, may perform only data entry and possess limited computer knowledge. The consultant who assumes that every secretary is computer-literate may present a speech far too complex for a large segment of the audience.

As you build your speech, don't make assumptions about the audience until you ask questions. If you understand the level of awareness about a topic, you can gear the speech toward more listeners by not isolating or losing any audience segment.

You also need to consider the attitudes of listeners toward your topic. *Attitudes* are prior inclinations people have about issues, and *opinions* are verbal expressions of these attitudes.[6] When you deliver a persuasive speech, for instance, you may have listeners who agree, disagree, or have no opinion concerning your point of view.

Suppose that you wanted to present a speech favoring capital punishment for drug dealers. You have conducted judicious research. You obtained statistical evidence from the United States Justice Department regarding the amount of illegal drugs entering the country every year. You also included some examples of specific drug dealers who have profiteered from the broken lives of dependent addicts. You even used some emotional appeals— "Would you want these drug dealers making profits off of your son or daughter, brother or sister?" But when you delivered the speech, you found yourself facing listeners with tight lips and unfriendly frowns. Once the speech ended, you discovered too late that most of your evidence and emotional appeals were irrelevant—your audience was strongly opposed to capital punishment, period. If you don't know how your audience feels about an issue, you are less likely to use your supportive data to best advantage.

It is important to know the strength of your listeners' attitudes so as to adjust your approach. Generally speaking, the stronger their attitudes against an issue or idea, the harder it is to influence the audience.[7] It is unreasonable to expect individuals to move from extreme opposition to approval after a five- or ten-minute speech. With hostile audiences, the best you can do is to establish common ground and focus on areas of agreement as well as the need for change. If people are mildly against your topic, you have a good chance of changing their minds—provided that the evidence is forceful. If your listeners are neutral, you are in the best position. Neutrality often means that the audience may not know enough about the issue, or has not yet formed clear opinions. You have a good chance of exerting influence through strong evidence and sound reasoning. And if the audience completely supports your viewpoint, you can change the focus of your speech to motivate them to act— to contact their legislators, form political action committees, or educate the greater public about the problem.

With many issues, you will find audience attitudes ranging from strong agreement to equally strong disagreement. If you found a variety of audience perceptions about capital punishment, for example, you would focus most of your persuasive appeals on the neutral group, including those who mildly agree and disagree. You would want to maintain contact with those who favor your position strongly and, at the same time, indicate that you respectfully disagree with your extreme opposition.

A SUCCESSFUL SPEAKER LINKS A TOPIC TO THE NEEDS AND MOTIVATIONS OF VARIOUS SOCIAL GROUPS WITHIN THE AUDIENCE.

Charles Kennard/Stock Boston

Motivations of the Audience

As they are listening to your speech, the audience will ask some mental questions: "Can I use this? Will this help me? Does the topic relate to my interests?" Your answer is to appeal to the needs that are most important to your listeners. Needs and goals provide incentives to your audience to become interested and involved in your information. When you focus on significant needs, audience members realize that they can benefit from the speech, that they have something to gain by allowing the speaker to influence them.

One way to discover your listeners' strongest needs is to understand their beliefs and values. *Beliefs* are conclusions people have about the world based upon observations, knowledge, and experiences.[8] The following statements would qualify as individual beliefs:

"An exercise program prolongs life."
"God answers prayers."
"Condoms help to prevent AIDS."
"Democrats are sympathetic toward social problems."
"Censorship violates the Constitution."

Collections of beliefs, called *value systems*, cause us to behave in certain ways and to achieve goals or states of mind.[9] Most people have general values in common—physical, social, love, ego, security, and moral needs. All of us have basic physical needs, such as food, water, shelter, rest, sex, and security—which include safety and social order. One researcher who recognized that needs are strong motivating forces in human beings was Abraham H. Maslow, a psychology professor at Brandeis University. He identified five levels of basic drives, called a "hierarchy of needs," which he felt influenced our thinking and behavior: physiological, safety and security, love, esteem, and self-actualization needs. Maslow felt that people must satisfy the lowest order of needs before they are able to progress to the next level.[10]

Even though all of us have similar needs, our value systems cause us to place these drives in different priorities. Some who put a high emphasis on family-type love needs will change jobs and move long distances to be near better schools or help sick relatives. Others, who value ego needs, will uproot families and change jobs to increase status and responsibility. Those who place strong emphasis on physical needs may spend a great deal of time exercising, choosing well-balanced foods, and getting the appropriate amount of rest. Individuals who place a high priority on moral or spiritual values may cherish religious services, daily meditation, and participation in religion-centered activities. When you analyze your audience, try to determine its values so that you can connect your topic to its most significant goals.[11]

The following list identifies five principal needs and provides several examples of appeals designed to motivate listeners. Notice how speakers phrased appeals to link topics to specific audience values.[12]

Physical–Survival Needs

I know what you're thinking—how can a radar detector be unsafe? Suppose you're driving down the highway and you have a radar detector, and Joe Schmo who's following you does not. What's the first thing that happens when your detector goes on? You hit the brakes, and Joe Schmo is your new trunk companion!

—SCOTT HIPP

Imagine. It's midnight, and you still have four chapters of sociology to study. You decide to take a break. You turn on the TV and all you see is food commercials. And what does your mind go to? Cheeseburgers? Naw. Chicken? Naw. PIZZA! Just a phone call away is a sauce-filled, cheese-covered, crisp-crusted pizza pie.

—EVAN FEINBERG

Social–Love Needs

Dr. Leo Buscaglia describes intimacy as the ability to touch totally, unabashedly, unashamedly, and to lay it on the line and expose your true feelings to someone and have them tell you at every turn, that it's all right. The only way we as human beings will ever know ourselves and develop is in an intimate relationship. But doing so is difficult because intimacy is not reinforced by society.

—ED MINCHER

Each one of us has experienced some isolation and loneliness in our lives. Well, magnify that experience and add to it the fact that this situation will never get better—and you will begin to approach the experience of many elderly and invalid people.

—NORMA FERRIS

Security Needs

Imagine your doctor shooting up drugs before your major surgery.

—HEATHER HAY

We are being financially abused by deceptive banking practices.

—MARIA MARSZALEK

Ego Needs

David Schwartz, a professor at Georgia State University and noted lecturer on motivation, writes in his book *The Magic of Thinking Big* about the multitude of suppressive influences at work in our lives. We've all heard things like, "It's not what you know, it's who you know." "Boy have you got a lot to learn —it really doesn't work like that in the REAL world." "Are you kidding? You can't do that!" He calls these people "the negators" and he says they're everywhere and seem to delight in sabotaging the positive progress of others. Is it any wonder then that we trip and fall on the road to success?

—Cynthia Holley

Not only will you feel better if you exercise, how would you like to look better?

—Kristine Ozgar

Moral–Commitment Needs

If Americans reduced their intake of meat by only ten percent—you guessed it—sixty million people could be adequately fed.

—Chris Clark

Without the volunteer coaches, officials, and huggers, the Special Olympics would not be able to operate. These Special Olympians would not be gaining the physical exercise and emotional support that is crucial to their self-esteem. As I've listened to your speeches over the last two months, I know that many of you are interested in athletics. Volunteering would be a great way for you to continue your love of athletics, and in turn you'd be helping others.

—Colleen V. Deitrich

In the preceding quotations, some people have used negative motivational appeals, some have been positive, and some presentations were designed to be psychologically threatening. Each approach, however, seeks to connect the topic to a *specific* audience need. Listeners' attention is aroused because speakers have motivated them to care by telling them that they are directly or indirectly involved with their topics.

Be certain that you really understand the beliefs and values of your audience without making false assumptions or stereotypes about them. *Stereotypes* are fixed notions or simplistic preconceptions applied to individuals or groups. Not all Democrats are equally interested in funding social programs. Not all people emphasizing moral values are responsive to quotations and examples from the Bible. Not all people who value health want an exercise program. To develop appropriate appeals to values, analyze your audience thoroughly and know the differences in their beliefs.

Impact of Social Groups Upon Listeners

Audience members belong to a wide variety of groups that can influence their perception of ideas. When you build a speech, you must understand the composition of the audience and the impact of specific social groupings upon listeners. Consider the following areas when you analyze the audience: age, sex, religion, cultural and ethnic origin, educational level, occupation, interests, income level, geographical location, and group affiliation.

Age When you prepare a speech, you will discover that your approach to a topic will change depending upon the age of the audience. If you were speaking about social security to a group of people in their early twenties, you would likely find listeners concerned about social security taxes as well as the reliability of the system. If however, your audience were in their sixties, they would be more interested in benefits, cost of living increases, and budget cuts affecting the system. When selecting examples, use those within the knowledge or experience of your listeners. If a speaker mentioned Watergate, the Korean War, or "Howdy Doody," and the audience consisted of people under the age of twenty-five, listeners would have little appreciation for the examples unless they were experts in history, or whizzes at the game of Trivial Pursuit. A speaker should either clearly define the examples, or use other illustrations from listeners' contemporary experience.

> Because of their experience not only on the job but in real life, older workers tend to have fewer accidents. According to a 1988 Bureau of Labor Statistics study, older workers account for 9.7 percent of work-related accidents while workers in your age group of twenty to twenty-four account for fifty percent of such accidents. You can see that there's no replacing life-long experience.
>
> People also age at different rates. There are neither biological nor psychological reasons to connect a number, such as sixty-five, to the onset of old age. Every one of you in this room is aging at this very moment and will face retirement sooner or later. When you face that time, retirement should be a decision that you make for yourself.[13]

Colleen Deitrich knew that her speech against mandatory retirement could be potentially uninteresting to her younger listeners in their early twenties. But she connected the topic to them by comparing accident rates of older workers to younger wage earners. Colleen also confronted her listeners with the issue by saying that they were aging "at this very moment."

Avoid alienating members of your audience by ridiculing their age and insulting their intelligence. Put-downs of any age group create animosity. A young speaker who referred to an audience of senior citizens as "you old people" would be met with anger and resentment. At the same time, if an older speaker were to describe a person under twenty-five as "just a twenty-two-year-old kid," listeners in the twenty-year-old category would probably react with equal hostility.

Eliminate assumptions and stereotypes about age. Older people are not necessarily wiser, and younger people do not necessarily lack experience. As an effective speaker, you want to influence rather than to alienate listeners. You can acknowledge generational differences yet bring people together and appeal to the audience by establishing a common ground.

Gender   The gender of your audience is an important factor to consider when you prepare a speech. With the changes in roles that men and women have experienced in the past two decades, it has become increasingly difficult to identify "women's" or "men's" topics. Women may be doctors, Army captains, truck-drivers, airline pilots, or devoted homemakers. Men may be chefs, florists, kindergarten teachers, or nurses. You can no longer assume that male and female audiences will be interested only in certain subjects.

An effective speaker should be sensitive to the subtle differences in women's and men's perceptions. While much research concerning gender appears to be inconclusive, there are a few generalities which present interesting implications for speakers. In a 1985 study, Patricia Andrews discovered that women often prefer more complexity while men frequently like simpler procedures and criteria. Faye Crosby and Linda Nyquist's research indicates that women tend to correct the grammatical or language use of others. In 1979 Janet Sanders and Willian Robinson found that men and women often differ in their discussions of sexuality and Judy Pearson, Lynn Turner and William Todd–Mancillas observed the existence of a "general pattern" that women tend to engage in more self-disclosure than men. Christiane Hoppe concluded in a 1979 study that males tend to be more aggressive than females, but according to Pearson, Turner, and Todd-Mancillas, research is mixed as to whether men or women use more assertive language patterns. Although it has often been assumed that women are more empathetic, research by Eleanor Maccoby and Carol Jaklin in 1974 indicates that there is no significant difference between men and women regarding the ability to empathize. While the preceding statements are based on research, it must be emphasized that such generalities have numerous exceptions, and speakers need to be aware of the unique qualities of gender in every audience situation.[14]

One classroom persuasive speaker defended the proposition that mothers who kill their babies as a result of postpartum depression should be given more lenient sentences. The audience listened carefully as the speaker provided evidence that postpartum psychosis is a psychological imbalance requiring treatment and understanding. During the discussion listeners were polarized based upon gender. Men generally felt that a woman who killed her own baby should be severely punished to the limit of the law. Women, however, were much more sympathetic and agreed that the offender should be given a program of treatment and rehabilitation.[15]

Another speaker described date rape, informing listeners what it is, how it happens, and what to do about it. While audience members appeared to listen intently to the horrifying examples, expert opinion, and statistics, reactions were mixed. Women felt that the topic was helpful and caused them to be more aware and enlightened. But males in the audience argued that they were left out of the speech and treated as if they were being implicitly linked to criminal behavior.

Both examples indicate the need of speaker sensitivity. In the first, the speaker needs to examine audience perception of the topic *before* the speech to understand potential polarization according to gender. In the second, the speaker should take a more inclusive and less hostile approach to connect to men as well as to women in the audience.

When presenting a speech, avoid stating prejudicial generalities or stereo-types that anger your listeners. To make remarks such as "A woman's place is in the home" or "All men are potential rapists" would arouse hostility in any audience. Carefully consider the sensitivities of your listeners and demonstrate that you care about them.

Religion Even in an audience of twenty people, there may be adherents of several religious attitudes and beliefs—Christians, Jews, agnostics, atheists, Buddhists, Muslims. Religious beliefs are a matter of deep personal conviction and must be taken into account if a speaker is going to touch upon religious subject matter.

> The book of Genesis advocates a vegetarian diet of fruits, grains, and nuts. Buddha commands, "Do not indulge a voracity that includes the slaughter of animals." The Hindu *Mahabharata* reads, "Those who desire to possess good memory, beauty, long life with perfect health, and physical, moral and spiritual strength should abstain from animal foods." The Islamic *Koran* prohibits the eating of "dead animals, blood and flesh." The ancient Greeks, led by Pythagoras and supported by Socrates and Plato, believed vegetarianism was natural and hygienic and necessary for healthy living. The Romans conquered the world with an army fed on vegetables, porridge, bread, and wine. These examples were gleaned from Gary Null's *The Vegetarian Handbook* and they illustrate how history has attempted to teach the philosophy and practice of vegetarianism in order to have a long, prosperous, and healthful life.[16]

After researching his audience, Jim Kilduff decided to identify a variety of religious philosophies to build an argument for a vegetarian lifestyle. Unlike Sinéad O'Connor's strategy, Jim's diplomatic approach helped to win enthusiasm for his topic by bringing philosophically diverse listeners together.

In any audience, avoid religious slurs which reflect prejudicial attitudes. These statements will arouse hostility and promote dissension among your listeners. It is important to unite the members of your audience and establish a sense of community.

Cultural and Ethnic Origin We live in a racially charged society where thought-less words or actions can not only injure feelings but can arouse animosity serious enough to ignite violence. Inappropriate ethnic humor, questionable examples, or a hostile delivery can alienate listeners and ultimately backfire on a speaker. An individual making a presentation to an audience must exercise extreme sensitivity when touching on controversial subjects that involve race, prejudice, or ethnic differences. One of the strengths of our society is its cultural diversity. The traditional Anglo-Saxon domination of America is rapidly changing and it is predicted that during the 1990s the white majority will continue to decline and that black, Hispanic, and Asian cultures will steadily increase in numbers. Demographers predict that by the year 2060, these three minority groups could actually become the majority.[17]

Because of this increasing diversity, speakers face interesting challenges when presenting messages. An effective speaker must not simply acknowledge but *understand* the cultural and racial background of the audience. Words, illustrations, concepts, events, and places must be chosen carefully to involve people of diverse backgrounds and help them to connect to the speaker's message.

Addressing an audience of public school science teachers in Hughesville, Maryland, Benjamin H. Alexander used the outmoded term "colored people," then said:

> Shocked? No, because you are scientists and you know you are not white— but people of color. Were you the color of this white sheet of paper that I am holding up, you would be void of melanin, and the ultra-violet rays from the sun would burn you up. Nor am I, or any other so-called black person in the world, black. Again, you are scientists and know that were we black, we would have an abundance of melanin—and be perfect receptors of the ultra-violet rays from the sun; our body temperature would quickly rise to over 108 degrees and into a fever so severe, we too would burn up. Because you have melanin in your skin—and so do I—it is factual that all people on God's green earth are people of color. God knows what He is doing when He makes no black or white people to inhabit the earth. He knows that if He had, some of them would always be fighting on this planet and disagreeing with the other. So He made a beautiful flower garden of people of all colors ranging from a pleasing cream to an exquisite sable.[18]

Alexander, a research chemistry professor at the American University, succeeded in shocking audience members by employing the term "colored." But having carefully analyzed the audience, the speaker quickly translated his message into scientific terminology that listeners could easily understand. He not only connected to his audience, he gave them a feeling of togetherness and pride by referring to them as "people of color" whom God made into a "beautiful flower garden."

Educational Level, Occupation, and Interests   When selecting a topic, a speaker must analyze the educational level, occupation, and interests of the audience.

Imagine a doctor using the following language in a speech describing the pancreas to an audience of businesspeople and musicians.

> The pancreas, an elongated gland situated between the spleen and the duodenum, secretes an external juice which passes through the pancreatic duct into the duodenum. It also creates an internal secretion, called insulin, which is produced in the beta cells and regulates carbohydrate metabolism.[19]

The speaker has talked over the heads of the lay audience and used terms that would be appropriate only if listeners were medical professionals. Many speakers create this kind of communication problem. But the topic has potential interest because it involves information about good health maintenance. In this situation, however, it is advisable for the speaker to use language that is easier to understand.

> The pancreas is a rather large gland located behind the stomach. It has two very important functions which are essential to the stability of our bodies. First of all, it secretes a fluid, called an enzyme, which helps in the digestion of food. Second, it produces insulin, which helps to reduce the amount of sugar in the blood and urine.

This example is superior because, the speaker has used terms appropriate to the audience's level of knowledge on the topic.

The key idea in understanding audience education, occupation, and interests is *speaker adaptability*. A good speaker who talks about "the treatment of childhood illness" must interest non-parents as well as parents in the audience. Referring to the non-parents' *future* role in child-rearing will probably help to gain their attention. If an accountant speaks to a mixed audience of medical people and air-transportation workers on how to manage money, the speaker knows that there is potential for success because almost everyone is interested in personal finances. A good speaker makes topics come alive for the audience by adapting to their education, occupation, and interests.

Income Level A married student decided to tell his audience how to obtain a home mortgage. He talked about the preliminary steps of filling out application and credit forms, as well as obtaining income verification. He discussed the property survey, insurance policy, and the termite inspection. Finally he described settlement costs, such as points, stamps, and recording fees. He told the audience that he was especially excited about the topic because he and his wife had just purchased their first home. But when his speech was over, audience members responded negatively. One student complained, "He seemed enthusiastic about his topic, but I couldn't get into it. I'm a commuter student and I live at home with my parents. Someday I'll need to know all of this, but right now I don't have a prayer of buying my own place—I just want to graduate so I can get a decent-paying job." That critique described almost everyone's economic situation in the class.

This example graphically portrays the problems that occur when a speaker does not consider the income level of the audience. In this instance, even the speaker's enthusiasm could not motivate the class. He would have been more successful if he had chosen a topic such as taking out a car loan, which would have enabled him to adapt to the needs of his audience.

Another key term for a speaker to remember is *audience sensitivity*. If you talk about joining a country club, or about gourmet cooking, to low-income people who can hardly afford to pay their rent, your feedback might be anything from indifference to hostility. Similarly, if you speak to a group of doctors or bankers and ridicule "rich people's fancy cars and expensive tastes," you may also find your audience switching you off quickly.

Geographic Location   Effective speakers take time to research the geographic location of an audience. When a speaker demonstrates knowledge about the audience's community, the speaker gains the admiration and respect of the listeners.

> It's an honor to address the Executives' Club of Chicago. Over half a century ago, the English writer G. K. Chesterton visited Chicago and recommended that everyone interested in the future should do the same. As Chesterton put it, "Although I won't venture a guess about the shape of things to come, if you wish to feel the pulse of things to come, go to Chicago."
>
> Chesterton's observation is still true. Despite the delays getting in and out of O'Hare [Airport], Chicago has the pulse of tomorrow.
>
> New Yorkers, of course, like to make a similar claim for their city. And while I'm a loyal resident of the metropolis, who cheered when the Giants took on the Bears, and will cheer again when the Mets beat the Cubs, I refuse to let civic loyalty get in the way of truth.[20]

The speaker, N. J. Nicholas, Jr. (co-chief executive officer of Time–Warner, Inc.), demonstrated respect for his hosts by using a complimentary quotation which put his Chicago audience in a receptive mood. A listener who is approached in this manner tends to think: "He's really interested in me," or "He's really gone out of his way to refer to my community."

Social Organizations   Audiences appreciate speakers who take the time to research some of the characteristics of their organizations. Notice how former Chrysler Corporation chairman Lee Iacocca refers to attorneys at a convention of the American Bar Association.

> Let me just say that it's an honor to be asked to be here. And a little bit of a surprise, to tell you the truth. When I got the letter from Mr. Thomas last

December, it said "It is my privilege to invite you..." and ended by wishing me "Happy New Year." Most of the letters I usually get from lawyers start out with "You are hereby summoned," and wind up with "Ignore at your peril." So this is a treat. And I'm glad to be here. I'm also a little curious because I've often wondered just what lawyers do when they have a convention. I know what *car dealers* do! I noticed, for example, that as soon as I sit down you're scheduled to get into something called "The Statement of the Assembly Resolutions Committee." Now, that sounds like *serious business:* Last year at our convention, my speech was the warm-up act for *Willie Nelson!* [21]

Iacocca's remarks were carefully designed to make good-natured fun of the legal profession as well as of his own industry. You can be sure that the attorneys appreciated his personal references to them.

Whenever you speak to a group or organization, there are certain identifiable catchwords and customs that will gain positive feedback from your audience. Knowing something about the PTA, the Longshoremen's Union, the Future Farmers of America, the Sierra Club, or the Young Republicans will help you use terms and phrases that will get the attention of your listeners.

Targeting Specific Groups One way you can arouse interest is to target segments of your audience. *Targeting* is the process of identifying selected groups of listeners and designing specific appeals to motivate them. Political candidates target urban voters, minorities, or senior citizens and appeal to their concerns about crime, drugs, or social security. Cosmetic companies market their products to teens worried about acne and to older consumers interested in hiding wrinkles.

You can also employ targeting in your speeches by using examples, statistics, or quotations that appeal to specific interests of listeners. If your topic is about proper nutrition and there are joggers in your audience, you can specifically refer to them as you explain the benefits of a healthy diet. You can formulate appeals to specific interest groups such as business people, young parents, part-time wage earners, church members, suburbanites, or inner city residents. Targeting helps you to motivate listeners in very personal ways to become involved with a topic.

Notice how this speaker targeted listeners and related their topics to his speech.

Several class periods ago, each of us had the opportunity to share something personal about ourselves to the class. I'd like to take a moment to revisit that night and review some of the topics we spoke about. Karen, you described your passion for art. Jennifer talked about sailing and Tom spoke about scuba diving, the final frontier. Madalen presented a speech about insurance rates and George explained what it's like to be a member of the state police SWAT team. Donna, you shared your feelings about returning to school—the pursuit of your dreams. Kelly described her passion for jigsaw puzzles, and

George discussed roller-skating for exercise. Bob presented his thoughts about friendship, and Elizabeth described her feelings about coming to the USA, and we're glad you did. Jean, you talked about Girl Scouts, truly an American tradition. Jagdish introduced medicine. Shannon, you described your college roommates, giving new meaning to the term "private property." Beth introduced skiing, and Michelle talked about playing the guitar. Lastly, and appropriately so, Rustin spoke about procrastination.

Is there a common link to these passions? I would say yes. Actually, there are three: a man, a date, and a piece of paper. The man's name is Thomas Jefferson, the date was the fourth of July, 1776, and the piece of paper was the Declaration of Independence. This document laid the foundation for the Constitution of the United States, allowing each of us the freedom to follow our dreams and pursue our passions.[22]

Dan Callahan listened closely to the topics presented by other classroom speakers, and used this personal approach to motivate the audience. After the speech, listeners commented that Dan's strategy of identifying their names and topics encouraged them to become involved with his topic.

Impact of the Occasion Upon Listeners

The occasion is a major influence on the audience, and a speaker must know how the environment will affect the speech. An audience subject to the antiseptic odors of a hospital will perceive a speech differently from an audience at a spring flower festival. Listeners on Christmas Eve display a contrasting mood from an audience on New Year's Eve. People have certain expectations of speakers; they want a judge to convey wisdom, a doctor to project confidence.

No analysis of the audience is complete unless you understand the impact of the speaking occasion upon listeners: the purpose, location, and expectations of the speaker.

The Purpose of the Occasion People exhibit a variety of moods and feelings depending on the purpose of the occasion. Listeners are festive at a ballgame or a Fourth of July celebration, and more serious at a professional convention or a lecture. Jokes and humorous sketches would be entirely appropriate at a retirement banquet but (usually) out of place at a funeral or memorial service.

Listeners are also influenced by upcoming holidays or by events of local and national significance. A reference to a tragedy in the community or to a special occasion such as Christmas, Veteran's Day, or the Great American Smokeout can help to make your speech more timely and meaningful to the audience.

Notice how John M. Scheb, Judge of the Second District Court of Appeals in Lakeland, Florida, referred to the occasion in a speech commemorating Presidents' Day.

As we reflect on the meaning of this Presidents' Day, our individual thoughts may focus on a particular president of the past. We all remember our history lessons about our early presidents—Washington, Jefferson, Lincoln, and the others who led our country up to the twentieth century. And then we have our own personal memories of more recent leaders. I can remember my parents speaking of President Hoover, and I have vivid memories of serving in the military under presidents Roosevelt and Truman during World War II. Most of us recall presidents Eisenhower, Kennedy, Johnson, Nixon, Ford, and Carter. And of course, we have fresh memories of Ronald Reagan and George Bush.

Our presidents over the years have differed philosophically, emotionally and culturally. But each wove a thread of love of country into his leadership. And although those threads have been different in strength and design, together they have formed a tapestry displaying cherished values of country and a willingness to serve. This tapestry is patriotism.[23]

Judge Scheb's references to past presidents helped listeners to reflect on the significance of Presidents' Day and prepared them for the theme of patriotism.

The Physical Location of the Event   The physical location of a speech can affect both the audience and speaker. An audience shivering in a drafty auditorium in the middle of winter will not listen effectively. A speech presented in the New Orleans Superdome requires a huge TV screen to project visual aids. A craft demonstration might require close proximity to listeners rather than a remote speaker's lectern. A speech given outside, at the county fair, may be subject to a sudden downpour.

An effective speaker carefully examines the physical location of the speech to anticipate and adapt to as many problems as possible. Below are some questions to ask when you are investigating a speaking site.

1. Is the event inside or outside?
2. What is the size of the room?
3. How many people will be present?
4. Is there a stage or raised platform for the speaker?
5. Will there be a speaker's stand or lectern?
6. Does the room have adequate heat, air-conditioning or ventilation?
7. Does the room have good acoustics?
8. Will there be a microphone, or will the speaker need to rely on strong vocal projection?
9. Could any possible external noise in or near the speaking area cause a distraction?
10. Will props or visual aids need to be set up before the speech?
11. Are adequate electrical outlets, thumb tacks, extension cords, chalk, erasers, easels, tables, or other devices needed for the speech available?

FIGURE 3.1

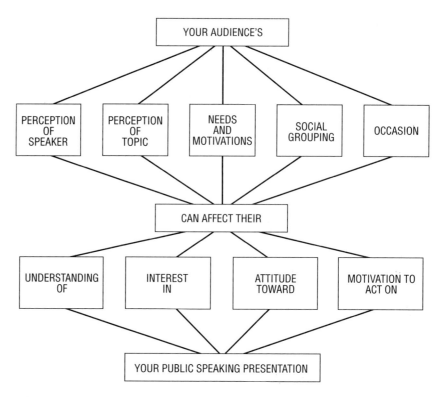

The Expectations of the Speaker Audiences attending events have certain expectations of speakers. They expect a graduation speaker to be warm and congratulatory. They expect a minister or priest to reinforce beliefs and include references to moral and spiritual values. They expect politicians to appear responsive to social and governmental concerns.

Audiences even have expectations regarding the speaker's appearance. During a televised speech on energy early in his presidency, Jimmy Carter wore a sweater as he told Americans to turn down their thermostats to reduce dependency on foreign oil. In this "honeymoon" period, public and press reaction appeared favorable to the speech. Over time, however, the public returned to more traditional expectations regarding Presidential appearance. Most Americans expect that the President of the United States will deliver an official speech "in proper attire"—meaning a conservative suit and tie.[24] President Carter never wore his cardigan again for a major address.

Whenever you present a speech, you need to know the expectations of your audience. To avoid "speaking surprises," ask questions. Here are points to cover when determining your speaking role on a particular occasion.

1. Do your topic and general purpose suit the occasion?
2. What is the order of speaking, and where is your speech in that order?
3. What time of day do you speak—morning, afternoon, or evening?

4. What is the time limit of the speech?
5. Who is the featured speaker?
6. Will you be introduced to the audience, or must you introduce yourself?
7. How is the ceremony organized?
8. Is someone clearly in charge of the event?
9. Are there any customs or traditions associated with the event which you will be expected to know or to perform?

Once you have gained as much information as possible about the purpose, location, and expectations regarding the event, you will be more confident that your speech will be appropriate to the occasion.

CONDUCTING AN AUDIENCE ANALYSIS

As a speaker you should conduct a thorough analysis of your audience in order to develop strategies that will help your speech to receive a favorable hearing. We suggest three steps to assist you in gathering, processing, and assessing information about your listeners.

Collecting Demographic Data About the Audience

Demographics refers to the science of gathering social and statistical information about any group of people. You can collect demographic data by surveying audience opinion or knowledge, circulating questionnaires, or by conducting personal interviews.

Surveys One way to determine the attitudes of your listeners is to survey the relative strength and weakness of their opinions. You can accomplish this by constructing a scale like the one below:

Audience Attitude Survey

Specific purpose: *Capital punishment should be strictly enforced for drug dealers.*

Do you agree, disagree, or are you neutral? Please place a check mark at the appropriate place on the scale that describes your attitude about the above specific purpose.

-10	-5	-1	0	+1	+5	+10
opposed			neutral			favor

This survey helps you to determine audience attitudes about controversial issues prior to a presentation. Circulate the survey to audience members while you are preparing a speech. When you get the results, carefully analyze how many in the audience agree, disagree, or are neutral. The range of audience attitudes will help you decide the types of supporting materials to use and even influence your persuasive approach.

Another type of survey can help you determine the degree of knowledge your listeners possess concerning your topic.

Audience Information Scale

Topic: *Computer Viruses*

How knowledgeable are you about the topic listed above?

1	2	3	4
I know a lot about it	I have some information about it	I've only heard about it	I've never heard of it

This scale is especially useful with informative speech topics. When you add and then average the score, you will have a good indication of how to gear your speech. A low audience average of 1.6 would indicate that listeners are quite knowledgeable about the topic. Your speech could then include examples and terms with a degree of depth and sophistication. On the other hand, a higher score of 3.4 would imply that your audience lacks knowledge and your speech should include definitions of unfamiliar terms and examples which are easy for listeners to absorb.

Questionnaires   Another way to get demographic information is to circulate a questionnaire. You can develop a list of open-ended questions about age, gender, religion, income range, nationality or ethnic origin, education, occupation, social groupings, experiences, and interests. You can then have the questions distributed to audience members well before your speech to collect the needed information. Data obtained through questionnaires can help you to determine the significant values, beliefs, and interests of your listeners and assist you in preparing motivational appeals that stimulate audience receptiveness.

Interviews   Personal interviews with audience members provide more flexibility than surveys or questionnaires and allow you to ask in-depth and follow-up questions.[25] In a personal interview, you also have the advantage of observing the listener one to one: you can watch an individual's reactions to questions, evaluate the person's use of language, and observe the audience member's appearance. One disadvantage is that a personal interview can be time consuming. If you have more than a hundred people in the audience, you may have difficulty interviewing each one. It might be more efficient to interview a cross section or sample of the group.

Processing the Data with a Computer

One effective way to process and organize demographic information about an audience is by using a computer. Speakers in government, business, and industry use a computer program called SPSS—Statistical Package for the Social Sciences—to assess demographic information and to develop profiles of audiences. This powerful program can process data according to key words or command names such as age, sex, occupation, or interest area. You can determine if there are relationships between audience interests and geographical region, or correlations among race, age, income, education, and social grouping.[26] If you have access to a personal computer and a statistical program, you can also enter demographic data and develop profiles using specific commands or key words.

Evaluating the Audience Profile

When you have a printout of your date, analyze and evaluate the information. Make some assessments about the audience and be able to understand some of the most significant qualities that could affect their perceptions of your speech. Develop specific appeals that relate to the most important interests and needs of your listeners.

SUMMARY

When building a speech, you need to understand some of the major influences upon your listeners and how these factors will affect your presentation.

1. Be aware of listener perceptions toward you as a speaker.
2. Assess audience perceptions of the topic.
3. Understand audience beliefs, values, and value systems. When you know the motivations of your listeners, you can develop specific appeals that link your topic to their needs.
4. Determine the composition of your audience according to age, gender, religion, ethnic origin, educational level, occupation, interests, income level, geographic location, and group affiliation. You can target specific groups of listeners by creating appeals that relate to their concerns.
5. Know how the occasion of the speech influences the audience and speaker.

Analyze the purpose of the occasion, the physical location of the event, and audience expectations of the speaker.

You can conduct an audience analysis by gathering demographic information, processing the data with a computer, and evaluating the audience profile.

EXERCISES

1. Conduct a complete audience analysis of your class. Gather your data through surveys, questionnaires, or personal interviews.
2. Analyze the elements of the speaking occasion that will affect your classroom speech. Are there any factors regarding the purpose, location, or expectation of listeners that could influence the speech in a positive or negative way? Will any of these influences cause you to make adjustments to your speech?
3. Once you have chosen a topic for a persuasive or an informative speech, survey the audience to determine their knowledge or attitude about the issue. What do the results of this survey imply about your choice of supporting materials and your delivery?
4. If you have already presented at least one speech, assess audience perceptions of you as a speaker. Gather information by reading and/or listening to critiques from your classmates and instructor. What are their expectations of you? Have they made any preliminary evaluations which you might want to change on the next speech?

NOTES

[1] See "Sinéad O'Connor Lambastes the Pope," *Christian Century*, October 21, 1992, pp. 927–928, and Janice C. Simpson, "People Need A Short, Sharp Shock," *Time*, November 9, 1992, p. 78.

[2] Roy P. Basler, ed., *Collected Works of Abraham Lincoln*, Vol. I (New Brunswick: Rutgers University Press, 1953), p. 273.

[3] William J. Stanton, *Fundamentals of Marketing* (New York: McGraw–Hill, 1981), pp. 35–55, 155–156.

[4] This definition is partially based upon a contribution from E. Joseph Lamp, professor of speech, Anne Arundel Community College, Arnold, Maryland.

[5] Compare an early analysis of the presidential primaries in "This Was the Least Desirable Outcome For Us," *Business Week*, March 2, 1992, pp. 28–29, with a later description in "The Survivor," *The New Republic*, April 27, 1992, pp. 15–20.

[6] Stephen W. Littlejohn and David M. Jabusch, *Persuasive Transactions* (Glenview, Illinois: Scott, Foresman, 1987), p. 54.

[7] Lawrence W. Hugenberg and Donald D. Yoder, *Speaking in the Modern Organization* (Glenview, Illinois: Scott, Foresman 1985), p. 182.

[8] Littlejohn and Jabusch, *Persuasive Transactions*, p. 46.

[9] Ibid., p. 56.

[10] Abraham H. Maslow, *Motivation and Personality* (New York: Harper and Row, 1970), pp. 46–47.

[11] For this section on audience needs and motivations, we used Paul D. Holtzman, *The Psychology of Speakers' Audiences* (Glenview, Illinois: Scott Foresman, 1970), pp. 50–63, and Abraham H. Maslow, *Motivation and Personality*, (New York: Harper and Row, 1970), pp. 46–47. Both authors identify specific needs and discuss hierarchies of needs or values. They differ in their approaches, however. Holtzman examines multiple values, whereas Maslow uses a five-level hierarchy of needs. Holtzman believes that audiences set priorities based on their goals; Maslow believes that people cannot achieve higher needs until they have fulfilled lower levels of needs.

[12] I am grateful to the following students who gave permission to use their motivational appeals as examples in this section: Scott Hipp, Evan Feinberg, Ed Mincher, Norma Ferris, Heather Hay, Maria Marszalek, Cynthia Holley, Kristine Ozgar, Chris Clark, and Colleen V. Deitrich.

[13] Colleen Deitrich, "Mandatory Retirement Should Be Illegal," speech to convince presented in speech class, Carroll Community College, Westminster, Maryland, 1991. Used by permission.

[14] Research cited in this section appears in Judy Cornelia Pearson, Lynn H. Turner, and William Todd–Mancillas, *Gender & Communication*, 2nd ed. (Dubuque, Iowa: Wm. C. Brown Publishers, 1991), pp. 36, 113, 110, 177, 182, 108, and 41 (in order of citation).

[15] Debbie Bosley, "More Lenient Sentences for Postpartum Moms," speech to convince presented in speech class, Carroll Community College, Westminster, Maryland, 1992. Used by permission.

[16] James Kilduff, "Vegetarianism Is a Healthier Lifestyle," speech to convince presented in speech class, Carroll Community College, Westminster, Maryland, 1989. Used by permission.

[17] Martha Farnsworth Riche, "We're All Minorities Now," *American Demographics*, October 1991, pp. 26–33, and Brad Edmondson, "American Diversity," *American Demographics Desk Reference*, July 1991, pp. 20–21.

[18] Benjamin H. Alexander, "The Uncritical Acceptance Today," *Vital Speeches*, July 15, 1992, p. 605.

[19] Adapted from *Dorland's Illustrated Medical Dictionary*, 25th ed., s.v. "Pancreas."

[20] N. J. Nicholas, Jr., "The Boob Tube Gets Smart," *Vital Speeches*, June 15, 1991, p. 535.

[21] Lee Iacocca, "In Order To," *Vital Speeches*, October 1, 1987, p. 745.

[22] Daniel Callahan, "Thomas Jefferson," speech to inform presented in speech class, Catonsville Community College, Catonsville, Maryland, 1990. Used by permission.

[23] John M. Scheb, "The American Patriot," *Vital Speeches*, April 1, 1991, p. 377.

[24] The Carter "cardigan speech" received much favorable reaction, although there were news accounts which reported some negative feedback to the sweater. Compare "Warm Words from Jimmy Cardigan," *Time*, February 14, 1977, p. 18, to "Pleasures and Perils of Populism," *Time*, March 21, 1977, p. 25.

[25] Stanton, *Fundamentals of Marketing*, p. 45.

[26] I wish to thank Marie Skane, associate professor of mathematics at Catonsville Community College, who provided me with information about the SPSS computer program.

READINGS

Arliss, Laurie, and Borisoff, Deborah, ed. *Women and Men Communicating.* Fort Worth: Harcourt Brace College Publishers, 1993. This book presents a compilation of articles by experts in communication and gender. It has a strong interpersonal emphasis, but several chapters are of interest to the public speaker: Chapter 9, "Communication and Gender in the Classroom"; Chapter 10,

"Communication in Corporate Settings"; Chapter 11, "Communicating in Legal Settings"; Chapter 12, "Communication in Health Care Settings"; and Chapter 13, "Gender and Communication in the Hospitality Industry."

Holtzman, Paul D. *The Psychology of Speakers' Audiences.* Glenview, Ill.: Scott, Foresman, 1970. A good book for additional information on audience analysis. Part II served as a basis for our approach in this chapter, and we added one additional aspect to Holtzman's "Four Listener Factors." In Part III, the author examines audience beliefs, values, and experiences, as well as the importance of speaker adaptation. This text can help you to adapt to persuasive as well as to informational audience situations.

Hugenberg, Lawerence., and Yoder, Donald. *Speaking in the Modern Organization.* Glenview, Illinois: Scott, Foresman, 1985. Chapter 3, "Preparing for Communication," contains a section on analyzing the context of the speech. The authors provide good suggestions for collecting data about audiences and include some exercises helpful in determining some of your own possible stereotypes in areas such as age, gender, and religion.

Pearson, Judy Cornelia, Turner, Lynn H., and Todd–Mancillas, William. *Gender & Communication,* 2nd ed. Dubuque, Iowa: Wm. C. Brown Publishers, 1991. A good text to read for more detailed information about communication and gender. The authors present conclusions supported by numerous studies on many aspects associated with gender. Although it tends to be theoretical, the book includes interesting exercises that provide the reader with helpful insights into self perceptions.

Thomas, David A., and Fryar, Maridell. *Successful Business Speaking.* Skokie, Ill.: National Textbook Company, 1981. This little book is especially helpful to students who plan to specialize in business-related careers. The text includes an overview of principles provided in this chapter, and an application of these principles to business situations.

Chapter Four

Improving Your Listening Skills

Key Terms

Active listening
Appreciative listening
Content
Delivery
Discriminative listening
Empathic listening
Evaluative listening
Passive listening
Listening barriers
Active listening behaviors

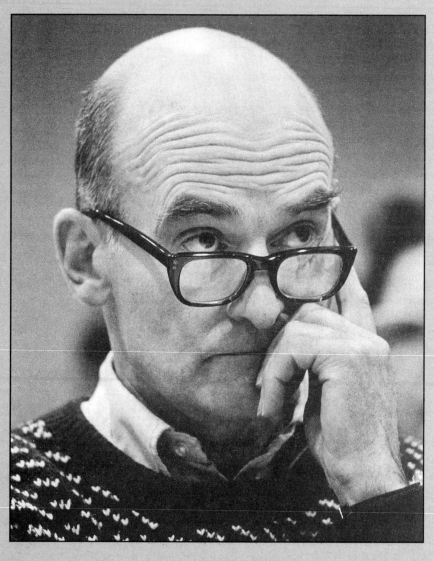

George Bellerose/
Stock Boston

"To listen is an effort, and just to hear is no
merit. A duck hears also."
—IGOR STRAVINSKY

*A*n advertisement for the Sperry Corporation showed a photograph of a little boy in a classroom. The caption read: "How can we expect him to learn when we haven't taught him how to listen?" The ad went on to discuss the need for education and training in listening at all levels of society and referred to research indicating that adults listen at only a "25 percent level of efficiency."[1]

The Sperry Corporation correctly identified the significance of effective listening in the communication process. Often our success depends upon how effectively we listen to directions and data, how carefully we evaluate and weigh information. Lives depend upon a pilot's ability to listen to flight instructions from the control tower, and upon a surgeon's ability to listen to other doctors or patients.

This chapter presents four kinds of listening and introduces the concept of active and passive listening, identifies seven behaviors which create barriers to effective listening, and discusses a four-point program to build better listening skills.

THE SIGNIFICANCE OF LISTENING

We spend much of our lives listening. In fact, research indicates that most communication activity is listening activity. A classic study conducted by Paul Rankin in 1928 examined the time spent in four communication-related behaviors: listening, reading, writing, and speaking. Rankin found that listening outranked all other communication activities. Listening took place 42.1 percent of the time, talking 31.9 percent. Reading accounted for 15 percent of communication behavior, and writing for 11 percent.[2]

A more recent study supporting Rankin's findings was conducted in 1977 at Auburn University. Researchers surveyed 645 students and found that listening occurred 52.5 percent of the time, speaking took place 16.3 percent of the communication day, while 17.3 percent of the time was spent reading, and writing occupied 13.9 percent of the communication day.[3]

Although we may spend the majority of our communication time listening, we don't always do it well. Poor listening is a fact of life in all professions and at every level of our society. Examples abound of problems created because individuals or groups refused to listen, didn't listen carefully, or listened only to information they wanted to hear. Here are a few concrete examples of the magnitude of the listening problem.

On January 25, 1990, Avianca Airlines Flight 025 ran out of fuel and crashed in Cove Neck, Long Island (New York), killing 73 of the 158 passengers aboard. The jetliner had missed an instrument approach to Kennedy International Airport, and was attempting to make a second attempt at a landing. After investigating the accident, the National Transportation Safety Board stated that "the flight crew did not adequately communicate its increasingly

HOW CAN WE EXPECT HIM TO LEARN WHEN WE HAVEN'T TAUGHT HIM HOW TO LISTEN.

It's ironic.

We teach children how to read, write and do arithmetic, but don't teach them the skill they need most to learn them.

How to listen.

(The bulk of a child's listening education consists of admonitions like "Pay attention!", "Open up your ears!", "Listen!")

And listening <u>does</u> need to be taught.

It's a difficult, intricate skill. And like other skills, it requires training. And practice.

In the few schools where listening programs have been adopted, listening comprehension among students has as much as doubled in just a few months.

We at Sperry are concerned about the listening problem. As parents. And as businessmen.

Denied a proper listening education as children, adults listen—according to research—at a pathetically low 25% level of efficiency.

And as a worldwide corporation with more than 87,000 employees, that's simply not efficient enough for us.

Which is why we've taken listening education into our own hands.

Listening has been a part of many Sperry training and development programs for years.

And we've recently set up expanded listening programs for Sperry employees worldwide. From sales representatives to computer engineers to the Chairman of the Board.

These programs are making us a lot better at listening to each other. And when you do business with Sperry Univac, or any of our other divisions, you're going to discover that they're making us a lot better at listening to you.

We understand how important it is to listen.

Sperry is Sperry Univac computers, Sperry New Holland farm equipment, Sperry Vickers fluid power systems, and guidance and control equipment from Sperry division and Sperry Flight Systems.

Test your listening skills.
Write to Sperry, Dept. 4B, 1290 Avenue of the Americas, New York, New York 10019 for a listening quiz that's both fun and a little surprising.

FIGURE 4.1

Based upon copyrighted material of Dr. Lyman K. Steil, president, Communication Development, Inc. St. Paul, Minnesota, for the Sperry Corporation. Reprinted with permission of Dr. Steil and Sperry Corporation (now Unisys).

critical fuel situation to airport controllers." The board also noted that one controller had not heard a portion of the pilot's transmission identifying the nature of the problem with the words ". . . We can't do it now, we, we will run out of fuel now."

In its conclusion, the safety board criticized the flight crew for not using the word "emergency" when referring to their critical fuel situation. But the report also stated that one probable cause of the accident was the "lack of standardized understandable terminology for pilots and controllers for minimum and emergency fuel states."[4]

An engineer supervising the manufacture of the space shuttle booster rocket repeatedly warned NASA officials that the booster rocket's "O–Ring" seals might not function properly in subfreezing temperatures. Four senior NASA officials did not listen to the warnings, and the fatal decision was made to launch the space shuttle Challenger on January 28, 1986 in sub-freezing temperatures. The O-Ring couplings failed to seal properly, causing the explosion that killed six astronauts and one schoolteacher. The Rogers Commission investigating the disaster concluded that "NASA's decision-making process was clearly flawed."[5]

At the time of the Watergate scandal, even a good listener could be deceived by the smokescreen of words and mangled concepts emanating from the Nixon White House. In 1974, historian and former presidential assistant Arthur Schlesinger presented a speech to the National Education Association advising his hearers to listen critically to the vague words and phrases used by the Nixon administration to describe Watergate activities. Phrases such as "toughing it out," "stroking sessions," "stonewalling it," "the limited let-it-all hang out," and "how do you handle that PR-wise?" were frequently used by Nixon and his appointees to manipulate language and to deflect criticism. Schlesinger also accused the president of manipulating meaning when Nixon released the transcripts of his tape-recorded conversations about the Watergate affair.

> The presidential speech preceding the release of the expurgated transcripts was grammatically correct, but it proclaimed in tones of ringing sincerity that the transcripts show exactly the opposite of what in fact the transcripts do show. "He unveils a swamp," as the *New Yorker* well put it, "and instructs us to see a garden of flowers."[6]

Sometimes listeners must work extremely hard to detect hidden meanings behind distorted and manipulated language.

In Jonestown, Guyana, on November 24, 1978, the Reverend Jim Jones persuaded 900 of his followers to commit suicide by swallowing a grape soft drink laced with cyanide. How could these people be so tragically manipulated? Part of the answer lies in understanding the dynamics of cults, charismatic speakers, and brainwashing techniques. But part of the answer also is explained by listeners' desires to hear what they wanted to hear and to deny the truth of what was occurring. In the following excerpt from Jones's suicide speech, notice the varying reactions among the listeners.

> *Jones:* What these people gone and done, and what they get through will make our lives worse than hell... But to me, death is not a fearful thing. It's living that's cursed... Not worth living like this.
>
> *First Woman:* I think there were too few who left for twelve hundred people to give them their lives for those people that left... I'm not ready to die. I look at all the babies and I think they deserve to live.
>
> *Jones:* But don't they deserve much more? They deserve peace. Please get some medication. Simple. It's simple. There's no convulsions with it. Don't be afraid to die. You'll see people land out here. They'll torture some of our children here. They'll torture our people. We cannot have this.
>
> *Second Woman:* There's nothing to worry about. Everybody keep calm and try to keep your children calm... They're not crying from pain, it's just a little bitter-tasting.

Jones: Please, for God's sake, let's get on with it... This is a revolutionary suicide. This is not a self-destructive suicide. So they'll pay for this. They brought this upon us. And they'll pay for that. I leave that destiny to them. (Male voices praise "Dad" [Jones]. Applause.) [7]

The first woman, who had absorbed the impact of what Jones was advocating, clearly protested his suicide solution. The second woman's supportive comment helped Jones carry out his aims, and the other listeners who expressed themselves exerted peer pressure by praising "Daddy Jones" and by applauding his words.

Perhaps the first woman became involved in Jones's cult by hearing what she wanted to hear—a promise of a better life. Perhaps, too, she began to listen more effectively only when it was too late. The second woman, brainwashed into believing that suicide actually offered a better life, heard what she wanted to hear instead of probing or questioning the ideas.

While these examples are extreme, they remind us of what can happen to an individual, a group, a nation, or an entire civilization if people don't listen critically.

KINDS OF LISTENING

Just as speakers have general speech purposes for sending messages, listeners also have goals for receiving them. We will examine four kinds of listening: discriminative, evaluative, appreciative, and empathic.[8] In addition, we will briefly describe the concepts of active and passive listening.

Discriminative Listening

When we listen discriminatively, we listen to learn, to be instructed, and to test theories. Discriminative listening can occur in formal settings such as in class, at work, or in a business meeting. If you are taking notes at a history lecture, receiving instructions on how to operate a new computer program, or hearing a committee report, you are acquiring instructional information for future use. Discriminative listening also occurs informally in the process of daily conversation. When you hear your lunch friends describing a new restaurant, the service manager explaining what is wrong with your car, or an insurance agent providing details of a policy, you have applied discriminative listening. Whether formal or informal, discriminative listening helps us to make distinctions, and to differentiate so as to become enlightened, informed, or educated.

Evaluative Listening

Evaluative listening is our response to a persuasive message. We listen to convincing, actuating, or stimulating messages, and formulate reactions based upon our needs and the strength of the persuasion. We are bombarded with persuasive messages daily. Advertisers on television, radio, and in magazines actuate us to buy products; family members persuade us to run errands, purchase gifts, or plan vacations; supervisors encourage us to use new strategies to enhance the company image or to improve sales; a colleague urges us to buy candy to help her daughter raise money for a class trip. Persuasion is often difficult because listeners have built up resistance as a result of the constant barrage of competing stimuli. Listeners ultimately evaluate persuasive messages and decide to agree or disagree based upon the credibility of the speaker and the material, the logic of the speaker's reasoning, the extent of the commitment exhibited by the speaker, and the need of listeners to buy into the speaker's goal.

Appreciative Listening

If you have ever been to a movie, listened to a favorite recording, taken a long walk in the woods, or just enjoyed hearing the sounds of the ocean at the beach, you have participated in appreciative listening. We listen appreciatively to hear the power and beauty of words, images, music, or environmental sounds. We may enjoy hearing the variety of instruments in a symphony; we might respond with strong emotion to the vivid language of an eloquent speaker; we may sit in passive contentment to the delicate trickle of a waterfall or to the patter of rain on a roof. We might hear the call of an owl at night, or the hiss of an alley cat springing off a garbage can. We learn appreciative listening as we become sensitized to new sounds and experiences. When we learn to listen appreciatively, we establish an emotional bond by responding to the works of others and we enhance our sensory enjoyment of life.

Empathic Listening

The primary goal of discriminative, evaluative, and appreciative listening is to benefit ourselves and contribute to our understanding, decision-making, and personal fulfillment. The goal of empathic listening differs, however, in that the objective is to understand and facilitate the needs and feelings of someone else.

We use empathic or therapeutic listening when we respond to the needs of a close friend, work associate, or family member who is sharing personal joy, anxiety, or concern. We could be hearing a friend who is describing a failed marriage, a family member sharing pride about a job promotion, or a relative describing a struggle with alcoholism.

Numerous businesses, professions, and volunteer organizations require their employees to possess skills in effective therapeutic listening. Lawyers assist their clients in developing the best defense after hearing the nature of the charges against them. Educators are required to plan strategies for growth after listening to the needs of students. Psychiatrists must provide therapeutic progress toward mental health when responding to the anxieties of patients. Volunteers often spend hours on hotlines listening to distraught individuals who describe suicidal feelings, spouse abuse, or rape. Hospice workers listen with love and devotion to the last cries and wishes of the dying. Empathic listeners must pay attention *completely* without giving in to distractions, without making irrelevant comments, and without ignoring the sender's message.

Active and Passive Listening

Most listening behavior is either active or passive. Active listening is attentive and involved behavior. Active listening is the kind of listening we should be using at work, in a meeting, or in class. Active listening is hard work—it represents complete mental commitment on the part of the hearer. Passive listening is relaxed or "easy" listening. Often when you listen to your stereo or watch a movie you are listening passively. Passive listening helps us escape from the pressures of everyday life. Most of us, however, are already accomplished in passive listening and probably not attentive enough to the demands of active listening. If you have ever received a poor grade on a test because you didn't take good notes in class, you have experienced the results of passive listening.

BARRIERS TO LISTENING

We all need to become better active listeners. But in order to improve our listening, we need to understand and analyze some of the poor listening behaviors we often practice. Seven barriers to effective listening are:

1. yielding to distractions
2. blocking out communication
3. failing to concentrate
4. piecemeal or selective fact listening
5. over-criticizing the speaker
6. faking attention, and
7. avoiding difficult listening situations.[9]

Yielding to Distractions

We've already discussed "noise" as a barrier to the communication process in Chapter 1. As a listener, you have a constant battle with distractions that result from external, internal, or semantic noise. If a speaker has a broken pair of glasses held together at the nose by tape, you are going to have difficulty listening to the speaker's remarks because of the external distraction. Equally distracting are your own internal "noises" such as anger at a person or situation, fatigue from staying up all night, or anxiety about an upcoming conflict, court appearance, or final exam. You also might not understand several of the terms that the speaker is using, or you might react negatively to an outdated word or phrase the speaker employs.

Blocking Out Communication

Sooner or later, most of us can be accused of "blocking out" information and of not listening. One of the most common stereotypes of blocking behavior is the husband who reads the newspaper and mutters "uh-huh" while his wife is trying to talk to him. We've probably all watched an exciting TV program and blocked out the phone talk or other conversation around us.

Sometimes blocking behaviors are purposeful, and sometimes they are habits acquired as a result of pressure, stress, and over-stimulation of the senses. Even conscientious, active listeners can be so bombarded by competing stimuli that they are forced to adopt blocking behavior as a survival mechanism. For example, you wake up in the morning and hear on the radio that several hundred people have been killed in an earthquake; at noon you hear about a fellow office worker's sudden heart attack; coming home you hear of another terrorist attack in the Middle East, and the evening news reports that violent crimes in your community have doubled in the past two years. At home, you discover that your little sister has broken her finger and there has been another family crisis. In these circumstances, you might well choose to block out information for awhile.

The problem occurs, however, when normally active listeners become so saturated by what they hear and see that blocking out stimuli becomes habitual, and they can no longer pay the necessary attention to *real* crises. When a husband or wife begin to block each other out in their marriage, or children cannot get through to their parents, serious communication barriers can be created.

Blocking can also result when a listener who disagrees turns off immediately when the topic of the speech is announced or when certain catch words are stated. Instead of giving the speech a fair hearing, a listener with an extreme bias will have a mental fight with the speaker about each point. A biased individual might not be able to get around the mere mention of the names Clinton or Bush, the terms *tax increase* or *supply-side economics*, the labels *Republican* or *Democrat*.

Sometimes an individual will block out the opposing speaker so that mental time can be spent storing up all of the verbal ammunition to fire back. The listener is not hearing the speaker, but is blocking out any opposing views so that the listener's position does not have to be examined.

"ISN'T IT ABOUT TIME TO STOP FOR A COMMERCIAL OR SOMETHING?"

Failing to Concentrate

Our society puts great emphasis on relaxation. Ads tell us to go on a vacation, take a coffee break, eat a certain candy bar, buy a VCR, or go to a movie. We are not condemning the practice of listening to relax. Listening to a good recording or watching a comedy can do wonders for your mental health. But many of us are very good at passive television listening and not very good at active listening that requires energy and work. Often the more time we spend in passive listening, the lazier we become in our active listening patterns.[10] It becomes easier and more fun to daydream and let our minds wander than to concentrate on more difficult information.

Piecemeal or Selective Fact Listening

Often we create a listening barrier when we try to listen for all of the details, and we don't catch the overall point of the information. An equal problem is the desire within all of us to hear what we want to hear, or to listen only to information that supports our own thinking.

Loan counselor: Now there are several types of mortgages you and your wife should consider before making your final choice.

Mortgage applicants: Could you explain the different mortgages for us?

Loan counselor: Well, there is the fixed-rate, fifteen-year mortgage; the fixed-rate, thirty-year mortgage; and several types of adjustable rate mortgages, called ARMs for short.

Mortgage applicants: Well, we really don't know anything about any of these, but all we know is that we want the best deal, and the cheapest mortgage with the lowest monthly payments.

Loan counselor: Well, you can always choose the fixed-rate mortgage which is nine percent. Of course, your monthly payments are going to start high and stay the same for the life of the loan. Now you can take any one of the ARMs which allow you the advantage of initial low monthly payments and don't really increase for several years. One of our ARMs, which I really think you'd both be interested in, starts at the low rate of six and three-quarters percent for the first two years, then increases to only eight and three-fourths percent in the third year. For the remainder of the loan the rate is set by the lender. *Imagine,* being able to have monthly payments of only six and three-fourths percent for two whole years!

Mortgage applicants: Sounds good to us!

The applicants in this example have unfortunately listened selectively when they should have been listening critically. The couple, clearly interested in "the cheapest mortgage with the lowest monthly payments," has focused on the loan counselor's enthusiasm and vocal emphasis: "Imagine, being able to have monthly payments of only six-and-three-fourths percent for two whole years!" These home-buyers think they have agreed to favorable mortgage rates, but because they only listened partially, they did not hear the "catch" to the agreement—that after three years, the mortgage rate will be set by the lender for the remainder of the life of the loan. Our mortgage applicants have not asked if there is any ceiling placed on the mortgage rate after the initial three years. It is possible, then, that for twenty-seven years these people could be paying monthly mortgage rates as high as thirteen, fifteen, or even sixteen percent, which will be set by the lender. Our buyers have now become victims.

Over-Criticizing the Speaker

We can criticize a speaker to such an extent that we can destroy any possibility of hearing the speaker's intentions or purposes. The speaker's appearance may be wrong, the speaker may lean too much on the lectern, or the speaker's tie may be the wrong color. Maybe we think the speaker shouldn't wear a tie, or the speaker's voice is too soft or too loud, or the speaker is too emotional or too logical.

Many listeners feel that communication is solely the responsibility of the speaker. If the speaker isn't exciting enough, attractive enough, funny enough, emotional enough, or logical enough, these listeners switch mental channels and perform their own mental activities.

The responsibility for effective communication must be *shared* between the speaker and listener. The speaker is responsible for encoding the feelings into symbols, structuring the message, and selecting the channels of communication. But the listener is responsible for decoding the message and for providing clear feedback, which signals to the speaker if communication is taking place, and how effective the communication has been.

An individual who over-criticizes a speaker often assumes that it is solely the speaker's responsibility to convey a message. Often these listeners develop the attitude that "Okay—here I am sitting in front of you. Do something to me. Interest me. Get my attention. Humor me." Not only is this poor listening behavior, it keeps the individual from shouldering his or her part of the communication transaction—to listen.

Faking Attention

Many of us are very good at faking attention. When we're involved in a boring conversation, we can smile, look interested, and nod our heads as if we are giving our complete attention. But in our minds we are performing some other activity, such as planning our weekend or finalizing the grocery list.

Students are very good at faking attention. A student can look straight at the instructor, smile and frown at all the appropriate times, lean forward and take notes (doodles on the paper), and generally appear to be involved in the class. The problem occurs, of course, when a question demands a specific response, or a pop-quiz is given on material just discussed. The faked response can quickly turn into embarrassment with an inattentive listener angry at being taken by surprise.

Faking attention is a bad habit that creates a barrier to communication. The faker loses, wasting valuable time that could have been spent growing in the sender-receiver communication process.

Avoiding Difficult Listening Situations

Sometimes we avoid listening situations we feel are too demanding. We feel insecure, and our lack of experience makes us dread the situation.

A poster in a college math department reads: "Mathophobia can cost you a career."[11] Underneath the caption is a list of careers such as commercial flying, dental technology, and engineering, which are inaccessible to individuals without skills in mathematics.

We could expand that caption to state: "Avoiding difficult listening situations can cost you enlightenment, growth, and fulfillment." Imagine someone canceling a trip to Greece or the Riviera due to insecurity about foreign languages.

Think of individuals passing up free tickets to a symphony concert because they don't "understand" serious music. Imagine an individual not learning how to use the computer because it appears too complicated. Unfortunately these situations can and do occur when individuals fear difficult listening circumstances.

Sometimes listening is a matter of rethinking and overcoming inner fears. Whatever you do, don't avoid situations that you think may be difficult. Overcome the difficulty by facing it directly. Open your mind up to the situation and allow yourself to receive communication. Take on the listening circumstance as a challenge: gain perspective by exploring an unfamiliar culture; develop sophistication from an aesthetic experience; gain satisfaction by acquiring a new skill. You will be surprised at your growth and achievement in a constructive environment.

BECOMING AN ACTIVE LISTENER

We now need to work toward the development of a program to become better active listeners. Here is a simple four-point program to help you increase your awareness of the way you listen:

1. Withhold judgment about the speech and the speaker.
2. Provide the speaker with honest, attentive feedback.
3. Eliminate distractions.
4. Evaluate the speech when it is over.

Withholding Judgment about the Speech and the Speaker

Keep an open mind. Don't turn off when you hear the speaker's name, the statement of the topic, or the purpose of the speech. Wait until the speaker has finished before you begin to evaluate the speaker or any portion of the speech. In withholding judgment about the speech and the speaker, you need to:

1. avoid the appearance trap,
2. not be easily swayed by the speaker's delivery and style,
3. give all topics a fair hearing, and
4. avoid extraneous mental activity during the speech.

Avoid the Appearance Trap. We are easily influenced by a speaker's physical appearance. It is easy to misjudge a sloppily dressed person, or to feel that someone who is neatly dressed in the latest fashion is more worthy of our time.

While it is important for a speaker to do everything possible to support the speech non-verbally as well as verbally, we must recognize that not all speakers share the same ideas about what constitutes effective speaking.

"Dressing for success" may be important to some speakers, but others might care very little about appearance. Recognize your own attitudes and standards about appearance, and try not to impose these attitudes on the speaker.

Don't be Easily Swayed by Delivery and Style. Don't allow yourself to become seduced or alienated by delivery and style. A speaker who has a soothing voice could be advocating ideas harmful to the audience, while a speaker with an irritating voice could be well-organized and coherent in logic and ideas. You also need to work hard not to let a speaker's hesitations, vocalized pauses, or monotonous delivery affect your judgments unfairly. In addition, don't be too easily impressed by a speaker's ability to use big words and flamboyant phrases which send you on a hunt through the dictionary.

Recognize that every speaker has limitations in delivery. Try to accept the speaker and learn as much as you can without mentally trying to change the speaker.

Give Topics With Which You Don't Agree as Fair a Hearing as Topics You Like. We all like some topics more than others. Don't let your own attitude for or against an issue prejudice your receptivity to a speech. You have nothing to lose if you keep your mind open to an issue. If you still disagree with the topic at the conclusion of the speech, you will have learned something—even if it is about the speaker's organization or research.

Force yourself to listen to ideas you oppose. Listening to different beliefs develops your active listening capacities, and helps you grow as a communicator.

Avoid Extraneous Mental Activity During the Speech. Some books and articles on listening advise people to take mental notes, make mental summaries, or write mental outlines while listening. Such mental activity is said to help the listener concentrate on what is being discussed, and more effectively retain the main points of the presentation. One author rejects these ideas and feels that such advice causes listeners to become distracted.[12] Some research indicates that when people are still thinking about a speaker's previous point (or making mental summaries) they are usually not listening to what the speaker is currently saying.[13]

It is important that listeners concentrate on what is being said and not think behind or ahead of the speaker. When you give the speaker a complete hearing, all of your mental activity will be focused upon the speaker, and you will postpone all other evaluation, summarizing, or inference-making until the speech is over.

Giving the Speaker Honest, Attentive Feedback

Work hard to listen actively to the speaker. Provide clear signals that show the speaker you are paying attention. Sit up straight. Make eye contact with the

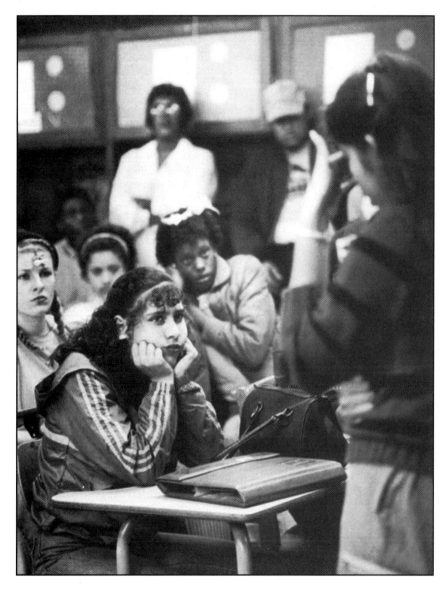

ACTIVE LISTENING
IS HARD WORK AND
REPRESENTS COMPLETE
MENTAL COMMITMENT
ON THE PART OF THE
HEARER.

Jane Scherr/Jeroboam, Inc.

speaker. Nod your head to let the speaker know you understand what is being said. Show interest in the speaker and in the speaker's topic. Give the speaker a smile when he tells a joke. Try to support the speaker as much as you can. If you don't understand a part of the speech, give the speaker a puzzled expression to indicate that you don't follow what is being discussed.[14]

Don't fake attention. Don't pretend to listen when you really aren't.[15] In Chapter 3, we talked about credibility and the necessity of trusting a speaker.

It is equally important that a speaker be able to trust an audience. The speaker needs to know that the speech is being actively heard and that the listener is providing clear, accurate, and sincere feedback to the speech.

In your speech class, you could conceivably deliver speeches exclusively to your instructor without class members present. In such a situation, your only concern would be to direct your speech to your audience of one (your instructor) and to get a good grade on each presentation. You could also conceivably deliver speeches to an audience commanded to fake pleasant facial expressions, giving you the false impression that whatever you said was positively received. But your speech instructor does not want a one-person audience or a fake audience. Your instructor wants every speaker to communicate to a "live" audience that is sincere, receptive, and attentive. Your position as a listener in your classroom is just as important as your position as a speaker. How well you listen can affect the learning atmosphere of the class as well as the success of each individual speaker.

Eliminating Distractions

Be conscious of the disruptions caused by external, internal, and semantic noise, and work hard to overcome them. You must continually remind yourself that your role as a listener requires you to share in the communication process and to be active in relation to the speaker. Don't allow yourself the luxury of daydreaming, making up the grocery list, or studying for an exam during a speech. Avoid the pitfalls created by these distractions. Remind yourself that, as a listener, you have the same responsibility of keeping to your task as does the speaker. Learn to block out the distractions—not the speaker.

Evaluating the Speech When It Is Finished

When the speech is completed, evaluate the presentation. Begin to ask questions, make mental summaries, and try to recall the main points of the speech. After you listen to the presentation, analyze both the content and the delivery. Speech *content* refers to the research, organization, and logical development of the topic. The *delivery* refers to the style or presentation of the speech. Here is a list of questions about content and delivery to use when you analyze speeches presented in your course:

Content

Was the speech well organized?

Did the speech reflect the existence and development of an outline?

Was there a clear specific purpose and/or a thesis statement in the speech?

Was there an introduction, body, and conclusion in the speech?

Were the main points in the body of the speech easy to follow?

Was the introduction interesting? Was the introduction designed to gain the attention of the audience?

Did the speaker use credible sources to support the main points of the speech?

Did the speaker use examples, case studies, illustrations or other supportive materials to explain some of the major points in the speech?

Did the speaker use statistics? Were these clear and easy to understand? Were the statistics logical, and did they support the main points in the speech?

Was the speaker's information accurate and current?

Was the topic appropriate to the audience?

Did the speaker attempt to adapt the topic to audience interests and needs?

Did the speaker define any unfamiliar terms?

Was the content of the speech generally well-prepared?

Was the conclusion interesting? Was the conclusion designed to wrap up the speech effectively?

Delivery

Did the speaker use eye contact?

Did the speaker use supportive facial expressions?

Did the speaker use gestures for emphasis and clarity?

Was the speaker's posture and body position appropriate?

Did the speaker use note-cards effectively?

Was the speaker spontaneous and conversational?

Was the speaker's voice easy to hear?

Did the speaker make use of vocal inflections?

Did the speaker appear to be enthusiastic and energetic about the subject?

Did the speaker's vocal tone, vocal inflections, and verbal emphasis indicate a commitment or belief in the topic? Was the speaker's articulation effective? Did the speaker have an understanding of English usage?

Was the language appropriate to the topic and the audience?

Did the speaker use external transitions to mark the main points of the body? Did the speaker make use of internal transitions within main headings?

If visual aids were used, did the speaker use the visuals effectively? Were the visuals easy to see, neat, clear, and were they an asset to the speech?

Did the speaker have any mannerisms that created external noise?

SUMMARY

Research indicates that people spend the majority of their communication time in listening-related activities. Problems occur when people don't listen effectively.

Listening can be identified as discriminative or instructional, evaluative or persuasive, appreciative or emotional, and empathic or therapeutic. Active listening is an attentive and involved activity, while passive listening is a relaxed behavior.

Barriers to listening include yielding to distractions blocking out communication, failing to concentrate, piecemeal or selective fact listening, over-criticizing the speaker, faking attention, and avoiding difficult listening situations.

To become a more active listener, withhold judgment about the speech and the speaker, provide the speaker with honest and attentive feedback, eliminate distractions, and evaluate the speech only when it is over.

Content deals with the research, organization, and logical development of the ideas in the speech, and delivery represents the style or manner used to present the content.

EXERCISES

1. Ask every person in your class to state his or her name and major. After you have finished hearing from the entire class, try to recall (in sequence) the names and majors from memory to assess how carefully you listened to each class member.
2. Keep a journal of your daily listening activities for two weeks. Write down the type of event you listened to, the amount of time spent listening to that activity, the kind of listening behavior you experienced, and your overall evaluation of how well you listened. In your journal, discuss any aspects of the listening situation that made it easy or hard to concentrate on the speaker.
3. By looking over your listening journal, write down those situations that especially interested you, list the situations to which you had difficulty listening, then list all the situations that bored you.
4. Look through your journal and make a list of any of the distractions (external, internal, or semantic noise) that made it difficult for you to listen. Did you give in to any of the distractions and allow them to take you away from active listening? Did you daydream, or did a speaker's comment trigger any extraneous mental activity on your part?
5. Go back through the journal and select the listening situations that you consciously or unconsciously blocked out. Ask yourself why you blocked out communication and what your emotional state was at the time. Were you tired, worried, under stress, or experiencing conflicts? Did you disagree with the speaker? Did you dislike the speaker, the speaker's style, or the way the speaker was dressed? Did something the speaker say make you angry?

6. Look over your journal and select a situation you listened to only partially. Why did you listen selectively? Did your lack of attentive listening cause you any damage in the situation? If so, explain.
7. Make a list of the subjects you find it hard to discuss or listen to. After looking over the list, try to find some areas for improvement.
8. Make a chart in a notebook to summarize your listening experiences during any one day. Put down the following information:
   a. The date
   b. The type of listening activity
   c. The amount of time you spent in that activity
   d. Whether you listened actively or passively in the situation (in some cases, you might have listened *both* actively and passively at various times during the listening experience—therefore, you would check *both* active and passive)
   e. Write a brief description of your listening behavior.
9. Take the listening test provided in this chapter.

Assessment of Listening Behavior

In the following test are fifteen statements that can help you determine how well you listen. Answer each statement by checking the box at the right under the word that BEST describes your behavior. The following five-point scale will be used to assess your total score:

Always = 5, Often = 4, Sometimes = 3, Seldom = 2, and Never = 1.

	Always	Often	Sometimes	Seldom	Never
1. I wait until a speech is over before I evaluate it.	❏	❏	❏	❏	❏
2. I keep an open mind when I hear a speaker's topic.	❏	❏	❏	❏	❏
3. A speaker's appearance does not influence my thinking.	❏	❏	❏	❏	❏
4. A speaker's delivery or style of speaking does not influence or affect my feelings about a topic.	❏	❏	❏	❏	❏
5. I keep my mind focused on what the speaker is saying at the moment rather than daydreaming about something else.	❏	❏	❏	❏	❏
6. I don't let distractions take my concentration.	❏	❏	❏	❏	❏

	Always	Often	Sometimes	Seldom	Never
7. I give the speaker some kind of honest and appropriate feedback while the speaker is talking.	❑	❑	❑	❑	❑
8. I work hard at listening to people.	❑	❑	❑	❑	❑
9. I don't block people out when they are speaking.	❑	❑	❑	❑	❑
10. When a speaker has finished, I find that I can mentally recall the main points of the presentation.	❑	❑	❑	❑	❑
11. I seek difficult listening situations that require a lot of effort.	❑	❑	❑	❑	❑
12. I don't fake attention when someone is talking to me.	❑	❑	❑	❑	❑
13. I don't mentally critique the speaker when the speaker is talking.	❑	❑	❑	❑	❑
14. I don't tune the speaker out if I hear a word, phrase, or idea that I don't agree with.	❑	❑	❑	❑	❑
15. I find that I listen completely and not selectively or in a piecemeal manner.	❑	❑	❑	❑	❑
Subtotal from each column	____	____	____	____	____

Grand total from all columns _____

Scoring:

65-75 total score indicates you are a good listener
55-64 total score indicates you listen sporadically and need to change weak areas
45-54 total score indicates you need to improve your overall listening behavior

NOTES

[1] Sperry advertisement, *Business Week*, February 4, 1980. Based upon copyrighted material of Dr. Lyman K. Steil, president, Communication Development, Inc., St. Paul, Minnesota, for the Sperry Corporation. Reprinted with permission of Dr. Steil and Sperry Corporation (now Unisys).

[2] Paul T. Rankin, "The Importance of Listening Ability," *English Journal* 17 (1928): 623–630.

[3] Larry Barker, Karen Gladney, Renee Edwards, Frances Holley, Connie Gaines, "An Investigation of Proportional Time Spent in Various Communication Activities by College Students," *Journal of Applied Communication Research*, 8 (1980), pp. 101–109.

[4] National Transportation Safety Board, *Aircraft Accident Report, Avianca, the Airline of Columbia, Boeing 707-321B, HK 2016, Fuel Exhaustion*, Adopted: April 30, 1991, pp. 6, 74, 75, 76.

[5] "Commission Finds Flaws in NASA's Decision-Making," *Science*, March 14, 1986, pp. 1237–1238.

[6] Arthur M. Schlesinger, Jr., "Watergate and the Corruption of Language," *Today's Education*, September–October, 1974, pp. 25–27.

[7] "Don't Be Afraid To Die," *Newsweek*, March 26, 1979, p. 53. From *Newsweek*, March 26, © 1979, Newsweek, Inc. All rights reserved. Reprinted by permission.

[8] Two sources were used as the basis for "Kinds of Listening": Florence I. Wolf, and Nadine C. Marsnik, *Perceptive Listening*, 2nd ed. (New York: Holt, Rinehart and Winston, 1992), pp. 88–103, and Andrew D. Wolvin and Carolyn Gwynn Coakley, *Listening*, 4th ed. (Dubuque, Iowa: Wm C. Brown, 1992), Part II, pp. 163–396. The authors of *Perceptive Listening* present five kinds of listening which include "self listening." In *Listening*, the writers identify five areas, but include a different type they call "comprehensive listening." We believe that the four listening types presented in this chapter are most commonly identified throughout the literature.

[9] This list of common barriers to listening is synthesized from two sources: Robert O. Hirsch, *Listening: A Way to Process Information Aurally* (Dubuque, Iowa: Gorsuch Scarisbrick, 1979), pp. 36–41; and Ralph G. Nichols, *Are You Listening?* (New York: McGraw–Hill, 1957), pp. 104–112.

[10] Peter Conrad, *Television, the Medium and Its Manners* (Boston: Routledge and Kegan Paul, 1982). Conrad makes some devastating and thought-provoking attacks on the invasion of television into our lives: "Talk on television isn't meant to be listened to. The words merely gain for us the time to look at the talker. The talk shows are theatres of behavior, not dialogues" (p. 48).

[11] Used by permission of the Mathematics Department, Toronto Board of Education.

[12] Charles M. Kelley, "Empathic Listening," in Jimmie D. Trent, Judith S. Trent, and Daniel J. O'Neill, *Concepts in Communication* (Boston: Allyn and Bacon, 1973), p. 270.

[13] Robert W. Norton and Loyd S. Pettegrew, "Attentiveness as a Style of Communication: A Structural Analysis," *Communication Monographs*, 46 (March 1979): 13–16.

[14] Ralph G. Nichols, *Are You Listening?* (New York: McGraw-Hill, 1957), p. 105.

READINGS

Kelley, Charles M. "Empathic Listening," in *Concepts in Communication*, p. 270. Written by Jimmie D. Trent, Judith S. Trent, and Daniel J. O'Neill. Boston: Allyn and Bacon, 1973. A compilation of interesting articles on many different aspects of communication. Kelley's article is useful in helping you to develop effective listening skills.

Steil, Lyman K., Barker, Larry L., and Watson, Kittie W. *Effective Listening*. Reading, Mass.: Addison–Wesley, 1983. An interesting book with many examples. Chapter 5, "Identifying Your Personal Listening Strengths and Weaknesses," is helpful in assessing your own listening behavior. In Chapter 1, the authors provide a listening quiz and classify some specific types of listening.

Wolff, Florence I., Marsnik, Nadine C., Tacey, William S., and Nichols, Ralph G. *Perceptive Listening*, 2nd ed. Ft. Worth: Holt, Rinehart and Winston, 1992. An especially good book about listening. Chapter 5 provides a detailed analysis of five kinds of listening–discriminative, evaluative, appreciative, empathic, and self. Chapter 10 discusses "Ten Listening Retraining Techniques," and the text is full of useful listening exercises.

Wolvin, Andrew D., and Coakley, Carolyn Gwynn. *Listening*, 4th ed. Dubuque, Iowa: William C. Brown, 1992. A good basic book on listening theory. Five types of listening are identified, and activities are provided for the reader.

Wolvin, Andrew D., and Coakley, Carolyn Gwynn. *Listening Instruction*. Falls Church, Virginia: Speech Communication Association, 1979. A small, readable book which provides a brief discussion of some of the listening types, and then provides thirty-eight different listening exercises helpful in understanding and improving your listening skills.

Chapter Five

UNDERSTANDING AND REDUCING YOUR APPREHENSION

Chapter Outline

Key Terms

"Awfullizing"
Communication apprehension
General adaptation syndrome
Negative self-talk
Positive self-talk
Systematic desensitization

Bob Daemmrich/
Stock Boston

"Courage is resistance to fear, mastery of fear—
not absence of fear."
—MARK TWAIN

*F*ormer First Lady Barbara Bush is a seasoned public speaker. She has spoken on behalf of numerous humanitarian and social causes from literacy to leukemia, received a variety of honors and awards, and served as a role model for many Americans. Because of her public poise and grace, it is hard to believe that she was extremely nervous when asked to deliver her first presentation.

> "She always knew what she believed in and she had always been able to meet and talk to people, but in the beginning she never thought of making speeches," said Mildred Kerr, who became Barbara's friend when the Bushes moved to Houston. Marion Chambers lived there by then, too, and Barbara arrived on her doorstep to say she had come to practice. "She stood in front of the fireplace and we both started laughing because we could hear her knees knocking," Marion said. "That was the last time I ever heard them knock."
>
> Said Barbara years later of her shyness, "For someone who has an open mouth on every subject now, it seems amazing."[1]

Barbara Bush's fears about public speaking parallel the attitudes held by many Americans. This chapter surveys the territory of speech anxiety: public speaking fears, research about anxiety, and ways to reduce your nervousness as you build your speeches.

SPEECH ANXIETY IS COMMON

A student began his first classroom speech. His voice trembled, his mouth seemed parched, and his hands visibly shook as he presented the introduction. At one point, he tried to control his quivering hands by placing them into his pockets; but he started to jingle his loose change, calling even further attention to his stage fright. When he decided to make an emphatic gesture, he had to suddenly withdraw his hand from his pocket, sprinkling the change all over the floor.

Another student came to the instructor at the beginning of the semester with these worried comments: "I am so nervous when I get up in front of people that I freeze up—I can't remember what I am going to say, and I start to fumble with my words. I live in fear that I will try to open my mouth and nothing will come out. I'm really good speaking in one-to-one situations, and I would do fine if I could just give my speeches to you in an empty classroom or in your office."

If you have ever felt this kind of anxiety, or if you have ever lost sleep because you had to give a report in class or in front of an organization—you are normal. A number of researchers have conducted studies to determine some of the greatest social fears among Americans. In a 1986 study of about 1,000 individuals, researchers discovered that people identified public speaking as their number-one fear. Public speaking anxiety outranked even such fears as going to the dentist, heights, mice, and flying.[2] In a study conducted in 1984, investigators asked 3,000 people to list situations which caused the most anxiety.[3] Individuals ranked fear of public speaking as their second greatest anxiety, and attending a party populated with strangers as their first social fear. Here is a summary of the fears identified in the survey.

TABLE 5.1 TEN SOCIAL SITUATIONS CAUSING GREATEST ANXIETY

Situations	Percent (%)
A party with strangers	74
Giving a speech	70
Being asked personal questions in public	65
Meeting a date's parents	59
First day on a new job	59
Victim of a practical joke	56
Talking with someone in authority	53
Job interview	46
Formal dinner party	44
Blind date	42

Almost everyone experiences some type of anxiety about public speaking.

Many famous or professional speakers have also experienced anxiety about public speaking. President John F. Kennedy was one of the most effective political speakers in this century. Yet even Kennedy could be nervous about delivering a speech. Biographer William Manchester cites a specific incident:

The President laughed, apparently relaxing. But he wasn't relaxed. In press conferences he could be at ease, despite the size of the television audience. Question-and-answer sessions were a challenge, a test of intellect. He had never learned to enjoy formal speeches, however, and his casual appearance was a triumph of the will. Unlike Lyndon [Johnson, then vice-president], he was not an extrovert. To his audiences his easy air seemed unstudied. Very few knew how hard he had toiled to achieve it. On a rostrum the illusion of spontaneity was almost perfect; only his hands would have betrayed him, and he was careful to keep them out of sight . . . they were. . . vibrating so violently at times that they seemed palsied. Now and then the right hand would shoot up and out, the index finger stabbing the limelit air to make a point. The moment it dropped the trembling would begin again. Several times he nearly dropped his five by seven cards. *Why, the President's nervous . . .* [4]

RESEARCH INTO STRESS AND COMMUNICATION APPREHENSION

As you begin to deal with your anxiety about public speaking, it is helpful for you to understand some of the research that has been done in the field.

In 1936, Hans Selye conducted research that has become a classic in the field of stress-reduction. From his laboratory experiments, Selye concluded that the human body reacts to stress in stages known as the general adaptation syndrome.[5]

The initial *alarm reaction* is a physical "call to arms" for the body to release a number of chemicals in response to the "fight-or-flight" situation. When you deliver your first speech, you will probably experience some of these physiological alarms:

Physical Symptoms of Nervousness

1. Increased heart rate
2. Thickening speech due to decreased flow of saliva
3. "Butterflies" in the stomach
4. Increased sweating
5. Tiredness or yawning
6. Jumpiness or jitteriness
7. Tightening of muscles
8. Shaky hands and legs, twitching in some muscles

Your body's alarm reaction is often the extra special shot of adrenaline that enables you to face your audience or allows you to perform superhuman feats of strength in times of emergency.

During the *resistance stage*, the body reduces the general physiological alarms, and channels energy to those organs that are most capable of handling the tension. The body stabilizes, maintains itself, and begins to adapt to the stress. For instance, once you have been speaking for a minute or two you may notice that your physical symptoms begin to decrease.

In the final *phase of exhaustion*, the body systems that were summoned to cope with the stress are depleted. The body can endure tension for only so long; when tension is chronic and continues for a period of days or years, serious damage can result. People under severe chronic pressure can develop ulcers, hypertension, and heart disease. Your public speaking class will not create any prolonged anxiety—only relaxation and mild fatigue after you have finished your speeches.

While Selye's conclusions represent a classic contribution in understanding tension, there is more recent research which is related to public speaking. In the 1970s, James C. McCroskey, a university speech instructor, coined the term *communication apprehension* to describe an individual's anxiety about speaking to another person or a group.[6] McCroskey found that most college students experience some level of apprehension about public speaking, and he also determined that at least twenty percent of these students experience high levels of anxiety.

But McCroskey also found that apprehension can be reduced. Many people who experience normal levels of anxiety can actually decrease apprehension and build self-confidence by taking and successfully completing a public-speaking course. For instance, the two anxious students mentioned in the opening examples were able to overcome many of their fears as they progressed through their speech classes. McCroskey also found that individuals who experienced high apprehension levels could lower anxiety through behavior modification techniques known as systematic desensitization.

In *systematic desensitization*, a trainer administers a test to determine individuals with high levels of communication anxiety. Subjects chosen for treatment are seated comfortably in a quiet room where they are told to close their eyes while a relaxation tape is played. When the tape is finished and individuals are relaxed, the trainer reads the first item on a list of anxiety-producing situations (such as presenting a speech, being interviewed for a job, conducting a meeting). There is a fifteen-second silence while subjects mentally visualize the stressful situation. If no anxiety is indicated, the trainer reads the next item from the list. If trainees report anxiety, they are asked to put the situation out of their minds while the trainer conducts additional relaxation exercises. The trainer then returns to the situation producing stress, repeating the process until no tension is indicated. McCroskey found that after five to seven fifty-minute sessions, almost all subjects had responded favorably to the process and reduced or overcome their apprehension.[7]

While you may not have severe apprehension, you will probably experience normal levels of speech anxiety. In the following section are eight areas which, if practiced, will help you to reduce your fear and build your self-confidence.

REDUCING COMMUNICATION APPREHENSION

Accept Anxiety Honestly and Face It

Try to understand your apprehension and determine your specific fears. Write down a list of things you fear about speaking in public. Here are some examples of common performance anxieties that students often express in speech classes:

I'm afraid I'll fall flat on my face.
I'm afraid I'll babble like an idiot.
I'm afraid that people will see my knees knocking together.
I'm afraid that people won't like me.
I'm afraid I'll make a mistake.
I'm afraid I'll forget everything I'm trying to say.
I'm afraid I'll make people angry.
I'm afraid I'll get sick.

When you've completed your list, take a good, long look at each statement and analyze it carefully. You will probably discover that you are creating irrational fears, and that most of your anxieties have no basis in fact. Anxieties are often worst-case scenarios. You will never literally fall flat on your face, although, yes, you will probably make a mistake every once in awhile. But who told you that you have to be perfect? A standard of achievement that is perfectionistic is unrealistic, irrational, and will probably cause you a lot of unhappiness. While you are very aware of your own nervous symptoms, many people in your audience will not detect your apprehension. So if your knees knock, you are probably the only one who knows it.

In a group such as a speech class, where you have a supportive group of people with a common purpose, the fear of people disliking you is also irrational. There will always be someone who disagrees with you and a few who may not like the speech. No one can, or should, try to please everyone. And you probably won't become sick unless you eat something that upsets your stomach.

Two well-known psychotherapists, Albert Ellis and Robert Harper, refer to the dread of the future as the concept of "awfullizing"[8]. The future is *awfullized* when people worry that something terrible will happen to them. These fears about tomorrow usually have no basis in fact. "Awfullizing" causes people to paralyze themselves with anxiety, to avoid situations thought to be unpleasant, and to stop performing constructive activities that are important to their growth.

Whatever you do in this speech class, don't run away from your fear or from your speaking experiences. Don't use some of the lines stated by students who try to avoid giving speeches.

I've lost my notecards, so I can't give my speech today.

I didn't have time to prepare my speech last week, so I just can't go through with it.

I've developed a severe headache—May I be excused from the speech?

I've been having car trouble all week and I'm terribly upset, so I don't think I'm in any condition to present a speech.

I have a terrible case of laryngitis, and there is no way I can talk today.

While we're not trying to ridicule legitimate problems that people may experience, it is human nature for people to create excuses to avoid fearful and unpleasant situations. If you run away from apprehension, you are simply creating a greater problem for yourself. In addition to postponing your performance, you will turn anxiety into a monster that will be more difficult for you to conquer the next time. Don't run away—face your fear. Stare down anxiety; you will discover that you can control the monster so that it won't control you.

Develop a Positive Attitude

When you begin to face your fear, you may also need to examine the attitudes you have about public speaking. Psychologists and speech instructors alike have discovered that many people fail at public performance simply because they think negatively and develop *negative self-talk.*[9]

I'm really not smart enough to speak in front of people.

I don't do well speaking in groups.

I seem to have bad luck.

I can't finish a coherent sentence in public.

I say some really ridiculous things at times.

Researchers have discovered that if people can transform their negative self-talk into positive self-talk, anxious people can unlearn old patterns and reeducate themselves into thinking more constructively.[10] Monitor the way you talk about yourself. Keep a journal or diary of the feelings you experience before every speech in your course. When you find yourself talking negatively about yourself, consciously begin to change your attitudes by writing down positive statements to replace the old negatives. The previous negative attitudes would become *positive self-talk.*

I'm intelligent and I usually have something to contribute to people.

I can do well speaking in groups if I try.

Good things happen to me all the time if I look for them.

I can finish my thoughts and my sentences if I'm patient with myself.

While I know I'll make mistakes at times, I know I'll also say some important
 things in my speeches.

In addition to thinking positively about yourself, begin to develop positive attitudes about your speech course. Look at this course as a challenge—an opportunity for you to grow from other people's experiences as well as from your own. You can even develop a positive attitude about the opportunity to make mistakes in a helpful, constructive climate. When your communication is critiqued in a supportive environment there is much less anxiety than in a competitive atmosphere such as your job. In your class, communication mistakes mean simply that you try to improve when you speak again. In your job, communication mistakes may mean that you lose your livelihood.

Begin now to replace negative self-talk with positive self-talk. By reeducating yourself in this fashion, you can start to think more rationally about yourself, and you can open yourself up to good experiences that will help you to grow.

One student placed these words of encouragement at the beginning of his speaking notes:

Calm yourself.

Look at them.

They are not vicious!

Take deep breath.

You can always do better next time.

Begin.[11]

Adopt Constructive Behaviors

Once you begin to think more positively about yourself, start doing something constructive related to your speaking assignment. Jot down speech topics when they pop into your mind. Think about some of your interests and abilities and ask yourself a few questions: *What ideas would I like to share with an audience? At what activities am I successful? What do I feel confident about? What subject areas would I like to know more about?* Go to the library and leaf through some magazines that interest you. Write down some ideas under a few different subject headings. Look at these rough outlines and decide which areas you want to pursue.

But whatever you do, *do something*.[12] Distract yourself from apprehension by performing constructive activities. Even if you do something that you may think is insignificant, sketching a rough list of ideas or doing a few deep-breathing exercises to relax, you will help yourself. Remember that apprehension is circular; it feeds on itself and defeats your growth. Develop an active program that helps you to make progress towards your goal. When you adopt constructive behavior, you will begin to forget your worries and start advancing toward your objective of successful speech-making.

Maintain a Healthy Body

Exercise can help us to relax and reduce stress. If you jog, lift weights, do aerobics, participate in team sports or have a consistent exercise program, you are already aware of the tremendous physical and mental benefits you gain from these activities. The night before giving a speech, it makes a lot more sense to exercise so that you can relax, feel tired, and get some sleep—rather than to drink five cups of coffee to stay up all night cramming for the presentation.

Occasionally in speech classes a student will say: "I think I need a couple of tranquilizers to relax before the speech," or "I think I'll fix a good stiff drink to loosen me up." The worst thing you could possibly do is to cloud your head with artificial "remedies" before you perform in public. You must learn to relax naturally rather than chemically. Remember that the body has its own unique chemicals which will give you the shot of energy you need.

To speak clearly, you need a clear head. There are even a few exercises you can do to help control your breathing and to relax. (Two relaxation activities are described at the end of this chapter.) If you don't have an exercise program, this is your excuse to start one. Physical activity can relieve tension and help you to maintain a healthy body.[13]

Be Thoroughly Prepared

One of the best ways to reduce anxiety is to be completely prepared for a speech. Being prepared means that you have worked on every aspect of the speech as much as you possibly can: the research, the outline, and the delivery. When you have selected a subject, you need to thoroughly investigate it. The more research you put into your topic, the more confident you will be when you speak about it. You must also prepare a clear and well-organized outline. When your thoughts are structured into a coherent and logical format you can relax, because you know where you're headed in the speech. It is also important that you practice the speech several times before you deliver it to an audience. While practice doesn't always mean you'll be perfect, it does mean that you will feel more comfortable with the wording of the speech when you're in front of an audience.

Many bright and capable college students do poorly in public speaking simply because they don't take the course seriously enough. The student who rushes into class late, or scribbles an outline down on paper five minutes before the speech, is not respecting the audience—or his or her own abilities. If you fail to research your topic, the audience will detect that you are delivering an impromptu rather than a prepared speech. If you don't outline your thoughts, you will be disorganized and rambling. If you don't practice the delivery, you will create unnecessary external noise such as vocalized pauses (and *ah's*), stumbling over words or sentences, and mannerisms.

There is no substitute for preparation; one thing you can control in a speech is the amount of time you are willing to invest. The more time you spend, the more confidence you will gain; the less time you spend, the more insecurity you'll experience. Careful research, clear organization, and a prepared delivery will help you to build confidence and security in each speaking assignment.

Reward Yourself

One public speaking student was a chronic worrier. She always sat on the front row, taking furious notes on every detail of classroom discussions. After presenting a speech she would focus on her negative points and never give herself credit for doing anything well. During the critique, the instructor would begin to point out some of the positive improvements in her speaking. She would react by saying, "Yes, but I know I did poorly—I just know it! My eye contact was rotten, I had all kinds of mannerisms, and I didn't state my purpose—How much worse can you get? Now I'm really going to have to work doubly hard to improve on the next speech."

It is important to take your public speaking course seriously, but not so seriously that you destroy the educational value of learning. This student was trying so hard that she was actually defeating herself and causing more anxiety.

When you have finally arrived at the night before the speaking assignment and you have done everything you possibly can to prepare, don't create more apprehension by dreading the assignment. Do something nice for yourself. Go out to a movie, go to dinner, or treat yourself to a hot fudge sundae. If it makes sense to prepare thoroughly for a speech, it also makes sense to relax so that you can take your mind off the event. Speaking shouldn't be drudgery—it should be enjoyable and positive.

But you should reward yourself only if you've worked hard and deserve it. If you have neglected some aspect of preparation or if you have waited until the last minute to cram for the speech, don't reward your negligence. If you have been successful, reward the success and you'll look forward to the next speaking event.

Let Go of Mistakes

You must face the fact that you will make mistakes some time when you speak in public. When you make a mistake, analyze it, understand it, and then let go of it. Life goes on. You'll have another chance to improve.

Even presidents make speaking mistakes which they'd like to forget. In a 1976 televised debate with his electoral opponent, Governor Jimmy Carter, President Ford stated that there is "no Soviet domination of Eastern Europe." Four years later, President Carter in turn said, in a debate with Governor Ronald Reagan, "I had a discussion with my daughter Amy the other day [to ask her about] the most important [governing] issue. . .She said she thought nuclear weaponry and the control of nuclear arms." Both Ford's and Carter's statements provoked derisive laughter. Even President Reagan had his share of speaking errors. While campaigning in the northwest United States, Reagan committed the blunder of saying, "Trees cause more pollution than people." And in the 1988 presidential campaign, Vice President Bush misstated an historic date when he said: "On this day, September 7, 1941, the Japanese attacked Pearl Harbor." (It was in fact December, unfortunately.)

All these mistakes were costly. Ford's and Carter's gaffes contributed to their election losses, and Reagan's error caused his support in northwest states to falter for a while. Political cartoonists enjoyed ridiculing Bush's minor lapse.

If presidents can make speaking errors, allow yourself to do so as well. Don't dwell on the past or on your failures—Just try not to repeat them. Whenever you prepare for a new speaking situation, try to profit from both

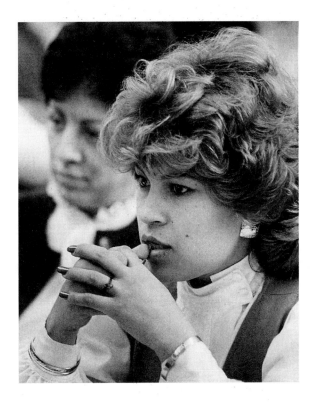

MOST INDIVIDUALS ARE APPREHENSIVE ABOUT PUBLIC SPEAKING. STUDIES INDICATE, HOWEVER, THAT SPEAKERS CAN REDUCE ANXIETY AND BUILD THEIR CONFIDENCE BY SUCCESSFULLY COMPLETING A SPEECH COURSE.

Jean–Claude Lejeune/Stock Boston

the positive and negative aspects of your past efforts. Don't place too much importance on any one speaking event; Each will benefit you in some way if you let it. Life will not end if you make an error—Pick yourself up and keep going. Letting go of mistakes helps you to keep your mind on improvement and makes room for success.

Accept Constructive Criticism

You are in a classroom situation in which you will probably be asked to evaluate other people. In these evaluations you will critique both positive and negative elements you have found in the speeches. You will be expected to be honest in your critiques but not personal or vindictive. Your classroom instructor wants to build a supportive atmosphere where every student can feel comfortable. You can help in this process if you accept constructive criticism from others. It is important that you listen to each critique as objectively as possible so that you can improve.

Sometimes people block out criticism by being defensive or by exhibiting hostile behavior. Here are a few common statements that block out criticism, create tension and inhibit growth:

Common Blocks to Criticism

Criticism in this class is destroying me.

I don't have poor eye contact—I don't care what anybody says.

I've seen good speakers slouch in public, and it doesn't bother me at all.

Politicians read their speeches word for word, so why can't I?

I already know enough about public speaking and I'm not going to learn much of anything in this class.

Speaking is a snap—All you have to do is throw a few things together.

People in this class don't know anything anyway, so why should I pay any attention to them?

Who do these people think they are, telling me what's wrong with my speeches?

I'll just sit here and let everybody say what they please. It doesn't matter anyway.

These types of comments can cause tension in a classroom and can be harmful to the individual who states them. Individuals who cannot accept constructive criticism cannot look at themselves honestly and cannot grow—They are held captive by their fear.

Help yourself and your class by allowing yourself to hear and absorb constructive criticism. Remember that criticism is meant to promote success and to help you overcome failure. Criticism might be hard to absorb at first, but you'll learn to develop the ability to bounce back and improve after hearing critiques of your speeches. If you accept constructive criticism you will help to create a positive classroom environment, and you will also help to reduce tension within yourself.

TAKING RESPONSIBILITY TO REDUCE APPREHENSION

Begin to adopt the preceding eight-point plan (summarized below) to reduce apprehension as you prepare to build your first speech. This approach can help you to overcome your anxiety by getting your mind on other issues related to the speech. When you use this plan actively, you'll begin to feel more confident. Recognize that reading theory is easy, but making theory work is totally up to you.

 SUMMARY

Most people fear public speaking, as several studies and McCroskey's research into communication apprehension have concluded. You must understand your fear and utilize this eight-point plan to help control and reduce your apprehension:

1. Accept your fear honestly and face it.
2. Learn to develop positive attitudes.
3. Adopt constructive behavior.
4. Maintain a healthy body.
5. Be prepared for your speaking experiences.
6. Reward yourself when you succeed.
7. Let go of mistakes.
8. Accept constructive criticism.

It is important for you to take responsibility for yourself and your own growth in public speaking by putting this program into effect.

EXERCISES

1. Here are two breathing exercises which can help you to relax.

Exercise 1
a. Place your hand over your abdomen (the diaphragm area).
b. Take a deep breath—You should feel your diaphragm *expand* as you inhale (if you are breathing properly).
c. Now hold the breath for just two or three seconds.
d. Exhale very slowly, vocalizing on the word "who" until your breath is almost extinguished.
e. Repeat this cycle once again.

Do this exercise two or three times before you rehearse a speech. This will help you to develop breath control, and it also helps you to relax your stomach muscles.

Exercise 2
a. Breathe in, and focus on one specific area of body tension.
b. As you breathe out, relax that specific area.
c. Progress through each muscle group of the body until your entire body is completely relaxed.

Muscle groups of the body to incorporate in the exercise:
1. Face and neck
2. Shoulders and arms
3. Chest and lungs
4. Stomach area
5. Hips, legs, and feet

This exercise helps you to relax the entire body.[14]

2. Keep a journal of your feelings as you progress through your speech course. After each major speaking assignment, compare what you've written with the previous assignment and determine if there has been any positive change.
3. Make a list of all of the fears you have about giving a speech. Take a close look at your "fears list" and then write a counter-list of positive ideas that represent opposites of the fears. Put this positive list in the cover of your text or notebook and take a look at it before every speech, or every time you get ready to develop a speech.
4. Select a book in the "Readings" section (below) that provides you with a number of stress-reduction exercises. Develop a breathing exercise, a mental exercise, and a physical exercise that will help you to cope with tension before every speech.
5. Interview a fellow student in your class. Find out some facts which the person considers to be significant. Prepare a two-minute speech of introduction which will acquaint the classroom audience with the individual.
6. Prepare a two-minute speech about one of your own interests, hobbies, or experiences. Write a rough outline on notecards, then practice the delivery so that you are confident before you present it to your class.
7. Divide your class into two teams. Play the game "Win, Lose, or Draw" using speech terms, famous historical or contemporary speakers, and current events as the topics.

NOTES

[1] Donnie Radcliffe, *Simply Barbara Bush* (New York: Warner Books, 1989), pp. 157–158.

[2] "Fears." Conducted by Bruskin Associates for Whittle Communications, Inc., 1986.

[3] W. H. Jones, "Situational Factors in Shyness." American Psychological Association, Toronto. Used by permission.

[4] William Manchester, *The Death of a President, November 20–November 25* (New York: Harper and Row, 1967), p. 85.

[5] Hans Selye, *Stress Without Distress* (Philadelphia: J. B. Lippincott, 1974), p. 38.

[6] James C. McCroskey, "Oral Communication Apprehension: A Summary of Recent Theory and Research," *Human Communication Research* 4 (Fall 1977), 78–96.

[7] James C. McCroskey, "The Implementation of a Large-Scale Program of Systematic Desensitization for Communication Apprehension," *The Speech Teacher* 21 (1972), 255–264. This article provides a detailed description of the process which McCroskey followed to help people who experienced high levels of communication apprehension.

[8] Albert Ellis and Robert Harper, *A New Guide to Rational Living* (Englewood Cliffs: Prentice Hall, 1975), pp. 102–112.

[9] Susan R. Glaser, "Oral Communication Apprehension and Avoidance: The Current Status of Treatment Research," *Communication Education* 30 (October 1981), p. 330.

[10] Maxie C. Maultsby, Jr., "Emotional Reeducation," in *Handbook of Rational–Emotive Therapy*, Albert Ellis and Russell Grieger (New York: Springer Publishing, 1977), pp. 231–247.

[11] James Elliot, from speaking notes used in speech class, Carroll Community College, Westminster, Maryland, 1989. Used by permission.

[12] Claire Weekes, *Peace from Nervous Suffering* (New York: Hawthorn Books, Inc., 1972), pp. 69–73.

[13] Dorothy Dusek–Girdano, "Stress Reduction Through Physical Activity," in *Controlling Stress and Tension*, Daniel A. Girdano and George S. Everly, Jr. (Englewood Cliffs: Prentice Hall, 1979), pp. 220–231.

[14] This exercise is based on a relaxation activity provided in Edward A. Charlesworth's and Ronald Nathan's *Stress Management–A Guide to Comprehensive Wellness* (Houston: Biobehavioral Publishers, 1982), p. 89.

READINGS

Charlesworth, Edward A., and Nathan, Ronald. *Stress Management–A Guide to Comprehensive Wellness*. Houston: Biobehavioral Publishers, 1982. Provides a detailed analysis of the body's coping mechanism under stress, and also provides some useful relaxation exercises.

Dusek–Girdano, Dorothy. "Stress Reduction Through Physical Activity," in *Controlling Stress and Tension*, Girdano, Daniel A., and Everly, George S., Jr. Englewood Cliffs: Prentice Hall, 1979. Written by several experts in the field of stress reduction and prevention, this book provides a number of chapters related to meditation, training for relaxation, biofeedback, and physical activity.

Eliot, Robert, and Breo, Dennis. *Is It Worth Dying For?* New York: Bantam Books, 1984. A readable book which provides questionnaires and tests that can help you to assess your level of stress. The authors also have a variety of relaxation techniques which can aid in stress reduction.

Ellis, Albert, and Harper, Robert. *A New Guide to Rational Living*. Englewood Cliffs: Prentice Hall, 1975. A comprehensive work on the nature of anxiety. Harper and Ellis believe that people feel the way they think and that individuals can conquer their anxieties by changing their thought processes.

Glaser, Susan R. "Oral Communication Apprehension and Avoidance: The Current Status of Treatment Research." *Communication Education 30* (October 1981), 321–341. This technical article is interesting because the author identifies a number of methods used to help individuals with high levels of communication apprehension.

McCroskey, James C. "Oral Communication Apprehension: A Summary of Recent Theory and Research." *Human Communication Research* (Fall 1977), 78–96. Although this is a fairly technical article, it is helpful if you want to understand some of the recent research into communication apprehension.

Pease, Victor. *Anxiety into Energy*. New York: Elsevier-Dutton Publishing, 1981. Provides a variety of mental and physical exercises to help you overcome stress.

Chapter Six

CONSIDERING THE ETHICS OF PUBLIC SPEAKING

Chapter Outline

Key Terms

Code of ethics

Ethos

Elements of virtue

Hidden agenda

Don West/
Picture Cube

"Believe those who are seeking truth; doubt
those who find it."
—André Gide

*I*n 1986, millionaire stockbroker Ivan Boesky delivered a speech to students in the Business School at UCLA. During the speech, he stated: "Greed is a good thing." At the end of the presentation he raised his arms in a V, symbolizing victory, and concluded with the line, "So here's to greed!" The students gave him enthusiastic applause.[1] About a year later, Boesky pleaded guilty to filing false statements with the Securities and Exchange Commission (SEC). His activities included insider trading, manipulating stock prices, and unlawful business takeovers. He received a three-year sentence and repaid $100 million to the SEC from illegal stock trading.[2]

"Greed is good" represents a clear standard or code that guided Boesky's thinking. Unfortunately, this "code" led him to behave unethically in his financial dealings.

This chapter considers the ethics of public speaking. We will examine the need for ethics, suggest ways to evaluate a speaker's ethics, and recommend some choices to consider as you develop your own speaking standards.

THE NEED FOR ETHICS IN SOCIETY

Interest in ethics and in ethical codes has been around for a long time. Centuries ago, Aristotle referred to character, which he called *ethos*, as "the most potent means of persuasion."[3] He also identified "elements of virtue" as "justice, courage, temperance, magnificence, magnanimity, liberality, gentleness, prudence, and wisdom."[4] These elements defined a clear code of ethical conduct for speakers in Greek society. Centuries before the Greeks, according to the Bible, God gave Moses the Ten Commandments on Mount Sinai. They were not, as TV commentator Ted Koppel has humorously observed, "the Ten Suggestions": they were, in fact, a guide for living.[5] In Roman times, the emperor Justinian revised the law for his empire. He was the first to incorporate ethics into the legal system and establish schools to educate lawyers concerning ethics, morality, and law. Medieval Germanic tribes recognized the need for ethical conduct and enacted the Salic Laws to codify common law and guide relationships. Following Justinian's example, Napoleon simplified French law and established a code of thirty-six statutes based upon the concept that all citizens, regardless of circumstances of birth or social stature, should be treated fairly and equally. And one of the most famous and widely respected documents is the American Bill of Rights, which identifies and guarantees our basic democratic freedoms. Indeed, every civilization has recognized the need for establishing laws and codes to guide human relationships and behavior.[6]

As we look at contemporary American life, however, it is often difficult to comprehend our ethical heritage. The 1970s, for instance, were labeled by the writer Tom Wolfe as "the Me Decade." As the economy prospered in the 1980s, scandals seemed to plague almost every aspect of society. Cincinnati Reds hero Pete Rose was ejected from baseball for gambling activities, and then sentenced to five months in jail for tax evasion. Washington Redskins defensive end Dexter Manley was banned from football for life as a result of his drug abuse. Wall Street stockbroker Michael Milken, who became wealthy trading in "junk bonds," was sentenced to ten years for insider trading. TV evangelist Jim Bakker was convicted on twenty-four counts of diverting monies from his "Praise The Lord" ministry to private use. Advisors to President Reagan were investigated for supposedly violating congressional laws in an arms-for-hostages deal. Senator Joseph Biden withdrew from a presidential campaign because of accusations he had plagiarized a speech, and Senator Gary Hart dropped out following a sex scandal. Improprieties such as these inspired editors at *Time* magazine to explore ethics in an article entitled "What's Wrong?"[7]

EVALUATING A SPEAKER'S ETHICS

It is apparent that the speaker and audience have special commitments regarding ethics in public speaking. It is the speaker's responsibility to practice ethics in every aspect of speech development, and it is the listener's obligation to determine whether the speaker lives up to ethical standards. Our purpose is not to prescribe rules or behavior, but to raise important issues pertaining to ethics and suggest areas for your consideration. We begin by analyzing a speaker's honesty, reliability, motivation, and policies.

Honesty and the Speaker

Our society places strong emphasis on honesty at all levels. The Constitution requires that the President swear to a thirty-six word oath of office to "preserve, protect, and defend the laws and Constitution of the United States." Courtroom witnesses must swear to tell "all the truth, and nothing but the truth." Contractual agreements are signed and sealed before notaries to reinforce the truthfulness of statements contained in the documents. Similarly, wedding ceremonies include vows of mutual love, loyalty, and fidelity, which couples pledge for a lifetime.

Too often, however, speakers violate these standards, causing devastating consequences. When probing the break-in of Democratic party headquarters, Watergate investigators asked, "What did President Nixon know, and when did he know it?" The sad answer was that Nixon engaged in a conspiracy to cover up the burglary. The House Judiciary Committee approved articles of impeachment, and Nixon was forced to resign from office. Upon assuming the presidency, Gerald Ford observed, "Truth is the glue that holds governments together. . . Our Constitution works."[8] Unfortunately, the Watergate scandal seriously eroded public confidence in government, and it was years before this trust was restored.

Here are two hypothetical examples, based upon factual experiences, that demonstrate how dishonesty can affect the lives of human beings with tragic results.

A manufacturing plant is in full compliance with local laws concerning the emission of toxic substances. One of the company's own scientific experts, however, has discovered new research indicating that the cumulative effects of plant emissions could pose serious health hazards to the public. Furthermore, if public officials knew about the information, they would enact stricter laws that would force the company to close in order to make drastic changes costing almost one million dollars. Arguing that a plant shutdown would contribute to severe economic loss for the company, employees, and community, executives decide to say nothing to local government officials about the new research. In addition, they demote their scientific expert, reprimand him for insubordination, and arrange for him to be transferred to another state. Still complying with local laws, the plant continues to emit toxins, now posing potentially devastating effects on the unknowing citizens of the community.[9]

When Benjamin turned sixteen, his parents adopted an infant they named Eva. After much discussion, the parents decided that it would be in the best interest of their little girl never to tell her about the adoption. They swore Benjamin to secrecy and advised him that family silence was necessary to protect his sister, allowing her to live a more secure life. Many years later, at the age of fifty, Eva became seriously ill with cancer and was informed by her doctor that she would need a life-saving bone marrow transplant from a close family member. Eva approached Benjamin, who delivered the astounding news that he could not be the donor because they were not biologically related. Eva was now forced to deal with anger over a lifetime of dishonesty in addition to her pain over the catastrophic illness.[10]

The unethical speaker often rationalizes dishonesty on the claim to be protecting the welfare of the community or another individual, when in fact the lie is self-serving. In the first example, the temporary hardship of the plant shutdown was of little significance when weighed against the long-term health effects of poisoning the community. Similarly, the second example, of parental rationalization, did not take into account the serious potential physical and emotional damage to the child. In both instances, the lies served the convenience of the speakers, and led to serious consequences.

There are occasions, however, when decisions pertaining to honesty are not so clear-cut. In 1976, Governor Jimmy Carter ran for president on the slogan, "I will never tell a lie."[11] But is this a realistic slogan in a presidential campaign? Are there times when presidents must choose between two evils to protect the lives of American troops or even ordinary citizens? Are there occasions when the president must withhold information, or give partial answers to questions from journalists, due to factors of national security?

Situations we face in our personal lives can also pose ethical dilemmas. When a family member is hospitalized with a terminal illness, what information should the patient be told? Should the patient be fully informed as to the extent of the incurable disease? Should the doctor or family withhold some data, thereby giving the individual (false) hope? Might the bad information help the patient to resolve emotions and relationships—or instead contribute to further deterioration?

While honesty is the best policy, you can also see that in some situations, there are no easy answers. Each speaker has the ultimate responsibility of choosing an ethical choice; but it is vitally important that the speaker think carefully and critically about the overall consequences of the choice.

The Reliability of the Speaker

One important standard for ethical evaluation is examining the reliability of the speaker. Audiences make judgments about speakers by measuring actions against words. What is the speaker's record? Does the speaker keep promises? Is the speaker committed to the ideas presented and willing to practice the deeds advocated?

Unfortunately, our political leaders are not always models of reliability. In 1988, Vice President Bush ran for president on the now famous slogan "Read my lips, no new taxes." Four years, a flat economy, and one tax increase later, voters held the president accountable for breaking his promise by removing him from office. Pledging to restore ethical standards in government, President Clinton nominated Zoë Baird to be the first female Attorney General. At her Senate confirmation hearings, however, the nominee acknowledged that she had hired two illegal immigrants and failed to pay their Social Security taxes. While Baird apologized for her actions, public opinion was strongly against the nomination. Committee senators asked whether an attorney general who had broken the law would be ethically able to enforce the very laws which she had violated. Baird ultimately withdrew her name from nomination.[12]

Now the individuals just mentioned in these examples are, in fact, fine Americans, and all have served government or business with distinction. But the instances indicate the high ethical standards that are expected of many public figures.

There are, of course, more blatant examples of speaker unreliability. The Reverend Jimmy Swaggart preached against sin, yet solicited sexual favors from a prostitute. Former Washington, D.C. mayor, Marion Barry advocated a drug-free city, but was caught smoking crack cocaine. TV evangelist

Jim Bakker asked for sacrificial offerings from loyal viewers, but spent money on extravagant homes and an air-conditioned dog house. In Louisiana, David Duke ran for governor pledging to serve all citizens, but his background included service as the Imperial Wizard of the Ku Klux Klan.

When an audience sees that a speaker does not abide by his or her own standards, many listeners are no longer willing to allow the speaker to have a significant influence over their lives.

Credibility, once destroyed, is difficult to rebuild. But under certain circumstances, audiences can be forgiving after a period of time. Charles W. Colson, a special assistant in the Nixon administration, was charged with obstruction of justice in a case involving Daniel Ellsberg, a Nixon adversary and an anti-war advocate. Colson pleaded guilty and served almost a year in prison. During that time he became a born-again Christian. To many cynical observers, his religious conversion and truth-telling seemed sudden and self-serving. But over a period of years, Mr. Colson has helped hundreds of prison inmates, and has established himself as a credible writer, speaker, and director of prison ministries. Colson's experience demonstrates that a "tainted" speaker can regain his credibility in another context.[13]

Even in a public-speaking class, a speaker's words are measured by actions. One student presented an informative speech about the dangers of second-hand smoke. While the material was enlightening, audience members had difficulty taking the topic seriously because the speaker's shirt pocket contained a pack of cigarettes. Another student delivered an impassioned plea for the homeless. The speaker urged listeners to bring donations of food

IF LISTENERS DETECT A DISPARITY BETWEEN A SPEAKER'S WORDS AND ACTIONS, THEY ARE UNWILLING TO ALLOW THE SPEAKER TO INFLUENCE THEM SIGNIFICANTLY.

John Moore Photo/Image Works

and clothing to a subsequent class period and assured them that she would distribute the goods at a local shelter. Class members faithfully brought their donations at the appointed time, but the speaker never arrived. Commenting that they felt betrayed by the speaker's lack of commitment, listeners returned home with their gifts.

When assuming the role of speaker, you have the opportunity of showing your commitment to an idea. While you are spending time and energy presenting your speech, remember that your audience is also devoting considerable effort to this experience. You can build trust and generate reliability if you are willing to live by your words.

The Speaker's Motivations

One area of ethics which is more difficult to assess is the motivation of a speaker. While the stated purpose may be obvious to an audience, there may also be an unstated objective, often called a *hidden agenda*. These internal agendas are present in all of us and they can actually be positive motivators. We take notes, study for exams, and maintain constructive relationships with faculty to pass courses and obtain degrees. We work hard, form positive relationships with supervisors, and present a neat appearance to advance in a company. We seek advancement in our position to provide greater psychological and financial benefits to ourselves and our families.

Problems occur, however, when the agenda is deceptive and would significantly alter audience attitudes if stated openly. Consider this hypothetical example.

> The new boss constantly praises the quality of your work and does everything possible to reward you with special opportunities and quick promotions. Several months down the road, however, you discover that the compliments have become more personal in nature, and eventually develop into inappropriate behavior. You begin to realize that the boss's initial favorable actions prepared the foundation for sexual harassment.

Here, the hidden agenda led to the exploitation and manipulation of the employee. Companies now have policies against such detrimental behavior, yet this deceptive practice still occurs too often in the American workplace.

The following is a true story which occurred several years ago.

> The Sundstrand Corporation, a company known for its high quality of manufacturing, is a major military and engineering contractor for the federal government. A few years ago, the company developed and adopted a code of ethics which set high standards for pricing, qualitative performance, and accounting procedures. An investigation into company practices revealed,

however, that the corporation engaged in a network of financial conspiracies which included charging the Pentagon for cost overruns, funding executive perks, and providing illegal gifts to government officials. In addition, Sundstrand channeled costs from its commercial business to the government, duplicating those costs in separate accounts, and billing the government. The company pleaded guilty to fraud, conspiracy, and criminal mischarging. It was fined $227.3 million in payments and contract concessions.[14]

The deceptive practices were in direct opposition to the published code of ethics that had been designed to make the company look good to the government and public. Sundstrand's new management succeeded in restoring a degree of trust, but the dishonesty caused the company severe damage.

Agendas are not always so hidden, and often members of an audience can easily assess a speaker's motivation. When hurricane Andrew devastated south Florida, over 100,000 people were left without homes, food, or clothing. Immediately after the storm, unscrupulous entrepreneurs sold water at $10 a bottle, exploiting the disaster.[15]

In this situation, the entrapped victims had no choice but to pay the high prices to survive. When a reputable business encourages its employees to give to worthy charities such as the American Cancer Society or the Red Cross, the company is demonstrating its social responsibility. But if company officials tell workers that there will be "unpleasant repercussions" for not making donations, the organization is openly engaging in exploitive tactics. You have already read about Ivan Boesky's public declaration that "greed is good." So too, did real-estate millionaire and hotel queen Leona Helmsley openly proclaim that "only little people pay taxes." Such obvious motivations are no less harmful than hidden deceptions.

Analyze a speaker carefully. Listen actively to stated objectives and read between the lines. Go beyond verbal pronouncements and evaluate a speaker's reasons for making a presentation. Know the speaker's background and proceed with caution before trusting information or submitting to persuasion.

The Speaker's Policies

A good indicator of a speaker's ethical standards are the policies and actions the individual recommends. Does the speaker exhibit concern for the welfare of the audience? Does the speaker advocate choices that are helpful to listeners? Does the speaker propose solutions that benefit society?

Unfortunately, America has its share of extremist groups such as neo-Nazis, skinheads, Klansmen, and street gangs that openly preach and practice hatred, fear, and violence. But an equally dangerous problem exists with groups that claim to be fighting for justice but encourage prejudice and engage in damaging behavior. Some extreme anti-abortionists condone the bombing or burning of abortion clinics "to save the lives of the unborn." Some speakers who believe homosexuality is a sin engage in gay-bashing and advocate discrimination in housing and employment. Racial violence is sometimes viewed by minorities as a justifiable remedy for past wrong-doing or present injustice. Speakers who advocate prejudice, hatred, stereotypes, law-breaking, or violence are not promoting ethical solutions to problems and show little compassion for the welfare of human beings.

A student presented a persuasive speech actuating audience members to buy radar detectors. He reasoned that "radar detectors will help you to avoid speeding tickets, get you to your destination more quickly, and allow you to enjoy driving at whatever speed your heart desires!" Another speaker demonstrated how to make fake identity cards. The student explained how to copy false information, forge signatures, and plasticize the phony document, making it appear realistic. She concluded her speech with the lines, "So remember, if you're under age and you want to get into that really neat club, you've got a solution—a fake I.D. You'll be able to drink as much as you want because nobody will be able to throw you out!"

These speeches are extremely unethical because the speakers are asking the audience to violate laws. In the first example, the speaker failed to mention that radar detectors are illegal in many states and seemed unconcerned that in using them his listeners could seriously injure themselves or others. The second speaker displayed similar disregard for her audience. Not only did she advocate making a counterfeit identification card, she also avoided describing the possibility of fines or jail sentences as penalties for possessing such a document. Finally, she seemed unconcerned about the physical consequences of drinking "as much as you want. . ." Both speakers lacked a sense of social responsibility, and were indifferent to the potentially damaging results of their recommendations.

Examine the policies that a speaker promotes. Think about the results of ideas or actions that a speaker recommends. Observe whether the speaker is interested in the well-being of the audience, and analyze the extent to which the speaker demonstrates concern for the well-being of society.

APPLYING ETHICAL STANDARDS

We have explored several ethical issues and examined some examples of unethical practice. It is now up to you as a speaker to formulate your own ethical standards. We suggest that you consider the following areas: honesty, concern for the audience, your motivations for speaking, and a personal code of ethics.

Be Honest

When you are building a presentation, be straightforward in every phase of speech development. Research information thoroughly, making sure that your material is accurate. Be sure that your research is complete and that you have taken the necessary time and energy to examine all the relevant sources. As you outline, be fair in reporting the data. Don't withhold portions of examples, statistics, or quotations if they are unfavorable to your ideas or viewpoints, but present these supporting materials in context. Stay away from twisting, distorting, or fabricating evidence if you can't find information to back up your issues. When you deliver the speech, give proper credit for direct quotations, and paraphrase information in your own words to avoid plagiarism. Here are some examples of quoted, paraphrased, and plagiarized material.

Quotation

"According to Paul O. Sand, Executive Director of the National Conference of Christians and Jews (quote): 'Very real ethical issues can also be found in reports about persons rifling through the desks of their in-house competitors searching for something to be used against them.'" [16]

Paraphrased Passage

"Paul O. Sand, Executive Director of the National Conference of Christians and Jews, mentions an example of unethical behavior when employees rummage through the desks of their colleagues looking for damaging information which can discredit or betray them."

Plagiarized Passage

"Ethical issues are found in reports about people who rifle through the desks of their competitors searching for something to be used against them."

In the first example, the direct quotation, the speaker gives credit to the author and restates the exact words by setting up the passage with the word "quote." In the paraphrase, the speaker uses different words to convey the intention of the author. The plagiarized passage merely eliminates a few words, but retains the original wording of the author. Notice also that the speaker presents no reference to the source of the material. The audience is led to believe that the words originated with the speaker. However, the passage would still be considered plagiarism even if the speaker added the name of the author to the last example. We emphasize that *a passage is plagiarized when the original wording is not changed or altered enough to recap the ideas in the speaker's own language.*

Be willing to take the necessary time to develop your speech. Avoid cutting corners or taking shortcuts that are unethical and dishonest. Give credit to the appropriate sources or individuals for materials, handouts, and audio-visuals used in the speech. At all times, provide honest information and present information honestly.

Advocate Ideas That Benefit Others

There are numerous topics and many points of view that are appropriate for speeches. Many controversial issues will generate a variety of opinions among listeners and often strong disagreement. We would expect such diversity of ideas in a free and open democracy. But we have already examined how public speaking can be used as a weapon to promote hatred, injustice, and law-breaking. As you approach topics and strategies for speeches, ask yourself some questions: How would you feel if a particular strategy or topic was used on you as a member of the audience? Do your ideas and recommendations benefit society? Do the actions you promote help people to work together towards solutions? Are you careful to avoid stereotyping groups, individuals, or cultures? Do you stay away from tactics that include name-calling or offensive language? Do you respect the needs and values of your audience? Do you care about people and do you demonstrate that concern in your speech?

Evaluate Your Motives for Speaking

All of us need to present positive images in order to gain acceptance from others. But as a speaker, you have more encompassing needs to meet than simply your own ego fulfillment. Before approaching the setting of your speech, examine carefully your motives for making the presentation. Determine whether or not your principal objectives are entirely self-serving, or if your motivations include interest in others.

Speakers are often tempted to exploit difficult situations for profit. Convicted felons who have been prominent politicians, religious leaders, sports figures, or entertainers often earn huge salaries on the lecture or talk-show circuit discussing their latest books or escapades. Such behavior is questionable and demeaning to the speaker–audience relationship unless the speaker can demonstrate that the objective is to educate others to avoid similar criminal activity.

Be willing to stand for principle rather than compromise your values to gain quick audience approval. Recognize that resisting opposition is often difficult and assumes a great deal of a speaker's energy. But when you are in the right, there are benefits to both speaker and listeners.

In the spring of 1992, Los Angeles exploded into a riot after a jury found four white police officers "not guilty" in the beating of an intoxicated, speeding driver named Rodney King. During this riot, Reginald Denny, a white truck driver, was stopped while hauling a load of sand and gravel through an intersection in south-central Los Angeles. He was pulled from his truck by several black males, and severely kicked and beaten. Other black citizens who witnessed the incident came to Denny's assistance and rushed him to the hospital.[17]

These heroic individuals looked beyond color to risk their lives for a fellow human being. Their actions took great courage, yet became a reassuring symbol to millions of Americans who anguished over racial tensions. Such speakers suffer initial setbacks, but often reap psychological rewards and satisfaction as a result of their bravery.

Take responsibility and be true to yourself. Avoid the hypocrisy of disguising questionable motives with superficial appeals. Make sure that your stated objectives and internal goals are in harmony. Constantly ask yourself, "What have I to give," rather than, "What have I to gain?"

Develop a Speaking Code of Ethics

According to a study by the Conference Board, more than 75 percent of the companies surveyed have now enacted codes of ethics for their employees.[18] While these codes are not necessarily the Ten Commandments, they are standards that act as guides for ethical behavior and practice. In a speech to a conference on business ethics, Richard R. Capen, Jr., Vice Chairman of Knight-Ridder, Inc., a publishing company, related his recommendations for an ethical code in business.[19] They are reproduced here *verbatim:*

1. *Build trust.* Getting along in today's pluralistic world starts with trust. Trust is an ultimate value that protects an orderly, civilized society from chaos and anarchy. Trust in marriage. Trust at work. Trust among friends. Trust in public life. Trust is never guaranteed. It must be constructed carefully, nurtured vigorously and reinforced daily.
2. *Be optimistic.* Attitude in the process of serving others is important. Often what happens in our lives comes down to the way we look at life. If we believe it will be a lousy day, it will be. If we believe there is no hope, the chances are there will be no hope. . . . On the other hand, if we believe we can win, the chances are we will. If we think we can make a difference in life, we will. The difference between such success—and failure—is usually a matter of attitude.
3. *Be an encourager.* Each week, dozens cross our paths crying out for help, for love, for encouragement. For them, it's a challenging, lonely world, and such people desperately need our love. In my business, I'm surrounded by special opportunities—big and small—to be a thoughtful listener, an enthusiastic encourager, a caring advisor, a special friend.
4. *Lead by personal example.* To be the best, leaders must be truthful and candid. They must be decisive and courageous. They must keep promises and be loyal to their family, friends, employees, clients and country.

We present these ideas as only a suggestion as you think about a speaking code. Whether you adopt Capen's model, the Golden Rule, or another viewpoint, begin to develop an ethical framework to guide you through the process of building your presentations. Remember that it is up to you as a speaker to set a responsible standard as you convey ideas and recommend actions to the members of your audience. Good speaking means good ethics.

James E. Perrella presented the following speech[20] to business students at the University of Illinois in Chicago. As an executive vice president of the Ingersoll–Rand Company, a construction manufacturing business, Perrella demonstrates his knowledge of business and ethics as he raises some important issues for the audience. In this edited speech, the speaker conveys a concern about his topic and an interest in the ethical choices of America's future business leaders.

THE RIGHT WAY: A MATTER OF PRINCIPLE

A Persuasive Speech

James E. Perrella

[1] To create suspense, the speaker avoids stating his topic until the last line of his introductory paragraph.

[1] Good afternoon. Professor McLimore's invitation to participate in this course with you today stirred a great deal of reflection as to the best subject for discussion. The number and variety of possible subjects seemed endless. Many subjects. Many ideas. Many possible directions. In this sea of subjects, one topic surfaced. It is a topic that touches on every other subject mentioned, a topic much in the news, a topic that affects our attitudes, a topic that touches our lives: Business ethics.

[2] The speaker cites two instances and refers to an article.

[2] Think about it for a minute. If you approach the subject, business ethics, in terms of Ivan Boesky or Dallas's J. R. Ewing, you may believe that "business ethics" is an oxymoron, or, as an article in *The Wall Street Journal* suggested, that "business" and "ethics" are mutually exclusive. Today, we need to ask: Are they?

[3] Perrella uses the humorous quote to support the point that fact and fiction suggest businesspeople are unethical.

[3] Certainly, in fact and fiction, there is much that says business is not ethical, and stories that even suggest that businessmen cannot operate ethically. Consider the case of Daniel Drew, a New York cattleman of the early 19th century. Stuart Holbrook tells the story in *The Age of The Moguls:* Mr. Drew "seems never to have denied his most celebrated piece of knavery, which he used for many years in his cattle business. As a big herd of anywhere from six hundred to a thousand

head of Ohio beef approached New York City, Drew had his drovers salt them well. Then, just before reaching the marketplace, he let them drink their fill. Cattle were sold live-weight. Drew's processing with salt and water added many tons to the average herd. 'Watered stock' soon become a term on Wall Street."

⁴ Mr. Drew seemed a follower of a 19th century parody of the Golden Rule: "Do unto the other feller the way he'd like to do unto you, an' do it fust."

⁴⁻⁵ The speaker draws a conclusion from the story and relates it to today's business world.

⁵ Mr. Drew's motives and actions can fit well with motives and actions prevalent in today's business world, or should I say, in today's world.

⁶ We seem to put ourselves first. Or try to. At almost any cost. The extreme of this "me-first" attitude is the drug addict who will take advantage of anyone and anything to satisfy his insatiable craving.

⁷ Think, for a moment, about every-day situations as well: The driver who tries to move ahead of other cars at every traffic light. The green grocer who puts the reddest strawberries on the top of the basket. The person who insists always on having the last word in any domestic argument. The doctor who prescribes more and more tests, not necessarily for the patient's benefit, but for protection against a possible malpractice claim. The salesman who thinks more of his commission than of his customer's needs. The student—certainly not anyone here—who cheats on an exam to gain a higher grade or rank. The politician who steals another's speech to make himself sound better or wiser. The individual who pays a tip to the maitre d' to get preferred seating. In every case, the action is a me-first action.

⁷ The speaker uses a series of interesting hypothetical examples which successfully connect to listeners.

⁸ Me first. A likely, or as many would say, the source of ethics problems.

⁹ In your career development, as you become our nation's business leaders, you will face the question: May business people use any means, fair or foul, to make a sale, to insure success, to take advantage of a customer, or to do a competitor in? In other words, to put themselves first.

⁹ Perrella poses a question to stimulate thinking.

¹⁰ In business, the Ivan Boesky/Drexel Burnham Lambert shenanigans keep reappearing in the nation's headlines. A recent lawsuit charges that Boeing used bogus misbranded bearings in commercial and military aircraft.

¹⁰ He mentions two examples of unethical business "shenanigans."

¹¹ While all sorts of special situations of this type have arisen, many people, I am pleased to say, still do things the old-fashioned way. In fact, many people still depend on a handshake to seal an agreement. A man's word is his bond. In many negotiations people trust each other completely. Even in complex business transactions. In today's business world, handshake deals have not disappeared. They

¹¹ Does the speaker adequately support these generalities?

are fewer, however, as people depend on written warranties and guarantees and exclusions and warnings in the most confusing language and in the tiniest type. In fact, "put it in writing" is a common request, accompanying the purchase of anything—from a baby buggy to a used car.

[12] The speaker makes a good point, but does it require more evidence?

[12] Lawyers love it. They sue people and companies. They defend. They challenge. They appeal. They seem to relish new opportunities in every business transaction. They try to put their clients, and themselves, first.

[13] Again, the speaker uses questions to get listeners to think.

[13] At the same time, they pose a new question for businessmen. They replace the question about business activity: "Is it right?"—with "Is it legal?"

[14] This trend, developing over years, as attorneys try to protect their clients in an ever more complex business world, has created a division between morality and legality, weakening, if not dissipating, the strength and significance of once-prevalent handshake agreements.

[15] The speaker continues to employ questions as a technique to involve the audience.

[15] In our Western civilization, laws and morals have strengthened each other since the time of Moses. Until now. Our question of today should be, What's the right thing to do? The right way to behave? The right way to conduct business? Don't just ask, Is it legal?

[16] He uses two hypothetical situations to promote critical thinking.

[16] Let me be the first to admit that the choice is not always easy. Consider, for instance, these questions from Scruples, a Milton Bradley game: The garage forgets to charge you for a six-dollar oil filter. You think the labor charge is too high, anyway. Do you mention the undercharge? In a parking lot you accidentally dent a car. Do you leave a note? You are applying for a job requiring experience you don't have. Do you claim you do?

[17] The speaker describes a simple ethical standard.

[17] Questions of this sort reach beyond legality. They raise the question of right versus wrong, not legal versus illegal. The answers require no legal knowledge. They require only common sense and the sense of fair play that we all learned as youngsters. You remember. I remember. Don't cheat. Don't steal. Don't lie. Don't take advantage of anyone's weakness. The Golden Rule. Do unto others the way you would have them do unto you. In other words, treat the other guy fair. That's the way to solve all ethics problems.

[18] The speaker uses gender to connect to listeners.

He resolves his earlier hypothetical examples, showing the positive results of ethical behavior.

[18] Have you considered what business would be like if we all did it? If every businessman (and businesswoman) followed the Golden Rule? Ripe, red strawberries would fill a box from top to bottom. Barrels would not contain a single rotten apple. My company would not have to file a complaint with the Federal Trade Commission charging dumping of other bearings in United States markets. Congress would not have to tighten curbs on insider trading. Companies

would not have to require employees to sign codes of conduct or establish strict guidelines for purchasing agents to follow. The Harvard Business School would not have to require that each entering student take a three-week course on business ethics. Drexel, Burnham, Lambert would not have to pay a $650 million fine.

[19]Many people, including many business leaders, would argue that such an application of ethics to business would adversely affect bottom-line performance.

[20]I say nay. The ideas we are considering today go far beyond the bottom line.

[21]If we do things right, because that's the way to do things, just imagine the effect we will have on customers. Mr. Iacocca showed the beginnings of the possibilities when he led Chrysler in new directions. Johnson and Johnson set a solid example when it pulled Tylenol off the shelves immediately during the crisis of a few years ago. H. J. Heinz and Squibb established a high standard of ethical excellence when they supported our nation's Pure Food and Drug laws early in this century. In these situations, the businesses and their leaders put the public and their customers first.

[21] The speaker uses three concrete examples of companies that have provided ethical leadership.

[22]I ask you to imagine the effect on the bottom lines of tomorrow if business were to follow these examples today. Good ethics, simply, is good business. Good ethics will attract investors. Good ethics will attract good employees. Moreover, good ethics will attract and retain customers, employees, investors, and build a quality reputation.

[22] He uses repetition to make a case for "good ethics."

In his conclusion, the speaker. challenges the audience. He points out that their actions can lead to positive or negative business ethics.

[23]As you begin your careers, please remember that you set your own standards. Your actions can lead to a Chrysler turnaround or to a Wedtech.

[24] In a real sense, the future is up to you. You can change the way things are done. You can make the critical choice. You can do what's right. Not because of conduct codes. Not because of rules or laws. But because you know what's right. I will applaud your decision.

[24] While his point of view is clear, he allows the listener to make the final critical choice.

SUMMARY

The study of ethics has been important through the centuries and is vital to the modern speaker. When evaluating a speaker's ethics, consider the speaker's honesty, reliability, motivations, and policies. When applying your own ethical standard, be honest, convey concern about others, assess your personal motives for speaking, and develop a speaking code.

EXERCISES

1. You are the press secretary to the President of the United States. You are told that during a routine physical examination, the president's doctor has discovered spots on the president's liver, requiring further tests. The president has important trips planned to Russia and China during the next two weeks, and he doesn't want anything to detract from ceremonies, which include treaty signings. The president has told you that he wants to appear vigorous and does not wish to alarm Americans; therefore, he asks you not to tell the press corps anything about the ominous medical news. At your daily press briefing, the press, knowing that the president has just completed his yearly physical exam, asks you about the president's health, and specifically whether the doctor found any irregularities during the physical. How do you respond? Explain your statements and actions.

2. You are the public relations officer for a large auto manufacturer. Your younger sister works at one of the company's assembly plants in New Jersey. She is a single parent and her assembly-line job is the sole means of support for her three children. You receive a confidential memo from company executives stating that the New Jersey plant has lost money for the past two years and is to be closed in six months. Top executives and the public relations officer are the only individuals to know about the decision. The senior vice-president has told you that "if any of this gets out now, the union will strike all of our plants all over the country, doing irreparable damage, possibly bankrupting the company." What, if anything, would you tell your sister who will be permanently laid off in six months? Explain your actions in this situation.

3. Find three newspaper or magazine advertisements that you consider to be unethical. What elements of the ads are unethical? Are the ads partially dishonest, or do they convey false implications? How could the ads be altered, making them ethical?

4. Evaluate the ethical components of a local, state, or national political campaign. Describe the ethical and unethical strategies used to "sell" the candidate and discredit the opposition.

5. Read the speech in this chapter entitled "The Right Way." Discuss your views of Perrella's ideas. Do you think his speech is simplistic? Does the speaker provide any suggestions or means of putting these ethical values into practice? Are the values advocated unrealistic in a complex world? If you were to give the speech, what ideas would you change?

NOTES

[1] See Charles W. Colson, "Right or Wrong in Today's Society," *Vital Speeches*, July 1, 1991, p. 556, and William A. Dimma, "The Decline of Ethics," *Vital Speeches*, February 1, 1991, p. 246.

[2] "Ever So Helpful," *The Economist*, December 26, 1987, pp. 33–34.

[3] Lane Cooper, ed., *The Rhetoric of Aristotle* (New York: Appleton-Century-Crofts, Inc., 1960), p. 9.

[4] Ibid., p. 47.

[5] As cited in Colson, "Right or Wrong in Today's Society," p. 561.

[6] I thank Paul S. Cunningham, professor of history and geography at Catonsville Community College, who provided valuable assistance for this section on history and ethics.

[7] *Time*, May 25, 1987, pp. 14–17.

[8] Waldo W. Braden, ed., *Representative American Speeches*, 1974–1975 (New York: The H. W. Wilson Co., 1975), p. 52.

[9] Preston Townley, "Business Ethics," *Vital Speeches*, January 15, 1992, p. 209.

[10] Josina M. Makau, *Reasoning and Communication* (Belmont, California: Wadsworth Publishing Company, 1990), p. 126.

[11] President Carter refers to this pledge in his 1980 concession speech. See "Transcript of the President's Concesssion Statement," *New York Times*, November 5, 1980.

[12] "Good Help Is Hard To Find, *U.S. News and World Report*, January 25, 1993, p. 14.

[13] Colson details these experiences in his book *Born Again* (Old Tappan, N.J.: Chosen Books, 1977). Also see Colson's speech in *Vital Speeches*, July 1, 1991.

[14] See Michael Oneal and Paula Dwyer, "Sundstrand Prepares to Pay the Piper—and the Pentagon," *Business Week*, January 23, 1989, pp. 35–36, and Louis A. Day, *Media Ethics* (Belmont, California: Wadsworth Publishing Company, 1991), p.33.

[15] Daniel Seligman, "Hurray for Avarice," *Fortune*, October 5, 1992, p. 146.

[16] Paul O. Sand, "Business Ethics," *Vital Speeches*, November 15, 1988, p. 85.

[17] Seth Mydans, "Four Held in Attack at Riots' Outset," *New York Times*, May 13, 1992, p. A20.

[18] Preston Townley, "Business Ethics," *Vital Speeches*, January 15, 1992, p. 209.

[19] These guidelines are quoted, in abridged form, from Capen's speech to the Conference Board Conference on Business Ethics in *Vital Speeches*, September 1, 1990, pp. 686–687.

[20] Perrella, James E., "The Right Way: A Matter of Principle," *Vital Speeches*, April 1, 1989, pp. 375–376. Used by permission of *Vital Speeches* and James E. Perrella, president, Ingersoll–Rand Co.

READINGS

Day, Louis A. *Ethics in Media Communications: Cases and Controversies.* Belmont, California: Wadsworth Publishing Company, 1991. Presents numerous cases that raise ethical issues and concerns. While the book emphasizes ethics in media, it assists you by posing questions that help you to make your own ethical decisions.

Mikau, Josina M. *Reasoning and Communication: Thinking Critically About Arguments.* Belmont, California: Wadsworth Publishing Company, 1990. An excellent book to help stimulate your thinking about ethics and persuasive arguments. We strongly recommend Chapter 6, "Argumentation and Communication Ethics."

Living Parlour

Hall

Bed-Chamber

Nursery

Great Parlor

Bed-Chamber

PARLOUR FLOOR

Unit Outline

Chapter Seven

SELECTING THE TOPIC AND PURPOSE

Chapter Outline

Key Terms

Brainstorming
General purpose
Specific purpose
Subject
Thesis statement
Topic

Jane Scherr/Jeroboam, Inc.

"There is a difference
between speaking much
and to the point."
—ERASMUS

*I*n her best-selling book *Talk Your Way To Success*, professional speech consultant Lilyan Wilder gives readers the following advice: "Whether you are going to be making a thirty-second toast or a thirty-minute speech, you begin by asking yourself what you intend to accomplish. . . What do you want your remarks to do? What do you want from the people you are addressing? The answers to these questions will give you a clear sense of purpose, an objective."[1]

Wilder is right. Developing a clear purpose is a vitally important part of building the foundation to a successful speech. In this chapter we examine the subject, the topic, the general purpose, the specific purpose, and the thesis statement.

GETTING IDEAS

> "I've listened to everything you've said in class, and I've read the book. But I just can't think of what to give my speech about. I'm not really a very unique person—I don't sky-dive or bake ethnic foods, I haven't traveled much, and I don't have hobbies or keep exotic pets. I'm just your average college student trying to get a degree. Please, please give me some ideas for a speech."

The inability to think of a subject is one of the most common complaints heard in speech classes. The same people talking with other students in the lounge or the cafeteria, or after class seem to have no problem coming up with ideas for conversation. But in a situation requiring public speaking and evaluation of abilities, the fountain of ideas seems to dry up.

There are a number of ways to search for speech topics. Here are some resources and techniques that can stimulate your thinking and help you to get started.

Your Own Knowledge and Experience

One of the best resources is your own knowledge and experience. When trying to think of speech subjects people often overlook their backgrounds. After thinking and worrying for several days, a student still had no subject for her informative speech. When asked about her interests, she responded: "Well I really like to square-dance. As a matter of fact, every week I go square-dancing, and my partner and I usually try to attend a square dancing contest once a month. I'm pretty good at it, but I can't talk about anything like that, can I?" When she finally realized that she could use some of her own experiences, she recognized that public speaking could actually be interesting.

Students have delivered speeches about traveling to India, climbing mountains, shearing sheep, "milking" poisonous snakes, studying fossils, training dogs, collecting coins, hang-gliding, making theatrical masks, excavating ancient ruins, recovering from alcoholism, serving military duty in war zones, stomach-stapling, and tattooing. These subjects were drawn from students' personal knowledge or experiences. Don't take your background for granted. Examine your unique experiences—you will often find something to expand into a topic that fits a particular assignment.

The Dictionary and the Encyclopedia

Another way you can gather ideas is to look through an encyclopedia or dictionary. In a copy of *Webster's New World Dictionary*, we searched under the letter "B." Here are just some of the subjects we found:

baboon	bat	blood	brass
J.S. Bach	batik	bloodhound	breast cancer
backgammon	Beaumont	blueberries	breaststroke
Badlands	beaver	boats	Brazil
badger	Bedouin	bobby	Britain
bagel	Beirut	bobcat	Buddha
bagpipes	Bermuda	Boise	buffalo
bail bondsman	Berlin	Bonaparte	bugle
Bahamas	Bible	Book of Mormon	buggy
Baltimore	bicycle	boomerang	Bull Run
Baseball	Bill of Rights	bordeaux	burlesque
bald eagle	biofeedback	Boston	butcher
banana	Bismark	Boy Scout	butter
balloon	blackjack	Braille	buzzard
barrier reefs	blindfish	brain	Byzantine

This list of sixty subjects was compiled in about fifteen minutes. These ideas can easily be subdivided into numerous speech topics. We caution you against copying material from dictionaries or encyclopedias; these are merely resources to help you get ideas and general background. You may find a subject that genuinely interests you and will fit your assignment.

Brainstorming

One technique to generate many subjects in a short time is brainstorming—the rapid and unrestrained listing of ideas. Take a pencil and paper and jot down anything that comes into your mind. Don't try to judge or evaluate the ideas when you list them—The goal of this exercise is to stimulate your thoughts and imagination. After a few minutes, you will have a long list of subjects on a variety of issues. Naturally, some of the subjects will seem ridiculous; but the purpose of the exercise is to generate a lot of ideas quickly. You can easily eliminate the irrelevancies later.

The *Readers' Guide* and the Vertical File

Additional places to look for subject matter are the *Readers' Guide to Periodical Literature* and the vertical file. (See Chapter 8 for a more extensive discussion.) The *Readers' Guide* is full of magazine titles listed by subject. As you look over the large green volumes, you will find it easy to come up with ideas for subjects; at the same time, the *Readers' Guide* will provide you with titles of periodicals you can investigate for further information. Most libraries also have a vertical file containing pamphlets and informational brochures from businesses, institutions, and self-help groups. The types of subject matter contained in the vertical file differ in each library; check your library to determine the material included.

Ask for Help

If you are having difficulty selecting a topic, ask for help from other individuals. Solicit suggestions from friends and family, or talk to your associates at work. Ask your instructor to react to several ideas or seek advice from fellow students. Talking to others helps you to verbalize feelings and restore your perspective on significant interests, abilities, and motivations.

There are plenty of subjects available if you actively look for them. Get busy and do something—Don't wait for inspiration. Examine your own experiences, try some brainstorming techniques, go to the library, or ask for suggestions from others.

SELECTING YOUR TOPIC

Once you have chosen the subject, you must narrow it down to a *topic*—the specific, limited issue which you can effectively develop into a five- to eight-minute speech. Here are five guidelines to consider as you build your speech.

It Should Be Sufficiently Narrow and Conform to the Time Limit

Most items in the previously cited list of subjects are too general for a five-minute classroom presentation. You could sign up for entire courses on Britain, barrier reefs, or Buddha. These subjects must be narrowed to more specific topics. For example:

The British presence in Northern Ireland

Types of plant life existing in a barrier reef

Some basic beliefs of Buddhism

Each of the above topics can be supported by several main points, and each topic can be made to conform to the time limit.

A speech on "The problem of mental health in the United States," for example, would be too broad, and could be narrowed down as the following list shows:

SUBJECT: MENTAL HEALTH IN THE UNITED STATES

Topics

Causes, effects, and treatments of impotence

Common phobias experienced by "average" people

Hyperactivity in children

Mental illness and the homeless

Myths about mental illness

Personal injury claims resulting from job stress

Problems of mental health insurance

Pro's and con's of mainstreaming the mentally retarded

The destructive effects of perfectionism

Unethical practices in psychiatry

Ten major speech topics are here generated from the one general subject, and many more are possible. Your topic must be limited so that you can develop it in sufficient detail within your allotted time.

It Should Interest You, the Speaker

You must be certain that the topic interests you. A speech is not like an assigned book report; the topic you select reflects your interests, your personality, and your motivations. You cannot go to the dictionary, close your eyes, pick out a random topic, and expect to feel positive about communicating it. You need to feel confident and challenged by your choice; you must be able to use appropriate aspects of delivery—vocal inflection, gestures, facial expression—to communicate your enthusiasm to the audience.

A student in the air-transportation curriculum asked his audience to play the role of passengers on a transcontinental flight. A few seconds into the presentation, the speaker (who played the pilot) stated that the aircraft was experiencing mechanical difficulty and that he would need to make an emergency landing. The "passengers" listened carefully as the "pilot" reviewed the safety precautions to take in flight and the emergency exit procedures to follow when the plane landed. The audience was fascinated because the speaker was interested in his topic and creative in his delivery.

You may be interested in a topic but you may not be very knowledgeable about it. Don't throw out the idea because you will have to do some additional investigation. One student, who had presented three very creative speeches during the semester, was having difficulty finding a dynamic topic for her final speech to inform. She had always been curious about ants, but didn't know very much about them. At first she thought her idea might be too trivial, but as she began to do research, she found the subject compelling. She became so involved that she even created some visual aids to support her narrowed topic, "Life in an ant colony." During the speech she was enthusiastic, animated, and extremely knowledgeable because of her extensive research. But her success started with her interest in the topic.

It Should Provide New Information

Successful speakers can make almost any topic interesting. With proper research and audience analysis, few topics are boring. But some topics can be classified as overworked or trivial, and should be avoided or altered. For example:

Toxic pollution is dangerous

How to make a cake by following the directions on the cake box

Drinking a beer

Registering for a course at this university

Transplants can help people

To involve your audience, alter these topics and provide new or more sophisticated information.

Home carpeting can contain toxic pollution

Secrets of making a perfect German chocolate cake

How beer is manufactured

Some of the most popular elective courses at the university

Improvements in bone-marrow transplants

These topics are not simplistic, they don't rehash information that is common knowledge, and they have the potential of providing additional knowledge.

A speaker began a presentation by identifying a process that was familiar to most audience members—decorating Easter eggs. But as the speech pro-

A SPEAKER WHO IS INTER-
ESTED IN THE TOPIC IS
MORE LIKELY TO PROJECT
ENERGY AND ENTHUSIASM
TO LISTENERS.

Jeffry Myers/Stock Boston

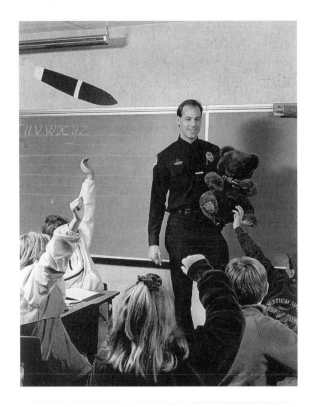

gressed, listeners soon realized that the speaker was not describing the ordinary Easter-time activity. The speaker's purpose was to demonstrate "How to make Ukrainian Easter eggs"—a centuries-old process requiring skill and dedication. The speaker briefly described Ukrainian traditions and demonstrated the application of intricate designs symbolizing Easter themes. The audience was completely involved: The speaker handled an overworked topic creatively and provided her listeners with new information.[2]

It Should Be Appropriate

While setting up visual aids for a process speech, a nursing student asked the audience for a volunteer, and a male student eagerly came forward. As the speaker proceeded with her introduction, it became clear that the purpose of her speech was to demonstrate how to give a bath to a hospital patient. The face of the male volunteer turned red, and the audience began to giggle nervously. Undismayed, the nursing student instructed her volunteer to lie down on the table as she proceeded to demonstrate in great detail how a patient is bathed. The speaker's topic was appropriate in a nursing classroom, but was extremely inappropriate in a speech class.

Appropriateness is highly subjective; what is appropriate to one person is not appropriate to another. An individual speaking about personal religious convictions might be on target in a church group, but the topic would be completely out of place at a secular meeting. Use common sense when you think about a topic, and select an issue that is appropriate for as many of your listeners as possible.

It Should Conform to the General Purpose: To Inform, Persuade, or Entertain

Once you have chosen a topic, you must then consider the *general purpose* or the direction of the material presented in the speech. You need to know whether your speech assignment is to inform, to persuade, or to entertain your audience.

Speeches to Inform   Informative speeches are presentations that enlighten and educate audiences. In speeches to inform, you can define concepts; develop personal experiences; demonstrate procedures; describe people, places, or objects; deliver business reports; or lecture on issues in which you have expertise.

If you were to define jazz, convey an experience such as sky-diving or life in the Marines, demonstrate how to make clay pottery, describe the life of Irving Berlin, discuss the principal historical sites in Boston, survey the effects of elephant's disease, report real estate projections for 1997, or lecture about the economic struggle in Russia, you would be contributing to audience awareness and understanding.

Speeches to Persuade   Unlike informative presentations, in persuasive speeches your goal is to influence the beliefs, feelings, or behavior of your listeners. While you must present accurate and well-researched material, you must also take a clear position regarding the information. There are three principal types of persuasive speeches: the speech *to convince*, which changes belief; the speech to *actuate*, which moves to action; and the speech to *stimulate*, which intensifies feelings.

Persuasive speaking is similar to taking one side in a debate. You tell your audience to do something ("plant a tree"), to believe something ("raise taxes to reduce the deficit"), or to feel something strongly ("support our football team in the bowl game"). Your goal is to build a case using logic and emotion to persuade the audience that your view is the correct one.

Speeches to Entertain   The purpose of the speech to entertain is to promote enjoyment and to amuse and divert the audience. Entertaining speeches could include an after-dinner speech, a roast of a boss or friend, or a monologue satirizing a person, place, or event. But entertainment does not mean a lack of research and preparation; often speeches to entertain are some of the most difficult to prepare and present. The speech to entertain requires creativity, competence in writing and organization, and skill in delivery.

College speech instructors tend to emphasize informative and persuasive speeches over speeches to entertain. But developing an entertaining speech is good experience; most people have an occasion sometime in their careers or personal lives to present a humorous speech—a friend's fortieth birthday, a toast at an anniversary, an office party spoof.

WRITING UP THE SPECIFIC PURPOSE

The *specific purpose* is the reason for the speech: This statement communicates the speaker's goal to the audience. When you state your specific purpose at the end of the introduction, your audience should clearly understand your topic and your intention.

Spend time developing your specific purpose so that it clearly defines and conveys your objective. Here are three guidelines to follow as you prepare the specific purpose statement.

Be Clear, Concise, and Unambiguous

The specific purpose should be phrased in simple and concrete language. Avoid wordy descriptions and vague terminology. The specific purpose should be easy to read and easy to verbalize. Most important, your audience must clearly understand your specific purpose. Some examples:

To inform you about the startling possibility of male pregnancy

To explain how you can help children afflicted with the disease called spinal bifida

To convince you that America should not tax Social Security benefits

The first specific purpose tells the audience that they will receive information about the topic, the second asks listeners to become actively involved with the issue, and the third requests them to agree with the speaker. The first may raise some eyebrows, but it promotes curiosity. The second introduces terminology which may be unfamiliar, but spinal bifida is clearly defined as a disease, and the third takes a strong position on a persuasive issue. Each statement is clearly worded and communicates the speaker's specific intention. Now look at the following specific purpose:

Poor: To tell you of the serious implications of central and obstructive sleep apnea and explain how these conditions impact the psyche and the physiology

This specific purpose is weak because it takes entirely too long to communicate. The sentence also introduces terminology—*central and obstructive sleep apnea*—unfamiliar to many listeners. The objective of the speech is not clearly communicated; we have the impression that the speech is about some type of sleeping disorder, but we're not exactly certain about the topic and we are not told whom it affects. This statement confuses audience members and discourages them from listening. Here's how the specific purpose can be improved:

Better: To describe the major causes and effects of a common sleeping disorder

Here the wording is clear, and the sentence moves logically and quickly to the point. The statement eliminates technical terms and ambiguous references to "psyche" and "physiology." The specific medical terminology can be identified and explained later in the speech.

Poor: To talk about M. C. Escher
To tell you about airline accidents
To inform you about blacklists

In each of these phrases, the subjects are not yet narrowed. A speaker who fails to make changes in these statements will probably speak overtime or jump from one topic to another. These are *better:*

To describe the stylistic influences on M. C. Escher, the pop artist

To explain how several airline crashes have contributed to stricter safety regulations

To convince the audience that computerized blacklists threaten individual privacy

These statements are improved because the subjects have been narrowed and the wording is more precise.

Include Only One Major Idea

A specific purpose should contain only one principal topic. If it contains more than one topic, the speaker will be developing at least two speeches.

Poor: To describe the effects of criminal behavior on the victim and explain the merits of crime compensation plans
To demonstrate how a dentist fills a tooth, performs a root canal, and cleans your teeth

To explain how Western nations sold technology to Iraq, encouraged Saddam Hussein to invade Kuwait, and triumphed over Iraq in Desert Storm.

To explain how computerized blacklists are compiled, and to convince you that these blacklists threaten our right to privacy

Often, beginning speakers are afraid they will not have enough material for a five- to seven-minute speech, so they include too many topics in their specific purpose statements. The first specific purpose contains at least two topic ideas. The effects of criminal behavior on a victim are at least one topic, and merits of crime compensation plans are another. The second sentence contains three separate demonstration speeches. A speaker cannot possibly demonstrate three dental procedures in six or seven minutes. In the third sentence there are numerous topics: the sale of technology to Iraq, the encouragement of the invasion, and the victory over Iraq. In the fourth statement, there are two distinct purposes. The first part of the statement is a speech to describe, and the last half is a speech to convince. Your specific purpose sentence clearly indicates whether the speech is informative or persuasive: it should not include both types.

Here is how each statement can be altered to incorporate only one main topic:

Better: To describe the merits of victim compensation plans
To demonstrate how a dentist performs a root canal
To explain the sequence of events in the U.S. victory over Iraq
To convince you that computerized blacklists threaten our rights of privacy

Each specific purpose statement includes only one major topic which can be developed adequately in a five- to seven-minute speech.

Phrase in a Sentence

The specific purpose should include a declarative sentence which contains the topic, the general purpose, and an infinitive phrase such as "to inform," "to describe," or "to stimulate." The following are poor examples:

Skin disease

Lead fishing-sinkers

African tribal body painting and how it is done

Prayer in public schools—pro or con?

Should the U.S. commit military forces to Bosnia?

In each of the above statements, the speaker has not clearly identified the goal of the speech. The first example merely names a broad subject; there is no topic, purpose, or sentence. Although the second example could be an adequate topic for a speech, it is not stated in sentence form with a general purpose; it has no direction or goal. The third example still is not complete because it lacks an infinitive phrase. The fourth and fifth examples raise questions when they should make clear statements as to the intention of the speech; we are not sure if the speeches are informative or persuasive. Here are better examples:

To provide the audience with an understanding of a disfiguring skin disease known as vitiligo

To demonstrate how to make lead fishing-sinkers

To demonstrate an African tribal ritual of body painting

To actuate the audience to support a constitutional amendment allowing voluntary prayer in public schools

To convince the audience that committing U.S. military forces to Bosnia is dangerous

These five examples have the following points in common: Each contains an infinitive phrase that clearly describes the intent and general purpose of the speech; each includes a precise statement of the topic; each specific purpose is phrased as a declarative sentence; no specific purpose is stated as a question. Each specific purpose statement will provide the audience with a clear understanding of the speaker's goal.

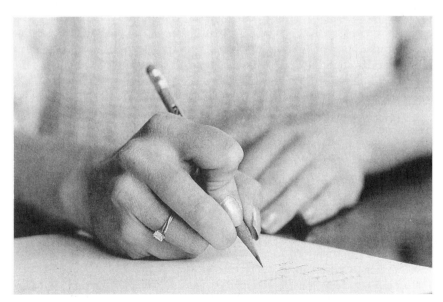

IDEAS FOR SPEECHES ARE OFTEN GENERATED AS A RESULT OF BRAINSTORMING, THINKING ABOUT PERSONAL INTERESTS, GOING TO THE LIBRARY, OR ASKING FOR HELP FROM FRIENDS.

Alan Carey/Image Works

WORDING THE THESIS STATEMENT

The *thesis statement*, often called the "central idea" or the "central objective," is the phrase that tells the audience the major points your speech will include. If a member of your audience walked in late, but just in time to hear your thesis statement, the listener would know exactly what your speech was to cover. The wording of the thesis statement is important because it acts as the organizational hub of your speech; all of the major headings of the body of the speech carry out the thesis statement. Here are two effective examples:

Topic: Communication of dolphins

General purpose: To inform

Specific purpose: To inform the audience about how dolphins communicate

Thesis statement: "Dolphins communicate through their sense of vision and through their sense of sound."

Topic: Meat "analogues" or substitutes

General purpose: To inform

Specific purpose: To inform you about the benefits of meat "analogues" or substitutes

Thesis statement: "Meat substitutes can be high in protein, low in cholesterol, and contain less fat."

In each instance the thesis statement expands and clarifies the specific purpose; it describes what will actually be covered in the speech. In the first example, the thesis tells the audience that the speech will include two points: (1) communication of dolphins through vision, and (2) communication of dolphins through sound. In the second example, the thesis tells listeners that the speaker will describe three benefits of meat substitutes: (1) high protein, (2) low cholesterol, and (3) less fat.

A speech is confusing or hard for an audience to follow when the speaker does not have a clear thesis statement in mind.

Topic: The insanity plea as a defense

General purpose: To convince

Specific purpose: To convince the audience that the insanity plea should be abolished

Poor thesis statement: "Insanity shouldn't be allowed as a defense because there are just too many criminals who have gotten off with that excuse and it just isn't fair to society or to the victims at all."

This thesis statement is a prescription for speaking disaster. The statement is merely a run-on sentence which does not include the main points of the body of the speech. The speaker will probably ramble on without much logic or organization, and the confused audience will probably stop listening. Here's how to correct the problem:

Better thesis statement: "Criminals can fake mental illness; psychiatrists can incorrectly diagnose criminals; and the judicial system loses control over criminals diagnosed as 'insane.'"

This thesis clearly introduces three areas to be covered in the body of the speech. The audience will be able to follow the speaker's organization with ease.

Problems with the Thesis Statement

If you have difficulties writing your thesis statement, it is possible that problems exist elsewhere in your speech.

Poor thesis statement: "I want to describe the religious rituals of the North, Central, and South American Indians."

This thesis contains a topic that is too broad. The numerous Indian tribes with their many religious practices would require an entire series of speeches. Here is a better thesis statement:

Better thesis statement: "I want to explain where and when the Sioux Indians lived, describe some of their religious practices, and explain what happened to them as a tribe."

This thesis is much improved because it incorporates a narrow topic and clearly indicates that the speech will contain three central points. Here is another difficulty often detected in student speeches:

Poor thesis statement: "I want to demonstrate how film is manufactured."

This is not a thesis statement; it is still the specific purpose sentence. If a speaker were to use this as the thesis, there would be at least ten main points in the speech—too many for a five- to seven-minute presentation. The speaker needs to write a thesis statement that expands the specific purpose and includes only a few main points.

Better thesis statement: "Film is manufactured by making a plastic base, coating the plastic surface with emulsion, and cutting the film into appropriate widths."

Here is another frequent difficulty in student speeches:

Poor thesis statement: "I want to describe the game board and the playing pieces of backgammon."

This thesis indicates that the topic is much too limited. The statement contains only one point—not enough for a five- to seven-minute speech. A speech given on this topic would only take about one minute. Here is how to correct the problem:

Better thesis statement: "I want to tell you where backgammon originated, some of the rules of the game, and how it is played."

This thesis is better because it broadens the topic and includes three main points in the speech.

If you are having trouble writing your thesis statement, you may not have enough information and need to do more research.

PUTTING IT TOGETHER

To help you build your own speeches, here are some examples of topics, specific purpose sentences, and thesis statements other students have used in their classroom presentations.[4] A brief commentary in the margin explains why the sample speech was successful.

Collecting comics was Dan Urton's hobby, and the audience could sense his enthusiasm for the topic. During the speech, Dan used some of his own comic books as visual aids to support key ideas. Listeners commented that the topic was "different—many were surprised to learn how valuable old comic books can be. The specific purpose and thesis statement made Dan's speech objectives completely clear to the audience.

Topic: Collecting comic books

General purpose: To inform

Specific purpose: To inform you about the value of collecting comic books.

Thesis statement: I want to give you some basic knowledge about collecting comic books, and tell you how to protect your investment so the comics will increase in value.

Topic: Making a cheesecake

General purpose: To demonstrate

Specific purpose: To demonstrate how to make a cheesecake

Thesis statement: Making a cheesecake requires understanding a recipe and using a step-by-step method to create a beautiful finished product.

Professional chef John Fields showed his audience how to make a cheesecake. John went to the trouble of preparing three cheesecakes in various stages of completion. His audience watched with fascination as he skillfully used his visuals to demonstrate the details of the general process he identified in the thesis. When he finished the speech, John revealed an elegant gourmet cheesecake which he divided among his delighted listeners.

Topic: Doctor-assisted suicide

General purpose: To convince

Specific purpose: To convince the audience that doctor-assisted suicide should not be legalized

Thesis statement: Doctor-assisted suicide violates the Hippocratic oath, encourages suicide, and can be abused.

Elizabeth Crawford used quotations from the U.S. Surgeon General, references to the *New England Journal of Medicine*, and personal experience to support the three reasons stated in the thesis. She described her father-in-law's victory over cancer and acknowledged the caring physicians who had provided treatment. In an emotional statement, Elizabeth concluded: "If Dad Crawford had encountered Dr. Kevorkian as his physician, the outcome of his illness might have been entirely different." Although not everyone agreed with this controversial proposition, the audience was deeply involved in the topic.

Topic: Amnesty International/human rights

General purpose: To actuate

Specific purpose: To actuate the audience to write letters to human rights violators

What impressed the audience about this speech was that Kelly Burns was committed to her topic. Kelly wore a T-shirt declaring "Human Rights Now" as she described her involvement with Amnesty International. Kelly touched the feelings of love and commitment within listeners when she spoke of children, stolen from their families, and illegally adopted in other countries. "Think of your own children, or brothers and sisters," she said, "and be glad this can't happen to them." Audience members were genuinely moved, and many offered to help Kelly with her cause.

Thesis statement: I want to define human rights, explain how Amnesty International works, and tell you what you can do to help those whose rights are being violated.

SUMMARY

In your search for speech topics, explore various areas.

Select a topic that is narrow in scope and will conform to the time limit, that appeals to your own interests as a speaker, is appropriate to your listeners, and conforms to your assigned purpose—to inform, to persuade, or to entertain.

The specific purpose is the overall objective of the speech. The thesis statement amplifies the specific purpose and tells the audience exactly what your speech will cover.

EXERCISES

1. Pick out what is wrong with the following specific purpose statements:

   a. To explain how volcanos form, some types of volcanos, and how a volcano actually erupts
   b. To inform you about three effects of TV violence on children and to urge your support of legislation which requires a TV rating system
   c. To convince you that the NCAA regulation called Proposition 42, which prevents academically "borderline" students from receiving college scholarships, is unfair, and that the NCAA should enact a fairer process
   d. To inform you about the Vietnam War.

2. Rewrite the following thesis statements so that they are more effective:

   a. I will describe the country of Greece and also tell you about the Greek Islands.
   b. I want to inform you about hearing-ear dogs.
   c. I want to tell you how to participate in home schooling.
   d. The purpose of the speech is to inform you about radon gas: what it is, the problems it can cause in your home, and how you can test for it.

3. For each of the following subjects, write a topic, a general purpose, a specific purpose, and a thesis statement.
   animals
   art
   lotteries
   music
   Albert Gore
   space exploration
   sculpture

NOTES

[1] Lilyan Wilder, *Talk Your Way to Success* (New York: Simon and Schuster, 1987), p. 76.

[2] Maria Marszalek, "The Art of Egg Decorating," demonstration speech presented in the Fundamentals of Public Speaking course, Catonsville Community College, Catonsville, Maryland, 1989. Used by permission.

[3] I am appreciative of the following students, who gave me permission to use their topics and specific purposes as examples in this chapter: Linda Carey, Jo Ann Dickensheets, Patricia Farquhar, Dawn Gyory, Stephen King, Lou Ann Pfister, Dwayne Mitchell, Sandra Prusin, Richard Renehan, Susan Stephan, Sherri Webb, and Tracey Weise. I also gratefully acknowledge the late Professor Stephen S. Hiten, who coined the phrase "Be clear, concise, and unambiguous" in his public speaking courses at Columbia Union College.

[4] Speeches in this section were presented in the Fundamentals of Public Speaking course, Catonsville Community College, Catonsville, Maryland, 1987, 1988, 1989, 1990, and 1992. All used by permission.

Chapter Eight

CONDUCTING RESEARCH

Chapter Outline

Key Terms

Credibility
Data base
General references
Primary source
Readers' Guide
Secondary source
Substantive reference
The Turabian style

Spencer Grant/Stock Boston

"Knowledge is power ...
knowledge is safety, and
knowledge is happiness."
—THOMAS JEFFERSON

*C*icero said, "There can be no true merit in speaking, unless what is said is thoroughly understood by him who says it." Cicero knew that a speaker must have an extensive knowledge of the topic to be effective. Without this knowledge, Cicero warned that the "volubility of words is empty and ridiculous."[1]

Cicero's thoughts about knowledge have applied in every generation. You cannot speak with confidence if you do not know your topic, and the audience will not trust you if you do not support your topic with research.

The principal focus of this foundation chapter is to examine the two types of reference tools you need to research a topic: the general references, and the substantive sources. In addition, the chapter includes discussions of source credibility, keeping accurate notes, conducting an interview, and recording a bibliographic entry.

PREPARING FOR RESEARCH

Going to the library does not have to be boring, nor does it have to waste hours of your time. If you know what you are doing, you can accomplish a great deal very quickly. The key to conducting good research is knowing where to look and what to look for on a particular topic. There are also times when doing research does not mean going to the library at all. But even in that case, you must know the alternatives available to make progress toward your goal of presenting an effective speech.

ESTABLISHING CREDIBILITY

The audience must be able to trust you as a speaker and to believe what you are telling them. This confidence, known as *credibility*, is developed when you support ideas with evidence which is verified by research utilizing sources that are respected, reliable, and relevant to the topic.

Sources exhibit varying degrees of credibility. Some, like reputable newspapers, newsmagazines, books, experts, trade journals, and encyclopedias are extremely authoritative and reliable. Others, like some autobiographies, TV talk shows, self-help books, well-meaning friends, or condensed publications containing only excerpts of articles, have less credibility.

Noncredible sources are easily detected by audiences. A student who presented an informative speech on the "positive existence of UFOs" made the statement: "There have been numerous sightings of UFOs according to a recent issue of the *National Enquirer*." Listeners tried to be polite and conceal their smiles. However, they eventually exploded into laughter because the speaker, who was entirely serious, did not perceive the credibility problem that the mention of this source had caused.

Here are some examples of other types of noncredible, hearsay, or "phantom" sources often cited in speeches:

"I got some information on diet from a muscle magazine which said..."

"I was talking to this guy, and he said..."

"Everybody knows that this is true..."

"Studies have proven it to be a fact..."

"Doctors recommend that..."

"I read in a movie magazine that..."

"There is some clinic in France, or Spain, or somewhere, that has developed a cure for AIDS."

"I was watching this TV show and it was real interesting, and it said that..."

"I saw this movie and it talked about..."

"The astrology magazine predicts a major earthquake in California in 1996..."

"I read this book written by a lawyer who has been born eleven different times over the past 1,000 years..."

If you want to establish credibility with the audience, cite reputable sources in your speech. Check the reliablity of authors and the authenticity of publications or so-called experts. Don't rely on hearsay, gossip columns, or fabrication for evidence. If you need a complete source, consult the original article rather than a condensed version. Be willing to spend the time researching ideas from sources that are credible and trustworthy. Cite specific sources, specific studies, and specific authorities to build confidence and believability with your listeners.

PRIMARY AND SECONDARY SOURCES

Sources can be either primary or secondary. *Primary evidence* is original, first-hand fact or experience. For instance, if your topic were "Racing for the America's Cup," a primary source would be a magazine article about a specific race written by Dennis Conner, skipper of the American yacht *Stars and Stripes*. Primary sources, however, are often difficult to obtain or unavailable. Hoping to obtain a personal interview with Dennis Conner is probably unrealistic and an article written by him may not exist.

For many topics, secondary research may be more accessible. *Secondary evidence* is information reported by an intermediary standing between you and the original source. You may find an article in *Sports Illustrated* written by a reporter who witnessed the America's Cup, or read a description of the race in

The New York Times. These sources would be extremely helpful to your speech and they could be obtained quickly through the library. You will probably use secondary evidence frequently as you research speech topics.

USING GENERAL REFERENCES

When you go to the library, you will use the *general reference* sources to begin your search for information. These references help you locate books, publications, or other sources which contain the information you need. The principal research tools are the catalog and the periodical indexes.

The Catalog

The catalog provides accessibility to all the books in the library. In some libraries, the catalog includes periodicals as well as audiovisual materials. Books are listed in the catalog according to author, title, and subject. If you know the author or title, it is easy to find your specific source. If, however, you are looking for a number of books in a general subject area, you will probably find a wide variety of sources to choose from.

Periodical Indexes

Periodical indexes reference a wide range of magazines, newspapers, and journals in popular subject-areas as well as in technical fields of study. The *Readers' Guide to Periodical Literature*, for example, is a general reference to articles in more than two hundred popular magazines such as *Time, Newsweek, McCall's, Science Digest, Popular Mechanics,* and *Parents Magazine.* This source, often called the "average person index," is one of the most important and most helpful references for speech research. The *Readers' Guide* is a yearly index starting in 1890 and extending to the current date. It identifies a general subject, then lists the titles of numerous articles appearing in periodicals relating to the subject. After you select the titles you want to research, go to magazine collections housed in bound volumes (or stored on microfilm) to read specific articles. During the semester you take public speaking, you will probably use this index as much as the catalog.

Periodical indexes in specialized fields are organized like the *Readers' Guide* and can help you find article titles in more technical areas. Here is a partial list of some of these specialized indexes; you'll need to consult your own library reference section to see which reference tools are available to you.

Applied Science and Technology Index   This index contains article titles in aeronautics, chemistry, computer technology, the construction industry, energy resources, engineering, fire and fire prevention, food and the food industry, geology, mathematics, machinery, mechanical arts, metallurgy, mineralogy, oceanography, petroleum and gas, plastics, physics, space science, the textile industry and fabrics, and transportation.

The Art Index   This reference includes titles appearing in periodicals from such varied areas as art-related archeology, architecture, art history, city planning, crafts, films, graphic arts, industrial design, interior design, landscape design, museology, and photography.

Business Periodicals Index   Article titles are included from major business fields such as accounting, advertising, automation, banking, communications, economics, industries and trades, finance, insurance, investments, labor, management, marketing, publications, specific businesses, and taxation.

Biography Index   This is an index to individual biographies and collections of biographies. It also indexes obituaries, letters, diaries, memoirs, and bibliographies. The index lists individuals in alphabetical order, provides their field of expertise, and then lists sources where more information can be found.

Cumulative Index to Nursing   Titles are listed relating to the following fields or professions: cardiopulmonary technology, emergency services, health education, health science librarianship, medical lab technology, medical assistant, medical records, nursing, occupational therapy, physical therapy and rehabilitation, physician's assistant, radiation technology, respiratory therapy, social services in health care, and surgical technology.

Education Index   This index references periodicals in many areas including pre-school, elementary, secondary, higher and adult education; multicultural and ethnic education; special education and rehabilitation; teacher education; vocational education; counseling and personnel service; teaching methodology; and curriculum.

Humanities Index   This reference contains titles in archaeology, classic studies, folklore, history, language, literary and performing arts, philosophy, political criticism, and religion and theology.

Index to Journals in Communication Studies   This is published by the Speech Communication Association and indexes fourteen professional speech journals in areas such as rhetoric and philosophy, broadcasting, education, forensics, and human communication research. It is an important source for the speech and communication major.

Index to Periodical Articles By and About Blacks This multivolume source indexes thirty-two periodicals relating to black Americans. Subjects include art, black studies, culture, discrimination, drama, family, health, history, law, literature, relationships, and religion. Subjects are arranged in alphabetical order, and articles which are referenced are of both general and scholarly interest.

New York Times Index This index lists all of the titles of news, editorial, and feature stories that have ever appeared in the *The New York Times*. Volumes of the index are listed according to year and month.

Psychological Abstracts This reference provides summaries of articles in the principal fields of psychology. Areas include applied psychology, communication systems, developmental psychology, educational psychology, experimental psychology (human and animal), general psychology, personality, physical and psychological disorders, physiological psychology, personnel and professional issues, psychometrics, social processes and social issues, and treatment and prevention.

Religion Index This reference includes 397 periodical titles in the area of religion. It is put out by the American Theological Library Association.

Social Sciences Index Titles in this index are from anthropology, criminology, economics, the environmental sciences, geography, law, planning and public administration, political science, psychology, social aspects of medicine, and sociology.

Women's Studies Abstracts Brief summaries of articles are presented on twenty-four areas related to women's issues. Subjects include abortion, employment, family, family planning, finances, history, literature and art, pregnancy, prejudice and sex discrimination, religion, philosophy and ethics, sexuality, sex roles, sex characteristics, the women's liberation movement, biography and criticism, and media and media reviews.

Accessing the Library by Computer

The computer has made libraries more efficient and much easier to use. Many college and university libraries have computer (on-line) catalogs that allow students to find books quickly and eliminate lengthy manual searches. The computer also facilitates finding books by allowing more key word-entry points. In the traditional card catalog, you search for a book by locating the

A SPEAKER MUST
UNDERSTAND HOW TO
USE GENERAL LIBRARY
REFERENCES TO LOCATE
CREDIBLE SOURCES FOR
PRESENTATIONS.

Pedrick/Image Works

appropriate author, title, or subject card. With a computerized system, there are more key-word access points such as the publisher, date of publication, or a word within a title or abstract.

Many libraries also have periodical indexes such as the *Readers' Guide* on computer. These are used the same way as the manual indexes, but they take less time and provide you with print-outs of periodical titles related to topics. They also provide extensive search options, allowing you to focus more specifically on topics or subtopics. Most of the periodical indexes already listed are available on computer. In addition, many libraries have various computer versions of periodical indexes which have been developed for specific markets. You may encounter some of the following software titles in your college, university, or public library.

Academic Abstracts

Academic Index

First Search

Infotrac

Magazine Article Summaries

Newspaper Abstracts Ondisc

Periodical Abstracts Ondisc
Uncover

These software systems have no print equivalent and enhance the general reference indexes of a library. Libraries choose combinations of software systems or indexes to meet their specific needs. For example, a large university with numerous graduate programs might select an index such as *First Search*, which accesses a variety of periodical indexes as well as books. These indexes are altered and updated frequently and it is advisable to check with your librarian for the most up-to-date information and accurate software titles.

Library research sources are now available through a home, dorm, or office computer. Many libraries network computer catalogs and data bases to faculty offices, residence halls, and classroom locations.

If you have a home computer with a modem (a device linking a computer to a telephone), you can access the *Knowledge Index*, which contains over sixty bibliographic data bases. The *Knowledge Index* includes periodical indexes such as the *Art Bibliography*, the *Magazine Index*, and *Psycinfo*, an electronic version of *Psychological Abstracts*. It also contains the *Books in Print* index, *UPI News*, and the entire King James version of the Bible. There is an hourly charge for this service, and the fee is less expensive after regular business hours. Since the *Knowledge Index* is a fee-based system, it is available from the library or home, but probably not in faculty office or dorm locations. Some libraries offer access to this program and to a similar system called the *Bibliographic Retrieval Service*.

RESEARCHING SUBSTANTIVE SOURCES

Unlike general references, *substantive sources* contain subject information and help you to locate more specific information. Biographies, directories, dictionaries and encyclopedias as well as almanacs, collections of quotations, books, and magazines, are substantive sources located in the library. Interviews with experts, as well as research using the resources of large institutions or specialized organizations, are substantive sources which require investigation outside the library.

Biographies

Biographies and biographical collections are good places to search for topics. A speech about a little-known American such as John Hanson, who was technically the first president of the United States, would be interesting. Biographies can also be helpful in providing background information about a person you intend to use as an authoritative source in your speech. These collections can assist you.

Current Biography Spanning five decades, these volumes provide detailed information about prominent individuals in almost every field of human achievement around the world. Each description is accompanied by a picture.

Dictionary of American Biography This source provides descriptions of important figures throughout American history. Volumes include supplements and a complete index.

Who's Who in America This multivolume reference contains biographies of those who are prominent in almost every aspect of contemporary American life. First published in 1952, *Who's Who* also includes dignitaries and officials of Canada and Mexico. Individuals must be living at the time of inclusion.

Who's Who of American Women American women who have attained positions of responsibility or who have made significant achievements are included in this source. First publication occurred in 1958, and subsequent volumes are printed in two-year intervals.

Who's Who Among Black Americans This four-volume set contains biographies of living African Americans who are leaders in occupations or professional fields and who have contributed signficantly to American life. The first volume appeared in 1975–76.

Directories and Handbooks

Directories can be helpful if you need information about specific agencies or institutions. These directories provide names, addresses, and services of all types of groups. The government also publishes an index called the *Monthly Catalog of Government Publications*, listing the numerous booklets and pamphlets put out by the U.S. Government Printing Office. You could use this source to find the names of pamphlets written about subjects such as AIDS, fire safety, or CPR. There are so many directories and handbooks that we can't mention all of them, but here is a brief list which might be helpful.

A Handbook of Services for the Handicapped This book helps readers to understand the difficulties of the disabled and describes resources which are available to meet these special needs.

Civil Rights Directory This source assists people who fear discrimination by age, race, sex, disability, religion, or national origin. It lists federal and state agencies which are responsible for handling these concerns.

Grant Seekers Guide This directory provides lists of foundations, philanthropists, and organizations which provide grants for groups seeking solutions to social or economic problems. It describes the name, nature and purpose of the foundation, and identifies the amounts distributed on a yearly basis.

National Directory of Youth and Family Services This directory lists treatment centers, hospitals, crisis centers, hot-lines and professional services. It includes both public and private agencies and is published every two years.

Occupational Outlook Handbook This book identifies the major occupations and professions in the United States. It describes the nature of the occupation, the working conditions involved, training and education required, statistics regarding employment, average wages or salary, and the projected job outlook.

The Help Book This guide lists numerous organizations which can provide assistance and intervention in difficult situations. Support groups are identified in areas such as battered women, rape, drug abuse, child abuse, peer counseling, pregnancy, insurance, smoking, family planning, food and nutrition, and victim's rights.

Dictionaries

In Chapter 1, we discussed misunderstandings in the speaker–audience relationship because of varying interpretations of a word's meaning. A good way for you as a speaker to overcome semantic noise is to be very clear about the meanings of the words you employ. Consult a good dictionary such as *The American Heritage Dictionary* or *Webster's New International Dictionary*. If you need to understand technical terms in a specific field, consult a specialized dictionary. *Black's Law Dictionary*, *Dorland's Illustrated Medical Dictionary*, and the *Scientific Encyclopedia* are examples of sources which can provide technical definitions in specialized areas.

Encyclopedias

Encyclopedias are often good places to start when you are researching a topic, because they provide you with an overview of a general subject very quickly. However, their information is not always comprehensive, and in many cases material is not up-to-date. Be careful not to base your entire presentation on information taken from encyclopedias or your speech might be superficial.

There are encyclopedias on literally every subject. Two good general subject encyclopedias are *Collier's Encyclopedia* and *World Book*. The *Encyclopaedia Britannica* is also excellent if you need a more scholarly source.

There are numerous specialized encyclopedias on subjects such as aviation, photography, and automotive repair. We have included a brief list useful for speech research.

Encyclopedia of Indians of the Americas Written to correct misinformation about Indians, this source contains information about the history, culture, artifacts, and architecture of North, Central, and South American Indian tribes.

Encyclopedia of Religion and Ethics Descriptions of world religions, customs, religious beliefs, and ethical systems are presented in this source.

Encyclopedia of World Art Paintings, photographs, sketches, and architectural examples of world art are included in these volumes.

Illustrated Science and Invention Encyclopedia This source provides information about scientific discoveries and technological advancements. It is helpful for descriptive and demonstration speeches.

International Encyclopedia of Social Sciences These volumes contain material related to anthropology, economics, law, geography, history, political science, psychiatry, sociology, and statistics.

International Library of Afro-American Life and History Arranged by subject area, volumes in this set emphasize African Americans in athletics, medicine, theatre, literature, Civil War times, and the struggle for equality.

International Wildlife Encyclopedia This encyclopedia classifies the wildlife of the world and describes animal behavior as well as evolutionary characteristics.

New Grove Dictionary of Music and Musicians This multivolume encyclopedia provides definitions of music terms, describes the origin and development of musical instruments, and includes extensive biographies of important composers and musicians. It emphasizes classical music.

Almanacs, Yearbooks, and Statistical Publications

Often you will need to find statistical information to give your speech credibility. Almanacs, yearbooks, and statistical abstracts contain numerical data on subjects such as crime, deaths, births, accidents, diseases, incomes, and budgets.

When you do statistical research, it is important to exercise care in your interpretation of the material. Be certain that you clearly understand the information as it is presented. Statistics can be presented in decimals, in percentages, in total numbers of cases, in means (averages), in medians (middle

number), or in modes (number occurring with greatest frequency). Know
what the statistics measure, and be able to draw clear and accurate conclusions
from the data before you decide to include the information.

Some of the most useful sources for statistics are:

Statistical Abstract of the United States This comprehensive statistical source
is divided into subject areas representing every aspect of American life. It is
published each year by the U.S. Department of Commerce.

Vital Statistics of the United States This series presents comprehensive data
in three areas: birth, marriage and divorce, and death. Three volumes are published annually by the U.S. Department of Health and Human Services.

World Almanac and Book of Facts This source contains world statistics in many
areas including births, deaths, and population. It also includes, for example,
articles, maps, actions of Congress, and information on baseball. It is divided
by subjects and published yearly.

Information Please Almanac This source presents articles in numerous fields
such as astronomy, family, and culture, and statistical information on Amercian
and international subjects. It is divided into subject areas and published annually.

Collections of Quotations

Many sources can provide you with the right quotation to introduce or conclude your speech. Quotations can often synthesize ideas that might take several lines for you to paraphrase. You might want to consult *Bartlett's Familiar
Quotations; Morrow's International Dictionary of Contemporary Quotations;* and
The Macmillan Book of Proverbs, Maxims, and Famous Phrases.

Books

One of the most obvious sources for a speech is an authoritative book written on your topic. Frequently you will find a collection of readings compiled
by one editor or author, which will be useful to your research. Be sure to
notice the date a book was published. If you were researching "Latest
Computer Technologies" in a book published in 1975, you would not find
much current information. If your topic were "History of Computer
Technology," the 1975 source might be excellent.

For some topics, using a rare book or a classic study might be more significant than a more recent source. In a speech about the *Titanic,* for example,

a speaker could quote an eyewitness from a book written in 1912 by one of *Titanic*'s survivors. In this case, the speech would contain material from an excellent primary source.

Some books, like the huge selection of self-help publications in bookstores, are popular with the general public, but many times authors of these publications are not experts—they are merely lay individuals writing from their own personal experiences about divorce, jogging, or making millions in real estate. That people have been enterprising enough to put their thoughts into print does not mean their words should be regarded with reverence. Analyze carefully what you read; examine how writers document and reference their material; and, above all, feel free to question and even discard information if other evidence proves data questionable or false.

Magazines, Journals, Newspapers

Newsmagazines such as *Time, Newsweek,* or *U.S. News & World Report* are excellent sources and will provide much of the information you need on current events. As you investigate these sources, however, be able to distinguish between fact and opinion. Many newsmagazines contain articles that report facts in a fairly objective manner. But these periodicals also include columns, such as editorials or features, which provide opinions and interpretations of facts. Also be aware of any political or social bias of the publications, and double-check articles with other news sources for accuracy.

Quarterlies and journals contain articles relative to specific disciplines. Periodicals such as *The Automobile Quarterly, The American Journal of Psychology,* and *The Criminal Law Quarterly* can be helpful in your research, even though they are written in the technical jargon of the discipline. Be certain that you clearly understand journal articles so you are able to communicate the information easily to the audience.

Newspapers will give you some of the most up-to-date information about current events and social issues. Check the political bias of the newspaper you research. The *Washington Post* and the *New York Times,* for instance, are considered liberal publications, while the *Wall Street Journal* and the *Christian Science Monitor* are more conservative. Be careful about using newspapers as comprehensive sources on issues. Since current events are constantly unfolding, one news story or article will rarely be complete. It is wise to cross-reference newspapers for accuracy.

Legal Research

You may need to cite a number of court cases to prove a point in a persuasive speech, or describe the details of litigation for an informative presentation. If so, don't be intimidated by the number of official-looking legal volumes in your library. You simply have to learn how to use these resources. If you know what information you need, a good librarian should get you to the right source.

Audiovisual Aids

In addition to books and periodicals, libraries have maps, atlases, and extensive media collections, which you can research to support ideas. A visual aid, such as a map, can quickly pinpoint a location and make a topic more understandable to listeners. Including a brief excerpt from a National Geographic videotape or playing a portion of a symphony may also add interest to particular speech topics. Audiovisual aids are effective because they help you communicate with listeners through additional channels. (Chapter 12 provides a complete discussion of the types and uses of audio-visuals in a presentation.)

Interviews with Authorities

For certain topics, your research will take you outside the library. Interviews with professionals such as physicians, lawyers, police officers, or child psychologists will yield invaluable primary source material—as long as the experts are authorities in their fields. If you are doing research about victims of rape, speak to an official in a community rape-crisis center. Your professional may be able to provide you with a wealth of supporting materials even in a brief telephone interview. Don't be content to include just a single interview—use several, so that your speech will contain a number of authoritative viewpoints.

You can also include *personal testimonies* from individuals who have actually experienced some aspect of the topic. A testimonial from someone injured by a drunk driver, or a brief quote from a person afflicted with AIDS, can vividly convey the impact of an issue.

Legislative and Governmental Research

You may have a topic that requires you to investigate specific legislation enacted by the state legislature or by the United States Congress. A quick phone call to the office of one of your representatives can help you to gather valuable information on a local or national legislative issue.

The Congressional Index is an excellent source if you want to know the legislation currently pending in Congress. This index gives you the current status of legislation: that is, whether the bill is in committee, if it has been passed by one or both chambers of Congress, if it has been signed into law or vetoed by the president, or if a presidential veto has been overridden by the Congress.

If you want to investigate the daily proceedings of Congress, consult *The Congressional Record*, which transcribes the floor debates and votes of the members of the Senate and the House of Representatives. (In addition, both houses of Congress now televise their daily proceedings, making a video record as well.)

When you need to understand how our Congress and the government spend our tax money, you can obtain a copy of *The Budget of the United States Government*, which can tell you how the Federal Government allocates more than $1 trillion in the current fiscal year. The budget is available in the library or through the Government Printing Office.

Institutional and Organizational Research

Many institutions and organizations have public relations or information offices which can provide you with material on specific subjects. If you need information on the eye bank, for example, contact the hospital specializing in this field. For data related to higher educational institutions, get in touch with your college or university's public relations office. If you're doing research on a foreign country, call the embassy or the foreign consulate office nearest you. Ask your state's department of motor vehicles for data regarding accident rates, insurance guidelines, or driving tests. To collect examples and statistical evidence concerning specific crimes in your community or state, consult the information office of the police department. If you need to know what people are doing to prevent drinking and driving, contact Mothers Against Drunk Driving (MADD). If you want to know what is being done to improve our nation's educational system, contact the National Education Association (NEA). Information from these institutions and organizations can provide more depth and substance to a speech topic. Here are three sources that can help you to find specific organizations or agencies.

Encyclopedia of Associations This source lists more than 23,000 national and international oranizations and associations. Published in several volumes, this set identifies the names, purposes, and addresses of mostly non-governmental agencies.

The United States Government Manual Published by the Office of the Federal Register (National Archives), this guide identifies the official names, purposes, addresses and phone numbers of all agencies in the legislative, judical, and executive branches of government. It also identifies those international organizations in which the United States participates.

State blue books, manuals, and almanacs Each state publishes a guide that lists agencies of the executive, judicial, and legislative branches of state government. You should consult your college or public library for the appropriate source.

Specialized Libraries and Museums

Many cities and communities have specialized libraries in law, medicine, literature, science, astronomy or agriculture. The Library of Congress is a comprehensive source that includes material from these libraries as well as anything that has ever been published in the United States. The Library of Congress and many other libraries have inter-library loan services that allow you to obtain materials from other libraries at your local institution. The only disadvantage of inter-library loan systems is that you may have to order information in advance. Check with your librarian for specific information regarding the inter-library loan system nearest you.

KEEPING ACCURATE NOTES

When you are doing research, it is important that you have a well organized system of note-taking so that you will use your time efficiently. Often people will go to the periodical indexes, jot down a list of sources, then look up articles and forget to write down the statistics or examples they wanted to use in their speeches. They have to return to their sources a second or third time and plod through the material all over again to recall their information. A good method of taking notes can help you avoid such a time-wasting process and assist you in making substantial progress towards getting your speech organized.

Get some 3×5 or 4×6 note cards. When you find a source you want to use, put a topic heading at the upper-right-hand corner of the card. Then at the upper-left corner put the type of supporting information you are listing on the card, such as statistics, quotation, comparison or contrast, and so forth. Then place a bibliographic entry on the next line, so that you will be able to identify the exact reference for later use in your speech or in case you ever need to investigate it again. Finally, jot down the specific details of the information. Include all the necessary statistical data, illustrations, or other material you want for the speech. When you follow this system, you will be able to build an index file of supporting materials that will be easy to use and will allow you to arrange in any order.

The following notes (see page 162) demonstrate how to identify the topic, the specific type of supporting data, the bibliographic reference, and pertinent details of the researched material.

THE INTERVIEW

Many of your speech topics will require you to interview people who are experts or authorities in their fields. You should know how to conduct an interview to get the material that you need from these individuals.

Statistics /   Decline in blue whale population —— Topic Heading
                                                                                Type of Support
Lipske, Michael. "A Whale of a Story."
   National Wildlife, February/ March, 1993, pp. 6, 12. ————————— Source

1. Blue whale is largest mammal in the world ———————— Statistical Data
   a. Newborn weighs 7 tons
   b. Adult blue whale weighs up to 150 tons
2. 250,000 blue whales and sub-species killed
   by whaling between 1920's and 1971
3. Maximum of 10,000 blue whales now exist

   Point: Largest mammal in the world has declined
   dramatically in population ————————————————— Conclusion

Quotation /   Tribute to Arthur Ashe —— Topic Heading
                                                                                Type of Support
Wilbon, Michael. "A Great Athlete, and a Very Great Deal
   More." *Washington Post*, February 8, 1993, p. C6. ——————— Source

"If you weren't paying attention, you could have missed so much
of what Arthur Ashe was. He never broke rackets or cursed
umpires or threw tantrums that hijacked the TV cameras or put —— Quoted Material
him at the top of the sports news . . . Not once did I ever see him
wave a finger to signify he was No. 1. Not once did I see him try
to upstage an opponent. Not once do I recall him whining or
alibiing, embarrassing himself or his family for any reason. As an
athlete, he won or lost, congratulated an opponent, and moved on.
Always with dignity, with his self-respect and sense of self intact."

                              –Michael Wilbon, sports writer, columnist —— Qualifications of
                                                                            quoted person

---

Example /   Amazing feats in advertising–bungee —— Topic Heading
                                   jumping GMC truck
                                                                            Type of Support
Bromer, Cliff. "Jumpin' Jimmy." *Popular Mechanics*, March, 1993,
   pp. 56-57. ——————————————————————————————————— Source
1. Bungee cord was attached to tail hook of GMC sport truck ——— Details of
2. Bungee cord also fastened to New River Gorge Bridge, Beckley,   Example
   West Virginia
   a. Bridge is 876 ft. high and has largest steel arch span in
      continental U.S.
   b. Engineers determined that bridge could sustain stresses of
      truck bungee jump
3. Bungee cord specially designed with 9 individual cords
4. Launch platform from bridge required stunt engineering
5. Jump was a success for a brief 30 to 60 sec. commercial
6. Truck had to be "reeled in" like a fish

Preparing for the Interview

When you interview an expert on your topic, you must be completely prepared by conducting preliminary research into the topic and developing a list of questions to ask. This kind of preparation will help you to conduct the interview more effectively and keep you from wasting valuable time.

When you have done your research and prepared your questions, call the interviewee to make an appointment. Be sure that the individual understands your topic and knows the reason for the interview. You might even tell the individual one or two of the questions you are going to ask, so that he or she can be adequately prepared with answers. When you set up the interview, you may want to double check the qualifications of the interviewee so that you are certain that you are talking to the appropriate expert. When the individual agrees to the interview, set a date and a time that accommodates the other person's schedule, and yet allows you to obtain all the information you need.

Conducting the Interview

Be sure that you are on time for the interview. Establish rapport with your interviewee by being friendly, courteous, and conversational. Demonstrate active listening skills—nod your head, sit forward, and show interest in the person you are interviewing. Let the individual know that you are easy to talk to, receptive, and noncombative.

Next, introduce your topic and state the purpose of the interview. Start by asking questions from your prepared list. As the interviewee introduces new or relevant information, think of other follow-up questions to ask. If the individual brings up ideas that are irrelevant to your topic, gently bring the person back on track by saying, "Let's go back to what you were saying before," or "Now, if you don't mind, I'd like to ask you another question." Remember that you do have a time limit, and you must gather the information you need.

Be sure that your interviewee adequately clarifies and explains material. One-word answers like "yes" or "no" will not really help when you need information in depth. Ask him or her to expand upon the issue by posing open-ended questions such as, "Can you give me an example of what you're saying?" or "How do you handle that type of situation?"

During the interview make verbal summaries to help you understand the material clearly, and also to allow the interviewee to correct any misinformation or misconceptions you may have. Keep the interview moving; if it gets bogged down, ask more questions or make additional comments to get the discussion going again. Don't monopolize the conversation; give the person adequate time to formulate a response. And don't interrupt the individual unless it is absolutely necessary. This practice is not only rude, it also interrupts the individual's thought process.

Conclude the interview on time. Don't stay longer unless you are specifically asked. The person has set aside a specific time for you in a busy schedule—don't impose any further.

Taking Notes During an Interview

During the interview, you should take notes that are accurate and complete. But remember that your writing should usually be notation—not a verbatim transcript of the entire conversation. If your interview covers detailed information that requires more careful transcription, ask for permission to bring a tape recorder—but never bring one to an interview unless you ask for prior permission. There will be times when taping will not be acceptable to an interviewee. For example, if you were talking with a rape-crisis counselor about specific case histories, the counselor might not allow you to tape the interview because of the need to protect confidentiality.

If you use a direct quote from the individual, make certain that everything you jot down is completely correct. Double-check the accuracy of the statement with the interviewee. Don't be afraid to ask questions to clarify an issue if you are not certain about the information.

After the interview is over, review your notes while the ideas are still fresh in your mind. Expand your notes by writing summaries and additional comments. At a later time you may want to make a follow-up call to clear up any unanswered questions.

The Bibliography: How To Record An Entry

When you write your outline, list the sources you have used to research the topic. And when you enter a book or magazine title in your bibliography, you need to use a style that is uniform and consistent. Many colleges and universities have their own style booklets which give their required bibliographic procedures. Your instructor may want you to use your college style system or another approach.

In this text, we have used the Kate L. Turabian stylebook *A Manual for Writers of Term Papers, Theses, and Dissertations.*[2] Since you will probably be using books, magazines, newspapers and interviews frequently, study these sample entries according to the Turabian style. Be sure to alphabetize the bibliography as you write each reference item.

Books : One Author

Rothman, Milton A. *The Science Gap: Dispelling the Myths and Understanding the Reality of Science*. Buffalo: Prometheus Books, 1992.

Books: Two Authors

Jaksa, James A., and Pritchard, Michael S. *Communication Ethics*. Belmont: Wadsworth Publishing Company, 1988.

Magazines: Article Without Author Provided

"Guns n' Riot." *People Weekly*, July 22, 1991, p. 46.

Magazines: Article With Author Provided

Simpson, J. "Before and After: Art for Art's Sake." *Architectural Digest*, September, 1991, pp. 82–89.

Newspapers: Article Without Author Provided

"Fischer Beats Spassky, Wins $3.35 Million in Controversial Chess Rematch." *The Evening Sun*, November 6, 1992, p. 3A.

Newspapers: Article With Author Provided

Ifill, Gwen. "Clinton Accepts Delay in Lifting Military Gay Ban," *The New York Times*, January 30, 1993, sec. 1, p.1.

Interviews

English, Phillip C. Vice-President for Communications and Technology, American Association of Community and Junior Colleges, Washington, DC. Interview, May 3, 1992.

SUMMARY

Sources should be credible and reliable; they may be primary or secondary.

General library references for locating sources are the catalog, the periodical indexes, and the computer. Substantive library sources are biographies, directories and encyclopedias, as well as almanacs, collections of quotations, books, and magazines. Interviews with experts and research into large institutions or specialized organizations are nonlibrary sources. An accurate system of note-taking should be used to collect research materials.

When interviewing experts, be prepared, conduct the interview skillfully, and take notes. Consult your institutional style guide or use the Turabian system to record a bibliography.[3]

EXERCISES

1. Select an individual in political life as the topic for a two- to three-minute speech to inform. The individual could be a member of Congress, or an elected official in your state or community. Gather some specific information about this person from three different sources: a biography, a news article (either in a magazine or newspaper), and an interview. Present the speech to your class. It is important for you to establish credibility in your presentation.
2. Select a current events topic for a two- to three-minute informative speech. Using the *Readers' Guide*, find articles in two periodicals that support your issue. Present the topic to your class, and try to integrate your sources effectively into your speech.
3. List your sources to Exercises (1) and (2) above using your departmental stylebook or the Turabian system. Make sure that you are accurate in every detail of your entries.
4. Identify a speaker who you feel uses credible research in his or her speeches. Write a brief paragraph explaining the reasons you trust the speaker's sources. Repeat the same exercise with a speaker you feel does not use credible research.

NOTES

[1] Lester Thonssen, comp., *Selected Readings in Rhetoric and Public Speaking* (New York: H. W. Wilson, 1942), pp. 65–67.

[2] Kate L. Turabian, *A Manual for Writers of Term Papers, Theses, and Dissertations*, 5th ed. (Chicago: The University of Chicago Press, 1987).

[3] I thank Bonita J. Preston, Associate Professor of Library Science at Catonsville Community College, for her guidance and advice regarding this chapter.

READINGS

Coco, Al. *Finding the Law: A Workbook on Legal Research for Laypersons.* Washington, D.C.: U.S. Government Printing Office, 1982. Helps you to understand the difference between statutory law and case law. It also identifies and describes some of the principal tools you need to investigate each area.

Elias, Stephen. *Legal Research.* Berkeley: Nolo Press, 1982. Uncomplicated and easy to read. It provides a brief description of the legal system and also identifies the various types of finding tools you need in legal research. The book also helps you to understand case citations and abbreviations.

How Federal Laws Are Made. Washington, D.C.: WANT Publishing, 1982. Describes how a bill is introduced into Congress and how it proceeds through both houses until it is sent to the president. It also describes the federal budget process and explains how to find laws in the *U.S. Code.*

Katz, William. *Your Library: A Reference Guide.* New York: Holt, Rinehart, and Winston, 1979. This excellent source helps you to understand some of the general and substantive reference tools available in the library.

Stewart, Charles J., and Cash, William B. *Interviewing: Principles and Practices,* 4th ed. Dubuque, Iowa: Wm. C. Brown, 1985. An excellent source to learn more about the interview process. The authors devote four chapters to preparing for the interview. In addition, Stewart and Cash identify and analyze six specific types of interviews: journalistic, survey, employment, performance, persuasive, and health care.

Turabian, Kate L. *A Manual for Writers of Term Papers, Theses, and Dissertations,* 5th ed. Chicago: The University of Chicago Press, 1987. The stylebook used for footnote and bibliographic references in this text. It is extremely helpful for any speech outline or research paper. You should check with your instructor for advice concerning the appropriate style source to use in your speech course.

Chapter Nine

CHOOSING SUPPORTING MATERIALS

Chapter Outline

Key Terms

Anecdote
Case study
Comparison
Contrast
Example
Illustration
Narrative
Observation
Personal experience
Poll
Quotation
Role-playing
Statistic
Survey
Testimony
Visual aid

Weiner/Gamma Liason

*D*uring his years as president, Ronald Reagan was often called "the Great Communicator." Reagan's genius was due partly to his ability to use supporting materials which created a strong emotional attachment with listeners. He could ignite feelings of patriotism by painting a vivid picture of the delegates to the Constitutional Convention; he could stimulate feelings of pride by describing the heroic actions of a young government employee rescuing the victim of an airline crash; and he could arouse sorrow by reading the letter of a daughter who had lost a father in World War II.

Reagan's use of supporting materials, however, has not always been entirely accurate. At the 1992 Republican National Convention, the former president attempted to quote Lincoln to support his contention that Democrats were trying to copy Republicans.

> They even tried to portray themselves as sharing the same fundamental values of our party! What they truly don't understand is the principle so eloquently stated by Abraham Lincoln: "You cannot strengthen the weak by weakening the strong. You cannot help the wage earner by pulling down the wage payer. You cannot help the poor by destroying the rich. You can not help men permanently by doing for them what they could and should do for themselves."

To research the quotation, Mr. Reagan used a book entitled *The Toastmasters Treasure Chest*, which incorrectly identified Lincoln as the source. Had Reagan further checked the accuracy of the lines with historians or librarians, however, he would have discovered that the quotation was taken from a book of maxims published in 1916 by William J. H. Boetcker, a Pennsylvania minister.[1]

This final chapter on the speech foundation considers several types of supporting materials. We include examples from student and professional speakers and make suggestions for you to apply to your own presentations. While we want you to build strong connections with your audience, we want you to use supporting materials accurately and appropriately.

MAKING THE APPROPRIATE SELECTION

When you research a speech, you must look for supporting materials. If you are talking about heart transplants, a quotation from a prominent heart surgeon builds credibility. If you are asking listeners to favor bicycle-helmet laws, you would use statistics to show that wearing helmets decreases fatalities. If you are educating the audience about the disease lupus, a disturbing story of a child's chronic suffering from it would paint a vivid picture. Whether your speech is informative or persuasive, you need information and credible examples to support your topic.

When you use supporting materials, it is usually advisable to mention the source for your information. While you certainly don't need to pepper your speech with "according to's," you do need to make it clear to your audience that your topic is based upon concrete evidence. If you use several facts or examples from the same source, you can make one reference which doesn't interfere with the flow of the speech. If you say "Some of my information today is taken from an article I read in the November, 1993 issue of *Consumer Reports*," you have shown your audience that your evidence is grounded in credible research.

Some of the most authoritative supporting materials are statistics, polls, and surveys; examples, stories, illustrations, and case studies; quotations and testimonies; and comparisons and contrasts. A speaker can use these materials to build a credible case for a persuasive speech or to provide verifiable support in an informative presentation.

Less verifiable, yet stimulating forms of support are personal experience and observation; humor, anecdotes and role playing. Speakers use these materials to enliven speeches and to maintain audience interest and attention. It is often difficult to validate experiences, humor, or skits with sources. But a speaker can enhance a speech if these forms of support are based upon realistic circumstances and combined with more authoritative statistics, testimony, or examples.

We will examine each type of supporting material and describe its potential use in a speech.

STATISTICS, POLLS, AND SURVEYS

One way to support a topic is by using statistical data. *Statistics* are a collection of facts in numerical form, *polls* are samplings of opinion on selected issues, and *surveys* are studies which draw conclusions from research.

Statistics can provide data about population, income, death, crime and birth. You can determine the increase in the number of deaths due to heart disease by looking at statistics over a fifteen year period. If you need to know how many people favor or oppose gay soldiers in the military, you can consult the *Gallup Opinion Poll* or the *CBS/New York Times Poll*. If you need to know how student performance compares in different racial or economic groups, you can investigate the conclusions provided in a specific study.

Using Statistics

You must be careful when you decide to use statistics, polls, or surveys as your supporting evidence. If you use too many complicated numbers, you'll bore your audience. Just stating that the federal budget in 1992–93 was approximately $1,473,742,198,427.27 is a mouthful. The audience would probably forget most of it by the time they heard the twenty-seven cents!

It is often advisable to round off your statistics to the nearest whole number so the audience can grasp the overall concept. Be sure that you draw conclusions from the data and relate the conclusion to your point. It is helpful to relate complicated statistics to a simpler concept. While few people could comprehend the staggering budget figure mentioned above, anyone could understand the number, if it were compared to a thousand dollar bills stacked several miles high.

If you need to be more precise with statistics, you can construct a visual aid or chart to display the data so that the audience can draw conclusions at a glance.

When you cite statistics, polls, or surveys, it establishes credibility to state who conducted the research as well as when and where the research was done. When presenting a survey, you might want to mention the purpose of the research in addition to the conclusions of the study.

In the following excerpt from an informative speech about the history of Coca-Cola, Jena L. Weigel used statistics to show the amount consumed by the public.

> I'd like to tell you some startling statistics I found about Coca-Cola in the book *Everybody's Business, A Field Guide to the 400 Leading Companies in America.* When Coca-Cola was introduced in 1886, the company sold only nine sodas a day. But almost one hundred years later in 1980, the amount of Coke sold would fill 213,000 Olympic size swimming pools. Researchers also estimated in 1980 that if you took all of the Coke ever consumed by the human race and poured it over Niagara Falls, the giant waterfall would flow at its normal rate for 23 hours and 21 minutes! That's a lot of the real thing, isn't it? Today, Coke is served more that 560 million times every day.[2]

Jena understood that raw data is not interesting unless listeners can relate to the numbers easily. The speaker made the statistics come alive by using familiar examples such as Niagara Falls and Olympic-size swimming pools. Jena also introduced a humorous note when she cited the slogan from Coca-Cola marketing campaigns. To give the data credibility, the speaker mentioned her source for the statistics.

During the presidential campaign of 1992, twenty million Americans watched as Texas billionaire H. Ross Perot used charts and simplified statistics to explain the problem of the national debt.[3]

> Now we have a four trillion dollar debt. Let's look at this map here. Look at the purple, and let me tell you what, if we had the four trillion still in the bank, we could do with it... We could buy a one-hundred-thousand-dollar home for every family in every one of those states. We could put a ten-thousand-dollar car in the garages of each of these houses. Then we could build one thousand ten-million-dollar libraries for a thousand cities in these states. We could build two thousand schools in these states costing ten million dollars

each and have enough left over to put into a savings account. And from the interest alone in that savings account pay forty thousand nurses and forty thousand teachers an annual salary of $32,760. And finally we'd still have enough from the interest income alone to give a five-thousand-dollar a year bonus to every family in those states. That's what four trillion dollars would buy. We just can't keep throwing money out the window.[4]

For his statistics, Perot used a two-color map of the United States to show how four trillion dollars could be applied in "the purple" area representing more than half of the country. While people could not readily understand the concept of several trillion dollars, Americans could easily connect to the numbers related in personal terms.

Speaker William L. Winter, Director of the National Press Institute, uses a poll from a credible source to support a point:

And finally, people are telling us that they just don't like the media very much. Poll after poll shows that readers, viewers and listeners believe the media are biased, that they have too much power, and that they wield that power arbitrarily.

This month's *Washington Journalism Review* reports the sobering findings of a survey done by the new University of Virginia-based Thomas Jefferson Center for the Protection of Free Expression. Nearly thirty percent of those polled said that freedom of expression did not extend to newspapers. Forty percent said that they didn't believe the First Amendment protected the arts and entertainment, or that protecting such expression was not as important as protecting the spoken word.[5]

In a speech about recycling materials, David Zebraski used a survey to demonstrate the problem of wastefulness.

Dr. William L. Rathje, an anthropologist at the University of Arizona, conducted a long-term study of the residents of Tucson. In research funded by the Environmental Protection Agency and the National Science Foundation, Dr. Rathje and his students actually collected samples of garbage from different economic neighborhoods in the city. He found that, overall, Tucson's residents throw away fifteen percent of their food, wasting eleven to thirteen million dollars per year. He also discovered that middle-income people throw away more food, tools, and appliances than do low- or high-income people. This study found that middle class people—individuals like you and me—are the most wasteful.[6]

In addition to stating the findings of the study, the speaker mentions the name of the researcher, the place where the study was conducted, two funding agencies, and even the process used for research. The results of the study credibly support the speaker's point about the average person's wastefulness.

EXAMPLES, ILLUSTRATIONS, CASE STUDIES AND NARRATIVES

When you conduct research you should look for examples, illustrations, case studies, or narratives to support your topic. An *example* is a brief factual instance that demonstrates a point; a *hypothetical example* is a fictitious situation that has a realistic application; an *illustration* is a long example that clarifies and amplifies an idea; a *case study* is an in-depth account of a situation or a set of circumstances; and a *narrative* is telling an experience or story.

A brief example or case can often demonstrate a point more dramatically than a long description of facts. People love a good story and appreciate research that stimulates curiosity. By combining a balance of theoretical facts with illustrations and examples, you keep your audience involved.

Using Examples

In a speech on drunk driving, a speaker might use one or two brief examples combined with a minute-long personal narrative about driving while intoxicated. In a five- to seven-minute speech, two brief instances and one long illustration would probably be sufficient. A speaker could also cite many brief examples of drunk driving. This type of rapid-fire approach is effective in communicating a great deal of information in a short period of time.

You build credibility in your speech if you cite references. Let your audience know if the narrative is from your own knowledge and experience or

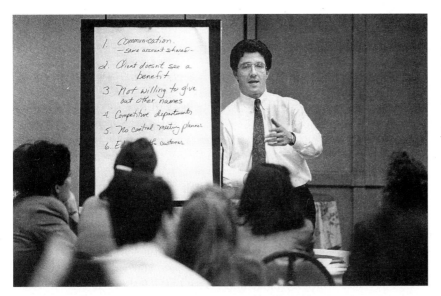

A SPEAKER PROVIDES CONCRETE SUPPORT FOR IDEAS AND CONCEPTS BY USING VIVID EXAMPLES, CASE STUDIES, AND ILLUSTRATIONS.

John Coletti/Picture Cube

from someone else's. State your sources for case studies, examples, and illustrations. Use a variety of sources and use a variety of instances. Don't base your speech on one personal narrative or on one brief example. Provide examples and cases that develop your topic in depth.

In the following speech, John E. Jacob, President and Chief Executive Officer of the National Urban League, cites a series of brief examples to support his point:

> Moving on to the political arena—We have made great gains in terms of the numbers of elected officials, in the numbers of black Congresspersons, and in the stature of the appointed positions we hold.
>
> It is a sign of how far we've come to realize that a black man, Congressman Mike Espy, was elected by black and white voters to represent Mississippi in Congress. The same state of Mississippi that cheered the assassination of Medgar Evers now has more blacks in its state legislature than any other state in the Union.
>
> A black man born and raised in the Bronx and a graduate of City College, General Colin Powell, is Chairman of the Joint Chiefs of Staff.
>
> A black doctor and university president is Secretary of Health and Human Services in the Cabinet.
>
> And, like it or not, a black man, Clarence Thomas, sits on the Supreme Court of the United States...[7]

This "rapid-fire" technique builds a strong argument, bombarding the audience with specific instances to show that African Americans have made progress in American politics.

The following illustration is an example of the use of a hypothetical situation. It is a powerful tool to use in a speech because it briefly allows listeners to experience blindness.

> I'd like you all to close your eyes for a minute. Imagine that it is early morning. The alarm rings, but you must feel for it to turn it off. You get up and search for your clothes. You go downstairs to make breakfast, but you touch the food to find out what there is to eat. After breakfast, you carefully go to the door, step outside and listen for the sound of oncoming traffic. Hearing none, you gingerly cross the street to the bus stop on the other side. You wait for the sound of the creaking brakes to stop in front of you. When the doors squeak open, you carefully make your way up the steps. You give what you hope is the correct change to the bus driver. You then feel for an empty seat. You've made it one more day! This is what it feels like to be blind. And

that's what we're talking about here—a *real* problem that happens to human beings just like you and me. You can open your eyes now.[8]

This illustration is more effective than simply describing the difficulties of blindness because the speaker simulates the experience by cutting off the visual channel. The speaker provides clear directions to audience members as to when they are to close or open their eyes. The "you" approach has effectively placed listeners in the sightless world of the blind: the speaker has successfully communicated his point through the use of a hypothetical illustration.

The next illustration comes from the real-life experience of the speaker's family.

Three months ago, I went to my cousin's wedding which lasted an entire weekend—Friday through Sunday. You'd be surprised though—I don't know where the time went. In India, a wedding is usually a two-day occasion, and everyone in the bride and groom's family plays a role in the wedding ceremony. The ceremony begins with the bride's and groom's parents in prayer. Heinrick Zimmer, in the book *Philosophies of India*, explains how the priest generally begins with an explanation of the union of two families with the groom present. The priest then calls to the bride, giving her one last chance to run away. Next the bride is given away by her uncle. The ceremony continues as the bride and groom walk around a fire in seven circles. During the first six turns, the groom is in the lead and the priest explains the significance: The wife will follow her husband in all the trials they go through in life, she will respect his decisions, and she will follow whatever he decides to do with the family. Then in the last turn, the bride leads, and undoes almost everything that was said during the first six circles. The groom vows to respect his wife, to love and cherish her, and always to include her as an equal in this partnership.[9]

Neha Badshah used an illustration to describe a portion of the wedding ceremony in her native India. The personal experience combined with a credible reference provided the audience with an interesting portrait of a different culture.

In the next example, Andrea Hoguet selected a case study from a local newspaper to support a persuasive speech.

It is one thing for children to have learned aggressive behavior at a young age, but it is quite another for a parent or a relative to contribute to this aggressive behavior. I read about a case in the November 13 issue of our local *Carroll County Times* newspaper. Mrs. Luella Wilson, a 91-year-old woman of Bennington, Vermont, was sued for $950,000. Here's what happened. Mrs. Wilson gave her nephew a large sum of money to buy a new car for his eighteenth birthday, knowing that he had a drug problem, and that he did not even possess a license. After drinking heavily and smoking marijuana one evening, the nephew drove the car off a bridge. The passenger riding with him was paralyzed, and finally had to have his leg amputated. The passenger sued Mrs. Wilson for negligence. She apparently knew about her nephew's problem with drugs, yet she still gave him $6,300 for a car. Should she be liable? Yes, she should! And apparently the jury agreed and awarded the victim almost one million dollars in damages. The case is currently under appeal.[10]

Andrea used this case to support the persuasive proposition that parents and guardians should be held accountable for the criminal actions of their children. The topic was controversial and some listeners disagreed with the speaker's viewpoint. But Andrea strengthened the evidence by describing the details of the case and by citing a credible source. The speaker used gestures, vocal inflections, and emphasis to stress her conclusion to the case: "Should she be liable? Yes, she should!"

The following narrative was related by Richard D. Lamm, former governor of Colorado:

Let me begin with a metaphor. The United States fleet was on the high seas. All of a sudden a blip appeared on the radar screen. "Tell that ship to change its course fifteen degrees!" said the admiral. The radio man did, and the word came back on the radio, "YOU change YOUR course fifteen degrees." "Tell that ship that we're the United States Navy and to change its course fifteen degrees," said the admiral. The radio man did and the word came back again, "YOU change YOUR course fifteen degrees." This time the admiral himself got on the radio and said, "I am an admiral in the United States Navy. Change your course fifteen degrees." The word came back over the radio, "You change your course fifteen degrees. *I* am a lighthouse!" We often expect the world to adjust to our course, but alas, we find we must adjust to the realities around us. I would go further—I believe it is the duty and the obligation of each generation to perceive the realities of their times.[11]

This kind of story makes the audience sit back, relax, and listen. The narrative is interesting and has a humorous punch line. But Governor Lamm draws a conclusion from the story and relates it to his overall theme—"the need to change course." If you choose to relate a narrative such as this one, you must be certain to deliver the story smoothly so that the details and punch line retain their vigor.

QUOTATIONS AND TESTIMONIES FROM AUTHORITIES

You can also build credibility by using quotations and testimonies from experts or authorities. A *quotation* is the exact restatement of a person's words, and a *testimony* is a statement or endorsement given by an expert or an individual with a logical connection to the topic. Quotations can be used to evoke emotion, synthesize feelings, and establish the authenticity of ideas. Often a politician delivering a speech on the Fourth of July will quote George Washington or Thomas Jefferson to arouse feelings of patriotism and pride within the audience. Baseball announcers are fond of quoting baseball heroes in a tense situation. During a tie game in the bottom of the ninth inning, you might hear the announcer say, "Yogi Berra once said, 'It ain't over till it's over.' That sure applies here." If, for example, you are giving an informative speech on brain surgery in newborns, a brief quotation from Benjamin Carson, a pioneer physician in pediatric neuro-surgery, could provide you with sufficient expert testimony.

Using Quotations and Testimonies

You need to be careful that you do not use too many quotes, or you may sound like a name-dropper. Select quotations with significance to your topic, and use them where they will have maximum emphasis. Often, a brief quote is more effective than a long, involved quotation that has to be unraveled with a lengthy explanation.

When using testimonies, be sure that the individuals you cite are qualified through experience or expertise to comment or represent your topic. Though Mark Lenzi may have been an Olympic gold medalist in diving, he is not professionally qualified to tell you which aspirin to take, or which breakfast cereal has more vitamins and nutrients. You should briefly tell the audience what qualifies the expert you have chosen to provide testimony on your topic.

When you use a quotation from someone who is not widely known, it is important to identify that person for your audience. If you are using that individual's exact words, it is a good idea to use the terms "quote" and "end quote" before and after the quoted material. A paraphrase is a general summary of the material in your *own* words. In that case, you would not use quotes. Be certain your quotation or paraphrase is accurate If you use only a portion of the quotation, don t change the author's meaning or intention by taking it out of context.

In choosing the following quotation to support a speech on free trade, President Clinton's speechwriters demonstrated a knowledge of his Japanese audience at Waseda University in Tokyo:

> Japan has, after all, a proud heritage of embracing bold change when the times call for it... And over 120 years ago, the leaders of the Meiji Restoration embarked on a series of rapid and successful initiatives that transformed a feudal Japan into a modern society, making it more open to the West and the broader world without sacrificing the uniqueness of the Japanese culture.
> On this campus today, there is a statue honoring one of the great statesmen of that period: this school's founder, Count Okuma. In his exhaustive narra-

tive of the Meiji Restoration, Okuma attributes the period's reforms—and I quote—"to thoughtful and farsighted Japanese leaders." And he concludes: "Even as the spirit of liberality has animated the Japanese race during the past half-century of its remarkable progress, so it will ever impel its march along the paths of civilization and humanity."[12]

As founder of Waseda university, Okuma was a figure well known to faculty and students in the audience. Clinton used the quotation to reinforce his point that trade between Japan and the United States should be free and open.

In this persuasive speech about buying American products, Kathy Birckhead paraphrased two experts to support her topic:

> Foreign imports are taking over a larger share in almost all markets. What is the effect on our economy? I interviewed Eddie Bartee, Vice President of the United Steelworkers of America—Local 2609—who told me that imported steel has virtually crippled the steel industry. I also spoke with Ted Baldwin, the public relations representative for Bethlehem Steel at Sparrows Point who told me that in 1970 Bethlehem Steel employed 26,500 people. At the present time they employ only 9,000.[13]

Since her listeners were unfamiliar with Eddie Bartee and Ted Baldwin, the speaker supplied the necessary information to build credibility. If you provide a brief phrase identifying your authority, you can quickly establish credibility.

In the following excerpt from a commencement address, Les McCraw, president of the Fluor Corporation (an engineering and construction company), used a quotation from a baseball player to arouse emotional feelings within his audience at Clemson University:

> Jim Abbott had a dream. It takes a special kind of person to make a dream come true against all odds. Jim is the 21-year-old rookie pitcher for the California Angels. He's a left-handed pitcher. He throws left-handed because he was born without a right hand. His parents raised this remarkable man by never treating him too remarkably.
>
> "When I was growing up," he says, "I always pictured myself as a baseball player, but I can't remember how many hands I had in my dreams. I just went out and did things." And he certainly has "done things." He earned the 1987 Sullivan Award as America's best amateur athlete, won the gold-medal baseball in the Seoul Olympics, was drafted number one by the Angels, and is pitching in the big leagues today.[14]

Notice that McCraw set the stage by describing the pertinent details of the ballplayer's story; then he used Jim Abbott's words to stir feelings of admiration and pride within his listeners.

COMPARISONS AND CONTRASTS

There will be times in your speeches when you will need to show similarities or differences in two or more things. *Comparisons* point out similarities in situations or events, and *contrasts* show differences.

Suppose you were giving a persuasive speech on the enforcement of drunk driving laws. You could contrast the enforcement of drunk driving laws in the United States with the enforcement of such laws in Scandinavian countries. In your research, you would probably find that American and Scandinavian laws are very similar, while the application of the law is very different in the two countries.

If you were persuading listeners to legalize gambling in your state, you could contrast the higher revenues in gambling states with lower revenues from non-gambling states. On the other hand, if you wanted to persuade the audience not to legalize gambling, you could focus on contrasting crime rates if they were higher in gambling states.

Using Comparisons and Contrasts

Using comparisons and contrasts can be tricky. You must be careful that what you are comparing or contrasting has similar principles or characteristics. A student tried to contrast gun control in the United States with gun control in England. His statement of contrast went something like this:

> The murder rate in the United States is five times greater than the murder rate in England. The reason for this is that England has a strict gun control law and we have none.

In Chapter 17, we will deal more extensively with logical reasoning. The information provided in this contrast is faulty and misleading. The United States does not have a *national* gun control law, but there are cities and states that do have some form of gun control. It is true that in the United States the murder rate is about ten for every 100,000, and in England, the rate is two and one-half murders per 100,000.[15]

However, the lower rate of murder in England could be due to other factors besides gun control. England has a homogeneous population with a lengthy common history. The British operate under different cultural rules than do Americans. British police do not wear guns, and it is rare for British police to be murdered in the line of duty. There appears to be an unwritten "agreement" between British criminals and British police that neither side will use violence when conducting "business."

In this excerpt, the speaker uses contrast to highlight the differences between Americans and Russians:

> I'd like to tell you about some of the specific differences between the American and Russian people. The statistics and examples are from *Almanac of the American People,* a Russian newspaper which translated, is entitled *Arguments and Facts,* and my own personal experience.
>
> In America there were 6.2 strict vegetarians [for every hundred people] in 1989. This is a practice which would be just unbelievable to the Russian people. In Russia, we eat many internal organs of a cow or pig such as the tongue, tail, and brains. But according to the *Almanac,* American's hate this type of food. In Russia, vodka is very popular and Russians drink on every occasion. But in America, only nineteen percent of men older than forty prefer vodka. Seventy percent of the American people get drunk once a year but in Russia, seventy percent of the people get drunk every day. There are also differences in exercise habits. Sixty-nine percent of Americans exercise and fifty percent enjoy walking for pleasure. Russians don't walk for pleasure—they just walk to buy things from shops. Russian people tend to be ashamed of exercise. They think bicycling, diving, and swimming are for children. You'll never see an elderly woman in tight pants on a bicycle riding through town. In my Moscow neighborhood, there was only one guy who went jogging every morning, and we all thought he was crazy![16]

Olga Norko was a recent immigrant from Russia to the United States. She combined personal experience with statistics and examples to create a fascinating series of contrasts for her classroom audience. By identifying her sources at the beginning of the contrasting examples, the speaker was able to strengthen the reliability of the information.

In another example, the speaker used both contrast and comparison as supporting materials:

> I think we're all aware of the enormous differences between the United States and Japan We're separated by geography; we're separated by language; and we're separated by culture. We go head-to-head in trade and often run up against serious frictions and conflicts. But our free and dynamic economies also afford us important shared values. No other economies in the world are as willing as the United States and Japan to embrace new ideas, new products, and new ways of doing business.[17]

Robert McCurry of Toyota contrasts the differences between the United States and Japan, but he uses these contrasts to show how diverse and competitive cultures can share common interests and goals. In this example, the speaker skillfully transformed contrasts into comparisons. The speaker was able to find a number of areas where the United States and Japan are similar.

PERSONAL EXPERIENCE AND OBSERVATION

Personal experience and observation can help to make your speech interesting. If you are giving a speech demonstrating how a volcano is formed, you create interest if you have an experience to relate. If you are informing your audience about poverty, you make your topic personal if you describe some of the impoverished conditions you have observed. *Personal experience* is the direct firsthand knowledge of a situation. *Observation* is a judgment based upon what an individual has seen.

Using Experience and Observation

Be sure that the experience you use is appropriate to your topic. Don't use too many personal experiences, and don't base an entire speech on one elongated experience. Sometimes speakers with an abundance of personal experiences don't use enough research to support their topics, hoping their observations and experiences will make up for their lack of hard evidence.

Don't try to improvise a speech by stringing together a multitude of observations. One effective personal experience combined with some factual research can make the topic interesting, and give you authority on your issue.

In June of 1973, I was diagnosed with leukemia and I had a one-in-three chance of seeing my next birthday. If I could survive that long, I had only a ten percent chance of living three years. Three years! Well, I wasn't about to buy that. There's something neat about being eighteen—you're feisty, rebellious, and out to prove people wrong. I underwent three years of intensive chemotherapy with mostly experimental drugs (which means I threw up for three years!). According to a pamphlet put out by the Leukemia Society of America, just twenty years ago, there was no effective treatment for any type of leukemia. And if you had what I had as recently as fifteen years ago, the outlook was so bleak that doctors questioned whether patients should even be treated. But now this disease has a sixty percent cure rate. Well I was still around about five years after the initial diagnosis, and the doctors started to admit that probably I was cured—which was something that my family and I knew all along. Now my oncologist brags that I have survived and have gone on to lead a "normal" life.

Well, since the day I shocked my husband Dave and my doctors by announcing that I was pregnant, my life has been far from normal. After twelve years of marriage, we have produced three healthy and active sons. Brian, Erik, and Shane's births are such rarities that they are being studied as part of a federally-funded research program analyzing the offspring of chemotherapy patients. Chemotherapy does many things to you, and one of them is that it kills your good and bad cells, including your reproductive cells. One of my doctors puts it this way: "For a past leukemia patient to give birth was uncommon, because survival was uncommon." I didn't think then that having leukemia and then having children was such a big deal—I just did what I had to do. But in 1981, the American Cancer Society awarded me with their Courage Award. This prestigious award is given to just one person in the country annually.[18]

Karen Anderson's personal experience gave the audience a first-hand account of the battle with leukemia. The speaker enhanced her credibility by quoting her doctor, providing information from the American Leukemia Society, and referring to her award from the American Cancer Society.

Audiences enjoy hearing factual experiences, and a speaker can usually maintain listener interest if the observation is told effectively, without verbal blunders or hesitations.

Gilven M. Slonim, president of the Oceanic Educational Foundation, used personal experience and observation to support a point about military readiness.

So tonight I suggest, rather than celebrate the fiftieth Anniversary of Pearl Harbor, we review what the nation is doing to prevent another Pearl Harbor.

I was there; I survived Pearl Harbor fifty years ago today. I'm here to tell you how dreadfully painful an experience Pearl Harbor was to live through. Had we been ready, for the crux was readiness, how simply it could have been handled!

Admiral Raymond Spruance, the most disciplined military leader I have ever known, wept openly, when he saw the destruction the Japanese had inflicted upon our fleet, upon returning to Pearl Harbor on the 8th of December with Halsey's Task Force. This was after their sweep of the sea in search of the Japanese fleet, they fortunately did not find.[19]

Slovin presented these remarks to the Richmond Council of the Navy League on the occasion of the fiftieth anniversary of the attack on Pearl Harbor. The "I was there" personal experience gave credence to his observation that the United States is not doing enough to prevent a similar military disaster in the future.

HUMOR AND ANECDOTES

Humor is the use of lighthearted, entertaining material in a speech to generate a reaction from the audience. An *anecdote* is a brief humorous story used to demonstrate a point.

Humor can be very effective in a speech. Telling a joke or a humorous anecdote can create a positive climate in a speaking situation. If your audience smiles and nods at your wit, you have them in a receptive mood. A humorous anecdote can frequently make a point more successfully than a long theoretical statement.

Using Humor and Anecdotes

Employing humor has some risks. There is always the possibility that the joke you tell does not get the response you might have expected. When you practice your speech, you need to be prepared for a variety of audience reactions. If listeners fail to laugh at your humor or groan at your attempts, you can joke about their response, relate "safer" humor that has worked previously, or acknowledge the response and move on. Don't let negative audience reactions destroy your confidence. You can still overcome momentary difficulties if you maintain your composure and keep to your stated objective Your audience might also respond by breaking up into laughter. Don't let a positive response catch you off guard. Pause after the joke or story, and wait for your listeners to enjoy the moment. Don't try to resume the speech until the laughter subsides.

It is best to use humor that can be related to your topic. Using irrelevant jokes simply to gain attention can often disappoint and even anger an audience. If you've ever inquired about a brand-new car for $4,999 described in a newspaper ad, remember how you felt when you discovered that the car was a stripped-down model without tires! Audiences, too, don't appreciate the tactic of "bait-and-switch."

Despite the risks, don't be afraid to use humor. If you're good at humor, use it to your advantage and develop it as a part of your style. Even if you do not feel comfortable with humor, try a few anecdotes. You might surprise yourself. A speech is not a stand-up comic routine, but you can look for ways to use humor appropriately.

Todd G. Buchholz, former associate director of the White House Economic Policy Council, used humor effectively in a speech on education:

> How do we teach children to distinguish heroes from villains, to pursue virtue instead of vice? Perhaps you've heard how Jack Kemp's grandson introduced him when the Secretary spoke to his Sunday School class. The boy shyly stepped to the front of his class and announced that he was proud to present his grandfather—a well-known public serpent![20]

Buchholz presented this speech at a conference on education held at the Russell Senate Office Building. The humorous incident about a cabinet member was appropriate to the audience of politicians. But humor was also used as a tool to promote critical thinking. The incident helped the speaker to introduce his point that storytelling, a powerful tool "for passing on values and developing virtue in children," is currently under attack.

In the following excerpt from a graduation speech, "Doonesbury" cartoonist Garry Trudeau used an anecdote to his advantage:

> I first learned about pertinent questions from my father, a retired physician... [whose] own practical experience frequently contradicted his worthiest inten-

tions. A man once turned up in my father's office complaining of an ulcer. My father asked the pertinent question. Was there some undue stress, he inquired, that might be causing the man to digest his stomach? The patient, who was married. . . allowed that he had a girlfriend in Syracuse, and that twice a week he'd been driving an old pick-up down to see her. Since the pick-up frequently broke down, he was often late in getting home, and he had to devise fabulous stories to tell his wife. My father, compassionately but sternly, told the man he had to make a hard decision about his personal priorities if he was ever to get well. The patient nodded and went away, and six months later came back completely cured, a new man. My father congratulated him and then delicately inquired if he'd made some change in his life. The man replied, "Yup. Got me a new pick-up."[21]

Trudeau presents his humor effectively and smoothly, logically developing the details of the story. The last sentence of the anecdote served as the punch line to stimulate a response from the audience. Trudeau used this anecdote to illustrate the point that an "unexpected or inconvenient truth is often the price of honest inquiry."[22]

Role-Playing

Role-playing is a technique using an individual to act out a brief skit, assume a character, or simulate a conflict. Role-playing can be a creative way of motivating listeners to become more personally involved with a speaker's topic. A skit portraying the effect of divorce on a young child might have more impact on an audience than a verbal description. One student, playing the role of a waiter in a restaurant, used two "customers" from the audience to demonstrate the proper and improper methods of taking orders and serving food.

Using Role-Playing Techniques

Speakers can use skits they have researched or they can create their own dramas. If the situation is taken from one of your sources, give the author proper recognition. If you write a brief dramatic piece, be sure that the skit is true-to-life and based on factual information. It is helpful if the situation is brief and to the point. Long, drawn-out dramas can bore listeners with unnecessary material and detract from the speech. If you need volunteers, rehearse them in advance, making sure that they are familiar with the script and know how to respond appropriately in the roles. Remember that role-playing is one of the less factual ways of supporting ideas; it should not be used as a substitute for cases, statistics, or verifiable sources. Role-playing is most effective when combined with other types of supporting materials.

Speaker Gina Alexander created a skit to demonstrate the proper and improper techniques of interviewing for a job. The speaker portrayed the applicant while a member of the audience played the role of the interviewer.

Interviewer: Can you tell me why you're leaving your present employer?

Applicant: Well, it's like, I'm so bored there, ya know? It's like I hate to go to work there everyday—I can't stand it. Ya ever felt like that?

Interviewer: Is it the work itself, or is it your environment?

Applicant: Yeeeah, both I guess, kinda, ya know?

What can I say? You do that, and you've probably lost the job right there. No matter what college you've gone to or what fancy degree you have, it's not showing. There's a better way to display the exact same message.

Interviewer: Can you tell me why you're leaving your present employer?

Applicant: Well, I'm considering leaving my present employer to seek new opportunities that they don't offer.

Interviewer: Is it the work itself, or is it your environment?

Applicant: Actually, it's a combination of both factors that are contributing to my desire to leave.

In the first example, I was sprawling all over the chair, I didn't appear interested, and it looked as if I wasn't paying attention. I used street jargon, and it appeared as if I had few language skills. Notice that I was running my fingers through my hair. This is an action which is very distracting. In some jobs, such as food-service positions, picking your face or touching your hair could lose you the job.

In the second situation, I said the exact same thing, but I displayed some intelligence. My posture was effective. I didn't sit like a soldier, but I sat up straight, appearing as an interested, active communicator who is open to new ideas. My vocabulary was precise, thoughtful, and I spoke in complete sentences. While I didn't stare, I maintained eye contact with my prospective employer.[23]

The skit was successful because the speaker conducted several rehearsals prior to the classroom presentation. While the skit was entertaining and humorous, it successfully demonstrated the speaker's point that language, organization, and poise, make a powerful persuasive impression on an interviewer.

SUMMARY

Gather supporting materials to create interest and to provide evidence for your ideas. Some of the most authoritative materials are statistics, polls, and surveys; examples, illustrations, case studies, and narratives; and quotations and testimonies from authorities. Less verifiable, yet interesting materials, are comparisons and contrasts; personal experiences and observations; and humor, anecdotes, and role-playing.

EXERCISES

1. Select a topic which can be supported by statistics and develop a one- to two-minute speech to inform. Be sure you understand the statistics and draw a clear conclusion from your data. After you present the speech in class, ask the audience to respond to the following questions:

   Were the statistics clear?

   Did the speaker understand the stats?

   Were the statistics related in a meaningful and understandable way?

   Did the speaker draw a clear conclusion from the data?

2. Choose a topic for a brief one- to two-minute speech to inform. Choose three different forms of support to reinforce the issue. Ask your instructor and your audience to evaluate the success of the presentation.
3. Read Garry Trudeau's graduation address (reprinted at the back of the book). Identify the various types of supporting materials he uses to back up his specific purpose. Does he use several different materials? Are his materials effective? Does he mention the sources for any of his information? Be specific in your answer.
4. Watch a videotape of several student speeches. Identify the kinds of supporting materials each student employs in the speech. Do the students mention their sources? Do the speeches appear to be credible?

NOTES

[1] "Lincoln Never Said That," *U.S. News & World Report*, August 31–September 7, 1992, p. 27.

[2] Jena L. Weigel, "The History of Coca-Cola," informative descriptive speech presented in speech class, Catonsville Community College, Catonsville, Maryland, 1991. Used by permission.

[3] "Prime-Time Perot," *Advertising Age*, October 19, 1992, p. 22.

[4] H. Ross Perot, "paid political broadcast, October 17, 1992.

[5] William L. Winter, "Putting the World in Perspective," *Vital Speeches*, March 15, 1991, p. 335.

[6] David Zebraski, "Recycling our Throwaways," persuasive speech to convince presented in speech class, Catonsville Community College, Catonsville, Maryland, 1989. Used by permission.

[7] John E. Jacob, "The State of Black America," *Vital Speeches*, June 15, 1992, pp. 533–534.

[8] Illustration created by the author.

[9] Neha Badshah, "The Indian Wedding Cermony," informative descriptive speech presented in speech class, Catonsville Community College, Catonsville, Maryland, 1992. Used by permission.

[10] Andrea Hoguet, "Parents Should Be Responsible for Their Children's Actions," persuasive speech to convince presented in speech class, Carroll Community College, Westminster, Maryland, 1989. Used by permission.

[11] Richard D. Lamm, "Time to Change Course," *Vital Speeche,s* October 15, 1985, p. 4.

[12] Bill Clinton, "U.S.—Japan Relations," *Vital Speeches*, August 15, 1993, pp. 645–646.

[13] Kathy Birckhead, "Buy American-made Products," persuasive speech to actuate presented in speech class, Carroll Community College, Westminster, Maryland, 1990. Used by permission.

[14] Les McCraw, "Nothing Much Happens Without A Dream," *Vital Speeches*, January 15, 1990, p. 217.

[15] George T. Kurian, *The New Book of World Rankings* (New York: Facts on File Publications: 1984}, p. 386.

[16] Olga Norko, "Differences Between the Russian and American People," speech to inform presented in speech class, Catonsville Community College, Catonsville, Maryland, 1992. Used by permission.

[17] Robert McCurry, "Competing With Japan," *Vital Speeches*, July 15, 1986, p. 593.

[18] Karen Anderson, "People Can Survive Cancer," descriptive speech to inform presented in speech class, Carroll Community College, Westminster, Maryland, 1989. Used by permission.

[19] Gilven M. Slonim, "Beyond Pearl Harbor," *Vital Speeches*, March 1, 1992, p. 308.

[20] Todd G. Buchholz, "Teaching Virtue," *Vital Speeches*, April 15, 1992, p. 396.

[21] Garry Trudeau, "The Impertinent Questions," *Vital Speeches*, August, 1986, pp. 619–620.

[22] Ibid., p. 620.

[23] Gina Alexander, "Effective Interviewing Techniques," speech to demonstrate presented in speech class, Carroll Community College, Westminster, Maryland, 1990. Used by permission.

UNIT OUTLINE

Chapter Ten

ORGANIZING THE BODY OF THE SPEECH

Chapter Outline

Key Terms

Cause–effect sequence
Chronological sequence
Coordination
Formal outline
Indentation
Informal outline
Mechanically parallel
Sentence outline
Spatial sequence
Subdivision
Subordination
Topic outline
Topical sequence

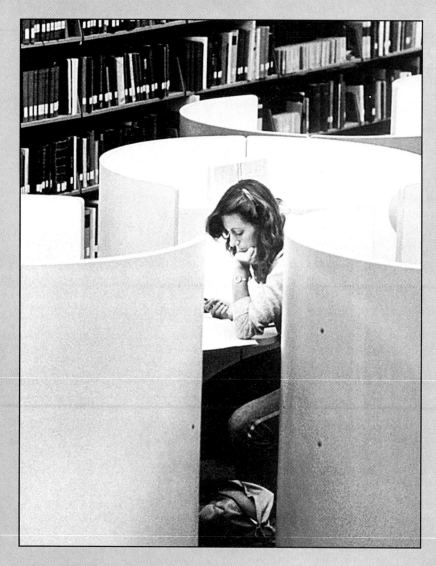

"Organize! Organize!
Organize!"
—CHARLES STEWART PARNELL

*A*s director of communications for the Miller Brewing Company, Patricia Ward Brash is often required to present speeches to various audiences. In 1992, she was a guest speaker at a conference for women in communication, and she entitled her presentation "Beyond Giving a Speech: Becoming a Poised, Polished Presenter." Here are a few of her thoughts about organization:

> Wherever possible, we should build our presentation around a few key ideas and feelings...
>
> We have a wealth of patterns to choose from when organizing the contents. Choices include chronological, spatial, topical, cause–effect, or problem–solution, as well as several other alternatives. We should use the pattern that best enables us to give the audience a comprehensive picture of what we believe and feel about a subject.[1]

Ward recognized the vital importance of logical structure and clear organization in public speaking. She also identified the importance of organizing information into *key ideas* that present the topic comprehensively to listeners.

An outline is just as important to you as it is to a professional speaker like Patricia Ward Brash. An outline is a structured plan of your ideas: It acts as a visual guide to the main and supporting elements in your presentation. You can think of the outline as the framework of your speech: It holds the speech together, keeps you within its boundaries, and clarifies the layout for the audience.

A speech has three parts: the introduction, the body, and the conclusion. It is the middle part, or body, which represents the major portion of the speech and will comprise about two-thirds of your speaking time. Once you have researched the topic, written your specific purpose, and worded your thesis, you should first spend your energies outlining the body of the speech. You can develop the introduction and conclusion after the meat of your presentation has been organized. This chapter presents ten principles that will help you to outline the body of your presentation.

APPROACHING ORGANIZATION LOGICALLY

The thought of outlining a speech might seem difficult at first, but if you think logically about the topic, sorting through your research will be less complicated. Some topics almost organize themselves. For example, if you were to give an informative speech on a historical issue such as the invention and development of the telephone, your research would fall into several categories according to years or periods. By contrast, a travelogue about Alaska could be organized using location or geographical regions such as the Arctic, western, southern, and interior areas as structural points. Research can also cluster around logical categories such as, in a study of comedy, the three types of clowns—straight man, joker, and character clown. Your research could also be outlined according to several major causes or effects.

What is important is that you begin to think in an organized manner. As Patricia Brash suggests, look for key ideas, patterns and trends in your research that are supported by examples, quotations, or testimony. Think in terms of the overall plan of your speech and don't try to fill in all details at the beginning of the process. After you develop your thesis statement, write a rough outline, making sure that the main points of the body carry out the statement adequately. Don't be afraid to adjust the major headings or thesis to make your plan clearer and more consistent. Try not to be intimidated or enslaved by the process. Remember that the outline is simply a tool for structure and clarity and should help speech construction to be more enjoyable and less complicated.

PRINCIPLES OF OUTLINING

If you carefully apply each of the following ten principles, your clarity of organization and speaking effectiveness will be greatly enhanced.

In this text the term *formal outline* refers to the body of the speech. We use the term *informal outline* when referring to the introduction, conclusion, bibliography, and other outline preliminaries.

I. The Body Should Contain Between Two and Four Main Points.

The thesis statement identifies how many main points you will have in the body of a speech. In a classroom speech with a five- to seven-minute time limit, the best guideline to use is to have no fewer than two and no more than four main points. If you have only one major point, your speech will be too short because you will not have enough supporting material to develop your topic. If you have six or seven points, you have the opposite problem—a lengthy speech with too much information to cover in the allotted time. Notice that the following thesis statement incorporates three elements:

Specific purpose: The purpose of the speech is to inform the audience about three funeral customs of the ancient Egyptians.

Thesis statement: Egyptian funeral customs included embalming, the use of coffins, and a process called "dry burial."

Body
  I. Explanation of Egyptian embalming practices
 II. Description of Egyptian coffins
III. Explanation of "dry" burial techniques [2]

The thesis statement tells you that there will be three main headings in the body: (1) an explanation of embalming, (2) a description of coffins, and (3) an explanation of burial techniques. The organization is tight, and there will be time enough to develop the main points in sufficient detail.

II. Main Points Should Be Structured Logically and Appropriately.

When structuring your main points, you can select an *organizational sequence* appropriate to the topic and which stimulates audience interest. You can organize main points according to chronology, space, cause–effect, topic/natural, or other sequence.

Chronological Sequence When you use chronological sequence, you arrange the main points according to time or order of events. For example, topics such as "Human Life from Fertilization to Birth," "How to Make Yeast Bread," or historical topics such as "American Exploration of Space" or "The Life of Salvador Dali" would be organized according to chronology:

Specific purpose: to inform the audience about the rise and fall of the American "Muscle Car"

Thesis statement: American muscle cars were introduced in 1964, increased in popularity during the late 1960s, reached a "high water mark" in 1970, and began to decline in the early 1970s.

Body
   I. The Early Years—1964 to 1966
  II. The Rising Popularity—1967 to 1969
 III. The "High Water Mark"—1970
 IV. The Decline—1971 to 1972

The topic is arranged according to chronology, by the historical events occurring over a period of years.

Spatial Sequence Space is the structuring of main points according to geography or location. Topics relating to the description of a building, a city, or a physical object are organized using *spatial sequence.*

Specific purpose: to inform the audience about four principal areas in the White House

Thesis statement: The interior of the White House includes executive offices, formal reception rooms, first family living quarters, and a kitchen complex.

Body

    I. Executive offices
   II. Formal reception rooms
  III. First family living quarters
  IV. Kitchen complex

You can see that in the above example each main point describes a different spatial area in the White House.

Cause–Effect Sequence Another way to structure the main points of your speech is by *cause-and-effect sequence.* This sequence simply arranges the main points according to cause and effect. You could inform your audience about several causes of drug dependency and then talk about the effects on the family and on the individual. Another example is:

Specific purpose: to inform the audience about the causes and effects of colon cancer

Thesis statement: While there are several known causes of colon cancer, there are advanced treatments that have significant effects on the patient.

Body

    I. Known causes of colon cancer
   II. Advanced treatments for the disease
  III. Effects of the disease on the patient

Here the first and last main point present causes and effects. Notice that "II" is not a cause or effect, but identifies a topic area necessary for the logical development of the speech.

    You could also structure the main points entirely by causes or by effects. A speech about child abuse, for instance, could expand upon three principal causes of child abuse, or describe three tragic effects of abuse on the victim.

Topical Sequence Another method of structuring the main points is by logical or natural sequence. This pattern can also be called *topical sequence.* On some issues, you will find that your research clusters around natural headings which can be earmarked for your outline.

Specific purpose: to inform the audience what it's like living in Dunoon, Scotland

Thesis statement: During the year I lived in Dunoon, Scotland, I got to know the town, learned how to negotiate the transportation system, became acclimated to a Scottish home, and enjoyed leisure activities.

Body

   I. Brief description of the town
   II. Transportation in the town
  III. Life in a Scottish house
  IV. Activities for leisure enjoyment

In this example, the speaker has discovered four logical headings that accurately describe her experiences and observations.

You can also create a natural sequence by identifying trends in your information. For instance, you could structure your main points from least to most important item, simple to complex, or familiar to unfamiliar. These types of arrangements not only create interest in the topic, but they also help your audience to remember your main points more easily. Consider these examples:

Least to Most Important

Specific purpose: to convince the audience that there are four reasons why HMOs do not provide quality health care

Thesis statement: Under HMOs, waiting rooms are impersonal, open enrollment is limited, immediate appointments with specialists are often difficult, and patients frequently experience inaccurate diagnoses and treatments.

Body

   I. Clinical, impersonal waiting rooms
   II. Limited open enrollment, requiring high premiums
  III. Immediate appointments with specialists difficult
  IV. Frequent inaccurate diagnosis and treatment

Simple to Complex

Specific purpose: to inform the audience about some troubleshooting techniques they can use when their car doesn't start

Thesis statement: You can learn to read and understand the instrument panel, identify possible difficulties with the starter mechanism, and know what to look for under the hood.

Body

   I. Understanding instrument panel
   II. Identifying problems with starter mechanism
  III. Looking under hood

Familiar to Unfamiliar

Specific purpose: to inform the audience about five types of stars in the universe

Thesis statement: Stars are grouped into five categories: stars, black holes, novas, binary stars, and neutron stars.

Body
   I. Stars—Glowing gas in the sky
  II. Black holes—Collapsed, former stars
 III. Novas—Exploding, bright and diminished stars
 IV. Binary stars—Revolving and eclipsed stars
  V. Neutron stars—Gaseous, atomic stars

In the first example, the speaker has arranged main points from least to most important reason. Numeral I, "Clinical...waiting rooms," is a good reason why HMOs don't provide quality health care, but it is least important of the four statements. Numeral IV, "Frequent inaccurate diagnoses..." deals with human life and is therefore the most important item. In the second example, "Understanding instrument panel" is the least complicated troubleshooting procedure, while "Looking under hood" is the most complex.

TO BUILD A SUCCESSFUL PRESENTATION, A SPEAKER MUST BE WILLING TO SPEND TIME DEVELOPING IDEAS, STRUCTURING THOUGHTS, AND WRITING A CLEAR, LOGICAL OUTLINE.

© Walter S. Silver/
Picture Cube

In the last example, the speaker assumes that the audience is most familiar with Numeral I, "Stars…" and may have some limited familiarity with black holes as well as novas. But the speaker has assumed that binary and neutron stars are the least familiar to the audience, and has arranged them as the last two points.

Other Sequences

There are a number of other ways to arrange the main points of the body. Many of these organizational patterns relate specifically to persuasive speeches which we will discuss in Chapters 17 and 18. But we want to briefly mention them now.

Problem–solution order is the arrangement of main points by identifying a problem and moving to a solution. The motivated sequence pattern is a five-stage system—attention, need, solution, visualization, action—to motivate the audience to act on an issue. The reasons organizational pattern simply arranges main points in the body according to reasons. There is also a comparative-advantages sequence, which develops each main point by stressing the advantages of a desired plan or idea.

III. Roman Numerals, Letters, and Arabic Numbers Should Be Combined with Indentation to Identify Main and Subordinate Levels.

Begin by using Roman numerals to outline the main points in the speech body. Remember that the Roman numerals carry out all the components of the thesis statement. Then introduce the next level of subordinate points with capitalized letters such as A, B, C, and so forth. Supporting points under capital letters should be introduced by numbers such as 1, 2, and 3. And if you need another level, items would be preceded by small letters like a and b.

Body

I. _____

    A. _____

    B. _____

        1. _____

           a. _____

           b. _____

        2. _____

II. _____

    A. _____

1. _____
2. _____
3. _____
      a. _____
        (1) _____
        (2) _____
      b. _____
  B. _____
III. _____
  A. _____
  B. _____
  C. _____

Each level of supporting points is indented so that the outline clearly indicates the relationship between the heading and the subdivision. Just by glancing at this outline, you can easily attach subordinate points to their appropriate headings. This is an important reason for good organization. A tightly structured outline helps to trigger your thoughts so that you can maintain eye contact with your audience.

This pattern is just a guideline of general outline procedure. The shape of every outline depends upon the topic and varies according to the number of main points and the amount of supporting items.

IV. Ideas in the Outline Should Be Carefully Divided into Major Elements and Subordinate Items, With No Overlap.

Coordination refers to the placement of equal ideas within the same level of an outline. *Subordination* refers to the placement of secondary, or lower-ranking, ideas beneath higher-order items. When you write the statements in your outline you must be sure that ideas are of equal importance in each level, that subordinate ideas logically support each heading, and that statements do not duplicate one another. Look at the following *incorrect* outline:

Specific purpose: to provide information that helps the audience to define and understand mental retardation

Thesis statement: I will define mental retardation, explain how it is classified, and identify some common misconceptions about it.

Incorrect

  I. What it is
    A. A definition of mental retardation

    B. Public myths about the mentally retarded
    C. Public fears of the mentally retarded
    D. Mental retardation *vs.* mental illness
       1. Mental illness conditions
       2. Mental retardation conditions
 II. Classifications of mental retardation
    A. Factors determining mental retardation
       1. Mental ability
       2. Adaptive behavior
       3. Physical development
    B. Degrees of mental retardation
       1. Mild to moderate
       2. Severe to profound
III. Common misconceptions about mental retardation

This outline is incorrect for the following reasons: Under Roman numeral I, item A ("definition") is not equal to other items in the same level: It is identical to the heading and must be eliminated. Items IB ("myths") and IC ("fears") are overlapping points which should be combined. And if you take an overall look at the outline, it appears that I contains points which are not supportive. "Fears" really belongs under III ("Common misconceptions"), and ID1 ("Mental illness conditions"), which does not define retardation, can also be categorized under III. Here is a more effective outline:

Correct

  I. Definition of mental retardation
 II. Classification of mental retardation
    A. Factors determining mental retardation
       1. Mental ability
       2. Adaptive behavior
       3. Physical development
    B. Degrees classifying mental retardation
       1. Mild to moderate
       2. Severe to profound
III. Common misconceptions about mental retardation
    A. Confusion with mental illness
    B. Fear of "different" behavior
    C. Inability to function in society
       1. Failure to have relationships
       2. Failure to be employed
       3. Failure to perform survival tasks

This outline now contains main and subordinate points that are arranged in their appropriate relationships.

V. Every Subdivision Must Contain at Least Two Items.

Under the concept of division, it is assumed that elements have been divided into at least two separate, equal categories. If there is only one item, there has obviously been no division. If you have only one supporting point under a heading, you have two choices: You can either look for a second item, or eliminate the one point and include it with the heading.

Specific purpose: to demonstrate how to juggle three objects
Thesis statement: I will explain the selection of objects and the process of juggling, and provide a brief demonstration.

Incorrect
   I. Selecting the objects
     A. Between four to six ounces
      1. Must not be too heavy
  II. Explaining the process
     A. Display visual aid describing steps
      1. Pick imaginary points
      2. Toss ball to points and catch
      3. Use opposite hand to throw ball
      4. Use steps B and C together
      5. Repeat the process
 III. Demonstrating the art of juggling

Under Roman numeral I there is an A but no B, and only one point under A. In II there is again only one A, but there are five items under A. Here's how to correct these problems:

Correct
   I. Choosing the objects
     A. Should weigh four to six ounces
     B. Should not be slick
     C. Should be able to bounce
  II. Explaining the process (using visual aid)
     A. Pick imaginary points
     B. Toss ball to points and catch
     C. Use opposite hand to throw ball

     D. Use steps B and C together
     E. Repeat the process
III. Demonstrating the art of juggling

Under I, Item 1 ("Must not be too heavy") has been eliminated because it can be included with A, "Between four to six ounces." An additional B and a C have also been created to further complete the subdivision. In II the original A ("Display visual aid") was eliminated because it can be incorporated with the heading. That change eliminates the need for numbers 1 through 5, which have been upgraded to the next level—A through E. The main and subordinate points are now correct.

VI. Each Statement Should Include Only One Thought or Idea.

Here is an outline that violates this principle.

Specific purpose: to inform the audience about preventing teenage suicide
Thesis statement: I will identify the warning signs of teenage suicide and explain how to help the individual.

Incorrect
  I. Warning signs of teenage suicide
     A. Direct suicide threats
     B. Indirect statements revealing desire to die
     C. Previous suicide attempts and sudden changes in behavior
       1. Social withdrawal
       2. Variable moods
       3. Severe depression and impulsive behavior
 II. Getting help to the individual
     A. Talk to the teen
     B. Show interest in the person
     C. Be certain teen can reach adult
     D. Solicit help from professional

Under I, item C, ("Previous suicide attempts and sudden changes in behavior") is clearly two ideas. The numbers under C seem to support "changes in behavior," but they do not clearly support "previous attempts." Item 3 also includes two separate thoughts—depression and impulsiveness. When ideas are mistakenly clumped together like this, the audience makes a brief attempt to put the pieces together, but often stops listening in confusion. The outline should be revised as follows:

Correct

   I. Warning signs of teenage suicide
      A. Direct suicide threats
      B. Indirect statements revealing desire to die
      C. Previous suicide attempts
      D. Sudden changes in behavior
         1. Social withdrawal
         2. Variable moods
         3. Severe depression
         4. Impulsive behavior

  II. Getting help to the individual
      A. Talk to the teen
      B. Show interest in the person
      C. Be certain teen can reach adult
      D. Solicit help from professional

Notice that a new item D ("Sudden changes in behavior"), has been added, as well as a new item, 4 ("Impulsive behavior"), to separate the ideas. The outline is now accurate. The audience will be more capable of sorting out one idea at a time.

VII. Main Points and Supporting Items Should Be Mechanically Parallel.

The sentence structure and wording in each level should be similar. For example, if your first main point begins with a noun plus a prepositional phrase (causes of pollution, effects on streams), or an infinitive phrase (to enjoy freedom, to participate in democracy), then other main points should begin in a similar manner. Subordinate points should also have parallel language structure: for instance, sub-letters A, B, C should be comparable, and sub-numbers 1, 2, 3 should show similarity.

Specific purpose: to demonstrate how to creatively use the Halloween pumpkin for decoration and for delicious food

Thesis statement: You can carve the pumpkin into a Jack O'Lantern and toast the seeds.

Incorrect

   I. How to carve a pumpkin
      A. Beginning the process
         1. Cut

Correct

   I. Making a Jack O'Lantern
      A. Initial preparation process
         1. Cut top

  2. Removing seeds
  3. Creativity with the face
  4. Flashlight *vs.* candle
  5. Placing in window
 B. Final preparation process
  1. Removing flashlight
  2. Foil and plastic
  3. Refrigerate
II. Toasting pumpkin seeds
 A. Initial preparation process
  1. Washing
  2. Soak
 B. Cooking process
  1. Draining
  2. To bake in oven
  3. Storage

  2. Remove seeds
  3. Cut out face
  4. Use flashlight—not candle
  5. Display pumpkin
 B. Final preparation process
  1. Remove flashlight from pumpkin
  2. Wrap pumpkin in foil or plastic
  3. Place in refrigerator
II. Toasting pumpkin seeds
 A. Initial preparation process
  1. Wash seeds in warm water
  2. Soak overnight in solution
 B. Final cooking process
  1. Drain in colander
  2. Bake in oven
  3. Eat (or store in cool place)

In the incorrect example, none of the main headings or supporting points are parallel. Notice the different wording and structure of the two main points: I begins with an adverb followed by an infinitive phrase, and II begins with an action verb ending in "ing" followed by a noun. Notice also that subordinate items are not mechanically parallel.

The incorrect example demonstrates improper outline form. These mistakes may actually impede the speaker's progress. The speaker is forced to read and decipher each item in detail while delivering the speech. This improper outline can then reduce eye contact and hinder the flow of ideas.

Now look at the correct example. Each main point begins with an action word ending in "ing" followed by a noun or modified noun. Subordinate items are also parallel with one another. Notice that it is not necessary that all levels be identical in sentence structure. For example, the items under IA are grammatically different from the items that support IB. You will find, however, that each level maintains internal structural consistency.

This parallel outline will be easier for the speaker to read, and will facilitate the speaker's eye contact and thought process.

VIII. The Outline Should Be Expressed in Either Sentences or Topics.

When you write the formal outline of the body, you should use either complete sentences or topics—never mix the two forms. If you begin using complete sentences for numeral I in the body, you must continue employing sentences throughout all main and subordinate levels to keep the outline consistent. If you begin with topics, again employ topics throughout the outline. Some speakers use a *topic outline* because they feel it keeps them from reading their outline word for word. Others use *sentence form* because they can get a more precise idea of the wording in the speech. Use either sentences or topics—whichever is most helpful.

Here are examples of the two types of outlines:

Specific purpose: to inform the audience about the increasing emphasis on sex in advertising

Thesis statement: Sex is increasingly used in advertising because of the economic benefits to advertisers.

Sentence Outline

I. Sex has invaded contemporary advertising.
   A. More men are shown as sexual objects.
   B. Women are now shown to be aggressors in sexual encounters.
   C. More nudity of both sexes is shown.
II. Provocative advertising benefits the advertiser.
   A. They receive positive feedback from consumers.
   B. Advertisers experience increases in their sales.

Topic Outline

I. The use of sex in advertising
   A. Men as sex objects
   B. Women as sexual aggressors
   C. Increased nudity of both sexes
II. Benefits of provocative ads to advertiser
   A. Positive feedback from consumers
   B. Increases in sales revenues

Even though one is a sentence outline and the other is a topic outline, each form is consistent throughout. The topic outline uses phrases—not just one or two words—to make each heading and subheading as clear as possible. Either form would be a useful tool to help the speaker successfully communicate to the audience.

IX. The Body of the Outline Should Identify Sources for Major Supporting Materials.

Portions of the outline that include significant examples, statistics, or testimonies drawn from your research should clearly identify sources containing the information. Indicating references on the outline reminds you of where you obtained the information and helps you to integrate sources more easily when you deliver the presentation.

Source notations can be abbreviated in the body of the outline since you will be including a more comprehensive bibliography at the end. Here is a suggested system you can follow when annotating your sources.

Specific purpose: to examine and explain the uses of four types of masks

Thesis statement: For thousands of years people have used masks for religious/ceremonial, theatrical, festive, and practical reasons.

Body

I. Religious/ceremonial
   A. American Indians
      1. Hopi tribe
         a. Katchina masks (Underhill, *Red Man's Religion,* pp. 90, 208)
         b. How masks were used
      2. Northwest Indians
         a. Half-man, half-animal mask
         b. How masks were used (Kondeatis, *Masks,* p. 11)
   B. Central African
      1. Northern Ba Kete mask
      2. Construction of masks (Segy, *Masks of Black Africa,* pp. 33–37)
      3. Function of masks

This outline clearly identifies sources. In heading 2b under numeral IA, the parentheses indicate that the material was researched in the book *Masks.* The abbreviated form lists only the last name of the author, the title of the book, and the page numbers. Notice that you don't need to annotate every item in an outline; only those headings and subheadings that include specific quotations or provide extensive data necessary to the development of the speech.

X. The Outline Should Include Transitions Between Main Headings.

Transitions are phrases that connect the major headings of your speech. These carefully crafted statements should tell listeners that one main idea is ending and another beginning. When you build the outline, write out the complete transitional phrase or sentence, placing it at the appropriate numeral.

Specific purpose: to inform the audience about one of America's passions—chocolate

Thesis statement: Chocolate, a sweet substance we all take for granted, has an interesting background, affects our health, and is the object of a love affair with the American consumer.

Body

  I. General background about chocolate

Transition: Now that you've heard about the history and background of chocolate, you need to know about chocolate and your health.

  II. Health issues related to chocolate

Transition: In spite of the health issues, American consumers have an ongoing love affair with chocolate.

III. American consumer's love of chocolate

 ## SUMMARY

Approach the organization process in a logical manner and follow these ten principles for outlining the body of your speech:

1. The body should contain no fewer than two, and no more than five, main points in a five- to seven-minute speech.
2. Main points should be organized in a sequence that is logical, interesting, and appropriate to the topic.
3. A system of Roman numerals, letters, and Arabic numbers, combined with indentation, should identify main and subordinate levels.
4. Divide ideas into major elements and subordinate items. Do not overlap.
5. Every subdivision should contain at least two items.
6. Each statement should include only one thought or idea.
7. Main points and supporting items should be grammatically parallel.
8. Use either complete sentences or topics. Do not mix.
9. Identify sources for major supporting materials.
10. Include transitions between main headings of the body.[3]

EXERCISES

1. From the following list of specific purpose statements, explain which method of organization you would use to arrange the main points in the body (either time, space, cause-and-effect, or topical order). Be able to support your answer.

    a. To inform about the life of John Birks "Dizzy" Gillespie
    b. To describe the interior of the Superdome
    c. To inform about the symptoms of AIDS
    d. To explain the origins and results of prejudice against Amerasian children
    e. To demonstrate how to develop 35 mm color film
    f. To describe the characteristics of the largest planets in the solar system
    g. To explain how superconductors can contribute to our lives
    h. To describe some of the myths about the homeless in America

2. There are a number of items in the following example that are not constructed according to correct outline procedure. Identify the incorrect areas and then rewrite or rearrange any heading or subdivision to reflect appropriate outline techniques.

Specific purpose: to inform the audience about the impact of new computer technologies upon today's music

Thesis statement: I will describe some of the new computer technologies and explain their impact on music.

  I. New computer technologies for music
    A. Synthesizers
      1. Recorded sounds of instruments
      2. Stored within memory
    B. Micro-chips
      1. The sound is burned into the memory.
      2. When the sound is retrieved, it is exact.
    C. Traditional instruments made obsolete
  II. Impact of new technologies on music
    A. Live concerts
      1. Music electronically assisted
      2. Performer must manipulate buttons
      3. Power blackout destroys performance
    B. Synthesizer goes beyond human abilities
      1. No mistakes and can play at any speed
      2. Tune can be played in any key
      3. Music mechanical
      4. Music lacks human feeling
    C. More people will learn instruments
      1. Can be hooked to home computer, providing instruction
    D. Performers learn computer programming
      1. Stop practicing scales

NOTES

[1] Patricia Ward Brash, "Beyond Giving a Speech: Becoming a Poised, Polished Presenter," *Vital Speeches*, November 15, 1992, p. 84.

[2] I am grateful to the following students, who gave me permission to use their topics and to modify their outlines for this chapter: Lisa Hilton, "Ancient Egyptian Funeral Customs"; Steve Hogue, "The American Muscle Car"; Joe A. Lloyd, Jr., "Colon Cancer"; Erin Ellis, "Major Causes of Child Abuse"; Mary Holmes, "Life in Dunoon, Scotland"; Richard Renehan, "HMOs and Quality Health Care"; Ralph Thompson, "Understanding Mental Retardation"; Richard Watson, "The Art of Juggling"; Tina Cerrato, "Teenage Suicide"; Deborah C. Brown, "Being Creative with Your Halloween Pumpkin"; Susan Stephan, "Sex in Advertising"; Tara Baker, "Four Types of Masks," courtesy of Mary Anne Rhoades, Associate Professor of Speech; Della Leister, "Chocolate—One of America's Passions"; and David Wildt, "New Computer Technologies and Music."

[3] I would like to acknowledge Leroy Giles, Professor of English at Catonsville Community College, for his helpful suggestions as I prepared this chapter.

READINGS

Hugenberg, Lawrence, and Yoder, Donald. *Speaking in the Modern Organization*, Glenview, Ill.: Scott, Foresman, 1985. Chapter 4 is excellent for additional information about speech structure. The authors discuss a number of organizational patterns for both informative and persuasive speeches. The chapter also includes procedures for outlining the body, and methods of introducing and concluding the speech.

Samovar, Larry A., and Mills, Jack. *Oral Communication*, 4th ed. Dubuque, Ia.: Wm. C. Brown, 1980. In Chapter 6, "Organization," the authors reinforce the ideas on outlining presented in this chapter. They also discuss the introduction and the conclusion, covered here in Chapter 11.

Chapter Eleven

Selecting the Introduction and Conclusion

Chapter Outline

Key Terms

Appeal, challenge
Humor
Illustration
Personal reference, compliment
Questions
Quotation
Reference to introduction
Reference to occasion
Shocking statement
Speaking notes
Statistics
Summary
Suspense

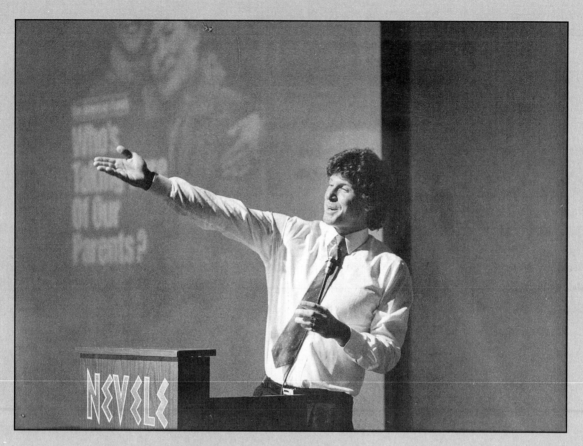

"Everything ends that has a
beginning."
—QUINTILIAN

Susan S. Suter, the director of the Illinois Department of Children and Family Services, delivered a commencement address to the graduates of Southern Illinois University. Notice how she introduced her remarks:

> Now before I begin my formal presentation, I have a favor to ask of the graduates of 1991. At the count of three, I'd like you all to say "Good afternoon, Director Suter." One...Two...Three...["Good afternoon, Director Suter."]
>
> Good afternoon, graduates.
>
> There's an ulterior motive behind this request. According to my office of employee services—DCFS will need to fill at least two hundred vacancies for social workers in the next year. And if you decide to apply for one of those jobs—*now* you can mention to the DCFS recruiter that you personally know their boss—and that you had a recent conversation with her.[1]

The speaker used audience participation to involve listeners who were concerned about finding jobs in unfavorable economic times. Suter realized a fundamental principle of public speaking. The audience forms its first impressions of your speech while listening to your introduction. If you are going to be successful throughout the speech, you must get your listeners' attention and stimulate their curiosity at the very beginning.

Speech introductions and conclusions are the focus of this chapter. It is important to know the purpose and structure of the opening and closing, as well as the various *ways* you can begin and end. Suggestions are given to help you construct your speaking notes, and an outline of an informative speech is provided as a model for your own presentations.

PLANNING THE INTRODUCTION

Every speech needs an entry point. The speaker does not want to start with, "My topic today is earthquakes and my purpose is to tell you how they happen—so here goes!" This type of beginning is certainly direct and to the point, but it is abrupt and uninteresting.

The purpose of the introduction is to provide a graceful entrance into your topic. You want to capture the attention of the audience, arouse their curiosity about your topic, and introduce your specific purpose and thesis statements.

The introduction must be thought out well and prepared very carefully. Since this is the place where the audience decides to listen or tune you out, it is a crucial part of your speech. A boring, poorly worded, or poorly delivered introduction can quickly destroy a speaker's credibility; on the other hand, an interesting, curiosity-provoking introduction can bring your topic to life.

An introduction isn't just one or two sentences placed together; it incorporates a carefully devised technique or variety of techniques to gain your listeners' interest. Generally, a good introduction is at least a paragraph long.

In this section we present examples of effective introductions and explain why they are successful. Some are taken directly from students' presentations in beginning speech classes, and some are excerpts from individuals who are experienced in delivering public speeches.

Examples, Stories, and Illustrations

You can always begin with an *example*, *story*, or *illustration*. Examples make your introduction vivid, and help your audience to quickly understand the reality of a person, experience, or circumstance. Notice how the following brief story creates interest and generates concern as it moves forward.

> This is a copy of my senior yearbook. Underneath the picture of each graduate is a caption that describes our personalities or our past school experiences. I'd like to show you one picture, and I'll read the caption under it. It says, "Is there no remedy?"
>
> Is there no remedy? Jerry Shafer still asks himself that question three years later. In March of 1984 Jerry was riding on a friend's motorcycle and someone ran a stop sign and hit him. He suffered a compound fracture of his arm and lost a large amount of blood. I went to visit him right afterwards in the hospital, and I can remember seeing the plasma bottle hanging over him with a tube going into his arm. Little did I know that this would be his killer.
>
> Between the years 1978 to 1985, [some] donated blood was HIV-contaminated— contaminated with the AIDS virus. Because of this, some exceedingly unfortunate people today are walking time bombs—and my friend Jerry is one of these individuals. AIDS—Acquired Immune Deficiency Syndrome—is a monstrous and terrifying disease that has deadly effects upon the body's immune system.[2]

Michael Black showed that he understood the purpose of the introduction when he used this example. The audience could sense Mike's concern and despair as he described the disease slowly seizing his friend Jerry. At the end of the speech one student said, "Mike's introduction really made me listen. He got my attention with the visual and he also made me curious—I wanted to listen to the story because I wasn't sure where it was headed. I really had a lot of sympathy for Mike and his friend. I didn't want to stop listening for a minute—I was so totally involved in the story."

Notice that the end of the introduction contains the thesis statement: "AIDS. . .is a monstrous and terrifying disease that has deadly effects upon the body's immune system."

In the next introduction, Gina Alexander uses a series of brief examples as her strategy:

- Susan's boss told her that her dress was too tight and too loud in color.
- Beth's supervisor pinched her every time she walked near him.
- Michelle was the object of many dirty jokes by her coworkers.
- John knew that making love to Norma, the vice-president of the company, was the only way to get that essential promotion.
- And Ralph had to endure hugs from his professor to get an "A."

Degrading, counterproductive, and criminal—these words describe sexual harassment in the workplace. This is the cancer of our workplace. Sexual harassment is a problem for both men and women. These harassers want power over us, and victims are unaware of how to cut off this power.[3]

This rapid-fire technique is effective because the speaker is able to convey several examples quickly in order to motivate listeners.

An example, story, or illustration helps to create immediate interest, because an audience can empathize with a vivid situation or specific experience.

Shocking Statement or Situation

A *shocking statement* or situation that shocks the audience is also an effective method of creating interest. In the following introduction to a speech on tornados, Michael Gerber used the first line to startle his audience:

It's raining toads and frogs. This may seem impossible but it is only one of the many astonishing feats of a tornado. Yes, toads and frogs have been sucked up by a tornado and poured out by a cloud. A railroad coach with one hundred and seventeen passengers aboard was carried aloft by a tornado and dumped into a ditch twenty-five meters away. A schoolhouse was demolished and eighty-five students were transported one hundred meters. Amazingly, none of these students was killed. Chickens have lost their feathers and straw has been driven into metal pipes. These are only a few examples of the meanest and deadliest wind of all—the tornado.[4]

The one-liner combined with the brief examples effectively set up the entire speech: Listeners were completely receptive and eager to hear other pertinent information about the tornado.

Here is another way to use a shock technique in the introduction. Before his speech began, Stephen King got the attention of his listeners by distributing a small white cup to each of his classmates. He then held up a "memo," which he began reading to his audience.

I'd like to read you a memo, from the dean of the university, which is dated today. "It has come to the attention of the administration and faculty that an increasing number of students have been abusing alcohol and illegal drugs on campus. In response, the university has adopted a policy of mandatory drug testing for all students. Since this is a serious problem—one that could cause the university to lose its state funding—all students, full-time and part-time, must submit to a witnessed urinalysis by the medical staff of the university by November 30. Should any student fail to comply with this test, he or she will be immediately dropped from class rolls. Moreover, any student who tests positive will also be immediately dismissed from the university and no longer allowed to attend class."

Now I've passed around some paper cups, and I'd like you to fill out your name and social security number on the labels provided, and make note if you are taking any prescription drugs. In the hall, stationed outside both restrooms, we have members of the medical department to witness your test. Now, I'd like to start at the rear of the room. One at a time please...

The memo I have just read is not real. But I'd like you to think for a minute how you would feel if it were. Would you be insulted, embarrassed, outraged? Would you say: What right do I have to ask you to do this? Who the hell do I think I am? Well, get prepared, because it's happening all across America. Sooner or later, don't be surprised if someone wants you to urinate in a cup like this. These drug tests violate our constitutional rights and invade our privacy.[5]

This type of method of using a startling situation was overwhelmingly successful. One student said, "I thought this was all true. The memo that he read sounded official, and I was going to take my little cup to the restroom for the sample." Another listener commented, "I was incensed that anyone would try something like this. It really drove the point home."

Steve used this method to get to the heart of the issue. He quickly communicated that the problem was real, and he placed his audience in a situation that forced them to examine the issues involved. He had his audience sitting on the edge of their seats.

Statistics

You can begin your speech by citing *statistics* to involve the audience.

Of the eighteen people in this classroom, nine were sexually molested as children—that's one out of every two, men as well as women—according to figures from Family and Children's Services of Central Maryland. Actually, there are only eight in the audience, because I'm the ninth person. And I kept that secret for thirty-six years.

I've been a rape crisis counselor for two years and I've put in one hundred hours working with sexually abused child victims. Victims of child abuse have no control over what happened to them. It is the secrecy surrounding the incident that causes significant damage. As parents and future parents, you need to know what sexual child abuse is, who the offenders are, how the victims are affected, and some preventative measures you can take to protect your children.[6]

Kathy Birckhead got immediate attention by using statistics to threaten the physical and emotional well-being of her listeners. Since the statistics she cited indicated that half of them were abused as children, audience members listened intently to learn more about the topic. Concern intensified when the speaker acknowledged her own abuse and established credibility as a counselor. Notice that Kathy involves the audience by connecting to parents as well as "future parents" when she states the thesis at the end of the introduction.

Questions

Another way to introduce a topic is by asking a question. *Questions* can be either rhetorical or open-ended. Rhetorical questions are self-answered: Listeners respond silently. In the following example, Kathleen Ward asked her listeners a rhetorical question to introduce the topic.

What do George Washington and Cleopatra have in common? Well, they are just two of the many different people who have braided their hair over the centuries. Braiding goes as far back as the Egyptians, who corn-braided their hair. Braiding is not just for females. Corn-braiding for the Egyptians included the males, and George Washington and many other men of his time had their long hair pulled back at the nape and braided. And according to Margot Liste's book *Costumes of Everyday Life,* many American Indians were known for braiding their hair. This book also stated that in the twelfth century, ribbons and different colored materials were woven through the braids, and it wasn't until the 1800s that these braids hung down and were uncovered. Until then, they were piled high or coiled around the head, and they were covered for a headdress. This process included both men's and women's styles. Braids have been popular in the last twenty years—I can remember seeing men wearing them in the 1970s. But today, it tends to be more of a woman's style. One of the most common braids that I see women wearing is the French braid—that's the way I like to wear my hair. To me it's great, because on a hot day like today, my hair isn't down around my forehead, and it isn't hanging on my shoulders or around my neck. So today I'd like to show you three variations of French braiding that I know—the inward plait, the outward plait, and the fish bone.[7]

Kathleen skillfully crafted an introduction with several audience-centered techniques. The rhetorical question stimulated the curiosity and interest of listeners. The brief history related the topic to men as well as to women in the audience. Kathleen documented her material with a source, stated a personal observation, and demonstrated her knowledge of the topic by wearing her hair in a French braid.

Questions can also be of the open-ended type, which stimulate a direct response from the audience. Asking open-ended questions can be effective, but you need to be careful with this method. Don't ask the audience for more than a show of hands or one-word answers. If you request more complicated information, you may find them taking control of your speech. In this example, the speaker asks for a simple show of hands to gain a response:

> By a show of hands, how many people in this room are Baptists? Okay, there are a few of you. I want you to listen closely, because what I'm about to read concerns you. By order of the governor, all Baptists have been proclaimed enemies of the state and must be exterminated, or driven from the state, if necessary, for the public good.
>
> This sounds crazy doesn't it? It's the 1990s and we live in the United States, and things like this just don't happen. Well, you're kind of right, they don't happen in the '90s, but they did happen in 1838. In the state of Missouri in 1838, Governor Lillburn W. Boggs issued an order of extermination for all Mormons. Today I want to talk about the three events leading up to that extermination order, namely, the existing anti-Mormon sentiment, the election-day riot, and the Crooked River incident.[8]

Michelle Allred decided to ask a question that seemed to invade her listeners' privacy. But the question combined with the hypothetical example helped the audience to understand the results of discrimination and religious persecution. When you seek an open-ended response, you must be clear that you want an answer from your listeners. In this instance, Michelle asked the question and told her audience the type of response she wanted. She also paused a moment to let the audience know she was waiting for their answer. The introduction then proceeded in a logical manner from the example to the 1838 extermination order which the speaker used to introduce her thesis. The strategy was extremely effective and helped the audience to connect to Michelle's historical topic.

Quotation

Another good way to introduce your speech is by using a *quotation* appropriate to your topic. In a nationally televised 1992 campaign speech, presidential candidate H. Ross Perot used a quotation to introduce a speech on the economy.

"The budget should be balanced. The treasury should be refilled. Public debts should be reduced. The arrogance of public officials should be controlled." These are not new words. Cicero said these words over 2,000 years ago, but certainly they apply to our country today.

Anytime we do anything, we try to learn from experience. We learned a lot from the first program from your comments. First, you wanted better charts that you can see the fine print on, and you'll have those tonight. Secondly, we had one news announcer [who] criticized the pointer that I used before. So, since we're dealing with voodoo economics, a great young lady from Louisiana sent me this voodoo stick, and I will use it as my pointer tonight. Certainly, it's appropriate, because, as you and I know, we're in deep voodoo![9]

Perot began with the quotation to stress the seriousness of the issue. But he interjected humor with the visual aid to motivate listeners and to connect them to a difficult subject. The combination of strategies was successful: Millions of Americans listened to his thirty-minute speech.

You can also include a longer quotation in the introduction, such as a poem, song, or other work that is appropriate to your topic.

I'd like to quote a poem, entitled "To Santa Claus, and little sisters."

Once . . . he wrote a poem.
And called it "Chops,"
Because that was the name of
his dog, and that's what it was all about.
And the teacher gave him an "A"
And a gold star.
And his mother hung it on the
kitchen door and read it to
all his aunts . . .

Once . . .he wrote another poem.
And he called it "Question Marked Innocence."
Because that was the name of
His grief, and that's what it
was all about.
And the professor gave him an "A"
And a strange and steady look.
And his mother never hung it
on the kitchen door, because
he never let her see it . . .
Once, at 3 A.M. . . . he tried another poem . . .
And he called it absolutely
nothing, because that's what it
was all about.

> And he gave himself an "A"
> And a slash on each damp wrist,
> And hung it on the bathroom
> door because he couldn't reach
> the kitchen.[10]
>
> This poem was written by a fifteen-year-old boy two years before he committed suicide. The National Institute of Mental Health recently reported that every ninety minutes a teenager commits suicide. We must know the warning signs of teenage suicide so that we can recognize them and intervene the next time a child cries out for help.[11]

In this introduction, Tina Cerrato immediately aroused the attention of her audience. They were completely involved as they listened to the poem; they were curious to find out the underlying meaning. Tina made them wait in suspense until the final sentences of her introduction. The beginning demonstrated that the issue was real, important, and required the full attention of the audience.

Suspense

You can make listeners curious about a topic by using *suspense*.

> A harness locks you into place. You move slowly forward and then upward, climbing to a height of fifteen stories. Next you drop fifty-five degrees, making you feel as if you just drove off a cliff at more than sixty miles per hour. You zoom through two sixty-foot-high loops, you are turned upside down, you gyrate through a two-hundred-foot corkscrew, and you are thrown like a boomerang into a final loop. You've been turned upside down and around six times, and pressed against your seat by the force—of gravity, that is, which is nearly four times your body weight.
>
> Is this some kind of masochistic exercise or strange ceremony? No, not really. You've just experienced the Vortex, the roller coaster ride at King's Island Amusement Park in Ohio as described by Kerry Hannon in an August 1987 issue of *Forbes* magazine. Today I'd like to give you some information that you may not know about the design and safety of these wonderful, whirling thrills.[12]

Karen Leonard did not identify her topic at the beginning of the introduction. Instead, she described a series of events designed to sustain the curiosity of audience members. Karen's strategy was successful even though most listeners had guessed the topic before she revealed it. After identifying her source of the descriptive statements, the speaker stated a clear thesis at the end of the introduction.

Personal Reference, Compliment, or Reference to Occasion

Another way to begin an introduction is by making a *personal reference* or by giving a *compliment* to the audience. There are occasions when speakers face audiences they do not know and places they've never been. In this kind of situation it is important for a speaker to establish a common ground. Effective audience analysis will help the speaker mention the appropriate catch words which will build a relationship with listeners. Notice how David Archambault, president of the American Indian College Fund, uses a personal reference in the following introduction:

> Thank you and good afternoon. Hau Kola. That is how we Lakota say "Greeting, friends." I am happy to be here today to represent Native American people. I am a Ikoeya Wicaska—an ordinary man. We think of an ordinary man as not superior to anyone else or for that matter to anything else. We— all people and all things—are related to each other.
>
> We begin our spiritual ceremonies with the phrase "Oni takuya Oyasi," which means "all my relations." We believe that all people are ultimately part of one nation—the nation of mankind—but that this nation is only one of many nations that inhabit the Mother Earth. To us, all living things are nations—the deer, the horses, things that crawl, things that fly, things that grow in and on the ground. All of these nations were created by the same Power, and none is superior to another. All are necessary for life. We are expected to live and work in harmony.[13]

Since he presented his remarks to an audience with few Indians, Archambault acquainted listeners with his culture by expressing warm greetings in his native language and by describing the spiritual philosophies of his tribe. The key to an effective personal reference is good audience analysis— if you understand your audience members, you will know the appropriate references or compliments to make in your introduction. In a speech class where you get to know everyone during the semester, you probably would not use this approach very often.

You can also begin your introduction by making a *reference to the occasion* of the speech. Mary Collins, associate minister for national defense in Canada, used a reference to the occasion as an introduction.

> President Hoxie, distinguished guests, ladies and gentlemen: It's a great pleasure for me to be here in Washington tonight, and to take part in your symposium marking the two hundredth anniversary of the American Bill of Rights.
>
> Fifty years ago, when he established a national "Bill of Rights" day, President Franklin D. Roosevelt reminded Americans, and the world, of the cost of the rights and freedoms being celebrated. "Those who have long enjoyed such privileges as we enjoy," he said, "forget in time that men have died to win them."

> For Americans and Canadians, alike, democracy, human rights and freedom
> are our heritage, but they do not have a life of their own. They must be lived, they
> must be nurtured, and they must be safeguarded through constant vigilance.[14]

As a Canadian, Mary Collins realized that her American audience would feel a sense of pride in celebrating the 200th anniversary of the Bill of Rights. She greeted the audience, acknowledged the occasion, and used an inspiring quotation from President Roosevelt to remind listeners of the precious cost of freedom. Collins ended the introduction on a note of common ground, stressing the similarity of Canadian and American ideals.

In your speech class you could refer to an upcoming holiday such as Christmas, Easter, Independence Day, or Thanksgiving, or a special event like Valentine's Day, Secretary's Day, or even April Fool's Day. An opening reference to the occasion can be related to the topic and simultaneously gain the attention and interest of your audience.

Humor

Humor is an excellent way to introduce a speech. Humor can establish goodwill between the speaker and the audience, and a joke or humorous anecdote can relax the audience and put the speaker at ease. Read this short introduction from a speech which Benjamin Alexander, president of Drew Dawn Enterprises, presented to the American Association of Retired Persons:

> It was twelve months ago that Mrs. Brown invited me to address this distin-
> guished group of retired Americans. My role is to speak to you; your job is to
> listen. If you should finish your assignment before mine is completed, and
> you wish to leave—please do so. But if too many of you begin to depart at
> the same time, let me know where you are going and if it sounds better than
> here, I will join you.[15]

The remarks are genuinely funny, yet they have a serious point. Alexander demonstrates his sensitivity to the speaker–audience relationship, and through the use of humor, tells the listeners that he intends to interest them.

Be certain that your humor gets the response you want from your audience. Humor can be tricky: A joke that flops or a poorly presented anecdote will defeat the purpose of the introduction. Be relatively sure that your humor will work by trying it out on friends or classmates in advance.

The Flexible Introduction

There will be times when your prepared introduction may prove inappropriate. Unexpected events sometimes create difficult situations making an audience unreceptive to a presentation. A humorous introduction might not be appropriate if an audience had just heard a wrenching testimonial about drug addiction; a sad story about adoption might not be effective after rollicking humor; an introduction presented to freezing listeners might generate very little positive response. You may need to alter your prepared beginning by presenting another introduction that puts listeners in a more receptive mood.

One student, who was among several scheduled to present a classroom speech, had planned a statistical introduction to a speech about recycling. By coincidence, however, another speaker presented almost identical factual materials on the same topic. The student with the second recycling speech adapted to the unwelcome situation with the following impromptu introduction:

> My topic is recycling as well. I was glad to see that someone else had an interest in the waste problem. (I was also shocked to see this!) That speech informed us about developments in recycling in different companies today, it showed that recycling is not developed as much here as in other places in the country, and it described the problems with dumping in the sea. I'll try not to reiterate the main points but rather, I'll try to reinforce the urgency and the need for recycling.[16]

Speaker Rick Trader did not let circumstances destroy his confidence. He transformed a negative situation by acknowledging the difficulty, by joking about the coincidence, and even by restating the previous speaker's thesis. He then reassured listeners that he would provide new information in addition to material already presented. The impromptu introduction worked. Rick's listeners were positive and supportive, and appreciated his different perspective on the same topic.

Combination of Methods

You will often find that it is useful to combine a variety of methods in your introduction. Chris Koeppen used a combination of approaches to stimulate his listeners' interest.

> When you were a kid did you ever play with building blocks like this? Well, I used to enjoy them, as I'm sure you did. I found blocks to be fun and educational, and I used to create all kinds of structures, like the one I've made here. Building these objects helped me to imagine larger structures. Consider, for example, that there are only six little blocks in my pyramid. Imagine that you had to put together two and one-half million of these blocks. Furthermore, instead of small blocks, imagine that each one of them weighed about five thousand pounds. That's the type of project that the ancient Egyptians undertook when building the Great Pyramid. What is equally amazing is that the exact reason for its existence remains a mystery. Thus the intrigue of the

Great Pyramid stems from the facts about its construction, and the theories on why it was built.[17]

The speaker asks the audience a rhetorical question and uses a visual aid to remind audience members of their childhood. The opening statements create suspense and the small pyramid provides an effective comparison to the Great Pyramid of Egypt. Finally, Chris mentions some startling statistics and ends with his thesis statement.

If you combine a question with a quote, or a statistic with a startling statement, you can develop an introduction both interesting and meaningful to your audience.

OUTLINING THE INTRODUCTION

The introduction is part of the informal outline of a speech. Remember that the purpose of the outline is to help you communicate the content of your introduction. While it is never advisable to mix sentences and topics in the formal outline of the speech body, it may actually be helpful to adopt this practice in your introduction. We are providing two different outline styles you can choose for your introduction. The examples below outline the story of Michael Black's friend who had acquired AIDS.

Style 1	Introduction
(First sentence)	I. "This is a copy of my senior yearbook."
(Strategy)	II. Story of my friend, Jerry Shafer
(Specific purpose)	III. To inform the audience about the disease AIDS
(Thesis statement)	IV. AIDS—Acquired Immune Deficiency Syndrome—is a monstrous and terrifying disease that has deadly effects upon the body's immune system.

This style of outlining is short but adequate if you know your introduction thoroughly. Numeral I includes the first sentence of the speech. It is important to write out the first line of your speech word-for-word so that you will be able to begin with confidence. Numeral II simply describes the strategy (or strategies) you are using for the introduction such as story, case study, quotation, or statistics. In this instance, the story mentioned in II will trigger the speaker's personal experiences. Numeral III identifies the specific purpose and numeral IV provides the thesis statement. Numerals III and IV remind you to state the purpose and/or thesis at the end of your introduction.

Here is a more detailed outline of the same introduction:

Style 2	Introduction

(*First sentence*)	I. "This is a copy of my senior yearbook."
	  A. Caption describes experiences
	  B. One picture with caption—"Is there no remedy?"

(*Strategy*)	II. Story of my friend, Jerry Shafer
	  A. Hit in a motorcycle accident in 1984
	  B. Received AIDS-contaminated blood transfusion
	  C. Has become walking time bomb

(*Specific purpose*)	III. To inform the audience about AIDS
(*Thesis statement*)	IV. AIDS—Acquired Immune Deficiency Syndrome—is a monstrous and terrifying disease that has deadly effects upon the body's immune system.

You can see that this outline has the same numerals as Style 1, but there is more detail. The detail obviously helps to keep you on track if you feel you need more information to guide you through your introduction. Use whichever style your instructor recommends to suit your particular needs.

PLANNING THE CONCLUSION

Just as a speech requires an introduction, a speech also needs a conclusion. We've often heard endings like this:

Well, uh, I guess, uh, that's about it!

And now in conclusion I'd just like to say that I hope you've learned something about holograms.

And now for my conclusion, I'll leave you with a quote: "All's well that ends well."

And so finally, in conclusion, I'd like to end by telling you that my last point is that you might want to pick up a kit to test radon gas the next time you're in the supermarket. Thank you.

These are not successful ways to end speeches. The "techniques" are abrupt, trite, awkward, or repetitious. Sloppy conclusions increase the speaker's apprehension and make the audience equally uncomfortable.

An effective conclusion gives finality to a speech. The speaker must choose a clear method or device which tells the audience that the topic has been resolved. A speaker must also clearly demonstrate in his or her delivery (voice tone, slower rate of speech) that the speech has ended.

You should not introduce new material in the conclusion; rather, you should choose a method which reinforces the information and ideas you have already presented. We will provide brief explanations and examples of a conclusion—summary, quotation, reference to the introduction, challenge and appeal, humor, question, story, and statistics.

Summary of Main Points

A *summary* of the main points can be an effective way to end a speech on complicated or difficult subject-matter. Summaries help to remind your audience of the major points and leave them with a sense of order. Meredith Kreczmer summarized her demonstration on creative photography and used a visual aid as reinforcement.

> The key to a good picture is not the number of lights or the quality of your camera and lens, but it is your ability to "see" and "think" in terms of pictures. Remember the simple steps on this poster:
>
> First, get to know your camera—
> > the viewfinder
> > shutter release
> > aperture
> > shutter
>
> Second, remember the key techniques—
> > Less is more.
> > Move around your subject.
> > Look at your background.
> > Close in on the subject.
> > Simplicity is never wrong.
>
> So snap away, and maybe someday you'll see your picture in *National Geographic!*[18]

The speaker used several visuals and described a number of techniques during the body of the speech. An ordinary verbal summary would have been adequate; instead, Meredith used words and cartoon sketches on a visual aid to remind her audience of important ideas stressed in the speech. The summary included both main and supporting points, since the body of this presentation included only two numerals. In longer, more complex speeches, however, speakers might tend to recapitulate only the numerals.

Don't use a summary conclusion simply because you can't think of any other approach. Remember that a successful speaker has a good reason for the type of conclusion he or she selects. Summaries are good with complex material, but they are not effective when you need to appeal to the audience or challenge their thinking in another way.

Quotation

A *quotation* is often an excellent way to end a speech. A quote can express feelings eloquently and reinforce the speaker's ideas.

Kim Jones combined an example with a quotation to end a speech commemorating Sojourner Truth, a famous black orator and reformer:

> Sojourner Truth fought for increased education, Negro rights, world peace, and women's rights. But some did not give her the respect that she deserved. According to William Jacobs' *Great Lives,* the newspapers started a rumor. Because she was six feet tall, they said that she was probably a man disguised as a woman. In order to prove her womanhood, they asked her to show her breasts. With quiet dignity, she opened her blouse before the stunned crowd and declared softly: "It is not my shame, but yours, that I must do this."
>
> Sojourner Truth died in 1883. A quotation in the Jacobs book presents a fitting tribute to the life of this great African-American. "With her arms outstretched, and her eyes aflame, she argued in a deep voice about women's rights: 'If the first woman God ever made was strong enough to turn the world upside down, all alone, then together we ought to be able to turn it back and get it right side up again and now they are asking us to do it, the men better let them.'"[19]

Kim cited this vivid example to demonstrate the courage and regal dignity that Sojourner displayed in the midst of humiliating circumstances. The end quotation resolved the speech effectively by painting an elegant portrait of a strong, compassionate, determined woman. Listeners experienced feelings of rage, empathy, and pride as Kim delivered the quotation slowly, with strength and emotion.

Quotations can also be used to provide authoritative support for the speaker's viewpoint. Notice how the following speaker integrated a quotation into her conclusion.

> Now that I've presented some information about the insanity defense, I'd like you to hear a story found in the book *Crime and Madness,* by Thomas Maeder. In 1882 Roderick Maclean tried to shoot Queen Victoria. At the trial, he pleaded not guilty by reason of insanity and he was acquitted of the

charge. When the queen heard about the result of the trial, she said, quote, "Insane he may have been, but *not guilty* he most certainly was not. If that is the law, then the law must be changed." As a result of this trial, the insanity law in England was altered. Under the changed law, jurors were directed to declare the defendant insane but also guilty of the crime. I think the queen had a pretty good idea.[20]

Stacey Solesha found a quotation from Queen Victoria that supported her view that the insanity plea should not be allowed as a defense. While the brief story put the quotation in its historical context, the speaker brought the incident up to date with her closing line, "I think the queen had a pretty good idea."

Reference to Introduction

One good way of concluding a speech is a *reference to the introduction*. This strategy can be used successfully with any type of introduction to promote unity within a presentation. Earlier we mentioned an introduction in which student Stephen King shocked his audience by reading an administrative memo requiring drug tests for all students. Steve ended that speech with this conclusion:

IN HIS FAMOUS SPEECH "I HAVE A DREAM," MARTIN LUTHER KING, JR., MADE SKILLFUL USE OF HIS CONCLUSION, WHICH INCLUDED THE RINGING WORDS, "FREE AT LAST! FREE AT LAST! THANK GOD ALMIGHTY, WE ARE FREE AT LAST!"

© Bob Adelman/
Magnum Photos, Inc.

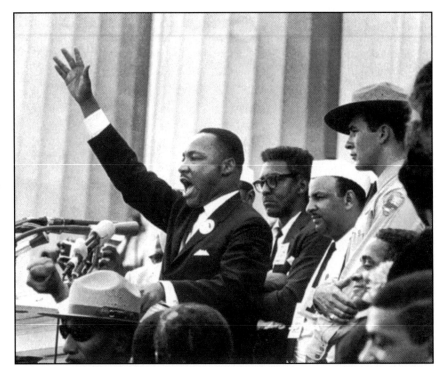

I want you to think about the urine cups you have in front of you. How does it feel to be looked upon as a drug user until you can prove your innocence? Suppose that your test came back "positive" and you were dismissed from college because of an inexperienced lab technician. Let's stop treating people as if they're being spied upon. Let's keep our Constitution strong and never relinquish our right to privacy. Let's stop drug-testing—now![21]

Stephen King effectively referred to his introduction and drew his class-mates' attention back to the injustice of the opening situation, reminding them of his specific purpose. He ended by challenging the audience to uphold the right of privacy.

Challenge or Appeal

In some speeches, especially persuasive speeches, you may need to conclude by issuing a general challenge or a specific appeal to the audience. A *challenge* is usually a broad, generalized summons to the audience to make some kind of effort to support the topic. A speaker telling the audience "We need to preserve liberty," or "We must protect our children," is using a general challenge in the conclusion.

Notice how Jacquelyn Shields ended her persuasive speech about increasing the length of the school year:

Last week I received notification of my eligibility to become a member of Phi Theta Kappa, the national honor society for community colleges. It's extremely ironic that I received this announcement while I was researching this speech. If I could walk into a Japanese classroom with my Japanese counterpart, a college sophomore, and be tested on my pool of knowledge, I would come up short. Each one of you must also consider how you would compare to your counterpart in Japan. And if you feel that you also would come up short, then you must remember that you are a product of the American educational system.

If you don't want your children to suffer in the future, I urge you to think about changing the system. Let's improve our educational process by lengthening the school year. Let's regain our economic and technological leadership by helping our children to compete with other nations on an equal footing.[22]

Jackie's reference to her membership in Phi Theta Kappa gave her credibility as an honor student. But the comparison of American and Japanese educational systems motivated listeners to think. In the final paragraph, she directly challenged the audience to improve American education. The challenge is general rather than specific; she allowed listeners to decide for themselves how to carry it out.

You can also end a speech by using a specific *appeal* to the audience. Unlike challenges, appeals are usually well defined for the audience. When a speaker asks you to vote for someone, give to a specific cause, or support a philosophy or issue, he or she is using a direct appeal.

Notice how Shelley Snyder used appeals to conclude a persuasive speech on racism:

> I hope all of you can admit that there still remains a problem of racism and that you can commit to taking a stand against it; that you evaluate yourselves, your preconceptions, your prejudices, and yes, your racist views. I really never thought of myself as a racist. I abhor violence. I abhor blatant discrimination and all the inequities I see. But in researching for this speech, I found that, in too many instances, I am racist. But my personal appeal, and the appeal I put before you is to understand where our attitudes come from, and to ask ourselves for a change of heart—to defend the victims of racism, to work to improve legislation for equal justice for all. I am going to hand out a test from a book entitled *The Day America Told the Truth*. I want you to take it in the privacy of your own home and assess yourself—honestly.
>
> Again, I ask you: Take a stand against racism. For, in the words of Martin Luther King, Jr., "to ignore evil is to become an accomplice to it." [23]

The speaker employed several appeals in this conclusion. Shelley asked listeners to stop racism by honestly evaluating their own views. But she did not simply make an accusation to the audience: The speaker was able to refer to her own "racism," making the persuasion even more powerful. Shelley urged listeners to take action by answering questions about racism and she combined her final appeal with a forceful quotation from the Reverend Martin Luther King, Jr. The appeals were highly successful with audience members. One listener commented: "Shelley really persuaded me to take a look at my own attitudes." Another observed: "I'm going to take the test, and if I don't like what I see, I'm going to do all I can to change. I guess we can't solve racism until we solve it within ourselves."

Humor

Humor that is appropriate to your topic can be a good way to end a speech. Telling a joke or brief anecdote can leave your audience in a good mood and can stimulate a spontaneous positive response at the end.

Kimberly Kittle informed listeners how to use substitute remedies for household problems when the appropriate products were too expensive or unavailable. She advocated using hairspray to remove ink stains, mayonnaise as a cure for brittle hair, and vegetable oil to keep car doors from freezing in winter. She ended the speech on a light, but cautionary, note:

> Even though these alternative remedies can work wonders, remember that nothing is one hundred percent foolproof, and one always has to be moderate and cautious. While some products can be used to solve common household problems, they can create even worse nightmares. For example, a man who thought he'd found the perfect way to absorb unsightly motor oil in his driveway, spread kitty litter on every inch of concrete outside his house. The remedy worked and the oil disappeared, but the poor man ended up creating a monstrous cat litter box which attracted every happy feline in town! [24]

The audience was enlightened by Kim's helpful hints and enjoyed laughing at the humorous punchline.

Your humor must be entertaining; stories from joke-books, or worn-out anecdotes, tend to backfire. Be certain that your humor is fresh, spontaneous, and appropriate.

Question

You can also conclude by asking the audience a *rhetorical question*. This approach tells the audience to "think about it" for a while.

Ernestine Cooper presented a convincing speech about the dangers of aerobic exercise. After providing statistics, examples, and a personal experience to support her point of view, the speaker delivered this conclusion:

> If you are thinking about getting into aerobics, listen to your body's signals. Check out your health clubs. Check out the floors. Wear the appropriate shoes. And most important, check out the instructors. Ask to see those credentials. Where did they receive their training? Will they address your needs on an individual basis? Remember, it is your body, your limbs that need to be protected. You have a right to know. Ask yourself, are the health benefits from aerobic exercise worth the pain? Do you want to wind up as a statistic in the next survey of aerobic injuries? [25]

Because of Ernestine's impressive evidence and the questions posed in her conclusion, the audience was persuaded to think seriously about the potential harm of aerobic exercise. The final question stimulated a silent "no" response within her listeners.

Examples, Stories, and Illustrations

Once you have provided your audience with extensive information about a topic, you can end with a *story*, an *illustration*, or a brief *example* to keep the audience interested and at the same time drive home your point. Notice how Norma Ferris concluded her speech about the Meals on Wheels program.

> But we often think, "Well there're so many problems in the world, and I'm just one person; what could I do?" With the Meals on Wheels program, there's no question that you can do something. You—just one person—can make a difference in someone's life—someone who would otherwise be forgotten.
>
> Let me tell you about one woman on my route who was a childless widow. It was Easter time, and while I was delivering her meal I saw someone selling flowers. So I picked up just a small hyacinth and brought it to her. She was so taken with it, she said, "No one but the Meals on Wheels people have treated me kindly in so long—I'm so grateful—I just wish there was something I could do for you." She thought for a minute, and she went back into her bedroom and she came out with an old mink stole—it must have been thirty years old. She said, "My husband gave this to me. Would you take it? Because I appreciate what you've done so much—I'm very grateful." Well, I couldn't take it. But it just goes to show you how important you can be to someone. With the Meals on Wheels program, you can make a difference.[26]

This brief story was drawn from the speaker's personal experience and gave the topic a powerful sense of credibility. The emotional quality of the story maintained audience interest and attention to the very end of the speech. Norma communicated the idea that the Meals on Wheels program was not just another charity begging for money. Listeners could see that their involvement would benefit the elderly, and would give those volunteering personal satisfaction and reward.

Statistics

A speaker can state or re-emphasize an alarming *statistic* to get the audience to think about an issue. Statistics are often effective when combined with other types of conclusions. In a speech about battered women, a speaker combined two approaches:

> We need to help these battered women. Often we overlook the problem just because it's not happening to us. Sometimes we overlook the problem because we don't want to get involved. Twenty women were beaten as I was giving this speech. I hope you all understand the importance of getting involved by hearing, seeing, or assisting someone in need of help. It's not okay. Don't let it happen. Help—please.[27]

Tresse Bailey asked her audience to provide volunteer help to shelters for battered women. She ended her actuating speech with an appeal and a simple, but powerful, statistic. The speaker was careful not to bombard listeners with complicated numbers; she simply related the one statistic to the time it took her to deliver the speech. The statistic was a dramatic reminder of the extent of the problem.

OUTLINING THE CONCLUSION

You can outline the conclusion in almost the same way you outlined the introduction. Here are two outline styles of the conclusion to the Meals on Wheels speech .

Style 1	Conclusion
(*First sentence*)	I. But we often think, "Well, there're so many problems in the world and I'm just one person; what can I do?"
(*Strategy*)	II. Story of an elderly lady
Style 2	Conclusion
(*First sentence*)	I. But we often think, "Well, there're so many problems in the world and I'm just one person; what can I do?"
	A. Involvement in Meals on Wheels helps
	B. Volunteers remember forgotten people
(*Strategy*)	II. Story of an elderly lady
	A. Woman given a flower
	B. Woman expressed overwhelming appreciation
	C. Woman offered volunteer mink stole

In both examples, I is the first sentence of the conclusion and II describes the strategy which the speaker employs for the conclusion (quote, story, question, summary, and so forth). Style 1 is the abbreviated form which can be used if you really know your conclusion well. Style 2 provides more detail to help you progress through each major idea in the conclusion. As we suggested when describing the outline of the introduction, use the style that is most helpful to you.

USING SPEAKING NOTES

Your *speaking notes* will include the introduction, the body, and the conclusion. Speaking notes are important because they are the tools which help you to communicate to your audience. You should construct your notes so that you can see where you're headed in one brief glance.

Select either 4" × 6" or 6" × 9" notecards and number them at the upper right hand corner. On the first card, write the outline of your introduction. Write legibly, use large lettering, and double-space between the lines. You may want to underline or occasionally use all caps for emphasis. You may even want to use different colors to highlight specific examples, statistics, or quotations. Use a reasonable number of notecards; don't cram too many phrases on two or three cards, and don't use too many notes. You don't want to squint as you read, and you also don't want to be flipping a card every few seconds. When you transfer your outline to notecards, remember that your objective is ease of communication; you want notes that help you communicate quickly and effectively.

Here are some notecards that represent an example of a clear, readable speaking outline:

1

INTRODUCTION

I. "On Nov. 2nd, 1988, at around 9:00 p.m., Robert Tappan Morris, a 23-year-old computer science student at Cornell University, pushed a single button on his computer keyboard and launched an attack."

II. A case study presented in a suspenseful manner

Thesis: "Participants of the top secret meeting in Fort Meade, Maryland, discussed the nature of an electronic virus, the threat computer viruses pose to universities, businesses, and the U.S. government, and what might be done to safeguard potential victims."

(more)

2

Transition 1: "When we think of a computer and the programs that run it, we usually think in terms of what it can do to help us, as an aid in gathering and sorting data. So what makes a computer virus different from other types of computer programs?"

BODY

I. General information on computer viruses
  A. Virus defined
  B. Two classes of viruses described
    1. Example of nuisance virus (*Time*, Sept. 26, '88, p.64)
    2. Example of destructive virus (*Business Week*, Aug. 1 '88, p.64)
C. Virus redefined for clarity

(more)

10

Transition 4: "Experts point out that computers, by their very design, must somehow exchange information in order for them to be a useful tool to mankind."

CONCLUSION

I "Because of this, we will continue to be afflicted with computer viruses as long as some computer programmers continue to develop and distribute viruses."

II. Summary with dramatic quotation for impact (*Time*, Mar. 20, '89 p.25)
   A. No safety measure is completely foolproof
   B. Computers must continue to transfer data
   C. Computer systems will remain vulnerable to virus creators
   D. Military expert compares threat of computer viruses to most devastating military weapons available

(end)

SAMPLE OUTLINE

Here is a complete outline of a speech to inform, presented by Christopher B. Kavanaugh:

THE COMPUTER VIRUS: DISEASE OF THE COMPUTER AGE [28]

Speech to Inform

Christoper B. Kavanaugh

Topic: computer viruses

General purpose: to inform

Notice that the speaker has chosen a cryptic title that educates and enlightens.

The speaker has identified the topic area and provided the general purpose.

The specific purpose describes the overall objective of the speech, and the thesis identifies the three main points in the body.

Specific purpose: to tell the audience about computer viruses

Thesis statement: "Participants of the top secret meeting in Fort Meade, Maryland, discussed the nature of an electronic virus, the threat computer viruses pose to universities, businesses, and the U.S. government, and what might be done to safeguard potential victims."

Each part of the speech is clearly labeled as introduction, body, or conclusion.

Introduction

Numeral I describes the first sentence—the very first line the speaker will say. Numeral II determines the strategy of the introduction. In this instance, the strategy is a case study followed by specific examples of research centers that were shut down. "Suspenseful manner" tells the reader that examples under II will be arranged to create expectancy. While the specific purpose in numeral III is not stated, the thesis (numeral IV) is taken directly from the speech. The introduction is an informal outline: it includes both sentence and topic form.

I. "On November 2nd, 1988 at around 9:00 p.m., a twenty-three-year-old student of computer science at Cornell University by the name of Robert Tappan Morris pushed a single button on his computer keyboard and launched an attack."

II. A case study presented in a suspenseful manner

III. To tell the audience about computer viruses

IV. "Participants of the top secret meeting in Fort Meade, Maryland, discussed the nature of an electronic virus, the threat computer viruses pose to universities, businesses, and the U.S. government, and what might be done to safeguard potential victims."

Transition 1 connects the introduction with the first numeral of the body.

Transition 1: "When we think of a computer and the programs that run it, we usually think in terms of what it can do to help us, as an aid in gathering and sorting data. So what makes a computer virus different from other types of computer programs?"

The body of the speech represents the formal outline. Unlike the introduction, the body does not mix topics and sentences. This outline contains only topics. Parentheses provide abbreviated sources. Here notation indicates that B 1 and 2 are taken from *Time* and *Business Week.*

Body

I. General information on computer viruses
   A. Virus defined
   B. Two classes of viruses described
      1. Example of nuisance virus (*Time,* Sept. 26,'88, p. 64)
      2. Example of a destructive virus (*Bus. Week,* Aug. 1,'88, p. 64)
   C. Virus redefined for clarity

Transition 2: "Now that you are armed with a general description of this electronic scourge, let's examine its *modus operandi* and why it's such a devastating threat to our technological way of life."

The external transition connects numerals I and II.

II. Characteristics of a computer virus
   A. Comparison and contrast with a biological virus (*Discover,* Jan. '89, p. 64)
      1. Comparison of virus multiplication
      2. Contrast in virus origin
      3. Comparison of virus transmission

This outline includes four levels: Roman numerals, capital letters, numbers, and small letters.

   B. Common means of virus movement
      1. Hypothetical example of disk infection from shared computers
      2. Electronic transference of computer virus
         a. Electronic transfer described
         b. Telephone modem described
         c. Electronic bulletin board explained

The three Roman numerals carry out the thesis statement. In this outline, main points are arranged in a topical sequence.

   C. Effects of the Morris virus
      1. Morris' original intention (*N.Y. Times,* Nov. 6,'88, sec. A, p. 30)
      2. Morris' terrible mistake
      3. The financial damage (*Personal Computing*, May,'89, pp. 85–86)
      4 Expert quote on implications of similar viruses (*Time,* Mar. 20,'89, p. 25)

Each level is mechanically parallel, all subordinate points clearly support their headings, every item contains only one basic thought, and each level contains a minimum of two items.

Transition 3: "*Scientific American* magazine reported in a March, 1989 article that future efforts to improve computer security are helped by examining the viruses that have struck in the past."

Transition connects numerals II and III.

III. What can be done for protection from viruses
   A. Change computer passwords (*Business Week,* Aug. 1,'88, pp. 66–67)
      1. Make passwords more complex
      2. Make passwords more confidential
   B. Close trap doors
      1. Specific example given
      2. Trap doors defined
   C. Install anti-virus programs (*Personal Computing* May,'89, p. 91)
   D. Take other precautions
      1. Making back-up diskettes regularly
      2. Not using untested "foreign" software

Sources are shown for III A and III C. Notice that the body includes many different types of supporting materials such as statistics, examples, cases, comparisons and contrasts, and definitions.

The final transition connects the end of the body with the beginning of the conclusion.

Transition 4: "Experts point out that computers, by their very design, must somehow exchange information in order for them to be a useful tool to mankind."

Like the introduction, the conclusion is informally outlined. Numeral I identifies the first sentence of the conclusion. Numeral II states the type of strategy used; in this case the speaker will use a summary followed by a quote from an expert conveying the potential harm of the virus.

Conclusion

I. "Because of this, we will continue to be afflicted with computer viruses as long as some computer programmers continue to develop and distribute viruses."
II. Summary with dramatic quotation for impact (*Time,* Mar. 20,'89, p. 25)
   A. No safety measure is completely foolproof
   B. Computers must continue to transfer data
   C. Computer systems will remain vulnerable to virus creators
   D. Military expert compares threat of computer viruses to most devastating military weapons available

The speaker has used a wide range of supporting materials from a variety of sources.

References are listed alphabetically and each source is entered according to correct bibliographic form.

Bibliography

Hafner, Katherine, et al. "Is Your Computer Secure?" *Business Week*, August 1, 1988, pp. 64–67, 70–72.
Markoff, John. "'Virus' in Military Computers Disrupts Systems Nationwide," *The New York Times,* November 4, 1988, sec. A, p. 1, 21.
Markoff, John. "The Computer Jam: How It Came About." *The New York Times,* November 9, 1988, sec. D, p. 10.
Rasch, Mark. Prosecuting Attorney, Fraud Division, United States Department of Justice, Washington D.C. Telephone interview, August 27, 1989.
"Spreading a Virus; How Computer Science Was Caught Off Guard by One Young Hacker." *The Wall Street Journal,* November 7, 1988, sec. A, pp. 1, 6.
(The complete bibliography appears in the Appendix.)

 SUMMARY

The introduction gains the attention of the audience, creates interest, and introduces the topic. There are a variety of ways to introduce a speech: (1) example, story, or illustration, (2) shocking statement or situation, (3) statistic, (4) question, (5) quotation, (6) suspense, (7) personal reference, (8) humor, (9) a flexible introduction, and (10) a combination of approaches.

The conclusion gives finality to the speech and communicates that the topic has been resolved. Types of conclusions are: (1) summary, (2) quotation, (3) reference to the introduction, (4) challenge and appeal, (5) humor, (6) question, (7) story, illustration, and example, and (8) statistics.

To outline your introduction, numeral I should be the first sentence, numeral II should identify the strategy you intend to use, numeral III should present the specific purpose, and numeral IV should identify the thesis statement. You can outline the conclusion in the same manner without numerals III and IV. As opposed to the speech body, the outlines of the introduction and conclusion are considered informal: They often combine sentences and topics.

EXERCISES

1. Read the informative speech on "The Computer Virus: Disease of the Computer Age" in Chapter 15. Evaluate the different introductions and conclusions provided with the speech. Are some more effective than others? Are there any other approaches you feel would be appropriate for this speech? Be specific in your answer.

2. After you have developed the body of your speech, write three different introductions and three different conclusions. Deliver just the introductions and conclusions for a classroom exercise.

3. Go to the library and do some research in *Vital Speeches* or *Representative American Speeches*. Look at a number of speeches and find an example of each type of introduction and conclusion that has been discussed in this chapter.

4. Read the two speeches listed in the bibliography. Write an analysis of the approach which each speaker uses to begin and end. Do the speakers use just one method to introduce and conclude their presentations, or do they use a combination of methods? Are the approaches used successful? Be able to support your answer.

NOTES

[1] Susan S. Suter, "Lessons From the Outside," *Vital Speeches,* July 15, 1991, p. 594.

[2] Michael Black, "Is There No Remedy?," informative speech presented in speech class, Catonsville Community College, Catonsville, Maryland, 1987. Used by permission.

[3] Gina Alexander, "Sexual Harrassment," speech to actuate presented in speech class, Carroll Community College, Westminster, Maryland, 1990. Used by permission.

[4] Michael Gerber, "Tornados—The Deadliest Wind of All," speech to inform presented in speech class, Catonsville Community College, Catonsville, Maryland, 1989. Used by permission.

[5] Stephen M. King, "The Right to Privacy," speech to convince delivered in speech class, Catonsville Community College, Catonsville, Maryland, 1987. Used by permission.

[6] Kathy Birckhead, "Child Sexual Abuse," speech to inform presented in speech class, Carroll Community College, Westminster, Maryland, 1990. Used by permission.

[7] Kathleen Ward, "Braiding Your Hair," speech to demonstrate presented in speech class, Catonsville Community College, Catonsville, Maryland, 1989. Used by permission.

[8] Michelle Allred, "The Anti-Mormon Campaign," speech to inform presented in speech class, Carroll Community College, Westminster, Maryland, 1990. Used by permission.

[9] H. Ross Perot, Paid Political Broadcast, October 17, 1992.

[10] "To Santa Claus and Little Sisters" from *A Cry for Help*, by Mary Giffin and Carol Felsenthal. Copyright © 1983 by Mary Giffin, M.D., and Carol Felsenthal. Reprinted by permission of Doubleday, a division of Bantam, Doubleday, Dell Publishing Group, Inc.

[11] Tina Cerrato, "Detecting Warning Signs of Teenage Suicide," informative speech delivered in speech class, Catonsville Community College, Catonsville, Maryland, 1987. Used by permission.

[12] Karen Leonard, "Roller Coasters," informative speech presented in speech class, Carroll Community College, Westminster, Maryland, 1990. Used by permission.

[13] David Archambault, "Columbus Plus 500 Years," *Vital Speeches*, June 1, 1992, p. 491.

[14] Mary Collins, "The Responsibilities of the New World Order," *Vital Speeches*, May 15, 1991, p. 457.

[15] Benjamin H. Alexander, "Before You Lambast This Generation," *Vital Speeches*, November 15, 1987, p. 70.

[16] Rick Trader, "Participating in the Nationwide Movement Toward Recycling," speech to actuate presented in speech class, Carroll Community College, Westminster, Maryland, 1989. Used by permission.

[17] Chris Koeppen, "The Intrigue of the Great Pyramid," speech to inform presented in speech class, Carroll Community College, Westminster, Maryland, 1991. Used by permission.

[18] Meredith M. Kreczmer, "How to Take Interesting Pictures," speech to demonstrate delivered in speech class, Carroll Community College, Westminster, Maryland, 1990. Used by permission.

[19] Kim Jones, "Sojourner Truth," speech to inform presented in speech class, Carroll Community College, Westminster, Maryland, 1992. Used by permission.

[20] Stacey Solesha, "The Insanity Defense," speech to convince presented in speech class, Carroll Community College, Westminster, Maryland, 1989. Used by permission.

[21] Stephen M. King, "The Right to Privacy," speech to convince delivered in speech class, Catonsville Community College, Catonsville, Maryland, 1987. Used by permission.

[22] Jacquelyn V. Shields, "Increasing the Length of the School Year," speech to convince delivered in speech class, Carroll Community College, Westminster, Maryland, 1990. Used by permission.

[23] Shelley Y. Snyder, "Let's Take a Stand Against Racism," speech to actuate delivered in speech class, Carroll Community College, Westminster, Maryland, 1992. Used by permission.

[24] Kimberly L. Kittle, "Helpful Ways to Use Everyday Products," speech to inform presented in speech class, Carroll Community College, Westminster, Maryland, 1992. Used by permission.

[25] Ernestine D. Cooper, "Aerobic Exercise Can Be Harmful," speech to convince presented in speech class, Catonsville Community College, Catonsville, Maryland, 1989. Used by permission.

[26] Norma Ferris, "You Can Make A Difference," speech to actuate delivered in speech class, Catonsville Community College, Catonsville, Maryland, 1987. Used by permission.

[27] Tresse Bailey, "Helping Battered Women," speech to actuate presented in speech class, Catonsville Community College, Catonsville, Maryland, 1989. Used by permission.

[28] Chris Kavanaugh, "The Computer Virus: Disease of the Computer Age," speech to inform delivered in speech class, Catonsville Community College, Catonsville, Maryland, 1989. Used by permission.

READINGS

Campbell, John Angus. "An Overview of Speech Preparation." *Modcom—Modules in Speech Communication.* Chicago: Science Research Associates, 1976, pp. 1–47. The author analyzes speech structure and presents a complete discussion (with examples) of the different organizational patterns of the body. The pamphlet includes sample outlines as well as some useful exercises to help you with your introduction and conclusion.

Kelly, Rex. "Speakers and the Bottom Line." *Vital Speeches,* November 1, 1987, pp. 47–50. The speaker is a general manager of communications at the Mississippi Power Company; he raises points about speaker credibility, preparation, and the human quality of public speaking. This is a good speech to read both as an example and for its helpful content.

Rackleff, Robert B. "The Art of Speech Writing." *Vital Speeches,* March 1, 1988, p. 311. An excellent speech about speech organization and development. Rackleff makes some important comments about each part of the speech. He is humorous, witty, and informative.

UNIT OUTLINE

Chapter Twelve

Using Audiovisual Aids

Key Terms

Audiovisual aid

Liquid crystal display (LCD)

Opaque projector

Overhead projector

Tiling

Transparency

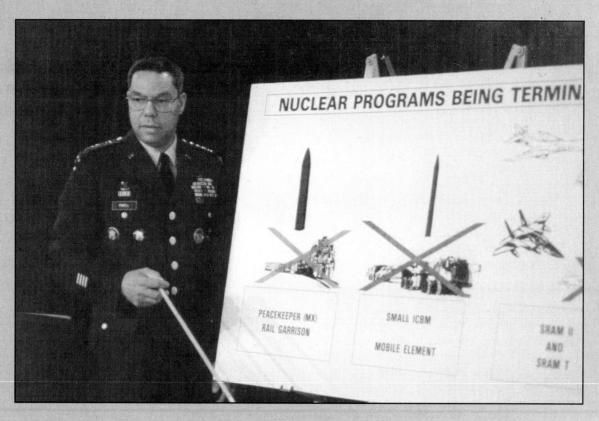

© Mark Reinstein/
Image Works

"On different senses
different objects strike."
—ALEXANDER POPE

*A*my had just ended the introduction to her speech by telling everyone that she would "demonstrate how a dentist makes a porcelain crown." The audience settled back for a new learning experience.

Amy unrolled three large posters identifying important stages of the process. When she rested the first poster on the base of the chalk board, it quickly rewound, fell to the floor, and bounced into a corner. Amy giggled nervously as she sensed audience reaction.

She picked up the poster and tried again. This time she climbed onto a chair she had scooted against the wall. As she stood on tip toes, she inserted the upper edges of the poster into two sliding metal hooks atop the chalk board. She steadied the poster with one hand, unraveled it slowly with the other, and climbed down from the chair, propelling it out of the way with her foot, which sent it tumbling across the room. As she rushed to rescue the runaway chair, Amy let go of her chart, which quickly rewound from bottom to top, snapping loose from the metal clips. Sailing through the air, it hit the forehead of a listener in the front row.

While audience members didn't learn much about porcelain crowns, they did have a new learning experience: Everybody discovered how *not* to handle visual aids.

This first chapter of Unit IV, "Refining the Appearance," will help you to avoid some of Amy's problems. Principal types of audiovisual aids are identified, and their effective use in a speech is discussed. Visual aids can be used in almost any type of speech to promote interest and clarity.

THE IMPORTANCE OF AUDIOVISUAL AIDS

Newsmagazines photograph members of America's basketball "dream team" embracing after their gold-medal win at the 1992 Summer Olympics. The U.S. government publishes a pie graph to explain how the $1½ trillion budget is spent. A guest actress on *The Late Show with David Letterman* brings a brief clip to plug her new film. The League of Women Voters uses a scale model to teach first-time voters how to operate a voting machine. Supermarkets play relaxing music to put customers in a receptive mood. VCRs at department-store perfume counters play glitzy commercials describing a particular fragrance. And the real estate supplement to the Sunday paper uses a line graph to display the upward or downward trend in home sales. People in every kind of institution or business understand the value of visual aids in communicating feelings, conveying information, and selling products.

Visual aids are also vitally important to the public speaker. During the 1962 Cuban Missile Crisis, U.S. Ambassador Adlai Stevenson displayed large aerial photographs at a United Nations Security Council meeting to prove the existence of Soviet missiles in Cuba. In 1977, President Jimmy Carter wore a sweater as he sat by a crackling fire and asked Americans to conserve energy. In his 1988 State of the Union speech, President Ronald Reagan lifted forty-three pounds of congressional documents to demonstrate the unnecessary red tape contained in many legislative actions. In 1991, U.S. General Norman Schwarzkopf used a diagram to illustrate the military offensive against Iraq in Operation Desert Storm. Research indicates that visual aids such as these increase the ability of listeners to remember information.[1] When you use a picture or an object to convey ideas, your audience will not only have a more concrete mental image, they will also recall your speech more completely.

TYPES OF AUDIOVISUAL AIDS

Audiovisual aids can help you to communicate ideas more effectively. When we use the term *audiovisual aids*, we refer to devices that may appeal to sight and to other senses as well: graphs, drawings and photographs, posters or chalkboards, mechanical media, models and objects, or some aspect of the speaker.

Graphs

Suppose that you need to show your audience how murders have increased over a three-year period in the United States. You could simply relate the statistics: 20,680 murders in 1988 increased to 24,710 in 1991.[2] The audience might hear you, but they would also soon forget the information. Another way to present the information is by constructing a graph to display the data visually. Graphs are helpful in explaining trends, showing comparisons, or indicating portions of a whole. We consider here three basic types of graphs which can reinforce information in a speech: the bar graph, the line graph, and the pie graph.

Bar Graph. A bar graph is helpful when you want to compare and contrast several causes or categories, such as the major causes of divorce or the main causes of heart disease. Bar graphs allow your audience to visualize similarities or differences among categories at a glance.

The bar graph in Figure 12–1 displays eight categories representing Americans' recreational spending habits. By looking briefly at the graph, listeners will learn that in 1990, Americans spent significantly more money on video, audio, and computer products than on other forms of recreation.

A bar graph like this is relatively easy to construct. You can use black on white, or highlight specific categories with color. Your bar graph must be clear and understandable so that listeners realize how it supports your point.

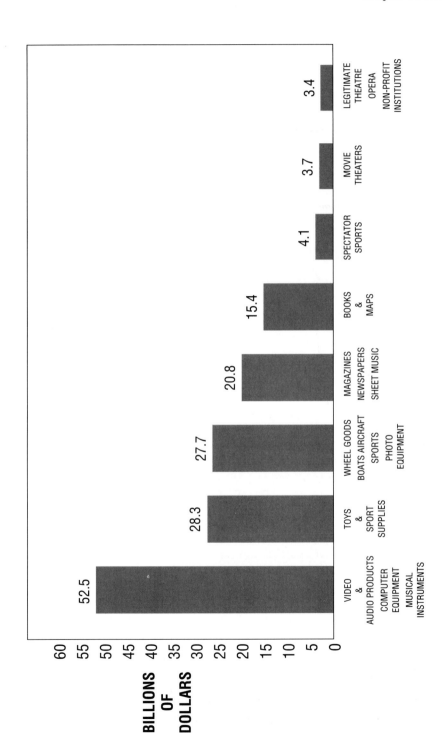

FIGURE 12.1

PERSONAL EXPENDITURES FOR RECREATION IN 1990

Source: Statistical Abstracts, 1992

FIGURE 12.2

U.S. Bureau of the Census

Interest Rates: 1970 to 1991

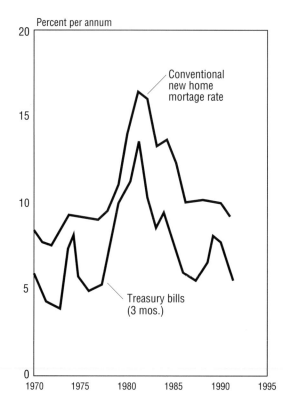

Line Graph. The line graph displays upward or downward trends over a period of time. Speakers use these graphs to show an increase or decrease in topics such as crime, disease, teenage suicide, income, inflation, or interest rates.

The line graph in Figure 12–2 indicates the rise and fall of interest rates over a twenty–year period. The audience can easily see that interest rates rose abruptly in the latter 1970s and early '80s, and declined steadily during the remainder of the decade. Notice that brief explanatory notes identify each line graph clearly.

Pie Graph. The pie graph displays portions of a whole sum. Pie graphs are helpful to speakers who want to show percentages. Where our tax money goes, how individuals spend their income, or the racial make-up of the U.S. population are among the many subjects that lend themselves to pie graphs.

A speaker used the pie graph in Figure 12–3 to display the breakdown of movie ratings since 1968. The audience could easily see that the largest number of films—47.8 percent—received "R" ratings, followed by "PG" films, which received 33.4 percent.

How the Movies Rate

Since 1968, the Classification and Rating Administration has rated 8,460 feature films. A breakdown by rating:

FIGURE 12.3

Reprinted by permission of *The Wall Street Journal*, © 1988 Dow Jones & Company, Inc. All rights reserved worldwide.

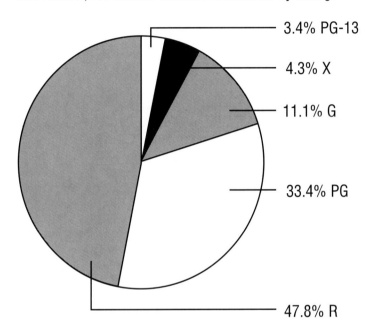

3.4% PG-13

4.3% X

11.1% G

33.4% PG

47.8% R

Developing Graphs. Before you construct any of these graphs, make sure you clearly understand the information and the statistics in order to report the data accurately. The *percentage* of crimes, for instance, is a far different concept from the *number* of crimes. Know what your data is saying in order to choose a graph appropriate for displaying the information.

When you understand the data, construct graphs that are simple and easy to read. Don't make the charts busy by drawing too many lines or numbers that can confuse listeners. Use color to emphasize different categories and bold lettering to convey meaning. Label the graph with direct and uncomplicated wording. Remember that the purpose of a graph is to help the audience understand concepts quickly.

Illustrations, Photographs, and Pictures

Imagine a speaker trying to explain how to use a computer keyboard without a diagram, or attempting to describe the Statue of Liberty without a picture. Without visual aids, the audience would not understand the impact of the speaker's message. Topics like these require communication on visual as well as verbal channels of communication. Drawings, photographs, and pictures enable listeners to visually complete their understanding of events and procedures.

Illustrations can be used to explain complicated topics such as the AIDS virus, or to portray elementary procedures like the basic tennis serve. Figure 12–4 describes in a simple diagram how the AIDS virus attacks the T cells of the body's immune system. Figure 12–5 points out how one student identified facial bones with a simple crosshatching system keyed to an index. And in Figure 12–6, a speaker used very elementary sketches to demonstrate the seven basic body positions in the tennis serve.

You don't have to be an artist to draw effective illustrations like these. The principal ingredient that contributed to each drawing was not talent, but time. Be willing to spend the hours necessary to create similar visuals that are neat, simple, and clear.

Photographs and pictures also provide listeners with vivid images. A speaker who describes starvation can generate more sympathetic feedback by

FIGURE 12.4

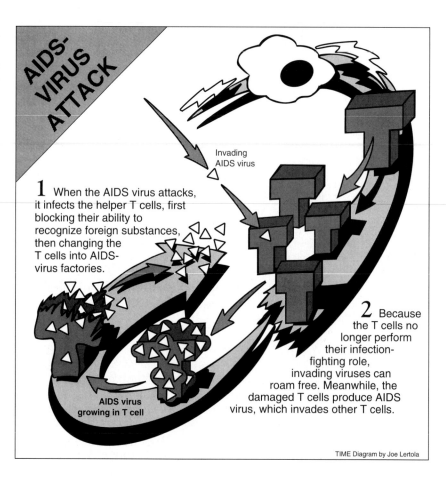

AIDS-VIRUS ATTACK

Invading AIDS virus

1 When the AIDS virus attacks, it infects the helper T cells, first blocking their ability to recognize foreign substances, then changing the T cells into AIDS-virus factories.

2 Because the T cells no longer perform their infection-fighting role, invading viruses can roam free. Meanwhile, the damaged T cells produce AIDS virus, which invades other T cells.

AIDS virus growing in T cell

TIME Diagram by Joe Lertola

FIGURE 12.5

Used by permission of Michelle Collins.

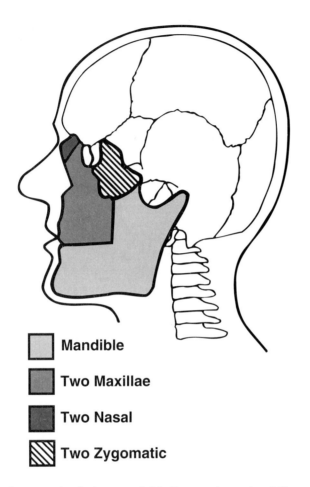

■ **Mandible**

■ **Two Maxillae**

■ **Two Nasal**

▨ **Two Zygomatic**

showing a photograph of a hungry child. One student who delivered a speech about sex in advertising displayed several magazine ads that used strong sexual images to sell products. And a student who described several types of drive-in businesses showed the audience a photograph (reproduced on page 257) of a drive-in funeral home.

Using Pictures. While pictures and photographs promote curiosity and interest, they must be large enough for the audience to see. Wallet-size pictures or tiny magazine photographs will not support a speech unless you make some adjustments. You can have the visuals professionally enlarged, which is often expensive, or you could have them photographed and made into slides. If an opaque projector is available, you can use the original picture or photograph with no additional expense. Be willing to take the trouble to communicate these important visuals so that all members of your audience can view them easily.

FIGURE 12.6

Illustration by George Goebel.

Posters and Chalkboards

Posters and chalkboards are also useful tools to help you convey ideas. Posters can support the steps of a process, reinforce main headings of a speech, or explain unfamiliar concepts. The poster in Figure 12–7 identifies three symbols used in weather forecasting. This visual is simple yet eye-catching

DURING AN INFORMA-
TIVE SPEECH ABOUT
DRIVE-IN BUSINESSES, A
STUDENT USED THIS
PHOTOGRAPH OF A "CON-
VENIENCE" FUNERAL
HOME TO STIMULATE
INTEREST AND CURIOSITY
AMONG LISTENERS.

Photo by Bruce Dale © 1981
National Geographic Society

Weather Symbols

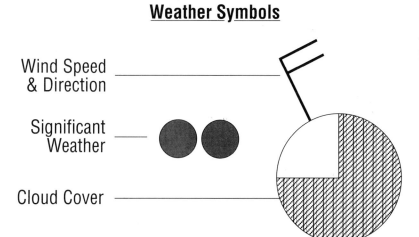

Wind Speed
& Direction

Significant
Weather

Cloud Cover

FIGURE 12.7

Used by permission of Michael
E. Gerber.

because the speaker used different colors to coordinate symbols with the appropriate explanations.

Unlike prepared posters, the chalkboard provides you with a great deal of flexibility as you are speaking. You can quickly write down unfamiliar terms, list the principal steps to a process, or draw a simple explanatory sketch.

Using Posters and Chalkboards.   If you decide to use posters, prepare them carefully. Lettering should be neat, large, and bold for easy reading. If you present the speech in a room that is 25 to 30 feet long, it is a good idea to use letters on your poster that are at least one inch high.[3] You also need to leave plenty of space next to words and between lines of print so that listeners can see the entire poster in a glance. Know where you are going to place your posters—taped to an easel, tacked to a bulletin board, held by a volunteer—so they will be easy to use during the presentation.

Even though you can be more spontaneous with a chalkboard, you still need to know how to employ it effectively. We've all suffered through the class where the teacher scrawls numerous concepts on the board with one hand, and erases everything with the other asking, "Did you all get that?" Avoid this problem by practicing with a chalkboard. Don't scribble down random ideas; write phrases neatly. If you need to draw a diagram, make sure it is clear and precise. Take the necessary time to plan your visual aids by placing information on the board *before* you speak, or writing ideas carefully *while* you are speaking. And allow the audience time to absorb the material before you erase it.

We've described the chalkboard in case you need it for brief or incidental use in a speech. We don't recommend, however, that you use it in a presentation such as a demonstration or a descriptive speech which is primarily dependent upon visual aids. Visual aids in these speeches require a great deal of time to plan effectively. Don't use the chalkboard as a shortcut for preparation; be willing to spend the time needed to create worthwhile visual aids.

Mechanical Media

The term *mechanical media* refers to any electrical devices which can be used as audiovisual aids. We'll consider two categories of media: projection equipment and recording equipment.

Projection Equipment.   The *opaque projector* can display a small drawing, photograph, or a picture from a book onto a large screen. This device usually has a built-in "arrow" you can employ as a pointer to refer to portions of the visual aid. But the opaque projector is large and somewhat bulky, and we advise that it not be used unless no other device is available for enlarging images.

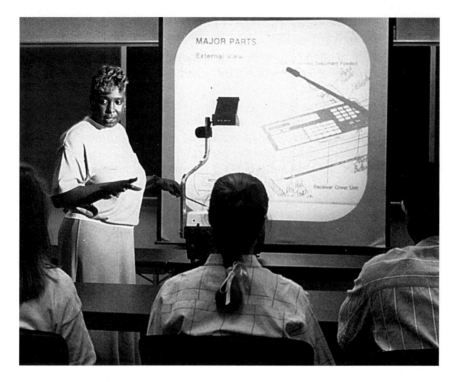

A SPEAKER WHO UNDER-
STANDS HOW TO USE A
VISUAL AID EFFECTIVELY
CAN INCREASE THE ABIL-
ITY OF LISTENERS TO
REMEMBER INFORMATION.

© Hal Rummel Photography

An *overhead projector* is useful if your speech requires you to add information to the visual aid as you speak. One speaker used the overhead to demonstrate how to fill out a tax form. The overhead allowed the speaker to add and subtract numbers to show listeners the steps involved in tax preparation. Another speaker used a series of interesting "overlays" to demonstrate the progressive stages of a corneal transplant. When you use the overhead, remember that you will need to transfer all of your information to acetate transparencies. Before the speech, it is a good idea to inspect the overhead and practice with the transparencies to be sure that everything is in working order.

If you need to display information from a computer monitor onto a larger surface such as a projection screen, you can use a device known as a *liquid crystal display* unit (LCD). The LCD is connected to a computer and then placed on an overhead projector, allowing an audience to see an enlarged version of the computer screen. The LCD is an excellent tool for projecting computer graphics, labels, procedures, or any type of computer program. If you use an LCD, be sure to check with a media specialist for instructions before using this device in your speech.

The *slide projector* can support a presentation if you use it with consideration for your audience. One speaker employed a slide projector to demonstrate how to bake chocolate-chip cookies. The student spent a great deal of time preparing and photographing the various stages of the process from mixing and baking to the finished product. The speech was interesting, well organized, and kept to the five-minute time limit. The speaker had to be certain that she allowed enough time to photograph the process and to develop the film to adequately prepare in time for the scheduled speech.

There are pitfalls to the use of slide projectors as well. Slides can be inserted upside down or backwards, bulbs can burn out easily, automatic focusing devices can malfunction, and changing mechanisms can jam. Problems can also occur if a room does not have a screen or proper surface for projecting slides, or the room can't be adequately darkened. Sometimes slide shows themselves are boring due to poor photography, needless repetition, or lengthy explanations. If you intend to use slides, rehearse your speech with the projector. Examine the equipment carefully, and test the projector in the room where the speech will be presented. Choose slides carefully, using enough to support your ideas, but eliminating those that are unnecessary.

Although film projectors aren't as popular as they once were due to VCRs, they can still be helpful in a speech. One student used a 1945 film clip to illustrate the destruction the atomic bomb caused to the cities of Hiroshima and Nagasaki. A brief segment like this can be effective; but you can't substitute a film for an entire speech. Like other visual aids, a film should only amplify portions of a presentation; you must develop the substance of the speech.

Recording Equipment. Tape or video-recording equipment can generate interest among audience members. One speaker, describing the history of jazz, used taped music as a background to her introduction. Another speaker showed a videotape of a diving experience to explain scuba gear.

Using Media. When you use recording equipment, your audio or video tape should be properly cued to each segment of your speech. If you want to play either kind of a tape while speaking, be certain you turn the sound down so that the audience can hear you comfortably. If the audio or video tape is the focus of the presentation, adjust the volume to reach all areas of the room or auditorium. A well chosen tape or video can add interest to a portion of your presentation, but media can also present problems. One speaker brought an extension cord that was too short to reach from the single outlet at the back of the classroom to the lectern at the front. Another student failed to inspect a VCR and discovered during his speech that he was not able to operate the complicated system supplied by the media department. A speaker who jammed a sluggish slide projector by banging it repeatedly finally gave up, saying, "Well, it worked at home, I can't understand why it doesn't now." One student confused an overhead with an opaque projector and placed a small photograph on the glass surface of the overhead, only to find that nothing happened on the screen.

Most of these disasters can be avoided by careful planning. Practice the speech with your visual aids. Know how the equipment operates. Examine the room for electrical outlets, projection screens, or tables for stationing equipment. If you use audio or video tape machinery, pay attention to set-up procedures. Check out batteries or extension cords. Allow extra time to carry in and to place heavy VCR equipment. Try to anticipate problems such as burned-out bulbs, unplugged cords, or inadequately darkened rooms.

Models and Objects

As a speaker, you can generate interest and stimulate curiosity with scale models, parts of objects, or the objects themselves.

Scale Models. Scale models reduce large objects or complicated procedures for easy visualization. College instructors use models of the eye or heart to help students understand vision or circulation. A student once used a model of a miniature volcano to explain how an actual eruption occurs.

Although scale models create interest, they must be large enough for all the audience to see. One speaker attempted to demonstrate a new trash-removal system that had been selected by several cities. Problems surfaced, however, when the speaker took out three tiny toy trucks from her handbag and pointed to the rear-end loader, the wheels, and the cab. Listeners leaned

THE DISPLAY OF OBJECTS CAN HELP SPEAKERS TO CONVEY IDEAS QUICKLY AND MOTIVATE AUDIENCES TO LISTEN.

© Robert Finken/
Picture Cube

forward and squinted in an effort to follow the process, but they soon gave up because of the inadequate visuals. Don't use scale models that are too small or too intricate; make sure that objects are large and practical enough for the audience to see and to comprehend easily.

Parts of Objects.   When it is impractical to bring the actual object, you can use a sample or a cross-section. A student demonstrated how to refinish furniture by displaying several pieces of wood in various stages of completion. Another student used a small cross-section of a studded wall to inform listeners how to wire an electrical outlet. Another speaker used pieces of shrubbery and small fir branches to explain how to do professional landscaping. Since it was not possible to bring in a china cabinet, half a house, or a nursery, each speaker sensibly chose to use *parts* of the object that could be managed easily in a classroom.

Actual Objects.   When listeners see a life-size visual aid, they are quickly motivated to listen. One student explained the process involved in decorating a wedding cake. Towards the end of the speech, she revealed a perfect three-tiered cake complete with a miniature bride and groom on top. The cake was an aromatic visual, appealing to the sense of smell as well as sight. A skydiver showed listeners his parachute, to demonstrate how to fold it before a jump. An antique gun collector brought out several muskets in explaining how American colonists used these firearms during the Revolutionary War.

Each of these speeches was interesting. But the life-size visual aids required a great deal of planning. The fragile wedding cake had to be transported to the classroom. The skydiver had to ask listeners to sit in a large semicircle to provide enough space to fold his parachute. The collector had to use a special gun rack to display the large muskets effectively.

If you want to use life-size objects, realize that they will take some added effort to the standard organization of a speech. Don't exhaust your energies in the visual aids alone; research, structure, and delivery remain the focal point of a public speech.

Yourself

Your own body movements, gestures, and actions can serve as visual aids in a speech. Imagine how body movements could simulate aerobics or weight-lifting, and how gestures could illustrate sign language or skin care. One student demonstrated how actors apply theatrical makeup to enhance their appearance under intense stage lights. The speaker's face and hands were the visual aids. He came prepared with a small mirror, which allowed him to put on layers of makeup while he explained the steps to the process.

While gestures and movements may seem easier to convey than other visuals, they require preparation. If you are demonstrating a detailed process, such as a golf swing or a karate move, your gestures and movements need to be precise and well defined. These actions should communicate so well that audience members could repeat them if necessary. Avoid sloppy gestures or vague actions; they lack clarity and will only create confusion. Run through the speech several times with the movements you intend to use. Refine and improve these actions until you feel confident that they will communicate effectively to your audience.

A volunteer from the audience can also be a visual aid. For example, administering the Heimlich maneuver, bandaging an arm, dancing an Irish jig, or throwing a curve ball are all procedures that require another person. When you work with an assistant, be sure that the volunteer knows exactly what to do. Rehearse the speech several times, so that both speaker and assistant are comfortable with planned actions and motions. Don't call on a volunteer from the audience unless you want a cold response. This uninformed assistant could be a detriment. Be sure that the volunteer really wants to help you, is adequately prepared, and will contribute to your speech.

USING COMPUTERS TO CONSTRUCT VISUALS

In today's business world, computers have become essential in the development of high quality visual aids. Workers using desktop publishing systems, for example, can make most decisions regarding the design and layout of visuals at computer terminals. They can employ a tool called a *mouse* to draw illustrations or write labels on computer monitors. If they are unable to create *original* designs, computer operators can work with lettering and graphics already provided in

COMPUTERS CAN BE USED TO CREATE MANY TYPES OF VISUAL AIDS FOR SPEECHES.

© John Nordell/Picture Cube

software programs. Employees can also develop graphs or charts, and make choices regarding the appropriate size of numbers, letters, and images. A student used a desktop publishing system to design the visual in Figure 12–8 for a speech demonstrating "The Proper Techniques for Giving Injections."

Computers are helpful in producing visuals because of their tremendous versatility. They can generate large posters through a process called "tiling" or reduce data for small brochures. They can copy photographs with the aid of special *scanning* equipment for use in reports or company handouts. Data for visual aids can be sent by a *modem* (a device connecting a computer to a telephone) to a facility for processing into slides or transparencies. Some computers can be used like slide projectors to convey data and images in timed sequence.

Although you may not have a computer with the capabilities of a desktop system, you can develop first-rate visual aids if you have access to a computer with a graphics package and a copy machine. You can design a graphic or chart on a computer monitor, print out the data, and then photocopy the material onto sheets of acetate instead of paper. The result will be high-quality transparencies which can be used on overhead projectors.[4]

FIGURE 12.8

Used by permission of Sherry Blye.

Angle of Insertion for Parenteral Injections

Five Guidelines for Using Audiovisual Aids

1. Talk to the Audience, Not to the Aid.

Some speakers become so involved with their visuals that they quickly forget to look at listeners. One classroom speaker turned her back on the audience and talked entirely to her poster for the majority of her speech. If you have practiced adequately, you shouldn't *need* to look at your aid. Remember that visual aids reinforce main ideas; they won't speak for themselves, and they are not substitutes for communication. Your job as a speaker is to present visual aids to your listeners and to help audience members understand them. Use a pointer, easel, table, or some other device that helps you to communicate your visuals effectively. Maintain frequent eye contact with listeners and, above all, talk to your audience—not to the aid.

2. Don't Pass Around Objects During the Speech.

A student who collected fossilized rocks described each specimen and then passed them to listeners during his presentation. The speaker had about 25 different examples, and listeners concentrated on looking at each rock and handing it to the next person. The problem, of course, was that the speaker lost listeners' attention because of the numerous interruptions. Develop other ways to convey visuals. The fossil collector, for instance, could have taken photographs of his examples and used a slide projector to describe the objects. Keep the attention of the audience focused on you, the speaker, and avoid circulating materials that could be distracting.

3. Be Sure That the Audience Can See Your Visual Aids.

Although it may seem obvious that visual aids need to be large enough for everyone to see, well-intentioned speakers sometimes take audience members for granted and neglect this important rule. Unprepared speakers often use photographs, objects, or scale models that are too small to read, posters with lettering too thin or tiny to read, or other visual aids that are obstructed from view. One speaker explaining how to make baklava, a Greek dessert, placed all the materials and ingredients directly in front of the mixing bowl, blocking the entire demonstration. The hard work that had gone into researching and structuring the speech was wasted because of the poorly executed visual aids.

In addition to these problems, listeners may not be able to see visuals because of the angles of the speaker's stand, the easel, TV monitor, or the room arrangement. If even one or two people in the audience can't see comfortably, the speaker should have done more careful planning. Depending on the setting, the speaker may need to readjust the visual aid, rearrange the seating area, or ask listeners to move forward. It is the speaker's responsibility to prepare visual aids and to plan an environment in which listeners can easily see everything a speaker wants to communicate.

4. Use Aids at the Right Psychological Moment.

If you have a lot of audiovisual aids, you may need to set them up before the speech so that you don't cause unnecessary disruptions during the presentation. But there will be times for which you can wait to reveal your aids—the right psychological moment, when the audience will be most interested.

For example, if you had three charts, you might decide to tape all of them onto the chalkboard prior to the speech. The problem with this arrangement, however, is that the audience will read the visuals before you want them to do so, and they may not listen to your speech because of the visual distraction. It would be more effective to reveal each poster as you talk about it. This method generates curiosity and helps to control the attention of your audience. Speakers can apply the same principle to a single poster by covering all of the information and then removing one portion at a time. Both techniques motivate your audience to listen.

It is important that you carefully think through how and when to use posters, charts, and objects during a speech. Talk about objects when you display them and, as a rule, don't reveal visual aids before you refer to them. Equally important, it is usually more effective to remove the aids from sight once you have finished referring to them. If you keep objects in front of listeners, you'll have a hard time directing their attention to other aids or back to your speech.

5. Be Clear at All Times.

Although audiovisual aids can support a presentation, they cannot speak for you. You will need to use clear explanations and precise descriptions to integrate them successfully into a speech. Explain the purpose of posters or charts: Point out relationships, show comparisons, or indicate contrasts in data. Draw conclusions from graphs or informational lists and relate audiovisuals to your ideas. Describe objects precisely, and reinforce physical actions or motions with verbal clarifications. When you employ photographs and pictures, integrate them smoothly by emphasizing significant areas or details. If you use a VCR or other mechanical media, set up the audiovisual segment with appropriate verbal descriptions. Provide brief explanations of slides and transparencies to amplify concepts and ideas. Your goal in talking about your audiovisual aids is to help listeners understand how they support your presentation.

SUMMARY

The term *audiovisual aid* refers to a device that may appeal to any of the senses: graphs (line, pie, and bar); drawings, photographs, and pictures; posters and chalkboards; mechanical media; physical objects; and you, the speaker. Posters are popular visual aids, and the chalkboard is effective if you use it for brief or incidental support of your speech. Mechanical media— such as overhead, LCD, opaque, slide, or film projectors, as well as audio and video tape-recording equipment—are useful in different situations. You can also include scale models, partial objects, or life-size objects in a speech. As a speaker, *you* are also a visual aid. You can incorporate your own body movements and actions into a speech, and you can ask someone to help you. The computer can help you to develop visuals quickly and efficiently.

Observe five general guidelines to use visual aids effectively:

1. Talk to the audience, not to the visual.
2. Don't pass around objects during the speech.
3. Be sure listeners can see your visual aids.
4. Use visual aids at the right psychological moment.
5. Be clear at all times.

EXERCISES

1. Research several newspapers and magazines such as *USA Today*, *The Wall Street Journal*, *Time*, *Newsweek*, and *National Geographic* to find clear and interesting visual aids for a speech. Present a two-minute speech in which you use the aid to explain an idea.

2. Choose a topic for a two-minute informative speech that can be supported with statistics. To get some ideas, consult sources such as *Information Please Almanac, The World Almanac,* or *Statistical Abstracts.* Plan and prepare a graph appropriate for displaying the data. Be sure to employ the visual aid effectively in your presentation.
3. Prepare a five- to seven-minute demonstration speech (see Chapter 16) using any of the audiovisual aids described in this chapter. Follow the suggestions we've provided for preparing and handling your visual aids.

NOTES

[1] Charles R. Petrie, Jr., "Informative Speaking: A Summary and Bibliography of Related Research," *Speech Monographs* 30 (June 1963): 82.

[2] The statistics regarding the increase of murders were obtained from the *World Almanac and Book of Facts,* 1993 edition.

[3] Donna Kirkley, "Visuals Help Communicate," video tape, 1975.

[4] I thank Stuart M. Singer, professor of computer graphics and applied art & design at Catonsville Community College, who provided valuable information about the use of computers in developing visual aids.

Chapter Thirteen

CONSIDERING LANGUAGE

Chapter Outline

Key Terms

Alliteration
Amplification
Antithesis
Connotation
Denotation
Euphemism
Metaphor
Mnemonic phrase
Simile
Transition

© UPI Bettman Newsphotos

"Eloquence is the power to translate a truth
into language perfectly intelligible to the
person to whom you speak."
—RALPH WALDO EMERSON

*I*magine that one of the most famous speeches in American history began like this:

Eighty-seven years ago our ancestors came to this land to build a new country dedicated to liberty and equality. But at the present time, we are in the process of a conflict which will prove if this new country or any new country founded on such principles can live on.

This passage may sound simple and straightforward enough. But listen to the way it was actually written:

Fourscore and seven years ago, our fathers brought forth on this continent a new nation, conceived in liberty and dedicated to the proposition that all men are created equal. Now we are engaged in a great civil war, testing whether that nation, or any nation so conceived and so dedicated, can long endure.

Abraham Lincoln chose his words carefully and refrained from using commonplace language in his famous 1863 address at Gettysburg. He realized that the words "fourscore and seven years" were more effective than "eighty-seven years ago." He also recognized that a metaphor could be effective in communicating the nation's origins. Instead of an impersonal reference to the nation's "ancestors," Lincoln humanized the reference to "our fathers" and continued the metaphor with the words "brought forth, conceived, and dedicated." Lincoln conveyed the image that our fathers and mothers "brought forth" or "gave birth" to a child, thereby implying struggle, labor, pain, and hardship. The words "conceived in liberty" extended the metaphor and revealed the sanctity of the new nation's purpose and ideals.

Lincoln's speeches demonstrate the power of language. In your own speeches your language can remain plain and ordinary or elevate the mind and stimulate thought. In this chapter we consider language which conveys your ideas with clarity, concreteness, style, and appropriateness. We also include a brief discussion of how language can make ideas more meaningful and interrelated. Choose language carefully to refine the appearance of your speech

DEVELOPING CLARITY

One of the most important rules of language use is to *say what you mean.* Use precise words to create mental pictures for your listeners, and use clear terminology which your audience will understand. Speeches that include obscure terms and flowery words may sound impressive, but aren't effective if they don't communicate to the audience. Former Vice President Spiro Agnew referred to Nixon administration critics as "nattering nabobs of negativism," "an effete corps of impudent snobs," and "pusillanimous pussyfooters."[1] While his flamboyant, alliterative style attracted public attention for a while, audiences soon tired of searching through the dictionary to find out what he meant.

One renowned speaker who enjoys using a large vocabulary and the full range of rhetorical devices is conservative writer–editor William F. Buckley, founder of *National Review* magazine. He demonstrates these qualities in this excerpt from a speech to the Ethics and Public Policy Center in Washington, D.C.:

> There is much room left over for argument, even as there is room left over, under this roof, for divisions about the impermanent things. But I tender you, Dr. Lefever, and your distinguished board of directors, and associates, this challenge. Deliberate the means of saying it in our public philosophy, saying that however much respect we owe to those who hold other ideas than those that are central to Judaeo–Christian postulates, we mustn't confuse any respect for their preternatural dignity for the fruit of their reason. How at once to do both these things—to respect a difference of opinion without undertaking a respect for different opinions? It is a searing challenge, in a world sensitive to cultural condescension, a world inflamed by the notion that *one man, one vote* presupposes one culture, any culture; one philosophy, any philosophy; one God, any God.[2]

It is likely that most of Buckley's highly educated audience knew what he was talking about. But the average mass audience would need a dictionary and an interpreter. It is important to direct your words in such a way that they will reach the particular audience before you.

Contrast the Buckley speech with this example:

> Mr. Chief Justice, my dear friends, my fellow Americans. The oath that I have taken is the same oath that was taken by George Washington and by every president under the Constitution. But I assume the presidency under extreme circumstances never before experienced by Americans. This is an hour of history that troubles our minds and hurts our hearts.
>
> Therefore, I feel it is my first duty to make an unprecedented compact with my countrymen. Not an inaugural address, not a fireside chat, not a campaign speech, just a little straight talk among friends. And I intend it to be the first of many.
>
> I am acutely aware that you have not elected me as your president by your ballots. So I ask you to confirm me as your president with your prayers. And I hope that such prayers will also be the first of many.

When Gerald Ford assumed the presidency on August 9, 1974, he took the oath of office under most difficult circumstances. For many months President Nixon and the Congress had been engaged in a constitutional crisis because of the Watergate scandal. When the House Judiciary Committee voted articles of impeachment, President Nixon resigned, and Gerald Ford, his appointed vice-president, was sworn in as the 38th president of the United States.

President Ford used simple language to express his ideas. He touched the hurt feelings within Americans, acknowledged his appointment to high office, and appealed for the goodwill and prayers of his fellow citizens.

Ford correctly realized it would be inappropriate to deliver an eloquent address filled with high-sounding phrases. He knew that, after Watergate, Americans wanted to hear the truth conveyed in a "little straight talk among friends." The introduction and the speech indicate that the president analyzed his audience accurately and used language effectively.

Avoiding Euphemisms

Sometimes people avoid saying what they really mean by employing inoffensive terms or phrases, called *euphemisms*. We tend to think that these veiled terms and phrases soften the blow of the underlying meaning. But often euphemisms are so vague that the essence is lost. Look at the following euphemistic words, phrases, or sentences used in a variety of occupational and social situations, and then read the "translation."

The following euphemism…	really means…
The government was disseminating disinformation.	The government was spreading deceit and propaganda.
I misspoke.	I lied.
She has a great personality.	She's ugly.
He's intelligent.	He looks like a nerd.
The Art Index can be found in Library, Media, and Telecourse Services.	The Art Index is in the library.
I'm going to the Physical Development Center.	I'm going to the gym.
She experienced a cerebral infarction.	She had a blood clot in the brain.
I need to consult the custodial engineer.	I'll get the janitor.
Your child needs help learning to use his leadership abilities more democratically.	Your kid is a bully.
Let me help you select a fitting memorial for the beloved.	Do you want to pick out a tombstone?[3]

Vague language seems ridiculous when matched with the intended meaning. While many of these examples may seem humorous, they are realistic.

Language is degraded and misused when people don't say what they mean. While bureaucratese and nonsense will never disappear, public speakers should be careful in their choice of generalized expressions. Eloquence doesn't mean using elaborate words and obscure phrases; it is more often composed of simple and direct language.

Read these excerpts from a speech delivered by Lieutenant Commander Drew Brown, an attack pilot with the U.S. Navy. Commander Brown visits inner-city schools plagued with drugs and gang violence. He represents a role model to young black teenagers who must stand up to the daily pressures of their surroundings. In this emotional presentation to students in a Los Angeles high school patrolled by police, Brown made his points emphatically:

> Michael Jackson goes around here saying he's bad. Mike Tyson thinks he's bad. You've got these gangs called the Bloods and the Crips and they think they're bad. They ain't bad—I'm bad. I'm bad because I can fly five hundred fifty miles an hour fifty feet from the ground and I can carry twenty-eight five-hundred-pound bombs under my wings. I have the expertise, the know-how, and the technology not to just take out this school, but to take out the whole neighborhood. But the point I'm trying to make is, you know what makes me bad? I'm bad because I have a college education! . . .
>
> You want to get high? You go to med school after college. You learn how to be a doctor, you save somebody's life. You watch the gleam in their eyes as they hand you a check for forty-eight thousand dollars when you can go and buy your big Mercedes that nobody can take from you—and you are toasted! . . .
>
> There is no black and white. But the bottom line is, black and white is in your mind, so if you blame your color on somebody else's color or somebody else's origin on your success or your failures, you are a loser![4]

Brown did not hide behind obscure language. His point was loud and clear: Don't give in to your surroundings—get an education. The audience might not have listened to the speaker had he used imprecise words or complicated sentence patterns. Brown was successful because he understood the kind of direct language and clear examples that would communicate his message to his teenage audience.

Your speaking will be far more successful if your words and phrases convey your feelings and objectives clearly. You will be effective if you analyze your audience well enough to understand the kind of clear language that will motivate them to listen.

USING CONCRETE LANGUAGE

When you use language, it's also important to be concrete. If you've ever had a friend tell you to "bring me the things when we get together tomorrow," you were probably puzzled if your friend didn't tell you what he or she meant by "things." Speakers who use vague language sound as if their vocabulary consists of no more than a few hundred words. Look at the wording used in the following demonstration speech:

> Okay. The first thing you want to do is to find out how much of this stuff you need. You measure the wall longways, and then this way, and then you come up with how much paper you need. Go behind the door or somewhere else where you can't see if you mess up. Take this baby here, and measure twenty inches from the edge like so. Then just mark a line up and down. With the same gizmo, go from the bottom to the top of the wall and add four inches onto everything so you can adjust it.

If you read between the lines, you may have understood that the speaker was demonstrating how to paper a wall. It was the vague language—*stuff, longways, this baby, like so, gizmo*—that made the demonstration sloppy and ambiguous. The speaker needed concrete words to describe materials and actions. Now read the more precise wording of the process:

> You need to know how much paper you need. It's very simple. You measure the height of the wall by the length of the wall, and you multiply them together and that gives the square footage. Do this on all four walls, add this together, and divide by sixty. That's the number of double rolls that you'll need. If this is your first job, I'd suggest that you get prepasted paper.
> Start with an inconspicuous corner, such as behind the door. With a metal ruler, measure twenty inches from the corner. The paper is twenty and one half inches. With the extra half inch, you will paper around the corner. Then take a pencil and a level, and at the twenty inch mark, draw a vertical line on the wall. Take the same metal ruler, measure from the floor to the ceiling, and add four inches. The extra inches give you two inches at the top and two inches at the bottom to allow for adjustment of the pattern.[5]

Denotation and Connotation

Knowing the difference between denotation and connotation can help to make your language more concrete and vivid. *Denotative* meanings are the dictionary definitions of words, while *connotative* meanings are their more personal and subjective meanings. For instance, a speaker who wanted to present an objective informational report about a proposed handgun bill might want to use words that generate denotative meanings within audience members:

City surveys in 1986 and 1987 revealed that from seventeen to twenty-five percent of all guns confiscated by our police departments were small handguns. The proposed handgun law prohibits the manufacture and sale of these weapons.

In this example, words such as *small handguns, prohibits, manufacture, sale,* and *weapons* are general terms which can generate denotative meanings. It is possible of course, that depending on the type of audience, the statistics could stimulate strong feelings.

But suppose this speaker strongly opposed the unregulated sale of handguns and wanted to persuade listeners to support the same handgun law.

Surveys done in 1986 and 1987 reveal that from seventeen to twenty-five percent of all guns confiscated by our city police department were Saturday-night specials. These sinister little weapons are cheap, dangerously inaccurate, and easy to hide. Many thugs prefer these badly made guns because they can be concealed in the palm of the hand like a straight-edge razor. As a matter of fact, one mini-derringer is no longer than four inches and fits inside a carrying case that looks like the electronic paging beepers which people carry on their belts.[6]

Words such as *sinister, Saturday-night specials,* and *thugs* evoke strong subjective meanings within listeners. The speaker can then suggest that members of the audience who feel strongly about the issue can support the law prohibiting the manufacture and sale of handguns.

Obviously the effect of these connotative meanings depends upon the audience. The second passage above could be very effective in some audiences but could backfire in other groups. As in any speech setting, you must analyze your audience well enough to know the type of language that will best evoke your desired response.

Here are a few examples of how a speaker can transform denotative or dictionary meaning into more subjective, connotative meaning.

Words from Their Most Denotative to Most Connotative Meanings

tall building	*steel skyscraper*	**towering deathtrap**
runner	*fleet-footed racer*	**Olympic-class sprinter**
dog	*puppy*	**adorable furball**
homeless woman	*bag lady*	**pitiful pauper**

As you move from left to right, the meanings become more connotative and subjective. If you want listeners to respond to your speech with strong mental images, use connotative words which have the capacity of stimulating feelings. Using specific names and images also has the same effect: For *tall building,* say *Sears Tower;* for *fruit,* say *luscious green grapes.*

BUILDING A UNIQUE STYLE

Style refers to the distinctive manner in which a speaker uses language to convey ideas and feelings. A speaker develops style with unique phrases, memorable lines, and technical devices designed to make language colorful, forceful, and dramatic. You can build an expressive style by including figures of speech such as *similes* and *metaphors*, and devices such as *alliteration, amplification, antithesis, repetition,* and *mnemonic phrases.*

Similes

A *simile* is a figure of speech in which the words *like* or *as* are used to show comparison. Here are some examples:

> Our current tax system is like an old inner tube that is covered with patches. We must replace it with a new, fair, simple tax system.[7]
>
> —H. Ross Perot

> Thank you very much. Inviting a physician to talk about the United States Constitution is a little like inviting James Madison to do an appendectomy. However, only one of us is going to be guilty of malpractice tonight.[8]
>
> —Harvey Sloame

> The fat cells are in your body just waiting, like Mr. Pac Man, to start eating. . .[9]
>
> —Vickie Chester

> As for annexing the island, I have about the same desire as a gorged boa constrictor might have to swallow a porcupine wrong–end–to.[10]
>
> —Theodore Roosevelt

These speakers used similes to make comparisons that were colorful, vivid, and interesting.

Metaphors

In the introduction to this chapter, we identified the "birth" metaphor that Abraham Lincoln employed in his Gettysburg Address. Like a simile, a *metaphor* is a comparison, but without the use of the words *like* or *as.* Here are some other examples:

> In order for any type of plant to grow, it must first have a healthy root system. But then it must be continually maintained in water to blossom. The same the-

ory of growth holds true for our major cities today. In order for them to grow, they too, need healthy root systems, and these roots lie in their downtown districts.[11]

—EDWARD L. BOKMAN

You remember the story of Chicken Little. She ran around the barnyard proclaiming that the sky was falling, and for a while she had all the other animals in a state of alarm.

Today, we have the Chicken Little theory of economics. This time it isn't the sky that's falling. Rather, America's middle class is disappearing; vanishing before our very eyes. And, guess whose fault it is? Yours, and everyone else engaged in a service business. Imagine that. You are performing magic tricks with the economy and don't even know it.[12]

—PAUL LAXALT

Epilepsy is a thunderstorm in the brain.[13]

—BRAD PIERN

The Student Government Organization is the sun, and the clubs, organizations, and committees are the planets which revolve around it.[14]

—BONNIE J. MCGREW

Metaphors can add life to the language of your speech. Don't be afraid to experiment with comparisons, but be certain that the comparison you make is sensible and consistent. Avoid mixed metaphors which shift comparisons midway through a presentation. A speaker who says "The ship of state is on the five-yard line, ready to go in for the touchdown" ought to stick with either the nautical theme or the football comparison.

Alliteration

Alliteration refers to the repetition of the same sounds to emphasize ideas in a speech. We've already referred to former vice president Agnew's alliterative "nattering nabobs of negativism." Some speakers have the ability to use this device with great effect.

Today when we *debated, differed, deliberated, agreed to agree, agreed to disagree,* when we had the good judgment to argue our case and then not self-destruct. . .[15]

—JESSE JACKSON

We are here, not only to *keep cool with Coolidge,* but to do honor to Alexander Hamilton.[16]

—WILL ROGERS

Provided that every effort is made, that nothing is kept back, that the whole *man power, brain power, virility, valor and civic virtue* of the English-speaking world. . . is bent unremittingly to the *simple but supreme* task. . .[17]

—Winston Churchill

A firm fruit is a friendly fruit.[18]

—Carol Denise Manis

Alliteration is a creative way to develop a vivid style but it is wise to use it sparingly.

Amplification

A speaker who employs *amplification* arranges words or phrases in order of importance to emphasize an opening or closing statement. For example:

I am in earnest—I will not equivocate—I will not excuse—I will not retreat a single inch—and *I will be heard.*[19]

—William Lloyd Garrison

We shall not flag nor fail. We shall go on to the end. We shall fight in France, we shall fight on the seas and oceans; we shall fight with growing confidence and growing strength in the air. We shall defend our island whatever the cost may be; we shall fight on the beaches, we shall fight on the landing grounds, we shall fight in the fields and in the streets, we shall fight in the hills; we shall never surrender.[20]

—Winston Churchill

In the first example, abolitionist editor William Lloyd Garrison used an ascending order of ideas to emphasize the final, most important line of his anti-slavery message: "I will be heard."

Winston Churchill also used amplification (as well as alliteration) in a speech defending the British withdrawal from Dunkirk in World War II. Even though British troops had suffered a defeat by the Nazis, Churchill wanted to rally the nation by repeating ideas which emphasized British determination "to not flag nor fail" and ending with the strong, emotional phrase, "We shall never surrender."

Antithesis

When using *antithesis*, a speaker combines contrasting ideas or qualities to convey a concept. Two examples are:

The race of man, while sheep in credulity, are wolves for conformity.[21]
—CARL VAN DOREN

Not often in the story of mankind does a man arrive on earth who is both steel and velvet, who is as hard as rock and soft as drifting fog, who holds in his heart and mind the paradox of terrible storm and peace unspeakable and perfect.[21]
—CARL SANDBURG

Carl Van Doren effectively combined opposite metaphors to describe the gullibility and like-mindedness of human beings. Carl Sandburg, speaking to Congress on the one hundred fiftieth anniversary of Abraham Lincoln's birthday, used contrasting metaphors as well as similes to characterize the paradoxes of our sixteenth president.

Repetition

Repetition of words and phrases is an effective way to emphasize key ideas, to increase interest, and to convey vivid images. Speakers throughout history have employed this colorful literary device to strengthen emotion and to summon courage. Here are excerpts from two speeches of the Reverend Martin Luther King, Jr., and President Franklin D. Roosevelt. Both employ repetition to intensify the feelings of their listeners.

Let freedom ring from the snowcapped Rockies of Colorado! Let freedom ring from the curvaceous slopes of California! But not only that; let freedom ring from Stone Mountain of Georgia! Let freedom ring from Lookout Mountain of Tennessee! Let freedom ring from every hill and molehill of Mississippi. From every mountainside, let freedom ring.[22]
—MARTIN LUTHER KING, JR.

Last night Japanese forces attacked Hong Kong. Last night Japanese forces attacked Guam. Last night Japanese forces attacked the Philippine Islands. Last night the Japanese attacked Wake Island. And this morning the Japanese attacked Midway Island.[23]
—FRANKLIN D. ROOSEVELT

In his famous "I Have A Dream" speech, delivered at the Lincoln Memorial during the 1963 March on Washington, King repeated the words "Let freedom ring" from the song "My Country, 'Tis of Thee." King used this repetition at the conclusion of the speech to summarize his dream that every part of America serve the cause of liberty and equal justice.

Franklin D. Roosevelt used repetition to energize his audience to support a different cause. After the bombing of Pearl Harbor on December 7,

1941, the president asked members of Congress to declare war on the empire of Japan. The repeated instances of Japanese military aggression quickly made an overwhelming case for the declaration of war.

Mnemonic Phrases

Speakers often develop ear-catching *mnemonic phrases* that summarize main ideas and help people to remember significant themes. We tend to remember phrases like "I have a dream," or "All we have to fear is fear itself." Some of the greatest speeches in history contain phrases that summarized the speaker's philosophy.

If the British Commonwealth and Empire last for a thousand years, men will still say, "This was their finest hour."[24]
—WINSTON CHURCHILL

With malice toward none, with charity for all, with firmness in the right as God gives us to see the right.[25]
—ABRAHAM LINCOLN

I know not what course others may take; but as for me, give me liberty, or give me death![26]
—PATRICK HENRY

When this is done, I will go to the king, even though it is against the law. And if I perish, I perish.
—QUEEN ESTHER

Let us never negotiate out of fear. But let us never fear to negotiate.[27]
—JOHN F. KENNEDY

I have always been fond of the West African proverb: Speak softly and carry a big stick; you will go far.[28]
—THEODORE ROOSEVELT

Each of these mnemonic phrases is effective because it captures the essence of the speaker's intention. In your own presentations, think of creative phrases which sum up your ideas. Recognize that memorable lines, if used sparingly in a speech, can stimulate thought and heighten audience feeling about your point of view.

BEING "APPROPRIATE"

Speech students often ask, "What exactly is inappropriate language? Shouldn't that decision be left up to the individual?" Certainly each of us uses a different standard to define inappropriateness. But a speaker must make perceptive decisions about the language he or she uses in a public presentation. A few suggestions can help you to avoid words, terms, phrases, and expressions that listeners consider ineffective and improper.

Avoid Offensive Terms.

When James Watt was Secretary of the Interior during the first Reagan term, he told an audience that he had appointed a commission made up of "a black...a woman, two Jews and a cripple."[29] His remarks caused a controversy that eventually led to his resignation. Former Arizona governor Evan Mecham described some reactions of Japanese businessmen by saying that "their eyes got round."[30] He was removed from office by the Arizona state legislature because of alleged illegal business deals—but his controversial statements were certainly of no help. Jimmy "the Greek" Snyder, a noted TV sports odds-maker, stated on national television that blacks have "been bred" to be athletes superior to whites.[31] The CBS television network immediately severed his employment contract. And Marge Schott, the owner of the Cincinnati Reds baseball team, was banned from the game for a year because of slurs against minorities.[32]

These speakers all had one thing in common; they each employed language that significantly offended large groups of Americans. Whenever a speaker uses words that attack an individual's race, religion, sex, or national-

THE MOST EFFECTIVE SPEAKERS STRIVE TO MEET THEIR AUDIENCES ON SHARED GROUND. HERE, REP. BARNEY FRANK (D–MASS.) ADDRESSES A HOUSING MEETING WITH THE HELP OF A SIGN–LANGUAGE INTERPRETER.

© John Nordell/ Picture Cube

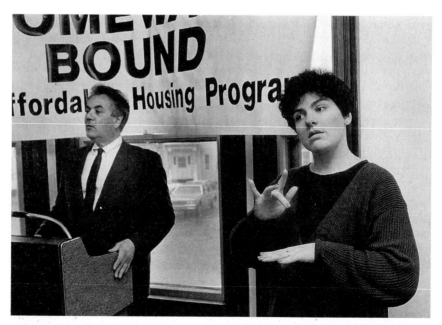

ity, the listener will react with hostility. As a speaker, you want to *win* listeners and *open* their minds to your ideas.

You should also avoid obscene words and phrases which can offend some listeners. During the latter part of the 1960s and early 1970s, many younger Americans discovered that they could gain public attention to their causes by shouting obscenities during rallies and protest demonstrations. But while demonstrators got attention, their language also helped to polarize listeners. Commentators often referred to "the generation gap" or the "age gap." In your own speeches, it is good to remember that you are being evaluated by your audience. If you utter four-letter words for their shock value, you will probably get many listeners to take notice, but you will also discover that many will be offended. Those who are insulted will judge you negatively and switch you off mentally. You may find your credibility damaged and reduced.

The guideline is to avoid language that offends your audience. Analyze your audience and respect their differences. Use positive language which wins them over to you, builds your credibility, and generates constructive feelings about you as a speaker.

Eliminate Irrelevant Language.

It's a good idea to avoid unnecessary verbiage or linguistic clutter. A speaker who constantly repeats words and phrases like "you know," "and so," and "well," or vocalized pauses like "um" creates external noise interfering with communication and frustrating the listener. President Ronald Reagan had the trademark habit of avoiding a silent pause by repeating the word "well" as he thought up responses to questions at news conferences. A student who had a problem with vocalized pauses discovered that several bored listeners devised ways to count the number of his "*um*'s."

It's also a good idea to avoid irrelevant details which are not important to the speech. In this example, a speaker attempts to explain the tools needed for professional painting but loses sight of the specific purpose:

> First, you set up a flat table for your materials where you want to do the painting. I set mine up in the family room. You know, my wife and children spend a lot of time there—they enjoy watching TV, playing games, or just reading. We find that the family room is a nice place to escape from it all. It's also a great place to have parties with friends.

This speech began as a demonstration of the steps involved in painting a room but soon deteriorated into a trivial description of "Life in the Family Room." Listeners will lose interest in presentations that get sidetracked.

Avoid Trite Expressions.

Our vocabulary frequently suffers from underuse due to peer pressure, lack of knowledge, or just plain laziness. Imagine how disruptive it would be for a speaker to constantly repeat slang phrases such as "it's bad," "real awesome," "outta sight," or "gag me with a spoon!" Audiences also become tired of hearing trite expressions such as "the moral of the story is," "to each his own," "the bottom line is," or "and now, in conclusion I'd like to say. . ."

We aren't suggesting that you *never* use slang in your presentations. The speech delivered by Lieutenant Commander Brown indicates that there are speaking situations where the use of slang can appeal to specific audiences and reinforce important ideas. But it's usually much more effective for a speaker to use inventive wording than to rely on cliches.

Eliminate Grammatical Errors.

Mistakes in grammar disturb listeners and tend to raise questions about a speaker's credibility. Imagine that after conducting a physical examination your doctor said, "Your X-rays don't show nothin'. Everything come out fine." Or suppose your pilot in a cross-country flight radioed to passengers that "I seen some turbulence up here." Your confidence in the doctor or your pilot just might deteriorate.

The same principle can be applied to your own speaking situations. If you go to a job interview and you claim to have a two-year or a four-year college degree, your prospective employer will expect you to communicate without major grammatical flaws. Your instructor will no doubt insist on the same standard in your speeches.

It is always possible to make a slip in noun–verb agreement as you move rapidly through a complicated speech in front of an audience. But it is important to avoid any consistent grammatical problems when you are delivering a speech. If you are weak in grammar, use the opportunity provided in your speech course to improve your skills. You may not be able to change all of your speaking difficulties in one semester, but you can reduce your grammatical mistakes by attending writing labs, taking a back-up course, or getting tutoring help.

You aren't expected to understand all the intricate details of the King's English, but you should know enough about language to be aware of the difference between good and bad grammar. A basic knowledge of a few grammatical principles will enable you to use English which will build credibility with your listeners.

Build Vocabulary Skills.

Do as much as you can to increase your vocabulary. Take the time to look up unfamiliar words in the dictionary. Good reference sources like *Roget's*

International Thesaurus or *The Random House Thesaurus* can help you to choose effective wording for your presentation. The more varied your vocabulary, the more interesting and colorful the speech will sound to your audience.

MAKING IDEAS MEANINGFUL AND INTERRELATED

Speakers can use language to create a sense of participation within an audience and to help listeners connect ideas smoothly. To achieve these objectives, you can employ personal pronouns and transitions.

Personal Pronouns

Listeners are more interested in a speech when they feel involved with the topic. An effective way to include the audience is to use personal pronouns like *you, your, us, our*. In the following example, notice how the speaker has excluded listeners:

> Not many people in this country can say that three generations ago their family was only American. Most people in this nation were originally from somewhere else. Whether it was Russia, France, Italy, or Ireland, immigrants came here seeking freedom—freedom of religion, freedom of speech, and freedom to contribute to this great country.

Many people and *immigrants* are vague and impersonal. The speaker does not allow listeners to feel any sense of involvement. Now read this altered example:

> How many of you can say that three generations back your family was "only American"? Almost all of our ancestors were originally from somewhere else. Whether from Russia, France, Italy, or Ireland, they originally came here seeking freedom—freedom of religion, freedom of speech, and freedom to contribute to this great country of ours.[33]

With some minor changes, the speaker has made the same passage much more personal. The introductory question addresses the audience directly—*you* and *your family*. Personal pronoun phrases such as *our ancestors*, and *country of ours* allow listeners to feel like participants. When it is appropriate in your speech, use these personal pronouns to relate to your audience. Avoid vague, third-person references such as *people, individuals*, or *they*. You want your listeners to feel they are a part of your topic whenever it is appropriate.

Transitions

Suppose you have ended the first of three main headings in the body of your speech. One way to end is by saying, "I've finished my first point. Now for point two." This external transition tells the audience they are about to hear your second main idea, but the line is abrupt and jarring. Improved language would enable ideas to flow more smoothly from one point to another. *Transitions* are connectives between major or minor ideas in a speech. External transitions connect main points while internal transitions join subordinate ideas. Here are some examples of external transitions:

Specific purpose: to inform the audience about circus clowns[34]

Thesis statement: "Clowning has a history, an educational process, and famous personalities."

Possible transitions to introduce Numeral I, "History of Circus Clowns":

1. Let me first tell you about circus clowns and their history.
2. Circus clowns have an interesting history.
3. I found out some really interesting aspects of clown history.

Possible transitions to introduce Numeral II, "College for Clowns":

1. Now that I've told you about clowns and their history, I want you to know that they also have their own college.
2. Circus clowns not only have a history: they also have a college.
3. While I found that clown history was interesting, I soon discovered that clown college was unimaginable.

Possible transitions to introduce Numeral III, "Well-known Clown Personalities":

1. Since I've told you about clown college, I'd like you to hear about a few well-known clown personalities.
2. But clowns are not complete without personality—and I'd like to talk about some of the most famous clown personalities.
3. After I discovered clown college, I came across some fascinating clown personalities.

Possible transitions to introduce the conclusion:

1. Now that you've heard about clown history, education, and famous clown personalities, I hope you will have a little more appreciation of this art the next time you see a circus clown.

2. In every part of the world, people of all ages have laughed at these interesting creatures called clowns.
3. I hope you've enjoyed some of the discoveries I've made about clowns.

Each external transition is a sentence that acts as a bridge to link the previous thought with the next main idea. Notice that a transition line after the
thesis helps to make a smooth connection between the introduction and
numeral I of the body. Similarly, an external transition after the last main
point of the body helps to bond the last point to the conclusion. External transitions flag main ideas and increase listener comprehension.[35] Remember
that members of your audience don't have copies of your manuscript or outline; they won't be able to distinguish major or minor points easily unless
you clearly indicate them.

External transitions are complete sentences that separate main points in
the body of the speech; internal transitions separate minor points under main
headings. Connectives such as *also, then, next* can tell listeners that a subheading has several items that are linked together. Here are a few examples
of internal transitions:

and	and so	in addition
then	finally	in addition to
next	first, second, third...	another
also	often	but

Be sure not to mix external and internal transitions. If you were to use *also,
and,* or *in addition* as your only connecting transition between two main points
in the body, you would confuse your audience, since they would not be easily
able to separate the major elements of the speech. Your presentation would
sound like one long numeral I, rather than a series of headings with subordinate points. If you use complete sentences as your external transitions between
main ideas, then one-word connectives will work effectively for internal transitions between supporting points.

SUMMARY

You communicate more successfully if your language is clear and direct,
rather than obscure or euphemistic. Concrete language is also more effective than ambiguity. If you want to evoke subjective feelings within listeners, use connotative rather than denotative language. A colorful and forceful
style can be developed by using figures of speech like similes, metaphors, and
devices such as alliteration, amplification, antithesis, repetition, and
mnemonic phrases.

The language of a speech should always be appropriate to the audience. Avoid offensive words and eliminate unnecessary language and extraneous verbal clutter. Avoid trite expressions and eliminate grammatical mistakes. Work to build a comprehensive vocabulary that enables your language to be more vivid.

A speech can be made more meaningful through the use of personal pronouns. Ideas can be linked together more effectively with the construction of external transitions to bridge main points, and the use of internal transitions to connect subordinate elements.

EXERCISES

1. Write an external transition sentence to separate each main point of the body in your speech. Be sure to include transitions between the introduction and numeral I, and between your final numeral and the conclusion.
2. Choose one of the role-playing situations listed below, and develop two skits with another student from your class. In the first skit, the individual playing the professional should communicate using the euphemistic jargon of the occupation. Then repeat the skit, this time communicating in language that everyone understands. Raise some questions with the class: Is there a place for euphemistic language? Are there times when euphemisms are unnecessary? When is it appropriate to use euphemisms?
   a. A doctor describing a surgical procedure that a patient must undergo.
   b. A funeral director describing the types of services offered to the family of the deceased.
   c. A lawyer explaining the steps involved in a legal proceeding (obtaining a divorce, drawing up a contract, writing a will).
   d. A fourth-grade teacher explaining to a parent that the child is a brat.
   e. A trucker explaining to another trucker over the CB radio that there is a problem on the road ahead.
   f. A weather forecaster explaining tomorrow's weather.
   g. An auto mechanic describing a problem with the car.
3. Prepare a one-minute presentation in which you describe an incident in neutral or "objective" language. Then describe the same incident in language that makes the same incident sound negative. Finally, use language to make the incident sound favorable. In each description use the same details, changing only your language. Were any presentations more denotative or connotative? Which presentation do you think would have been most persuasive to the audience? [36]

NOTES

[1] "Leaves from a Lurid Lexicon," *Newsweek*, September 28, 1970, p. 24.

[2] "Buckley's Remarks at Gala," *National Review*, December 31, 1986, p. 24.

[3] Terence P. Moran "Public Doublespeak: On Beholding and Becoming," in *Language Awareness*, 2nd ed., ed. Paul Eschholz, Alfred Rosa, and Virginia Clark (New York: St. Martin's Press, 1978), p. 54.

[4] ABC, "Incredible Sunday," October 30, 1988.

[5] Norma Ferris, "Papering a Wall," speech to demonstrate presented in speech class, Catonsville Community College, Catonsville, Maryland, 1987. Used by permission.

[6] The statistics and examples used in this passage were based on two articles entitled "The Gun Law: Maryland's High-Powered Issue," *The Sunday Sun* (Baltimore), October 30, 1988, p. A1.

[7] H. Ross Perot, Paid Political Broadcast, October 17, 1992.

[8] "Jefferson, Madison, and Franklin," *Vital Speeches*, May 1, 1988, p. 445.

[9] "Overcoming Obesity," speech to inform presented in speech class, Catonsville Community College, Catonsville, Maryland, 1987. Used by permission.

[10] Henry F. Pringle, *Theodore Roosevelt* (New York: Harcourt, Brace and World, 1956), p. 206.

[11] "The Proposed Football Stadium at Camden Yards," speech to convince presented in speech class, Carroll Community College, Westminster, Maryland, 1988. Used by permission.

[12] "Chicken Little is Wrong Again," *Vital Speeches*, October 1, 1987, p. 741.

[13] "Epilepsy," speech to inform presented in speech class, Carroll Community College, Westminster, Maryland, 1990. Used by permission.

[14] "The Student Government Organization," speech to inform presented in speech class, Carroll Community College, Westminster, Maryland, 1991. Used by permission.

[15] "Common Ground and Common Sense," *Vital Speeches*, August 15, 1988, p. 650. Emphasis added here.

[16] "Wealth and Education," in Lewis Copeland and Lawrence Lamm, eds. *The World's Great Speeches* (New York: Dover Publications, 1958), p. 730. Emphasis added.

[17] "Address Before United States Congress," Copeland and Lamm, *World's Great Speeches*, p. 452.

[18] "Cooking With Vegetables," speech to demonstrate presented in speech class, Carroll Community College, Westminster, Maryland, 1991. Used by permission.

[19] William Lloyd Garrison, quoted in Sol Chaneles and Jerome Snyder, *That Pestilent Cosmetic Rhetoric* (New York: Grossman, 1972), p. 98.

[20] "Dunkirk," Copeland and Lamm, *World's Great Speeches*, p. 439.

[21] Carl Van Doren and Carl Sandburg from Chaneles and Snyder, *Rhetoric*, p.114.

[22] Martin Luther King, Jr., "I Have A Dream," in Lester Thonssen, ed., *Representative American Speeches: 1963–64* (New York: H. W. Wilson, 1964), p. 48.

[23] "For a Declaration of War Against Japan," Copeland and Lamm, *World's Great Speeches*, p. 531.

[24] "Their Finest Hour," Copeland and Lamm, *World's Great Speeches*, p. 446.

[25] "Second Inaugural Address," Copeland and Lamm, *World's Great Speeches*, p. 317.

[26] "Give Me Liberty, or Give Me Death!" Copeland and Lamm, *World's Great Speeches*, p. 234.

[27] "Inaugural Address," Thonssen, *Representative American Speeches*, p. 38.

[28] Edmund Morris, *The Rise of Theodore Roosevelt* (New York: Coward, McCann and Geoghegan, Inc., 1979), p. 717.

[29] "James Watt's Last Gaffe?" in *Newsweek*, October 3, 1983, p. 45.

[30] "Inside the Wacky World of Evan Mecham," *U.S. News & World Report*, February 22, 1988, p. 29.

[31] "An Oddsmaker's Odd Views," *Sports Illustrated*, January 25, 1988, p. 7.

[32] See, for example, "Schott Visits Reds Camp Before Suspension Starts," *Baltimore Sun*, February 27, 1993, 5C.

[33] Evan Feinberg, "Making English the Official Language," persuasive speech presented in speech

class, Catonsville Community College, Catonsville, Maryland, 1988. Used by permission.

[34] Julie Balick, "Circus Clowns," informative speech presented in speech class, Catonsville Community College, Catonsville, Maryland, 1988. Used by permission.

[35] Charles R. Petrie, Jr., "Informative Speaking: A Summary and Bibliography of Related Research," *Speech Monographs* 30 (June, 1963): 81.

[36] This verbal exercise is adapted from a written exercise in Paul Escholz, Alfred Rosa, and Virginia Clark, eds., *Language Awareness*, 2nd ed. (New York: St. Martin's Press, 1978), p. 152.

READINGS

Eschholz, Paul; Rosa, Alfred; and Clark, Virginia, eds. *Language Awareness*, 2nd ed. New York: St. Martin's Press, 1978. This excellent book on language is a compilation of readings by a variety of experts in law, journalism, education, and business. The articles are interesting, and the editors list some helpful discussion questions and exercises at the end of each reading. Authors include Edwin Newman, H. L. Mencken, and S. I. Hayakawa.

Farb, Peter. *Word Play*. New York: Alfred A. Knopf, 1981. Enjoyable to read and includes numerous examples. A number of chapters are helpful: "Speech Situations," which describes speech communities; "The Speakable and the Unspeakable," a discussion of appropriateness, euphemisms, and connotative language; and "Man at the Mercy of Language," which presents general *semantics*, the science of word meanings.

Chapter Fourteen

DEVELOPING THE DELIVERY

Chapter Outline

Key Terms

Appearance
Articulation
Body movement
Clavicular breathing
Diaphragmatic breathing
Eye contact
Facial expression
Gesture
Inflection
Pause
Phrasing
Pitch
Pronunciation
Quality
Rate
Volume

© Dirk Halstead/
Gamma Liaison

"Even the most timid man can
deliver a bold speech."
—SENECA

Before facing each other in presidential debates, political candidates work feverishly to develop images that will project favorably to voters. They review briefing books on the principal campaign issues, and rehearse catchy one-liners describing the failures of their opponents. Candidates also hold mock debates with stand-ins to practice fielding questions and presenting rebuttal remarks. Each side worries about its candidate's appearance and delivery on camera. Campaign staffs argue about the color of the background, the height of the speaker's stand, and the intensity of lighting. Media consultants try to improve candidates' gestures or vocal delivery, and wardrobe specialists give advice on appropriate clothing. The candidates make every effort to create a positive, dignified presidential image to the public.

Politicians know that extensive preparation is necessary because of the impact of past presidential debates upon voters. In the 1960 Kennedy–Nixon debates, Richard Nixon's pale face with its "five o'clock shadow" contrasted poorly against John F. Kennedy's tanned, relaxed image. Kennedy's visual success in the debates helped to give him the edge in a very close election. In the only 1980 debate, Governor Reagan—who was older than his opponent, a tired-looking President Carter—appealed to voters by asking, "Are you any better off now than you were four years ago?" And when Senator Dan Quayle compared his age and experience to that of John F. Kennedy during the 1988 vice-presidential debates, Senator Lloyd Bentsen responded with the retort, "Senator, you're no Jack Kennedy." These debates indicate that a speaker's delivery and style can significantly influence an audience.

In this, the last chapter of Unit IV, we identify the skills you need for an effective speaking delivery. We discuss some of the important aspects of your vocal and visual delivery, and we include some brief suggestions to help you develop your delivery techniques.

DELIVERING THE SPEECH

Students often ask public speaking instructors, "Is delivery or content more important in a speech?" Our usual answer is, "Yes." The problem with this question is that it assumes delivery and content are somehow isolated and that a speech can successfully depend upon one or the other. An eloquent delivery is not helpful, however, if the message is disorganized or poorly researched. At the same time, well-researched and clear ideas can fail to communicate if the delivery is poor.

You need effective skills in both delivery and content to succeed in communicating your message. Martin Luther King's famous "I Have a Dream" speech would have been only moderately interesting had it been published in a book or magazine. It was the civil rights leader's ringing style of delivery that projected King's ideas forcefully to his audience.

There are two aspects of delivery—the vocal and the visual (or non-verbal). Imagine a speech that you hear over the radio. You listen to the speaker's increase and decrease in volume, quickening or slowing of the speaking rate, and emphasis on key words and phrases. Now picture a televised speech with no sound as the speaker gestures, smiles or frowns, and makes visual contact with the audience. The radio or the silent TV speech can have a degree of success, but unless the vocal and visual aspects of delivery are combined, meaning will not be fully projected over all the available channels of communication. For example, those who heard the Kennedy–Nixon debates on radio in 1960 thought Richard Nixon had been the most effective speaker. But a majority of those who watched the debates on television thought Kennedy was the clear winner. Vocal and visual delivery are equally important when you present a speech. If one channel is blocked, communication can be significantly altered.

PROPER BREATHING FOR VOCAL DELIVERY

You need a supply of air not only to survive, but also to produce the sound needed for an effective vocal delivery. It is the diaphragm that is primarily involved in inhalation. The diaphragm is a dome-shaped muscle attached to the base and sides of the lower ribs separating the abdomen from the chest. When you inhale, the diaphragm contracts and moves downward, while the ribs move upward and out, increasing the size of the chest cavity. At the same time, air flows into the lungs filling the vacuum. As you exhale, the diaphragm slowly begins to relax, and the abdominal muscles exert pressure upward to force air out of the lungs, through the trachea and into the larynx where the air vibrates the vocal folds producing sound.

If you gasp for air or raise your shoulders when you inhale, you are possibly using *clavicular breathing*, or respiration from the top of the lungs. Slouching or leaning over a lectern can interrupt the natural process of inhalation and contribute to improper breathing. Clavicular breathing causes unsteadiness in the air supply and creates tension in the neck and throat. If you place your hand over your abdomen and inhale, you should feel the stomach muscles move forward in *diaphragmatic breathing*. A good, steady breath from the diaphragm produces the constant supply of air needed to produce sound.[1] The following exercises can help you to breathe properly and to establish breath control.[2]

Exercise 1. Sit in a chair that is comfortable but firm and has good back support. Stretch your hands on your abdomen immediately below your ribs, with your thumbs pointing to the rear and fingers pointing forward. Sit erect but relaxed, with your feet firmly on the floor. Inhale slowly, then exhale. When you inhale, you should feel your stomach muscles push forward, and when you exhale, they should pull in. Now repeat this exercise, but this time take about five seconds to inhale. Then take ten seconds to exhale. If you run out of breath before ten seconds, try the exercise again and exhale much more slowly. Repeat this exercise several times.

Exercise 2. Stand up straight with both feet firmly on the floor. Inhale normally and then exhale on the sound *s*. Maintain the sound as evenly as possible for about ten seconds. Repeat the exercise and exhale on the sounds *sh*, *th*, and *f*.

VOCAL DELIVERY

We will examine the following elements of vocal delivery: volume, articulation, pitch, quality, rate, pronunciation, pausing, emphasis, and phrasing.[3]

Volume

Volume is the intensity, or loudness and softness of your voice. If you have ever been approached by a person who shouts a ten-minute sales pitch at you, or if you have ever strained to hear a speaker in a large auditorium, you are already aware of the importance of volume in speech delivery. Either of these situations is irritating, and listeners will block out a speaker who fails to adjust volume to meet the needs of a particular speech setting. If you present a speech in a gymnasium without a microphone, you'd better be prepared to project your voice so the individual on the last row can hear you comfortably. Conversely, you may need to speak more softly to a handful of people in a small conference room.

In speech classes, people rarely have the problem of projecting too much volume; more often, individuals aren't loud enough. It takes experience and training to develop vocal sensitivity. Experienced actors and actresses can project their voices, even in a whisper, without amplification in cavernous playhouses or in vast open-air amphitheatres. Unless there is a physical problem, most of us have the ability to develop good vocal projection. By doing some vocal exercises and practicing diaphragmatic breathing, you can control the intensity of your voice so that the audience can hear you comfortably.

Adjusting your volume can also be an effective way to emphasize significant portions of a speech. You can increase or lower your volume for dramatic emphasis when you convey startling information or emotional examples. Leo Buscaglia, an educator, author, and public speaker who tours the country lecturing on love and human emotions, told this story of a smiling girl "with kind eyeballs" who was a student in one of his huge lecture classes at the University of California:

> And about five weeks into the semester this beautiful young girl was not in her seat and when Monday Wednesday Friday Monday Wednesday Friday

came, I became curious and I went down and asked the people around her what had happened to her. And do you know that in something like six weeks of school, they didn't even know her name? . . . .And so I went to the Dean of Women and I asked about her. . . [and she said] "Oh Leo, I'm sorry, haven't I told you? This girl went to Pacific Palisades (which is an area where many of you know where sheer cliffs fall into the sea), and there were people there having a picnic on the grass and they saw her drive her car up and she left the ignition running and zombie-like, she walked across the grass and without a moment's hesitation, threw herself off onto the rocks below." She was twenty-two.[4]

When he used this example, Buscaglia increased his volume on the words "they didn't even know her name" to show anger and disgust. Then he contrasted that emotion by softening his voice almost to a whisper on the line "and threw herself onto the rocks below" to reinforce the tragedy and shock of the story. Volume can be an effective device to shade meaning.

Articulation

Another aspect of delivery is *articulation*, which refers to the clarity and enunciation of words, phrases, and sentences in a speech. Americans often exhibit sloppy enunciation; we frequently eliminate vowels and consonants, run words together, and mumble sentences. The unfortunate result often sounds like some kind of verbal jumble that not even fellow English-speaking citizens can easily understand. The following exchange could take place on almost any college campus in the country. See if you can decipher some of the garbled words and phrases.

Man:	Haryadoin?
Woman:	Fine. Whatchurnam?
Man:	Laryowns—urz?
Woman:	Molyilsn. Whouwerkfor?
Man:	Blakndeckr. Wheryagodaskool?
Woman:	Eescampus.
Man:	O. Imonweseye. Wheryagoinow?
Woman:	I dunno.
Man:	Yasingl?
Woman:	Yeh.
Man:	Yawannagodamyplas?

Although the example may be humorous, it makes a serious point. In order to communicate effectively, a speaker must enunciate clearly. The audience must be able to understand words and phrases easily without having to guess at the meaning. When you speak, you should make the effort to open your mouth and use clear articulation. Remember that words have vowels and consonants, and some words must be distinctly separated in order to be understood. Try to pronounce each of the following words containing difficult sound combinations: [5]

fifths	grasped	asks
frisked	answer	fists
sixths	oaths	months
thousands	depths	twelfths
widths	lengths	hundredths

Many problems of articulation are simply a result of bad habits caused by verbal laziness. There are some serious problems, however, such as stuttering, cleft palate, or aphasia, that may have emotional or physical causes requiring extensive speech therapy. Individuals with these speaking disorders need patience, love, and understanding in addition to good speech therapy to build confidence in their communication abilities.

Many articulation problems can be improved through simple vocal exercises and by opening the mouth and speaking more distinctly.

Pitch

Pitch is the vocal element that refers to the highness or lowness of sound. If you spoke in a normal voice and struck a note on a piano corresponding to

A SPEAKER'S STANCE, BODY LANGUAGE, AND POISE CAN CONVEY ENTHUSIASM AND INTEREST IN THE LISTENER.

© MCM Nita Winter/ Image Works

your vocal note, you would find your approximate pitch. Children have high-pitched voices, women have lower voices, and men's voices tend to be still lower. Changes in pitch, called *inflections*, are important in effective vocal delivery. A presentation in which a speaker uses a variety of inflections sounds interesting. If you have ever had to endure a speaker who delivered an entire speech using the same monotonous pitch, you know how bored and frustrated you felt. The most interesting written material can often seem tedious if a speaker uses a monotone. Here is an exercise underscoring the contrast between the two styles of delivery. Read the following lines to a children's story using only a monotone.

> Once upon a time, deep in the forest, there lived a talkative owl, a one-legged grasshopper, and a turtle who could climb trees. One day the owl swooped down near the ground and discovered the grasshopper hobbling along.
>
> "Wholoo there," said the owl perched on the lower limb of a tree. "I've been very lonely lately because I've had no one to talk to. Why don't you jump up on this limb, climb on my feathers and we'll go for a ride?"
>
> "I can't," said the grasshopper slowly and sadly. "I lost a leg in a fierce battle with a kitten, and now I can hardly do anything at all."
>
> "Ha ha," said the talkative owl, "at least you're still alive!"
>
> "Not funny," clicked the one-legged grasshopper. "Not funny at all. At least you can fly."
>
> "Oh yes," said the owl, "and I can turn my head all the way around, and I have sharp sharp claws, and I am very, *very* wise."
>
> "I've heard enough from you," said the one-legged grasshopper who began to limp away.
>
> "Wait," yelled the owl. "You can do all sorts of things that I can't do. You can sneak under doors and get into people's houses, you can crouch into corners and not be seen, and best of all, you have a lovely, *lovely* voice to sing with. As a matter of fact, why don't you sing and entertain me right now?"

Now do it again, this time using a lot of vocal variety and different voices for each character as if you were telling the story to an audience of pre-schoolers. If you let yourself go during the reading, your pre-schoolers would probably have been fascinated. Vocal variety helps you to emphasize meaning and to create interest in the material.

You will get a similar result when you use vocal variety in your speeches. If you vary your inflection, your listeners will be much more interested and involved in your topic.

Quality

Voice *quality* refers to the sound or timbre of the voice. It is the element that makes each speaker's voice unique. No doubt you have heard speakers whose voices sounded harsh, nasal, breathy, gravelly, melodious, seductive, or hollow. Think of the differences in vocal quality of Bill Clinton, Jesse Jackson, Madonna, Joan Rivers, Marilyn Monroe, Michael Jackson, Connie Chung, Bruce Springsteen, James Earl Jones, Charlton Heston, and Pee-wee Herman. We recognize each of these individuals by their unique trademark—the sound of their voices.

Vocal quality can add to or detract from an individual's speech. If you've ever picked up the telephone and heard a nasal, "Hallow—Haw are yoooooo?" you probably had difficulty concentrating on the message because the nasal sound was so annoying. On the other hand, you probably listened actively to a speaker who greeted you in a rich, mellow voice.

The voice quality of most adults is usually established by long-term vocal habits. Frequently, however, some bad habits that are responsible for unpleasant voices can be altered through tension-reduction vocal exercises. A good voice and diction coach should be consulted for treatment.[6]

Rate

The *rate* of speech refers to the number of words an individual speaks every minute. Your speaking rate can affect the audience's comprehension of your meaning. If you rush through your speech, listeners cannot grasp your ideas or keep up with you. One student, who delivered a speech too rapidly, told a joke and was surprised to discover the audience laughing several seconds later, when he had moved on to more serious information. A speaker needs a comfortable rate of delivery that allows ideas to sink in. The most desirable speaking rate falls somewhere between 125 and 150 words per minute.[7] Anything significantly more or less than that is either too fast or too slow. Because of apprehension, many beginning speakers unconsciously speed up their rate. If this happens to you, try to make a conscious effort to slow down so that your listeners can absorb your ideas. Use dramatic pauses to break up important thought groups and to give listeners time to think about your ideas.

Rate can also be important in the interpretation of a speech. You can increase your rate when you want to create suspense and generate emotional feelings. You can slow down at the conclusion or during climactic points in the speech to demonstrate finality and resolution. Read the following dramatic incident aloud and adjust your speaking rate to reinforce the meaning of the material.

> The woman escaped from her assailant and ran out of the house. She ran up the street and began yelling and pleading, "Will anyone help me? Please, please, protect me. Someone's trying to kill me!" She kept running and glancing over her shoulder to see if the assailant was coming after her. She ran around a corner and spotted a police car two blocks ahead. She ran the last two blocks waving her arms wildly. "Please, save me," she screamed. Finally,

finally, she saw the beautiful car with the red and blue revolving light coming toward her. She slowed to a half-run, half-walk. Between her sobs and heavy breathing she whispered, "Thank God!"

If you followed the events in the narrative closely, your speaking rate was probably rapid at the beginning. As the pace of the story quickened, you may have increased your rate, and as the events concluded, your pace decreased. Your rate of speech is a valuable tool you can employ to emphasize and to interpret meaning.

Pronunciation

Pronunciation describes the combinations of vowels, consonants, syllables, and accents a speaker chooses to emphasize in a specific word. It is important to know how to pronounce common English words and difficult terminology you employ in a speech. Stumbling over words or making frequent errors in pronunciation interrupts the flow of ideas and raises questions about a speaker's credibility. Knowing how to pronounce a word means understanding the generally accepted pronunciation. While pronunciation can differ remarkably depending upon the region of the country, a good dictionary should be a helpful guide to the preferred pronunciation.

As part of your standard speech practice, you should check the pronunciation of any difficult words or terms unfamiliar to you. Here are some common words that are frequently mispronounced. Read the list carefully, and make sure that you are able to use the generally accepted pronunciation of each word.

adjective	mischievous
aluminum	nuclear
cavalry	particularly
congratulate	pumpkin
escape	recognize
gesture	statistics
	veterinarian

Pauses

Pauses are breaks or interruptions in speech that separate thoughts and ideas. Dramatic pauses are intentional breaks or silences between major ideas that can bring out the meaning of a specific passage. Dramatic pauses can help a listener to focus on a startling fact, or create a moment that allows a listener to experience an emotion. Notice how the following passage reads when you place dramatic pauses in strategic parts of the story.

> Melanie was a bright, seventeen-year-old girl. She was a straight-A student, she had numerous friends, and she was extremely attractive. Everything seemed to be going well for Melanie. But Melanie had one problem that few people knew about. [*pause*] Melanie was an anorexic [*pause*] and it was killing her!

You can use pauses effectively in a number of places to bring out the meaning of this passage. If you pause briefly at each punctuation mark and then use longer pauses at the brackets, the punch line to the story is dramatically emphasized. Read it several more times and experiment with different combinations of pauses. Experiment in your speeches as well. Use pausing where it is most likely to enhance and emphasize emotional examples, startling statements, and colorful quotations.

Vocalized pauses are verbalizations such as *uh*, and *um* that cause distractions in speaking. Speakers sometimes use vocalized pauses because they are nervous or because they may be uncomfortable with silence. The three Kennedy brothers all earned reputations as effective public speakers; but the late President, his brother Robert, and Senator Ted Kennedy all developed the bad habit of incorporating vocalized pauses in many of their speeches. Try to eliminate this habit from your verbal delivery. Vocalized pauses are annoying and keep listeners from concentrating on your presentation.

Remember that you don't have to verbalize 100 percent of your speaking time. Use silences to your advantage when you deliver your presentations. Dramatic pauses can help you to separate thoughts and to provide the audience with some time to grasp your ideas.

Emphasis and Phrasing

You use *emphasis* in a speech when you make alterations in your rate, volume, and pitch to highlight significant words and sentences. In phrasing, you group words and sentences into units of thought that make ideas easier to understand. Both emphasis and phrasing help to make a speech interesting and clear. In the following example, emphasize the italicized words by increasing your volume and slowing your rate. Use pauses wherever you see the caret.

> The U.S. national debt is four trillion dollars.
>
> ᴧ *Think* of it. *Four trillion dollars.*
> ᴧ   ᴧ   ᴧ   ᴧ

You can hear how verbal emphasis helps to underscore important words and thoughts, and how phrasing helps to clarify the meaning by grouping sentences into smaller thought units. The following markings reflect the emphasis and phrasing each individual used to deliver the following passages.

And so my fellow Americans, *ask not* what your *country* can *do* for *you,* *ask*
what *you* can *do* for your *country.*

—JOHN F. KENNEDY

I have a dream that my four little children will one day live in a nation where
they will not be judged by the *color* of their *skin* but by the *content* of their
character. I have a *dream* today.

—MARTIN LUTHER KING, JR.

The only thing we have to fear is *fear itself.*

—FRANKLIN D. ROOSEVELT

The ideas are dynamic enough. But each speaker used his unique
delivery to promote an even clearer understanding of his words. The
results were powerful. If you re-read each quotation using different
emphasis and phrasing, the meaning is altered, and the overall effect is
much less dramatic.

Your ideas can be emphasized in many ways, and your words can be
grouped into a variety of patterns. Choose the emphasis and phrasing that
most effectively reflects your intention and which will, in turn, contribute to
the audience's understanding of your meaning.

VISUAL DELIVERY

Visual delivery refers to the nonverbal aspect of communication. Your
eye contact, appearance, gestures, facial expressions, body position, and
movement can significantly affect the audience perceptions of your communication.[8]

Eye Contact

Eye contact is a very important aspect of your visual delivery. Through the
eyes you can reach the intellect and emotions of your audience and gauge their
feedback to your ideas. Research indicates that poor eye contact may even
have a negative impact on the amount of information an audience compre-
hends during a speech.[9] Any audience wants the speaker's recognition and
awareness. A speaker who reads word for word, without ever looking up, will
promote indifference and boredom.

The teacher arrived for every class period just three minutes late. She always sat down gingerly, pulling her chair up very slowly under the desk. She tugged three times at her skirt, making certain that it was stretched over her knees. She then began the lecture, without ever once looking at her students. "Today we are going to discuss the dangling participle," she droned in a monotone, "...an exciting lesson in rhetorical dysfunction." One student commented at the end of the semester, "She never looked at me any time during the whole course. I don't think she ever knew I was alive. The trouble is, I'm not sure that she was alive."

Contrast this experience with one of your most interesting instructors. You'll find that the professor who is an effective communicator uses a great deal of eye contact. The good instructor is always aware of student reactions and knows when to repeat ideas, ask questions, or proceed to new information. This instructor combines good eye contact with many other techniques of effective delivery. The communicative professor walks around, gestures, uses facial expression, and shows interest in students who respond by becoming actively involved and interested in class discussions.

When you deliver a speech, you must establish visual contact with your audience. While you aren't expected to memorize the speech, you should have rehearsed enough to free yourself from too much attention to notecards. It may take some practice and repeated experience to discover how often to glance at notes and how much visual contact to make with listeners. When you look at the audience, sustain eye contact long enough to let them know you see them and are following their reactions. Look at each area of the audience at some point in your speech. Avoid bobbing your head up and down between notecards and audience. This practice detracts from your speech and doesn't establish eye contact. If you feel insecure in front of people, find several friendly, attentive faces at the right, center, and left. Begin by looking at these supportive individuals, and gradually expand your field of vision to other audience members. Practice your speech thoroughly so that you will feel confident enough to look away from your notecards and establish rapport with your audience.

Appearance

Your *appearance* can support or detract from the communication process. A student who worked as a school crossing guard gave a speech informing the audience about the duties and responsibilities of her job. On the day of the speech she wore her school guard uniform, complete with hat, badge, and whistle. She spoke of her role as a protector and guardian of "her kids," and firmly reminded the audience that it is her job to stop traffic whenever it is in the best interests of the children. The speaker's words and feelings conveyed commitment to the topic, while her appearance communicated authority and dedication on a non-verbal level.[10]

Politicians carefully analyze speaking situations when they make decisions about their appearance for important speeches. A governor eating chicken and politicking for votes at the local county fair may wear blue jeans and suspenders. But the same governor will probably choose a conservative suit with red, white, and blue accessories for the inaugural address at the state capitol.

You create a positive impression when you dress appropriately for your speech. Avoid distracting styles: straps that fall down, skirts that ride up, jewelry that dangles noisily, hair that hides eyes or face, shoes that skid or squeak. An appropriate appearance—neat, clean, neither too formal nor too casual—lets the audience know that you care about the speech and that the occasion is important to you.

Gestures

Enhance your speeches by using *gestures* to emphasize words or phrases, to describe physical objects or events, and to point out directions or locations. In the early part of this century there was an emphasis on elocutionary speaking, which involved the study of vocal production and gesturing in speech delivery. Speakers practiced complicated vocal exercises and studied manuals containing illustrations and definitions of gestures. From this analysis, speakers learned to project their voices in large assembly halls and to use gestures forcefully in their presentations. In the early twentieth century, William Jennings Bryan, Teddy Roosevelt, and Robert LaFollette were prominent elocutionists whose booming voices and animated delivery influenced millions of Americans.

Although these speakers were effective in their era, their speeches would seem overdone today. Radio, television, and microphones have enabled speakers to be more conversational and to use more descriptive gestures in speech delivery. Modern speech educators feel gestures should be spontaneous and reflective of an individual's feelings and energies.

While it's not advisable to memorize gestures like some of the elocutionists, you can increase the effectiveness of your gestures through practice. Successful gestures are precise and punctuate your words and ideas clearly. Think of the varieties of gestures you might need to describe tying a shoelace or giving directions to your home.

Beginning speakers are sometimes afraid to use gestures in their presentations. They often stand with their arms stiffly at their sides, clasped behind or in front of them, or resting rigidly on the speaking lectern. If you make a conscious effort, you will find that gestures can help you work out some of your nervous energy in a speech. Don't let yourself be controlled by nervous mannerisms such as distracting hand, arm, or body movements. Show enthusiasm and project confidence to your audience by using gestures to punctuate ideas and to describe objects and concepts.

Facial Expression

Each of us has a wonderful set of muscles in our faces which can be used to smile, frown, show anger, or express love and joy. Our facial expressions help to reinforce our words. If you were to say "I love you," and convey anger in your expression, your listener would either be confused or interpret the message negatively. If you had a blank facial expression, your listener might wonder if you had any feelings of love at all. A student presenting a speech about the importance of seatbelts smiled broadly as he said: "If you were involved in a traffic accident and you didn't wear your seatbelt, you might die!" The audience didn't take the speaker seriously, because his facial expression wasn't appropriate.

Your *facial expression* should clearly support your verbal message. If you talk about parental kidnapping, your expression should reflect anger and concern; if your topic is space exploration, your face should convey adventure and curiosity; if you are speaking about chronic illness, your face should show empathy and hope. Your facial expressions cannot be mechanically planned in advance. Like gestures, they should be spontaneous and reflect your natural feelings. Practice your speech in front of a friend or, if possible, a video camera to get some clues about your expressions and determine if they support your verbal messages. A speaker who projects emotion about a topic through facial expression will tend to receive a similar emotional response from the audience.

A SPEAKER COMMUNICATES COMMITMENT VISUALLY BY EMPLOYING FACIAL EXPRESSION, EYE CONTACT, AND GESTURES.

© Bob Daemmrich/
Image Works

Body Position and Movement

Your stance, posture, poise, and *body movement* can also contribute to your communication. An individual who has good posture appears to be more prepared than a speaker who slouches or leans on the lectern. Standing on both feet gives a speaker greater stability than shifting from one leg to another. Good posture also allows a speaker to breathe more effectively to produce sound.

A student was in the process of presenting an informative speech about learning disabilities. She had researched the topic well, and she had found a number of interesting examples, statistics, and testimonies to support her main points. During her speech, however, she would wrap one leg around the other the way a contortionist does at the circus. The audience was fascinated as they watched her legs tangle and unwind. It's obvious, of course, that the awkward body movement was a distraction which kept the audience from hearing the speech.

It's good speech practice to develop posture that is both relaxed and erect. Practice using your stance and body position to your advantage. A tall speaker with good posture can use height as an added means of persuasion. A short speaker can stand beside the lectern and develop greater intimacy with the audience. Be sure that your stance and posture add to your presentation and do not interfere with the message.

When you become a confident public speaker, you can develop some variations in body movement to emphasize the transitions in your speech. Here are some suggestions:

Specific purpose: to inform the audience about dyslexia
Thesis statement: Dyslexia has several causes and effects which can be described in a case study.

BODY	SUGGESTED MOVEMENT
I. Causes of dyslexia Transition line 1: "I've just told you about some of the major causes of dyslexia; now I want to go into some of its effects on children."	Move to right of lectern.
II. Effects of the learning disability Transition line 2: "Now that I've considered some of the effects, let me tell you an experience that happened to my family."	Move in front of lectern.
III. Case study of dyslexia	

In this presentation, the speaker begins the introduction and numeral I of the body standing behind the speaker's lectern. When transition line 1 is stated, the speaker moves to the right of the lectern, reinforcing the change in thoughts. Again, when transition line 2 is delivered, the speaker moves in front of the lectern, standing closer to the audience. This final action not only supports the change in ideas but also establishes greater intimacy with listeners during the presentation of the personal experience. You may want to gain some confidence behind the speaker's lectern before you try some of these suggestions; experiment with body movement when you become comfortable with your audience.

COMBINING VOCAL AND VISUAL DELIVERY

Vocal and visual delivery are combined in the enthusiasm and vitality which a speaker projects to an audience. An enthusiastic speaker uses vocal inflection, volume, pauses, eye contact, gestures, and facial expressions to convey a feeling of involvement in his or her topic. Audience members experience the speaker's energy visually and verbally and think, "This person really cares about the topic—I'd better listen."

In the second 1992 presidential debate, a voter asked how the national debt had personally affected the lives of each candidate. President Bush's

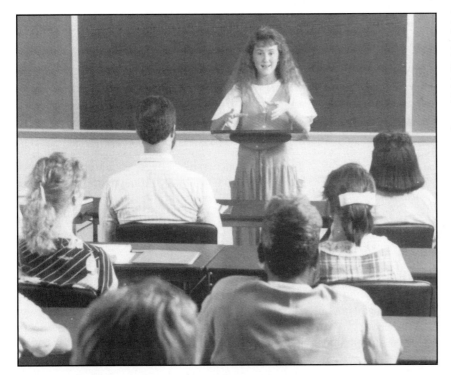

EFFECTIVE SKILLS IN VOCAL AND VISUAL DELIVERY ALLOW A SPEAKER TO PROJECT IDEAS WITH CLARITY, PASSION, AND STYLE.

© Hal Rummel Photography

response included the comment, "I'm not sure I get it." This reaction demonstrated the President's difficulty in communicating his concern about the economic hardships suffered by many Americans. By contrast, Governor Clinton used facial expression, body movement, and gestures to convey his emotional response: "In my state when people lose their jobs, there's a good chance that I'll know them by their names." An individual does not have to be a vibrant public speaker in order to be president, of course. America has had many presidents who have not been effective speakers, including Calvin Coolidge, Lyndon Johnson, Richard Nixon, and Jimmy Carter. But some of our strongest leaders have been dynamic public speakers—among them are Teddy Roosevelt, Franklin Roosevelt, John F. Kennedy, and Ronald Reagan.

To be successful in a speech, show that you care about the topic. Employ good eye contact with the audience; use your facial muscles to show appropriate emotion; alter your pitch for vocal variety and adjust your volume, rate, and phrasing for emphasis; use gestures to reinforce your ideas, and reflect your commitment in your appearance. Combine all of the vocal and visual aspects of delivery into a speaking performance which is enthusiastic and energetic.

BUILDING SKILLS IN DELIVERY

Here are a few suggestions to help you develop your skills in speech delivery.

Know the Material

One of the first principles of an effective delivery is to be knowledgeable about your material. Your research should be thorough, your sources should be credible, and your understanding of the topic should be extensive. Know how to pronounce difficult names, terms, or concepts, and be familiar with your supporting materials. One key to a successful delivery is confidence in your material, which can free you to relay the topic to your audience.

Be Well Organized

You need a good outline written on note cards to deliver a speech effectively. Make sure the outline is clear and complete. Know exactly how you are going to begin and end the speech. Be certain that your specific purpose is defined and that the main points of the body are identifiable. Check your notecards for ease in reading. Write large enough to see comfortably, and double-space between phrases and sentences. Number your note cards at the upper corner to keep them in the proper order.

Mark Your Notes

A high school instructor marked his lecture notes with phrases like "insert joke here," "use gesture now," or, "show grimace." While this type of preparation can be helpful, it might promote a memorized or mechanical delivery. We don't suggest that you plan every detail of your delivery, but we recommend that you develop your own system of marking to indicate areas of verbal and visual emphasis. Use a simple system of underlining, circling, and arrows similar to this example.

Here just a few lines and circles indicate emphasis, and some slanting lines and arrows show increasing rate and volume. You don't need complicated notations. You merely need to be consistent in order to translate your markings into effective gestures, expressions, and verbal emphasis.

We need to do something <u>now</u> about this problem. If we don't stop dumping in our oceans, <u>there won't be</u> any more beautiful beaches, <u>there won't be</u> any more coral reefs, and <u>there won't be</u> any more deep-sea fishing. We've got to get Congress to enact strict laws with STRONG EMPHASIS <u>severe</u> penalties that deter hospitals, cities, states, and corporations from dicarding their posionous wastes into the sea. [Our oceans are SOFTLY a fragile part of the ecological system.] We can preserve them for PAUSE ourselves and our children, ∧or we can <u>destroy</u> them∧<u>forever.</u> [Think SLOWLY about it. What will your choice be?]

Practice the Delivery

When you have organized your material and you know what you want to emphasize, practice the speech several times. Whenever possible, it is helpful to practice in an environment similar to your speech setting. Stand behind a speaker's lectern so that you can rest your notecards and practice some gestures. Rehearse the speech aloud and work on your vocal inflections, volume, articulation, and speaking rate. Rehearse your phrasing to develop pauses between the appropriate thought groupings. If you have a tape recorder, use it in your practice sessions. Replaying the speech can help you to evaluate your vocal delivery and detect vocalized pauses, improper pronunciation, and monotonous pitch.

It is also helpful if you can practice your speech in front of a friend or video camera. You can determine the success of your eye contact, facial expressions, gestures, and body movement as you deliver the presentation.

Notice how often you need to look at your cards and how comfortably you manage your notes. Try to develop a visual delivery that reinforces every aspect of your material.

Situations frequently arise where speakers cannot engage in practice sessions. Executives, physicians, and business or sales people are often too busy with scheduled appointments to devote time for speech rehearsal. In such cases, it is helpful to have a "think through" session on the corporate jet or in the car on the way to the speech setting. In these brief sessions, the speaker can mentally review the main points of the presentation or jot down a few notes on a legal pad to organize the thought process.

Whether you have a "think-through" session or a formal rehearsal, work to project enthusiasm and confidence during the speech. While it is appropriate to use your prepared notes, know your material well enough to maintain eye contact with your listeners without reading word for word. Concentrate on your ideas and be natural and spontaneous. Your goal is to refine all of the elements of your delivery into a smooth, unified presentation.

SUMMARY

In this chapter we have described proper breathing practices needed for an effective vocal delivery. We have also described the aspects of vocal delivery: volume, articulation, pitch, quality, pronunciation, pauses, including dramatic pauses and vocalized pauses, emphasis, and phrasing. In addition to vocal aspects, we've stressed the importance of the visual, or nonverbal, aspects of delivery. A good speaker maintains eye contact with the audience, dresses appropriately for the speech, and uses gestures, facial expressions, and body movement. When you combine all aspects of delivery, you should project enthusiasm and vitality. Four simple guidelines to help you develop delivery skills are: (1) know your material, (2) be well organized, (3) mark your notes, and (4) practice the delivery.

EXERCISES

1. Choose a selection from a favorite piece of literature such as a lyric from a song, a poem, or a prose selection and develop a one- to two-minute reading for class. Work on your vocal and visual expression, emphasis, eye contact, and gestures. Practice the selection aloud several times. Experiment with various interpretations until you feel your reading reflects the author's intended meaning.

2. Choose a situation for a two- to three-minute pantomime. Develop your facial expressions, gestures, and body movements to portray the details of

the experience. Communicate all of the elements of the pantomime without props. Here are some ideas for pantomimes.

Visiting the dentist
Getting stuck in an elevator
Washing windows on a skyscraper
Doing acrobatics in an airplane
Styling hair at a unisex shop
Applying make-up
Receiving an Olympic gold medal
Driving a small car on a busy freeway
Getting a ticket from a police officer
Participating in a drug bust
Walking an unruly dog
Toilet training a child

NOTES

[1] For this section on the production of sound, we used five sources you can consult for more detailed information: (1) Virgil A. Anderson, *Training the Speaking Voice* (New York: Oxford University Press, 1961), pp. 21–54; (2) Jon Eisenson, *Improvement of Voice and Diction*, 2d ed. (New York: Macmillan, 1965), pp. 15–41; (3) Hilda B. Fisher, *Improving Voice and Articulation*, 2nd ed. (Boston: Houghton Mifflin, 1975), pp. 3–24 and 89–105; (4) Giles Wilkeson Gray and Claude Merton Wise, *The Bases of Speech*, 3d ed. (New York: Harper and Row, 1959), pp. 135–199; and (5) Arthur Lessac, *The Use and Training of the Human Voice*, 2d ed. (New York: Drama Book Specialists, 1967), pp. 9–16.

[2] These exercises were selected from Eisenson's *The Improvement of Voice and Diction*, p. 45–47.

[3] Fisher, *Improving Voice and Articulation*, pp. 3–36. We have based our definitions of vocal delivery upon Hilda Fisher's definitions, which she provides in Chapter 1 of her text.

[4] "The Art of Being Fully Human," Public Broadcasting Company video, Washington D.C., 1980.

[5] This exercise is drawn from a longer list provided in Anderson, *Training the Speaking Voice*, p. 405.

[6] Fisher, *Improving Voice and Articulation*, p. 67. Hilda Fisher recommends exercises which help the muscles of the larynx to relax. If you have some concerns about the quality of your voice, try some of the exercises she suggests on pages 64–72.

[7] Charles R. Petrie, Jr., "Informative Speaking: A Summary and Bibliography of Related Research," *Speech Monographs* 30 (June 1963), p. 81.

[8] Shelly Chaiken, "Communicator Physical Attractiveness and Persuasion," *Journal of Personality and Social Psychology* 37 (August 25, 1978), pp. 1387–1397. This article contains some interesting research about the impact of physical attractiveness on persuasion. The author concludes that "The present research indicates that physical attractiveness can significantly enhance communicator persuasiveness" (p. 1394).

[9] Ibid., p. 82.

[10] Example based upon a speech delivered by Marie E. Miller, Catonsville Community College, Catonsville, Maryland, 1988. Used by permission.

SELECTED READINGS

Fisher, Hilda B. *Improving Voice and Articulation*, 2nd ed. Boston: Houghton Mifflin, 1975. A comprehensive book on vocal delivery, including diagrams and illustrations which describe physical breathing and sound mechanisms. The author includes numerous exercises for breathing, vocalization, resonance, and articulation.

Linklater, Kristin. *Freeing the Natural Voice*. New York: Drama Book Publishers, 1976. Written by a British actress and world-famous voice teacher, this very interesting book contains many vocal and breathing exercises which have been used successfully by both American and British stage performers.

UNIT OUTLINE

Chapter Fifteen

SPEAKING TO INFORM

Chapter Outline

Key Terms

Description
Demonstration
Definition
Informative speaking
Lecture
Personal experience
Report

© Martha Stewart/
Picture Cube

"The best way to send information
is to wrap it up in a person."
—ROBERT OPPENHEIMER

W hile vacationing in the unfamiliar territory of Nags Head, North Carolina, we decided to eat at a restaurant several miles out of town. At a local grocery we received the following directions:

> *Grocery store attendant:* Well, you jest keep goin' straight, till you get to a "crook" in the road. Then you veer off to the left. Restaurant should be... Oh...I guess I'd say, 'bout five or ten miles down that way.

We headed down "that way" for the next ten miles, searching for our destination. We counted five sharp curves, three angles, and two dips, but no "crooks" and no restaurant. Once more we asked directions.

> *Ice cream store clerk:* Yep. I know jest where you're talkin' about. Now you go to the third traffic light, see, beside the twelve mile marker—and turn left. Now you stay on that road 'til you come to a "Y"—Take the right fork—don't take the left one or you'll be in trouble. The restaurant is on the left after you make the "Y."

Thanks to these precise instructions, we found our destination quickly. You've been confused by inaccurate and imprecise information too. Communicating information isn't easy—There is an art to being clear, accurate, and concrete.

This first chapter of Unit V helps you develop your informative speaking skills. We examine the difference between information and persuasion, consider several categories of informative speeches, and present some guidelines to help you build the informative descriptive speech. We also provide an analysis sheet to help you evaluate an informative presentation.

THE DIFFERENCE BETWEEN INFORMATION AND PERSUASION

As you begin to build your speech to inform, clearly recognize the difference between information and persuasion. Some rhetoricians agree with Aristotle that all speaking is persuasive; speeches differ only in the relative strength and weakness of the persuasion. This text, however, draws a distinction between communication that is informative and communication that is persuasive.[1]

Overall, an informative speech promotes understanding, enlightenment, and education about a topic; a persuasive speech seeks to influence and alter the beliefs, feelings, or behavior of listeners. Specifically, speeches to inform can be grouped into the following categories: description, demonstration or process, definition, personal experience, the report, and the lecture.

We've listed three topics below and indicated how the specific purpose sentences would be phrased as informative and persuasive presentations.

Topics to Inform	Topics to Persuade
To define "libertarianism"	to convince the audience that the Libertarian Party is potentially dangerous to the American constitutional system
to describe four of the most notorious serial killers	to convince the audience that serial killers should automatically receive the death penalty
to explain the process of interviewing sexually abused children for courtroom testimony	to actuate the audience to support efforts to change courtroom procedures for child witnesses

The topics on the left generally provide information on an issue, while the topics at the right seek to influence the audience to agree with the speaker's point of view. In the list of informative topics, "libertarianism" would be considered a speech of definition, "serial killers" would be a descriptive speech, and "interviewing sexually abused children" would be considered a process speech.

Some communication specialists feel that informative speeches are "factual" while persuasive speeches are more "emotional."[2] We would like to caution you, however, about making this distinction. It is true that informative speeches can contain supporting materials such as statistics, surveys, or polls, and visual materials such as graphs, maps, and charts. But informative speeches should also incorporate emotional elements such as personal experiences, illustrations, and examples that interest the audience. And while persuasive speeches should make use of strong emotional appeals, persuasive speeches should also be grounded in supporting evidence which incorporates sound logic and fact.

Recognize also that speeches are not always strictly informative or persuasive. Informative presentations often contain elements of persuasion which modify the thinking or behavior of listeners over a period of time. In persuasion, speakers often include large portions of informative material to educate and enlighten listeners before asking them to change attitudes or take action. Speeches frequently exist on an informative–persuasive continuum, with some presentations clustering around the informative end, and others tending towards the persuasive.

Up to this point we've been talking about defining informative speeches in terms of the topic. But there are also times when the audience will determine whether a topic is informative or persuasive. For example, after conducting careful research, you present an informative speech with the stated intention "to acquaint the audience with some interesting biographical data about Candidate X," a Democrat. Your listeners, however, might have different ideas. If the audience consisted of either Republicans or Democrats who favored other candidates, they might feel that your speech was persuasive rather than informative.

TYPES OF INFORMATIVE SPEECHES

In this Chapter, we will consider three categories of information: (1) description, (2) definition, and (3) reports, lectures, and personal experiences. A fourth informative type, the demonstration speech, will be presented in Chapter 16.

The Descriptive Speech

In *descriptive* presentations, speakers choose topics related to persons, places, objects, or events. Under *objects* we are including both the animate and inanimate, and we are defining an event as an incident or occurrence. Here are a number of examples in each area:

Person(s)   To describe the personal life of J. S. Bach
           To describe Andy Warhol's contributions to pop art
           To describe the culture of the Eskimo
           To describe influential women speakers in American history

Place(s)   To describe a film studio
           To describe the Baseball Hall of Fame
           To describe Mackinac Island, Michigan
           To describe life in Japan
           To describe the largest mall in America
           To describe the planet Venus

Object(s)   To describe the destruction from the civil war in Bosnia
           To describe repetitive stress injuries
           To describe the relationship of color and personality
           To describe the effects of the bombing of New York's
               World Trade Center
           To describe the history of trademarks
           To describe killer wasps
           To describe the wonderful, wily cat

Event (s)   To inform an audience about the religious conflict in
               Northern Ireland
           To inform an audience about rebuilding in south Florida
               after Hurricane Andrew

To inform an audience about radon gas
To inform an audience about violence in football
To inform an audience about drug education programs
To inform an audience about unusual advertising feats
To describe the benefits of the Special Olympics

An Example

In the following example, the speaker attempts to describe some of the highlights of Mexico City with mediocre results:

Mexico City is a huge city in the mountains inhabited by millions of people. The city contains artifacts dating back to the ancient Aztecs, buildings constructed by the Spaniards, and structures which reflect modern Mexico.

In this example, terminology is only denotative. Words such as "huge," "artifacts," "buildings," or "structures" do not create mental images. The speaker employs vague generalities and uses no concrete supporting materials. This description will have little impact; the speaker has lost a wonderful opportunity to arouse interest. Notice the improvement:

In today's Mexico City, you can sample a tasty enchilada made with white cheese; feel the rough chisel marks of an ancient Aztec pyramid; take a leisurely stroll through the cool green palms and curving lakes of Chapultepec Park; experience the excitement of the clubs, cabarets, and

INFORMATIVE PRESENTATIONS CAN EDUCATE AND ENLIGHTEN LISTENERS ABOUT OBJECTS, PLACES, PERSONS, OR EVENTS.

© Shelley Gazin/
Image Works

BUILDING THE DESCRIPTIVE SPEECH

Since a descriptive speech is one of the major types you will probably deliver in your speech course, here are some specific guidelines to help you build this presentation.

1. **Choose an interesting topic.**
   a. Choose an innovative topic providing new information.
   b. Select a topic that is interesting to you, the speaker.
   c. Examine your personal interests, experiences, and knowledge.
   d. Avoid repeating information the audience already knows.
   e. Choose a topic which is appropriate to listeners.

2. **Conduct careful research.**
   a. Review personal experience for primary source material.
   b. Use sources that are accurate, reliable, and up-to-date.
   c. Avoid sources lacking in credibility such as "house and garden" or condensed magazines for medical or scientific facts.
   d. Conduct interviews with experts.
   e. Build credibility with accurate examples, statistics, testimony, and audiovisual aids.
   f. Check details such as events, numbers, dates, and quotations for precision and accuracy.

3. **Organize the speech in a logical sequence.**
   a. Develop a creative introduction with a clear thesis identifying the main points in the body.
   b. Choose an organizational plan appropriate to the topic.
      (1) Use external transitions to emphasize major headings.
      (2) Employ internal transitions to link supporting ideas.
   c. Construct an interesting conclusion conveying finality.

   (1) Choose a poem, quotation, or example which resolves or summarizes the topic.
   (2) Avoid providing new information during the conclusion.

4. **Employ vivid language.**
   a. Use clear, colorful, connotative language.
   b. Employ images that evoke mental pictures and appeal to the senses.
   c. Avoid trite phrases or vague jargon such as "to each his own," or "stuff like that."

5. **Use concrete supporting materials.**
   a. Humanize the topic with realistic supporting materials.
   b. Round off statistics for easy comprehension.
   c. Employ colorful quotations.
   d. Avoid stringing together lists of statistics or hard facts.
   e. Use audiovisual aids for variety and interest.

6. **Develop a clear, personal delivery.**
   a. Pronounce difficult names and technical terms correctly.
   b. Define unfamiliar words or phrases.
   c. Avoid extensive technical terminology, using words and phrases that listeners understand.
   d. Maintain eye contact with the audience.
   e. Use personal pronouns such as "you," "we," and "us," to include listeners.
   f. Be conversational, use extemporaneous delivery, and avoid reading word-for-word.
   g. Make effective use of your eyes, face, hands, and voice.
   h. Stimulate feedback by using humor, asking rhetorical or open-ended questions, and employing emotion.
   i. Be sensitive to audience feedback, making minor adjustments to content or delivery based upon audience response.
   j. Practice the speech to gain confidence.

outdoor cafes in the Zona Rosa; browse through shops filled with mounds of solid silver jewelry; contemplate the classic beauty of the oldest Spanish church in the Americas; navigate the flowered canals of the Xochimilco; and dance to the melodies of a hundred Mariachi groups in Garibaldi Square.

This description is effective because the words are connotative, and the speaker uses numerous sensory examples as supporting materials. Vivid language such as "tasty enchilada," "rough chisel marks," "flowered canals," and action words such as "feel," "sample," "navigate," and "dance" invite listeners to participate with all their senses. Words that identify objects in terms of color ("white cheese," "green palms"), shape ("curving lakes"), and size ("mounds of...silver") add to the visual imagery. Notice the foreign names that the speaker needs to pronounce correctly. The speaker has successfully created a variety of mental images.

Outlining the Descriptive Speech

When you develop the outline for the descriptive speech, you should follow the organizational principles suggested in Chapter 10. Remember that the main points of the body should be arranged according to chronology, space, cause–effect, topic, or a combination of sequences. Here are three examples that show how these sequences can be combined.

In the following descriptive topic, the speaker combines chronological with spatial order:

Specific purpose: to describe the Baseball Hall of Fame at Cooperstown, New York

Thesis statement: The Baseball Hall of Fame, with exhibits in the first, second, and third floors, preserves the legends of baseball for posterity.

Body
 I. Brief history of museum
 II. First floor Hall of Fame gallery
 III. Second floor history sections
 IV. Third floor rooms of memorabilia

Notice that subheadings under I would be arranged according to order of events and that II through IV are arranged according to location of rooms in the museum.

In the next example, the speaker has organized main points using a combination of chronological and topic sequence:

Specific purpose: to describe the wonderful, wily cat

Thesis statement: Cats were respected in Egyptian times and feared in the

Middle Ages; they are equipped for savage battle, yet make loving members
of any family.

Body

   I. Cats in Egyptian times
  II. Cats in the Middle Ages
 III. Cats as hunters
 IV. Cats as pets

The speaker uses chronology for the history in I and II, then incorporates a
topical sequence for the last two headings.

    In the next example, the speaker combines topic with cause–effect
sequence:

Specific purpose: to inform you about the dangers of steroids

Thesis statement: I want to provide an explanation of steroids, describe their
intended purpose, and identify their desired effects as well as their damaging
consequences.

Body

   I. General explanation of steroids
  II. Intended purpose of steroids
 III. Desired effects
 IV. Damaging consequences

    Numerals I and II are arranged in topic sequence, while III and IV char-
acterize the issue in terms of its effects.

The Speech of Definition

In a speech of *definition*, you inform your audience about a philosophical
concept such as a theory or idea, or a more concrete subject like a science
or art:

Science or art	What is cryonics?
	What is electronic music?
	What is impressionistic art?
	What is a phobia?
	What is Romantic music?
	What is vegetarianism?

Theories or ideas	What is "pure Marxism"?
	What is apartheid?
	What is Basque separatism?
	What is Shi'ite Islam?
	What is evolutionism?
	What is creationism?
	What is libertarianism?

With any of these topics, the thrust of your information would be to explain the meaning of an unknown term to your audience. When defining such terms, follow guidelines suggested for the descriptive speech. Be concrete and accurate, use plenty of supporting materials, and work to maintain the interest of your audience. Remember that definitional speeches are not simply intellectual explanations of dry theories or complex subject-matter; these speeches must be just as creative and alive as any other informative presentation.

Here are two structural examples of speeches defining terms. The first example uses chronological sequence; the second employs topical order.

Example 1: Chronological Sequence

Specific purpose: to define Shi'ite Islam

Thesis statement: Shi'ite Islam is a religion having its origins in the Middle Ages and exhibiting specific characteristics today.

Body
  I. Shi'ite Islam in the Middle Ages
 II. Characteristics of the movement today

Example 2: Topical Sequence

Specific purpose: to define the term "vegetarian"

Thesis statement: Vegetarianism is a dietary practice which includes vegans as well as lacto–ovo–vegetarians, and has clear advantages as well as disadvantages.

Body
   I. Vegans—eliminating all animal foods
  II. Lacto–ovo–vegetarians—using eggs and dairy products
 III. Advantages of the vegetarian diet
  IV. Disadvantages of the vegetarian diet

Notice that the Shi'ite Islam speech is organized according to chronology, and that the one on vegetarianism is structured according to the natural headings reflected in the research.

In these topics, speakers can motivate listeners by using effective supporting materials. A presentation on Shi'ite Islam could incorporate visual aids and examples relating to current events taking place in revolutionary Iran and other Middle Eastern countries. A speech about vegetarianism could relate the topic to the physical health and welfare of listeners. In both topics, speakers can provide new, interesting, and helpful information to members of their audiences.

Other Informative Types

We will consider three other types of informative speeches briefly: the report, the lecture, and the personal experience.

The *report* is often required in business or industry. You may already have had to present reports to supervisors, committees, or clients. In this important speech the quality of your presentation can improve or hinder your chances for success. Topics for reports are usually based on limited issues such as "the decrease in sales for the third quarter," "decisions of the search committee," or "marketing committee actions."

In many cases, your report will summarize the work of a committee or other employee unit. You need to be completely accurate, and your comments must reflect the collective decisions of the group. Even though your report is

SPEAKERS MUST CONVEY INFORMATION WITH CLARITY, ACCURACY, AND PRECISION.

© George Gardner/ Image Works

technical, it should still be interesting, clear, and well organized. Know your material thoroughly, maintain contact with your audience, interject humor when appropriate, and use concrete examples.

Business reports often incorporate visuals: transparencies with overhead projectors, chalkboards, white boards with magic markers, and easels. Remember that effective use of visuals can create the perception among co-workers that you know what you're doing.

Lectures are presentations given by experts for instructional or educational purposes. Colleges and universities often receive grants to invite well-known authorities in science, humanities, and industry to speak on topics of national interest. Lecturers frequently read lengthy presentations from manuscripts and incorporate question-and-answer sessions at the end.

You already know from your own classroom listening experience that a two-hour lecture can seem like minutes or days depending upon the speaker's organization and enthusiasm. Some campus student groups publish evaluations rating faculty lectures according to interest, enthusiasm, and scholarship. Lectures don't have to be boring. They can be fascinating if the speaker is knowledgeable, structured, and communicates new or complicated information creatively. You will probably give a lecture, however, only if you are an expert in a particular field.

The *personal experience* speech provides information about an encounter or observation. Travelogues, harrowing adventures, or expeditions are good subject areas for personal experience speeches. These presentations are often exciting and interesting; they are also potentially boring. Use good judgment in developing the topic and be sensitive to your listeners.

In your speech class, your instructor may ask you to present a brief personal-experience speech. But remember not to substitute one lengthy personal experience for a major informative speech that requires a variety of research materials.[3]

ANALYSIS SHEET FOR THE INFORMATIVE SPEECH

Introduction

Curiosity device   Did the speech contain an effective device for building curiosity such as a case study, question, or shocking statement?
Did the end of the introduction contain a clear specific purpose and/or thesis statement?

Content

Topic   Was the topic sufficiently limited and innovative?
Was the topic appropriate and interesting to the audience?

Organization	Were main headings and supporting points structured in a clear, logical, and interesting manner? Were main headings thoroughly developed?
Accuracy	Was the information accurate, up-to-date, and verified by credible sources?
Supporting materials	Did the speech contain a variety of clear, concrete, and creative, supporting materials?

Delivery

Language	Did the speaker use connotative words and vivid language to create mental images? Was the speaker's language appropriate to the topic? Did the speaker's language reflect good English usage?
Clarity	Did the speaker use external transitions to "flag" main points, and internal transitions to connect subordinate points? Did the speaker adhere to the topic and keep ideas moving in a logical sequence? Were steps in demonstrations clear and understandable? Did the speaker define and clarify unfamiliar terms?
Vocal delivery	Did the speaker enunciate words and phrases clearly? Did the speaker pronounce difficult terms effectively? Did the speaker's volume, rate, and vocal inflections enhance the speech?
Visual aids	Did the speaker spend time and effort developing audiovisual aids? Did the speaker know how to use the visual aids? While using visuals, was the speaker able to keep the speech moving without awkward "dead space?"
Enthusiasm	Did the speaker's voice, eye contact, facial expression, gestures, and posture reflect enthusiasm for the topic?
Emphasis	Did the speaker employ verbal emphasis and/or repetition to highlight important areas? Did the speaker support verbal emphasis with appropriate gestures, movement, and facial expression?

Other   Did the speaker display any other effective or ineffective
                            techniques (pauses, mannerisms, movement, appearance)
                            which would enhance or detract from the delivery?

Conclusion

Method of   Did the speech contain a clear device (quotation,
ending   summary, story, question) to provide closure to the topic?

Constructed by an advanced public speaking student, this speech includes
numerous supporting materials to describe the threat posed by electronic
viruses. In addition to this descriptive presentation, Christopher Kavanaugh
has developed several alternative introductions and conclusions to demonstrate the variety of creative approaches available for a single speech.

THE COMPUTER VIRUS: DISEASE OF THE COMPUTER AGE

Informative Descriptive Speech

Christopher B. Kavanaugh

[1] The speaker begins the introduction with a case study to gain audience attention and to promote curiosity. The events in the story are arranged to create suspense.

[1] On November 2nd, 1988 at around 9:00 p.m., Robert Tappan Morris, a twenty-three-year -old computer science student at Cornell University, pushed a single button on his computer keyboard and launched an attack. Two of his targets were the research and science centers at Berkeley, California and Cambridge, Massachusetts. Around 10:00 p.m. Princeton University was hit. By midnight NASA's Ames Research Center in California, the University of Pittsburgh, and the Los Alamos National Laboratory in New Mexico became victims. Around 12:30 a.m., Johns Hopkins University in Baltimore was struck, and by quarter after one in the morning the attack reached the University of Michigan in Ann Arbor.

[2] At 2:30 that morning a frantic computer scientist in Berkeley sent out a message to computers around the country which began with the words, "We are currently under attack..." The message noted other locations around the country that had been affected by the attack, and provided a brief description of the way the attack was taking place. At the time, the "only help" the scientist could offer to others in danger was a recommendation to shut down their computer systems in order to protect themselves.

[3] Now you may be asking yourself what could attack so many locations in such a short period of time. It was neither a series of guided missiles nor a test of the "star wars" laser beam; it was a phenomenon known as a computer virus.

4 The story I just described was reported in great detail on the front page of the *Wall Street Journal* on November 7, 1988. That incident prompted an emergency meeting of computer scientists and representatives of twelve government agencies, including the FBI, the CIA, the Department of Defense, the Air Force, the Army, and the National Security Agency. Participants in the top-secret meeting in Fort Meade, Maryland discussed the nature of an electronic virus, the threat computer viruses pose to universities, businesses, and the U.S. government, and what might be done to safeguard potential victims.

5 When we think of a computer and the programs that run it, we usually think in terms of what it can do to help us, as an aid in gathering and sorting data. So what makes a computer virus program different from other types of computer programs? Put simply, a computer virus is a type of disruptive program that someone places secretly into a computer system. Victims of computer viruses typically report that unwanted, often damaging, disturbances occur in infected computers.

6 An electronic virus can produce effects as benign as a simple picture and message on your computer screen. A September 1988 issue of *Time* magazine reported the case of several thousand Macintosh computer users who turned on their machines on March 2, 1988 to find a picture of the earth and a "universal message of peace" on their computer screens. The message disappeared quickly and never returned, and the virus responsible for the spontaneous greeting card caused no lasting damage.

7 But a computer virus can also be sinister in nature, created with the intention of deleting some or all of the data stored within a computer system. *Business Week* gave an example of a more destructive virus in its cover story article on August 1, 1988. A man named Donald Burleson was fired from his job as a computer programmer for a securities trading firm and decided to get revenge.

8 Shortly after he was fired he wrote a virus program and secretly planted it in the company's computer system. The program was designed to wipe out all the records of sales commissions once a month. Burleson's electronic virus was discovered only two days later by the company's programming analysts, but before it could be eliminated, the virus had destroyed 168,000 records in the computer's memory bank.

9 Whether the results are disastrous or merely distracting, it is important to remember that a computer virus is a foreign element—a sort of devious computer program—which secretly enters a computer system. Once inside, it activates hidden instructions that alter the performance of the computer.

4 Chris carefully documents the story with a credible source.

The speaker has skillfully crafted his thesis statement at the end of the introduction.

5 The first external transition introduces numeral I about the nature of the computer virus.

6 Throughout the speech, Chris uses specific references to back up his ideas.

The brief example of the "universal message of peace" helps the audience to visualize the symptoms of a "benign" computer virus.

8 The case study enables listeners to understand a "sinister" virus.

[10] The external transition connects numerals I and II.

[10] Now that you are armed with a general description of this electronic scourge, let's examine its *modus operandi* to determine why it's such a devastating threat to our technological way of life.

[11] The speaker uses an effective comparison and contrast to describe similarities and differences of computer and biological viruses.

[11] The science magazine *Discover* noted in its January 1989 issue that a computer virus is similar to a biological virus, because both contain built-in instructions to duplicate themselves repeatedly. The biological virus achieves this chemically, based on genetic coding. The computer virus works electronically, using computer coding called machine language. One significant difference between the two viruses is that a biological virus usually occurs naturally, but an electronic virus must be intentionally created by someone to infect computers.

[12] Both viruses need to find a way inside the "host" before infection can take place. The human body is the "host" for the biological virus, whereas the computer operating system is the "host" for the computer virus. Just as a person (without realizing it) can transmit infectious germs during a friendly handshake, a computer can also pass on its form of virus to other computers. A computer infection occurs when two or more computers share or transfer information.

[13] To understand exactly how serious the virus threat is, we need only look at our increasing reliance on computers to perform everyday tasks. In the past, most records were kept on paper. Once we recognized the advantage computers provided by allowing immediate access to information, computers replaced many of our filing cabinets and typewriters.

[14] Chris develops an interesting hypothetical example to help listeners understand how a computer virus could affect them. Because the speaker indicates that an electronic virus can pose a threat to their computers, audience members are motivated to listen.

[14] Some of you use a computer as a word processor for your class assignments. It is possible that the following scenario could happen to you: imagine that you have just spent eight weeks and countless hours on a major term paper. All of your research and rough drafts are stored on your computer disk and the finished paper is due tomorrow. You run into the college lab to make some last minute adjustments and as you prepare to print out the final copy, you look up to find that your computer screen has suddenly gone blank. No matter what you do, you can't retrieve your work. Now you remove your disk and take it to a friend's house so you can check it on his computer. When you place your disk in his computer, all of the data stored in his machine also disappears. Both of you are now victims of a computer virus. In this example, the lab computer, whether by accident or on purpose, had been infected with a virus. When you used the lab computer, the virus automatically copied itself onto your computer disk. Later, by inserting your infected disk into your friend's computer, you inadvertently transferred a copy of the virus into his machine. You can see how using many different machines and freely swapping computer disks increases your risk of becoming a computer virus victim.

15 Another method exists for someone to spread a computer virus. As our society demands faster ways of communicating information, many people have abandoned the old method of sending information through the mail. We can now transfer data at mind-boggling speeds by linking computers. Computers are quickly becoming our electronic mailmen.

¹⁵ The speaker uses the metaphor of the "mailmen" and the "envelope" to describe the computer and the computer disk.

16 The computer disk is the new envelope, and the data stored on it has replaced the document. Modern technology enables us to zip off a letter to a friend without leaving our computer keyboards. Now you may ask, "How can a computer transfer data across the country?" say, from Portland, Oregon to Portland, Maine, for example. The answer is by telephone. The same phone system which transmits your voice and the tones from your telephone push-buttons can also carry a message right out of your computer.

¹⁶ For variety, the speaker poses a rhetorical question to keep the audience interested and involved in the topic.

17 Computer users often exchange data by using a simple device called a telephone modem. A modem makes it possible for two distant computers to be linked electronically. A telephone modem transfers computer messages by using special frequencies and electronic pulses. If you were to listen to a computer message coming through a modem, you would hear nothing more than buzzes and bleeps. But when the telephone modem is connected to your computer, it decodes the incoming sound waves so that your computer can understand them. In a matter of seconds the bleeps and buzzes are transformed into words on your computer screen.

¹⁷ After analyzing his student audience, Chris recognizes the need to define unfamiliar terms such as "modem" and "electronic bulletin boards."

18 Today, large networks exist so that computer users can call nationwide central computers. These massive central units are known as electronic bulletin boards, which are used to distribute information. If you used a computer to call a bulletin board you would find an amazing variety of information. The contents of an electronic bulletin board can range from singles dating advertisements to the latest medical techniques for treating AIDS—and practically everything in between. If you saw something that was particularly interesting in the vast library of information, you could easily copy that file directly into your computer with the press of a button.

¹⁸ The brief explanation describing the contents of electronic bulletin boards— "singles dating ads" and "techniques for treating AIDS" provide interesting concrete examples that listeners easily understand.

19 Unfortunately, electronic bulletin boards are a prime breeding ground for most computer viruses. One of the easiest ways for a computer virus to invade your computer system is to masquerade as a legitimate program or file, known as a Trojan horse virus. Just as the ancient Greeks secretly placed soldiers inside the wooden horse, an unscrupulous programmer can plant a hidden computer virus inside what appears to be a simple file of information. Anyone who copies that file can bring the virus into their system. Computer users, like the unsuspecting citizens of Troy, are often too late in realizing their mistake—the damage has already begun.

¹⁹ The speaker uses a simile to compare the computer virus to the ancient Greek Trojan horse.

[20] The speaker explains the automatic transmission of bulletin board files by making a comparison to the Morris virus.

Chris uses statistics from the *New York Times* article to indicate the widespread effect of the virus.

[20] Some bulletin boards even send electronic mail to thousands of machines automatically, just as advertisers send junk mail to your house. If a computer mass mailing became infected with a hidden virus, it would automatically transmit thousands of virus copies as an extra, unwanted bonus. To illustrate this point, the plague Robert Morris started began when he sent an ordinary piece of electronic mail. Even though it looked harmless, the message he sent contained an elaborate virus. His virus was automatically designed to multiply and spread to every machine linked to a national computer network. According to a *New York Times* article dated November 8, 1988, the Morris virus infected over 6,000 computers nationwide in less than twelve hours, shutting them down completely. It is the most dramatic example to date of the potential danger of computer viruses.

[21] The speaker provides further explanation and clarification of the Morris virus and the damage it actually caused.

[21] Many experts classified the Morris virus as mild when they considered the damage that might have occurred, since it did not destroy any of the files inside the infected computers. However, it did cause the computers to "freeze up" so that no work could be performed on them. Friends close to Mr. Morris say his intention in releasing the virus was merely to track its growth as it spread; he was reportedly horrified by the results.

[22] It appears that after he released his virus through the telephone line, he discovered he had made a terrible mistake in his math computations. The virus was only supposed to make a single copy of itself in each computer. Instead, it multiplied hundreds of times in every machine. The error caused his virus to rapidly consume all the available computer memory in the infected machines, until they were overloaded and rendered useless. The tracking system Morris designed quickly reflected that something had gone wrong, but by then he could do little more than sit and watch as the casualties mounted across the nation.

[23] The speaker has skillfully related the statistics by figuring out the hourly wages of Robert Morris and how long he would have to work to repay the $100 million damages.

[23] An article in *Personal Computing* magazine described the consequences of the Morris virus in its May 1989 issue. It was estimated that all the costs involved with removing the virus totalled approximately $100 million dollars. Now just imagine if Mr. Morris had to repay everyone for the damage his virus created. Morris would have to earn $274 dollars an hour, working twenty hours every day without a single day off for fifty years! Keep in mind that all that expense came from what was considered to be a mild, nuisance-type virus. If the virus had been more destructive in its programming, it could have wiped out millions of files forever, and the costs could have run into the billions.

[24] A quotation from an expert is used to support the claim made about the potential threat posed by an electronic virus.

[24] In this "Age of Information" computer viruses threaten the very lifeblood of our society. Banks, universities, hospitals, satellite networks, telephone systems, law enforcement agencies, and the U.S. armed forces are only some of the insititutions that now depend on computer information in order to function. Stephen Walker, former director of information services at the Pentagon said, "If someone at NORAD (the North American Aerospace Defense Command)

wanted to do what Robert Morris did… he could cause a lot of damage." You can understand why computer scientists and government security experts are studying ways to protect computers from viruses.

25 *Scientific American* magazine reported in a March 1989 article that future efforts to improve computer security are helped by examining the viruses that have struck in the past. As a result of this research, several safety measures now exist for businesses and individuals to protect their computers.

26 *Business Week* magazine points out that one important measure is to do away with simple computer passwords, and to make new passwords more confidential. Basic passwords like "open" and "hello" are far too common among computer networks. Virus programs can be written to attempt entry using the most common passwords, as was the case with the Morris virus, and once inside the system the virus is free to do its programmed damage.

27 *The Wall Street Journal* provided another clue towards solving the puzzle created by computer viruses. When the Morris virus struck, AT&T's Bell Laboratories avoided infection because they had already closed what are known as "trap doors" in their computer programs. "Trap doors" are openings within a computer operating system which allow a programmer to make changes quickly. These "trap doors" are often built into the system because new programs need modification in the first few months, but many times a company will forget to secure the secret entry point once a program is running smoothly. Robert Morris's virus searched for and found "trap doors" in many of the machines that it infected.

28 *Personal Computing* magazine recommends the use of an anti-viral program which can set off an alarm when it detects that a new or unusual computer command is trying to enter your computer. There are now dozens of anti-viral computer programs available, and some will even automatically shut down your machine to prevent a virus from reaching your computer operating system.

29 Other practices, like making backup copies of computer disks daily, and not allowing new and untested copies of software to be loaded onto central computers, can reduce the risk and the spread of viruses. Incorporating some or all of these changes into your computer system will lessen your vulnerability to a virus attack.

30 None of these measures, however, are competely foolproof. Experts point out that computers, by their very design, must exchange information in order for them to be useful tools. Because of this, we will continue to be afflicted with computer viruses as long as some computer programmers continue to develop and distribute viruses. The current threat of computer viruses was best described by a military expert in computer security who was quoted in a March 1989 *Time* magazine article, and I would like to leave you with his ominous

25 This external transition links numerals II and III.

26 The speaker describes the first method of protecting computers.

27 The description of the second method involves defining unfamiliar terms.

28 The speaker uses a source to support almost every explanation of the alternative security systems. He states only the periodical name and avoids repeating the previously mentioned date.

30 The concluding quote from the computer expert dramatically conveys the potential damage of a computer virus. The speaker uses the phrase "I would like to leave you with…" to set up the quotation. A better way to introduce

the quote would be, "... a military expert in computer security who made this ominous statement in a March 1989 issue of *Time* magazine. He said that..."

Chris has made a technical topic interesting by providing meaningful examples, clear statistics,and expert testimony.

words. He declared that, "The potential for offensive use of viruses is so great that I would have to view the power and magnitude as comparable with that of nuclear or chemical weapons."

ALTERNATIVE INTRODUCTIONS AND CONCLUSIONS TO THE SAMPLE SPEECH

Here are several alternative introductions and conclusions constructed by Christopher Kavanaugh. Each example is designed to demonstrate a different opening and closing technique for a speech. Every introduction ties into the speech at paragraph #4, which presents the thesis statement. Each conclusion is inserted at paragraph #30 following the line, "Experts point out that computers, by their very design, must somehow exchange information in order for them to be useful tools to mankind."

Introduction 1: Shocking Statement

[1] This introduction begins with a shocking statement, which leads into the story about the computer virus created by Robert Morris. The shocking statement quickly gets audience attention.

[1] "We are currently under attack!" Those were the first desperate words of a message sent out to warn research facilities, universities, and military installations around the country. A computer scientist at NASA's Ames Research Center in California sent the emergency bulletin after struggling to control a renegade computer program that had somehow entered NASA's research computers. This was the nightmare that many computer experts had hoped would never happen, but on the night of November 2, 1988, their fears came true.

[2] An unknown computer operator had created and unleashed a terrorist program into a massive national network of over 60,000 computer terminals. In just a few hours, the terrorist program—commonly called a "computer virus"—had brought several thousand computers around the country to a standstill. Investigators frantically began searching for clues to discover who had perpetrated this unprecedented attack on the computer network.

[3] The result of the investigation proved astonishing. The computer virus was not caused by agents from the KGB or the PLO, but by a U.S. college student. The virus creator, twenty-three-year-old Robert Tappan Morris, was a computer science graduate student at Cornell University. On a lark, Morris wrote what he thought was a harmless virus and then sent it out through his computer terminal.

Introduction 2: Series of Statistics

1 By September of 1988, twenty-five different types of them had been documented. Two major corporations have been terrorized by people who threatened to unleash them unless ransom money was paid. One expert estimates that 40 percent of our nation's biggest industrial corporations have been struck by them at one time or another, and in one nine month period alone, over three hundred universities, corporations, and other institutions had been victimized by them. Even homes have been attacked, with estimates soaring as high as 250,000. You may think I'm talking about bombs, missiles, or burglaries, but actually I'm talking about computer viruses. The threat of these electronic viruses is increasingly alarming.

1 In this introduction, the speaker presents a series of statistics creating suspense. The introduction has listeners wondering what could do so much damage and potentially affect their homes. The speaker satisfies audience curiosity by explaining that the problems were caused by computer viruses.

2 The Jet Propulsion Laboratory in Pasadena, California has been infected with computer viruses four times in a single year. Computer virus attacks have been aimed at both FBI and CIA computer systems. The National Security Agency and the CIA have even admitted that the U.S. government had "experimented" with infecting the computer systems of other nations.

3 In 1988 a Cornell University student named Robert Tappan Morris placed a computer virus into an unclassified military computer network with explosive results. The computer network, established in the late '60s by the Department of Defense's Advanced Research Projects Agency, electronically links over 60,000 computer terminals from all over the country. Thousands of computers on the network were brought to a halt by Morris's computer virus in a matter of hours, and the U.S. Department of Defense ordered the entire network shut down temporarily so the dangerous computer program could be completely removed from the system.

4 Immediately following the Morris virus infection, computer scientists and military security experts from twelve government agencies hastily gathered together to examine the growing problem.

Introduction 3: Rhetorical Questions

1 Have you ever stopped to appreciate just how convenient your life is because of computers? Have you ever used the computer lab on campus to complete an assignment? Have you ever withdrawn money from an automatic teller machine? How many of you have placed a long distance phone call using direct dialing? Have you ever bought concert tickets over the phone, or made reservations for an airplane flight or a train trip? All of these are examples of the way in which computers influence your daily life.

1 This introduction begins with a series of rhetorical questions to create attention. The technique successfully generates curiosity and interest in the topic.

2 But computers also keep track of countless other pieces of information that we rarely think about. Stocks and commodities exchanges, air traffic control systems, corporate payrolls, and strategic military bases are other prime examples of operations that rely heavily on computers and the information stored within them. Think what would happen if we suddenly lost control over the computer systems we use every day. Sound far-fetched? Not at all. In fact, there is already something in our midst which threatens to change the way that you and I do business. I am referring to the problem of computer viruses.

3 Did you know, for example, that on November 2, 1988, a college student by the name of Robert Tappan Morris wrote a computer virus and sent it into a national computer network? The network Robert Morris managed to infiltrate with his computer program connected over 60,000 computer terminals from military installations, research facilities, and universities from around the nation. In only a few hours, Morris' virus program had brought the entire network crashing down, infecting and disabling thousands of individual computers. If this example worries you, consider this: most experts agree that the damage caused by Robert Morris was slight, and perhaps the next computer virus will be far worse. As a result of the concern raised by the Morris virus, computer scientists and military security experts from twelve government agencies held an emergency conference.

Introduction 4: Quotation

[1] This quotation stimulates curiosity by revealing only a portion of the information.

1 A man by the name of Stephen Ross said, "The virus problem is potentially unlimited. The era of the firecracker virus that goes off without any purpose or gain is coming to an end, and the era of the directed virus is close upon us." Ross isn't a doctor, and he wasn't referring to a new strain of Hong Kong flu. Mr. Ross is a senior manager with Deloitte, Haskins & Sells, one of the nation's largest consulting firms, and he was talking about something called a computer virus. Computer viruses are becoming more numerous, and they are gaining the attention of corporations, the U.S. government, and the media.

2 *The Wall Street Journal* reported a sensational example of a computer virus attack in the autumn of 1988. A Cornell University student named Robert Tappan Morris released a computer virus that infected a military network of computer terminals. The U.S. Air Force Logistics Command office at Wright Patterson Air Force Base, NASA's Ames Research Center in Moffett Field, California, the Naval Research Laboratory in Cabin John, Maryland, and the Air Forces' Electronic Systems Division at Hanscomb Air Force Base were only some of the military installations that were struck by the Morris virus. Major universities, including Berkeley, Purdue, M.I.T., Johns Hopkins, and Princeton were also infected by the computer virus that Robert Morris created. Several thousand computers were literally shut down by the Morris virus program overnight.

Conclusion 1: Brief Story

[1] Some of you may still be thinking that the computer virus problem only affects huge corporations and the U.S. Government, so let me remind you that individual computer users are equally at risk. To give you an idea of how threatening viruses can be to you, the individual, I'd like you to consider what happened to a newspaper reporter in Providence, Rhode Island. In 1988, Froma Joselow placed a computer disk into her terminal. Her disk contained interviews and notes she had compiled for articles, representing six months worth of work. As she attempted to call up files at her terminal, the message "DISK ERROR" kept flashing on the screen. Up until that moment she had never experienced any problem with her disk, yet suddenly six months of her career were irretrievable.

[2] Later, while examining the disk, a computer systems engineer discovered that most of the data stored on it had been devoured by a hidden virus. Still more frightening was the discovery that the particular virus which wound up on the reporter's computer disk had been created two years earlier in Lahore, Pakistan. No one knows exactly how the Pakistani virus reached Providence, Rhode Island.

[3] It is because of stories such as this that many experts are now saying that we, as a society, have reached the crossroads where our needs for convenient technology are conflicting with our needs to secure that very same technology. Most are predicting that by necessity, concern for protecting our information will eventually take precedence over the convenience we have previously enjoyed. The days of sitting down at a computer terminal and immediately beginning to work may be numbered. In the future, we may have to go through an elaborate and time-consuming ritual of confirming the integrity of our data every time we use a computer.

[1] This conclusion contains a brief story, which the speaker uses to remind listeners how viruses can affect them.

Conclusion 2: End Question

[1] Throughout our investigation of computer viruses, I have given you information concerning Robert Morris and the virus he created. But there is one more thing that you should know. Remember when I mentioned that the Morris virus attacked computers connected to a large national network? How would you feel if I told you that the network that he infected, ARPANET, is controlled by the U.S. Department of Defense's Advanced Research Projects Agency and is the largest unclassified military network in the U.S.? Dozens of our nation's top military research facilities and even a few of our strategic installations were infiltrated by a college student who didn't even have to leave his dorm room to accomplish his deed.

[1] Throughout this conclusion, the speaker asks listeners several questions.

[2] Some computer scientists say the onslaught of computer viruses like the one Morris released are the price we pay as a society that relies heavily on technology. Experts agree that it shouldn't be so easy to do what Robert Morris did. A

[2] The final question is thought-provoking and keeps the audience thinking about the impact of the virus on

[2]their own lives, even after the speaker has completed the presentation.

few have even predicted that without more significant changes in computer security, we will be afflicted with viruses that, by comparison, will make the Morris infection look like child's play. In light of what you now know about computer viruses, you might ask yourself this question: "Am I prepared for the possible consequences of a virus attack in a computer that I use?"

Conclusion 3: Summary

[1]The speaker develops a summary to the speech. Notice that the summary is not simply a listing of main points; it touches on some of the significant information provided in the speech.

[1] In a nation where an entire generation has been raised with computers which can teach them to read and spell, to add and subtract, and even to entertain themselves by playing games, it should be no surprise that many of these same individuals have acquired a rather sophisticated understanding of computers and their operation. Due to this increase in computer literacy, we now have more people capable of creating computer viruses, and unfortunately we are seeing a steady increase in the number of computer viruses that are being written and released. In an attempt to deal with the recent surge in computer sabotage, new laws have been passed which make the misuse of a computer a criminal offense. Robert Morris became the first person ever indicted under a federal law concerning computer security, and Morris's indictment reflects a growing sentiment in our country. By holding Morris accountable for his actions, the government has said that we, as a society dependent on critical information systems, will no longer tolerate computer misuse, even when it is done in "harmless" fun. There is too much at stake.

Conclusion 4: Reference to the Introduction

[1] This means that we will probably continue to be afflicted with computer virus programs.

[2] In this conclusion, the speaker completes the story about Robert Morris, which was started in the introduction.

The reference to the introduction combined with the end quote from the prosecuting attorney, provides more information about the case study.

[2] Many of you may be wondering what happened to Robert Morris. He became the first person ever indicted under a federal law dealing with the issue of computer security. The legislation, enacted by Congress and known as the Computer Fraud and Abuse Act, provides stiff penalties for the misuse of government computers. The Morris legal case may drag on for years within the court system, but if found guilty of the felony charge, Morris could be sentenced to five years in prison and ordered to repay all of the costs incurred by his virus attack. The legal action being taken against Morris signals a change in our attitude towards computer mischief. In the past, viruses like Morris's would have been celebrated for their ingenuity, but today, we recognize them as threats to our information systems. I spoke with Mark Rasch, a prosecuting attorney with the Justice Department in Washington, D.C., regarding the Morris case, and he summed up the situation with eloquent simplicity. He said, "A computer is a tool, just like a crowbar is a tool. And although a tool can be used in a beneficial manner, it can also be used to commit a crime."[4]

SUMMARY

When you deliver speeches to inform, you seek to educate and enlighten your audience—not to influence their beliefs, feelings, or behavior.

Three categories of informative speeches are: description, definition, and other informative types (reports, lectures, and personal experiences). The descriptive speech is related to a person, place, object, or event. A speech of definition identifies and explains a theory or subject area. Three other informational types are the report, which is used primarily in organizations and institutions; the lecture, which is presented by experts; and the personal experience.

EXERCISES

1. Choose four topics and write one informative and one persuasive specific purpose for each.
2. Choose a topic and present a five- to seven-minute descriptive speech. Use a minimum of three sources and ten supporting materials to establish your credibility.
3. The following specific purpose sentences contain worn-out topics. Rework the topics to provide new information which motivates audience members to listen.
   a. to inform you that AIDS is a deadly disease
   b. to explain the hazards of cigarette smoking
   c. to describe the benefits of an exercise program
   d. to define *democracy*
   e. to demonstrate how to make a cake by following the directions on the back of the Pillsbury cake box
4. Evaluate an informative lecture of one of your instructors. Comment on the following areas:
   a. Is the instructor clear and well organized?
   b. Does the speaker maintain the interest of the audience?
   c. If visuals are used, does the instructor incorporate them effectively into the presentation?
   d. Does the speaker have an effective delivery?
5. From your own experience, choose a term that is familiar to you but perhaps unknown to your audience. Develop a speech of definition using this term as your topic. Make sure that your listeners understand the definition and become interested in the speech.

NOTES

[1] Thomas H. Olbricht, *Informative Speaking* (Glenview, Illinois: Scott, Foresman and Company, 1968), pp. 15–16. Our discussion of the difference between information and persuasion coin-

cides with Olbricht's analysis of the "traditional means of distinguishing informing from persuading" in his second chapter.

[2] Ibid., p. 15.

[3] I thank Kara Jenkins and Tom Pfeffer for permission to use portions of their outlines and Kelly O'Connor, Joan Stark, and Tresse Bailey for topic ideas.

[4] Christopher B. Kavanaugh, developed from an informative descriptive speech presented in speech class, Catonsville Community College, Catonsville, Maryland, 1989. Used by permission.

READINGS

Olbricht, Thomas H. *Informative Speaking.* Glenview, Illinois: Scott, Foresman, 1968. Contains material relating to the development of informative speeches. Olbricht includes chapters on audience analysis, organization, visual aids, verbal reinforcement, and language. While it is an older text, it is an excellent reference when you prepare your informative presentation.

Samovar, Larry A., and Mills, Jack. *Oral Communication Message and Response*, 4th ed. Dubuque, Iowa: Wm. C. Brown, 1980. Contains a chapter on informative speaking which parallels many of the ideas presented here. Samovar and Mills list some excellent guidelines for the use of visual aids and provide extensive discussion of the organizational patterns used to structure informative speeches.

Chapter Sixteen

SPEAKING TO INFORM: DEMONSTRATING PROCEDURES

Chapter Outline

Key Terms

Chronological sequence
Demonstration

© Grant LeDuc/
Stock Boston

"...whatever be the process to that end..."
—SAMUEL JOHNSON

*M*ike Mason was a scuba diver and trainer on the Kona coast of Hawaii. As senior divemaster, Mike's job required him to conduct training programs for advanced divers, tourists, and students. His duties almost always involved demonstrating procedures with visual aids. Here are just a few of the processes that Mike demonstrated in the course of one work day: handling and maintaining diving equipment; assembling and donning scuba gear; using proper equalization techniques; executing descents and ascents; achieving neutral buoyancy; learning underwater communication techniques; executing emergency and safety procedures; using dive tables; disassembling equipment. As a skilled professional, Mike recognized that lives depended on the effectiveness of his presentations. A clear, well prepared demonstration could enhance diving skills; a poorly organized, ambiguous presentation could contribute to a diving tragedy.

Even though lives may not depend on the quality of your classroom demonstration, you will probably be required to present, evaluate, or participate in numerous process speeches during your occupational life. This chapter helps you to develop, organize, and evaluate this informative speech.

THE DEMONSTRATION SPEECH

One important type of speech to inform is the *demonstration*, which usually includes a variety of audiovisual aids to show the steps of a process. In most businesses, institutions, and professional organizations, employees at all levels are required to present or participate in programs that explain procedures and processes. Seminars are conducted to teach workers how to use new telephone systems, fax machines, or laser technologies; how to fill out purchase orders, application forms, or government documents; how to confront sexual harrassment, use new sales techniques, or handle consumer complaints; how to treat new diseases, implement new manufacturing procedures, or conform to safety standards. These training sessions protect the company and employee, help to maintain a company's competitive edge, and improve workers' productivity or efficiency.

No matter what your career or profession, you will probably be required to explain how something works, how something is made, how something is done, or how something happens.

How something works

to demonstrate how the eye works

to demonstrate how to operate a personal computer

to demonstrate how a carburetor works

to demonstrate how a Revolutionary War musket operates

How something is made

to demonstrate how the violin is constructed

to demonstrate how the Chinese weave rugs

to demonstrate how to make Greek moussaka

to demonstrate the art of Japanese origami

How something is done

to demonstrate how pianos are tuned

to demonstrate how to shear sheep

to demonstrate how to mine rubies

to explain how to rig a sailboat

to explain how an airplane flies

How something happens

to explain how geysers develop

to explain how dreams occur

to explain how pearls form

to explain how Parkinson's disease attacks the body

AN EFFECTIVE
DEMONSTRATION SPEECH
INCLUDES CLEAR
EXPLANATIONS, PRECISE
GESTURES, AND CAREFUL
PRACTICE WITH
AUDIOVISUAL AIDS.

© Spencer Grant/Pictue Cube

BUILDING THE PROCESS SPEECH

Demonstrating a familiar process may sound easy, but when you are in front of an audience, many things can go wrong. Lack of preparation can cause misplacing or dropping a visual aid or displaying objects that are too small for the audience to see. To help you avoid these and other difficulties, here is a list of guidelines for building the process speech.

1. **Choose a topic from your experience or knowledge.**
   a. Examine your professional expertise and life experience.
   b. Choose a topic in which you teach, train, or educate.
2. **Investigate the location of the speech.**
   a. Does the room or auditorium have everything necessary to support audiovisual aids?
   b. Do you need to bring extra equipment or supplies?
   c. Can the audience see your visuals easily?
3. **Develop a logical outline.**
   a. Include all required structural elements: an interesting introduction, a purpose statement, a well-organized body, and a clearly-defined conclusion.
   b. Combine information in the body of the demonstration into overall categories like "gathering materials," "preparing for the process," or "finished product."
   c. Use chronological sequence to arrange events in order of occurrence.
   d. Employ any type of conclusion, using a summary to reinforce complicated or unfamiliar procedures.
4. **Apply principles of effective delivery.**
   a. Be clear.
      (1) Verbally emphasize important points and repeat steps, key ideas, or complicated material when necessary.
      (2) Use gestures to point out significant details.
      (3) Clarify main headings in the body with external transitions.
      (4) Use internal transitions—*then, next, finally*—to connect steps grouped beneath main headings.
      (5) Employ simple terms, defining unfamiliar words and pronouncing difficult terms correctly.
      (6) Speak slowly enough to allow listeners to follow the steps of the process.
      (7) Relate ideas to listeners with concrete examples.
   b. Keep the speech moving.
      (1) Keep talking as you demonstrate, avoiding awkward pauses or silences.
      (2) Be prepared with additional comments if the procedure takes longer than expected.
      (3) Keep to the time limit.
      (4) Include only essential elements of the process, eliminating unnecessary detail.
   c. Know how to use audiovisuals.
      (1) Set up visuals in advance if possible.
      (2) Use enough visuals to support the process, avoiding too few or too many.
      (3) Reveal visuals at the right psychological moment.
      (4) Avoid distractions by not passing out objects while you speak.
      (5) Be sure that visuals are large enough for listeners to see.
      (6) Integrate visuals smoothly into the speech, eliminating awkwardness.
      (7) Remove visuals quickly if there are other speakers following your presentation.
   d. Be prepared.
      (1) Rehearse with all the audiovisuals you intend to use.
      (2) Show enthusiasm and interest through vocal variety, facial expression, and gestures.
      (3) Maintain eye contact with the audience.

An Example

Demonstrations are not simplistic show-and-tell speeches: they are sophisticated presentations that include carefully crafted visuals which support the process.

A student who was an avid mountain climber demonstrated how to do rappelling—descending a steep incline with a secured rope. He took the speech class outside to an eight-foot-high retaining wall on campus, where he described the necessary equipment and the proper procedure to descend the wall. Class members watched and listened intently as the speaker slowly lowered himself down the wall, carefully explaining each step of the process. Listeners commented that the speaker's creative approach made the speech important and "alive."

OUTLINING THE DEMONSTRATION SPEECH

Most process speeches incorporate numerous steps or phases often difficult for listeners to recall. For example, "Developing Color Film" would probably include more than 15 steps, and "Decorating a Wedding Cake" could incorporate more than 23 procedures. The body of a demonstration should never contain 15 or 23 numeral headings. In order to keep the process simple, group the steps into categories:

Specific purpose: to demonstrate how the digestive system works

Thesis statement: The digestive process includes the mouth, the stomach, the small intestine, and the large intestine.

PROCESS SPEECHES REQUIRE A COMPREHENSIVE KNOWLEDGE OF THE TOPIC AND A CLEAR UNDERSTANDING OF THE USE OF AUDIOVISUAL AIDS.

© Walter S. Silver/ Picture Cube

Chronological order

Steps grouped by categories
  I. The mouth

Steps of the complete process
    A. Food enters mouth
    B. Food chewed by teeth
    C. Salivary glands secrete digestive enzyme
    D. Valves in larynx keep food from passing into windpipe
    E. Food passes through esophagus to stomach

  II. The stomach
    A. Sphincter prevents regurgitation
    B. Food mixed with gastric juices

  III. The small intestine
    A. Food enters small intestine
    B. Food mixed with bile from liver
    C. Food mixed with enzymes from pancreas
    D. Food molecules absorbed into blood stream for transport to body tissues

  IV. The large intestine
    A. Food enters large intestine
    B. Receives undigested food

                                                C. Water absorbed from food
             residues
        D. Residues converted into solid
             mass for elimination
        E. Elimination through anus[1]

Notice at the right that there are at least sixteen separate steps in the digestive process. Like any other five- to seven-minute speech, process speeches should contain no fewer than two and no more than four numerals in the body. On the left, you can see that the digestive process can be grouped into four principal steps which incorporate all sixteen items. The four headings make the demonstration clear and easy to follow.

Notice that main points in the body of most demonstrations will be arranged according to some form of chronological sequence—by time or events. In the above example, main points are organized according to the order of occurrence. Some topics can be organized by combining chronological sequence with another arrangement. For example, Ann Foley combined topic sequence with chronology in the following demonstration of fingerprinting:[2]

Specific purpose: to demonstrate the science of fingerprinting

Thesis statement: Fingerprinting, an important science which identifies individuals' finger print types, is an interesting process used in police work.

Body

    I. The importance of fingerprints
        A. Identify fugitives
        B. Identify victims
        C. Provide unmistakable verification
   II. Different types of fingerprints
        A. Plain arch
        B. Fented arch
        C. The loop
        D. Plain whorl
        E. Central pocket loop
        F. Double loop
        G. Accidental (no set pattern)
  III. The process of fingerprinting
        A. Insert fingerprint card in card holder
        B. Use small amount of ink on roller
        C. Apply thin ink coat with roller to glass inking plate
        D. Place subject approximately one forearm away from fingerprint card
        E. For right hand, stand to left of subject
        F. Take right thumb and roll on inking plate

G. Place inked thumb on fingerprint card
H. Roll thumb from left to right for complete rounded print
I. Continue with rolling process for other fingers
J. Take prints of four fingers without rolling
K. Repeat entire process with left hand

Ann chose a topic that could be demonstrated rather quickly. In order to provide more depth to her speech, she spent a few minutes explaining the importance of fingerprints and identifying the various types. Ann arranged her three main headings in a simple topical sequence. Then in III, "The process of fingerprinting," she used chronological order for the subdivisions. Because of her organization, Ann included enough material for an effective six- to seven-minute process speech.

The following speech was presented by a student in the basic speech course. "Having a Heart," by Henry Humm, is a demonstration explaining the delicate heart transplant surgery the speaker experienced at age sixteen. Visual aids provided with the speech indicate how supporting materials can clarify and enhance a process.

HAVING A HEART

An Informative Speech to Demonstrate

Henry Humm

1 Three years ago, I was trying out for my high school soccer team, and I was required to have a physical examination. Little did I know that the routine physical I took would lead to the most dramatic event that ever happened in my life. Through that physical and a series of tests, I was diagnosed as having what was called a dilated cardiomyopathy. Now that may sound like a 50 cent word to you, but I want you to know that a dilated cardiomyopathy is very serious—the heart becomes globular in shape and is enlarged in size. The heart may increase as much as twice the size of a normal heart. Also, the left ventricle around the heart becomes thinner than normal.

[1] While there are many ways to introduce a speech, Henry's personal story is probably the most effective method for this topic. The personal experience generates curiosity and establishes the speaker's credibility. He defined the unfamiliar medical term to keep his audience with him.

2 Well, from this diagnosis, I was told I needed to have a very serious life-saving operation—a heart transplant, which is what I'm going to demonstrate today. I'm going to tell you about matching the donor organ with the recipient, removing and transporting the heart, preparing the patient for surgery, and performing the actual transplant itself.

[2] Both the specific purpose and the thesis statement clearly conveyed the main point and the areas the demonstration would cover.

3 Let me briefly explain something about matching the donor and the recipient. First the patient must be placed on a waiting list with other heart recipients. This

[3] Henry clearly identifies numeral I of the body. His use of the the internal transitions "first," "next," and "finally," allows the audience to follow the numeral (I) subheadings easily.

waiting list is based upon the severity of the illness and each case carries a rating of one to four—one standing for those with the greatest need and four representing the least. Next the blood type of the donor heart must either match the recipient's or be compatible. Finally, the donor heart must be the right size for the patient's chest cavity. As long as the heart fits it is suitable for the transplant. In my situation, for instance, I was small and I could not have a large heart, so I had to wait for a donor organ for five-and-a-half weeks. I should also tell you that if a heart were too small, it would have to work twice as hard to pump blood throughout the body. So you can see how important it is for doctors to select a heart which corresponds to the patient's chest cavity.

[4] He uses an effective transitional phrase to connect numeral I and II of the body.

4 Okay. I've talked about matching the recipient—Now let me tell you about removing and transporting the heart.

[5] The speaker cites a primary source to provide credibility. Since listeners are not acquainted with the expert, Henry briefly provides her qualifications.

5 According to Sharon M. Augustine, who is a Transplant Nurse Practitioner at Johns Hopkins, the hospital gets a call that a donor heart is available for transplant. Members of the transplant team immediately fly to the person who is brain dead to remove the organ. In order for this procedure to occur, team members hurry to the heliport located on top of the hospital and fly to the airport. Once they arrive at the airport they fly by private jet to the city where the donor heart is located. They drive to the hospital where they remove the organ. It is important for team members themselves to make this trip in order to be sure that the heart has not suffered any previous damage, or is not damaged during removal. You can imagine the incredible amount of time, energy, and resources that would be wasted if the transplant team did not examine the heart first-hand to determine its suitability.

[6] Henry keeps his topic moving in a chronological sequence. He uses concrete examples (like the Igloo Cooler) to make the topic come alive for his listeners.

6 Once the organ is examined and then removed, it is placed in a tupperware container with an iced saline solution. The saline solution keeps the organ cold, at about four degrees centigrade. The organ is cooled to keep the metabolism of the heart down to a minimum. The tupperware container is then packed into sterile ice with saline and placed into an Igloo cooler—the type of cooler you take to a picnic or to the beach! Finally doctors are ready to return to the hospital of the anxious recipient.

7 The transplant team takes the heart by ambulance to the airport and flies back to the city where the transplant will be performed. State police pick up the doctors and the heart and take them back to the hospital by helicopter. Once they have returned, the special job of these team members is finished and other members of the transplant team take over to perform the actual surgery.

[8] Again, there is a clear transition between numeral II and III of the body.

8 I've described how doctors transport the heart to the hospital—Now I want you to know what happens to the patient right up until the transplant procedure. As the team leaves to bring back the organ, the recipient is called to the hospital. When the patient arrives, doctors take chest x-rays and do blood work to check the H.L.A.—that is, the Human Leukocytes Antigens. These antigens are

checked against a panel of antibodies to see whether the donated heart will reject its new body. Doctors then give the patient an injection of a drug called Cyclosporin A which helps to prevent rejection of the donated heart. This injection is given before the surgery so that anti-rejection drugs will already be circulating in the patient's system. When all these procedures are complete, the patient is wheeled into a room where he waits until the donor heart arrives.

9 When the heart arrives, the patient is taken into surgery where an IV is started. Once the patient is heavily sedated and the donor heart is reexamined, the chest cavity is then opened. I'd like you to look at my first poster which shows the steps involved in opening the chest cavity.

10 As you can see from Figure 1, surgeons must make a 9-inch incision in the skin of the chest. Then, as Figure 2 indicates, they take a saw and cut the sternum.

The speaker continues to explain terms unfamiliar to his audience.

OPENING THE CHEST CAVITY

FIGURE 16.1

Figures 1–4: Opening the Chest Cavity

Illustration by
George Goebel

[10]Each visual is simple, effective, and clearly labeled. The speaker carefully explains his visuals and uses humor to generate audience feedback.

[11]Henry uses another external transition as he introduces the transplant process. Although the topic is based on a personal experience, the speaker has provided primary research sources such as the interviews with the doctors to supplement his own knowledge.

[12]The speaker directs his listeners to the next poster and uses the diagram to point out each step in the process. He emphasizes the section of the drawing ("I want you to notice") that he wants listeners to remember in preparation for the next illustration.

FIGURE 16.2

REMOVING THE
DISEASED HEART

Illustration by
George Goebel

(The sternum is another word for the breastbone.) After they have cut the sternum, Figure 3 shows surgeons using the rib spreader to separate the ribs in order to allow access to the chest cavity. (I hope nobody gets queasy!) Finally, they gain access to the chest cavity, and they are ready to begin the actual transplant, as you can see in Figure 4.

[11]You've heard how the patient is prepared for surgery and seen how the chest is opened—Now I'd like to show you the steps involved in this remarkable transplant procedure. I interviewed my surgeon, Dr. William A. Baumgartner, and chief cardiologist, Dr. Thomas A. Traill, of Johns Hopkins Hospital, who told me that there are basically three major steps involved with a heart transplant.

[12]I'd like you to look at my next poster, which shows the removal of the diseased heart. In the first step, surgeons hook the patient up to a pulmonary bypass machine. Notice the tubes running from the heart to the heart–lung machine at the left. The bypass machine takes the place of the heart as the old heart is

REMOVING THE DISEASED HEART

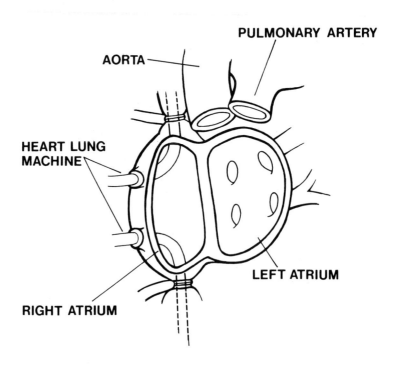

being removed. Second, the surgeons remove the diseased heart, which has already been done in this drawing; but I want you to notice that the diagram indicates that surgeons do not remove the entire heart—They have left the back of the left and right atrium along in here and parts of the pulmonary artery and aorta, as you can see at the top of the drawing.

13 Once the diseased heart is removed, surgeons can begin to surgically transplant the donated heart. The third and most delicate part of the surgery is the attachment of the donor organ to the remaining portions of the patient's heart. This step must be performed in four precise stages, which you can see in my next drawing.

[13] The speaker mentions the label of the diagram for reinforcement and for clarity.

14 1. Here is the first step, where surgeons sew the donated heart to the left atrium, along these suture lines. (Don't try this at home!)

2. Next they sew the heart to the right atrium, as you can see by these dotted suture lines here.

3. Then the most important step is sewing together the pulmonary artery (along these dotted lines), which is the heart's main blood vessel that takes blood from the heart to the lungs to get oxygenated.

[14] The speaker carefully identifies each step by number, pointing out the areas which need special emphasis. His use of "here," "next," "then," and "finally," helps the audience to follow each stage in the process. The use of humor generates audience feedback, and relieves the tension of a potentially intense topic.

FIGURE 16.3

ATTACHING THE NEW HEART

Illustration by George Goebel

ATTACHING THE NEW HEART

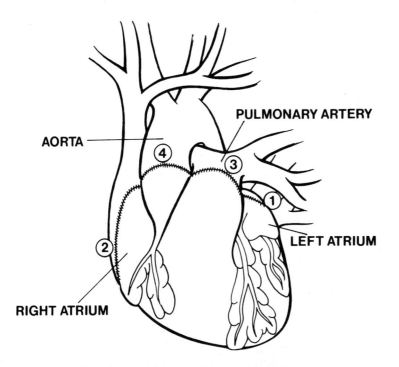

4. Finally they sew the heart aorta, which you can see with the suture lines in this area.

[15]Once the heart is attached in the four proper places and is checked to make sure there is no leakage, doctors can begin to close the patient's chest.

[16]The conclusion effectively summarizes additional obstacles of transplant patients.

[16]I hope you realize that getting a new heart does not mean everything will be easy. There are many obstacles transplant recipients face on a day-to-day basis. In my case, for instance, I must take medication for the rest of my life. And this medication often has unpleasant side effects. There is also the constant fear of infection and rejection of the new organ. Doctors must monitor my health closely and I'm required to return every few months for periodic checkups and heart examinations.

[17]The final paragraph, revealing Henry's personal feelings, ends the speech on a powerful note.

[17]But all this is a small price to pay for what I have. I've been living on my donated heart for three years, and I can honestly say I've never felt better. I would just like to someday tell the family who lost their child how grateful I am for their gift of life![3]

SUMMARY

Demonstration speeches use carefully crafted audiovisual aids to explain how something works, how something is made, how something is done, or how something happens. Demonstrations are not simplistic show-and-tell speeches; they are sophisticated presentations with detailed steps which are grouped into categories, often using chronological sequence.

EXERCISES

1. Choose a topic from your own knowledge and experience for a five- to seven-minute demonstration speech. Make extensive use of audiovisual aids to convey the process clearly. Be sure that you know how to develop audiovisuals and how to employ them effectively.

2. Watch a program on public television that demonstrates a process such as cooking, home building, or auto repair. Evaluate the effectiveness of the speaker's organization and delivery, clarity of the process, and quality and management of audiovisual aids. Describe what was successful and unsuccessful about the presentation.

NOTES

[1] Information from the *Encyclopedia Americana* was used for this section on the digestive system.

[2] Ann Foley, "Fingerprint Identification," demonstration speech presented in speech class, Catonsville Community College, Catonsville, Maryland, 1988. Used by permission.

[3] Henry Humm, "Having A Heart," demonstration speech, presented in speech class, Catonsville Community College, Catonsville, Maryland, 1987. Used by permission.

Chapter Seventeen

SPEAKING TO PERSUADE

Chapter Outline

Key Terms

© Henri Dauman/
Magnum Photos, Inc.

"What thou hast spoken,
thou must prove it."
—SADI

*P*ersuasion is a fact of life at all levels of a democratic society. Highway billboards picture the "pleasures of drinking" while TV commercials portray the disastrous consequences of drunk driving. Magazine ads motivate us to buy expensive cologne to make us more appealing. Twirling TV raisins invite us to taste their "sun-ripened" California flavor. Husbands and wives debate the merits of having small or large families. Celebrities appear with starving children to raise money for famine relief. Streetcorner activists trumpet their favorite candidates or political issues. Children pester their parents to buy candy and gum at the supermarket.

We use persuasion consciously and subconsciously. Whether we are asking a supervisor for a promotion, listening to a eulogy, or explaining a speeding ticket to a judge in traffic court, we are involved in persuasive activities.

We must understand and acquire the skills necessary for persuasive effectiveness. This chapter considers the nature of persuasion, the different types of persuasive appeals, persuasive organization, and provides some guidelines to help you construct your persuasive speech to convince.

AN AUDIENCE CAN BE PERSUADED BY ETHICAL, EMOTIONAL, AND LOGICAL APPEALS.

Beringer–Dratch/
Image Works

THE NATURE OF PERSUASION

Persuasion can be defined as communication that influences and changes the beliefs, feelings, or behavior of a listener. Persuasive speeches convince, stimulate, and actuate. To develop the correct speech for the appropriate persuasive situation, you must know how each of these types of presentation differs.

Speeches to Convince

The goal of the speech to *convince* is to alter the beliefs and judgments of an audience. A prosecuting attorney tries to convince jurors that a defendant is guilty. A legislator attempts to convince other lawmakers that a tax increase is the best way to solve the deficit problem. A parent tries to convince the PTA to consider adding sex education classes in elementary grades. While a convincing speech may lead an audience to take some future action, it is important to emphasize that the immediate goal of a speech to convince is to obtain mental agreement with the speaker's position. In a speech to convince, a speaker persuades an audience to believe that a problem exists, that a proposed solution is a better alternative, or that some future action may be required.

Speeches to Stimulate

In a speech to *stimulate*, the speaker seeks to reinforce and intensify the beliefs or feelings of listeners. A coach gives the football team a pep talk at half-time to generate enthusiasm and a winning spirit. A religious leader reminds the congregation about basic beliefs to strengthen faith. A political leader makes a Veterans Day speech to rekindle patriotic feelings. Therapeutic groups come together for mutual reinforcement. Members of Alcoholics Anonymous, drug rehabilitation centers, or parental stress organizations relate their personal experiences for empathy, encouragement, and positive change. As a rule, agreement already exists between speaker and audience about basic beliefs and goals. It is the purpose of the stimulating speech to focus on these sentiments and bring them to the surface.

Speeches to Actuate

Speeches to *actuate* motivate audiences to act. A salesperson selling a product, a candidate asking for votes, or a humanitarian appealing for donations to a worthy charity are all seeking to affect the behavior of the audience. Highly effective thirty to sixty second commercials motivate children, teenagers, young adults, or senior citizens to buy products designed "with you in mind." In a speech to actuate, a speaker generates curiosity, clarifies a problem, identifies a solution, and then persuades the audience to perform a specific action related to the solution. The action the speaker solicits is clear, direct, and observable.

Selecting the Persuasive Topic

When you begin to build your persuasive speech, your first task is to choose a topic with potential to influence your audience. Begin by analyzing some of your interests, concerns, and activities. You might have a concern about the pollutants in our oceans. You might be an avid hunter and resent gun-control legislation. Or you might be upset by the leniency of the courts toward criminals. Hundreds of issues would make excellent topics for persuasive speeches. The key to your success, as in any speech, is your degree of commitment to the issue, your ability to select appropriate supporting materials, and your competence in organizing and delivering your thoughts.

Wording the Proposition Statement

Once you have selected a topic, write a statement called a *proposition*, an arguable resolution phrased in a declarative sentence. The proposition acts as the focal point for your arguments and supporting materials. Like the specific purpose sentence, the proposition statement relates the overall objective of the speech at the end of the introduction. But unlike the specific purpose, the proposition reveals a clear point of view on a controversial topic.

To convince your audience that a relationship exists between TV violence and the behavior of young children, you could state several propositions:

Violence on television contributes to violent behavior in young children.

Violence in TV cartoons has harmful effects on young children.

TV violence can contribute to severe emotional trauma in young children.

You would select one of the above statements and conduct research to find supporting evidence—statistics, testimonies, and examples. You would need to be certain that the evidence did indeed back up your proposition. If it did not, you would be faced with three choices: (1) conducting a more extensive search for evidence until you found suitable data; (2) rephrasing the proposition to correspond to existing evidence, or (3) looking for another issue.

Once you had written your proposition and gathered your evidence, you would construct logical arguments to support your point of view. (We will consider logic and reasoning later in this chapter.) Thorough research and appropriate evidence are extremely important to your success as a persuasive speaker. Your speech will have a significant impact on your listeners if they feel your proposition is validated by careful research and good evidence.

Propositions of Fact, Value, and Policy   You can select any of three proposition statements for a persuasive speech: propositions of fact, value, or policy. In a *proposition of fact*, you develop a statement you believe is true and must be verified by evidence. Here are some examples:

Propositions of fact

America is in decline.

Free trade agreements with Mexico and Canada have contributed to fewer American jobs.

Victims of rape are treated as criminals by the judicial system.

Bans against controversial art exhibitions violate the First Amendment.

There will be a major volcanic eruption in Alaska within the next five years.

National health insurance will increase taxes.

The above propositions are not actual facts, but facts as they are perceived by the persuasive speaker. If you took a survey in most audiences, you would probably find a variety of opinions about each statement. It is the speaker's job to gather evidence which persuades the audience that the perceived fact stated in the proposition is correct.

In a *proposition of value*, you are required to judge or evaluate an issue. You ask the audience to believe something is right or wrong, good or bad, effective or ineffective.

Propositions of value

Home schools are damaging to children.

Homosexuals are responsible soldiers.

Athletic scholarships are beneficial to colleges and universities.

Aspartame is not the safe sugar substitute that we have been led to believe.

The president's economic policies are ineffective.

National health insurance is harmful to the consumer.

Notice that these propositions contain words like "damaging," "responsible," "beneficial," or "harmful" which contribute to judgment or evaluation of the issue. If you choose a proposition of value for your persuasive speech, you must support it with appropriate evidence.

If you were to select a *proposition of policy*, you would advocate the adoption of a future action or behavior.

Propositions of policy

Prices for prescription drugs should be strictly regulated.

Borrowers who default on student loans should be given jail terms.

Boxing should be declared illegal.

Term limits should be enacted for members of Congress.

Taxes should be raised to pay for national health insurance.

English should not be the official language of America.

Each proposition contains the word "should" and proposes an action or a change in future policy. Each issue requires extensive evidence to persuade the audience to believe that the intended policy is the correct course of action.

Spend some time developing your proposition statement. Choose simple words and clear phrases so that the statement flows evenly and conveys your viewpoint on a debatable issue regarding a fact, value, or policy.

ETHOS, *PATHOS*, AND *LOGOS:* THE MEANS OF PERSUASION

The Greek rhetorician Aristotle wrote that there are three means of persuasion: "The first kind reside in the character [*ethos*] of the speaker; the second consist in producing a certain attitude [*pathos*] in the hearer; the third appertain to the argument proper [*logos*]."[1] While in ancient Greece these three elements were considered as separate structures, today we view them as interrelated. Think of ethos, pathos, and logos as a pyramid which is not complete without any one of its three sides. Persuasion without ethos has no credibility; a speech without pathos generates no feeling; and a speaker deficient in logos reasons without sound argument. While we will consider each area separately, it is important to remember their interconnection.

Ethos: The Ethical Appeal

Ethos represents that dimension which causes us to trust and believe the individuals persuading us. We have confidence in speakers when they are sincere and knowledgeable about issues, show commitment to their persuasive goals, and demonstrate concern for the welfare of others. Ethos involves ethics, character, and credibility. To Aristotle, ethos was "the most potent of all the means to persuasion."[2]

A student remarked in class, "I believe that the most important thing in persuasion is the number of individuals the speaker is able to influence. If the speech changes the opinions or behavior of a lot of people, then it was successful, don't you think?" The problem with this idea is that it measures persuasion in terms of outcomes, without considering the means to the ends.

The success of a persuasive speech must not be measured entirely by outcomes, or civilization will continue to nurture madmen such as Adolf Hitler and Jim Jones. A persuasive speech should be judged by the ethical means speakers use to influence listeners. When Saddam Hussein delivers a speech, most Americans react with hostility because of Iraq's aggressive activities in the Middle East. When Russian president Boris Yeltsin presents a speech, however, we listen sympathetically because of his advocacy of democratic reforms. Because of her unselfish service to humanity, people of all spiritual beliefs respond to the words and deeds of Mother Teresa. If a speaker advocates ideas that benefit others, demonstrates commitment to persuasive goals, and possesses personal actions consistent with stated beliefs, the persuader will be establishing a positive foundation for ethical appeals.

In a democratic society, citizens expect ethical persuasive practices. To help you become more aware of unethical persuasive techniques, here is a partial list including some brief explanations and examples.

Unethical Persuasive Practices

Advocating Harm: Withholding information necessary for people's welfare; inciting people to violence; scapegoating; or isolating groups according to ethnicity, race, religion, gender, or other characteristic for the purpose of assigning blame. Prior to World War II, Hitler blamed the Jewish people for all of Germany's problems. Scapegoating was just one sinister tactic Hitler used to prepare for the Holocaust.

Name-Calling: The so-called *ad hominem* argument that attacks the character or personality of an individual; the use of loaded words to attack an individual or group. In the 1950s Senator Joe McCarthy wrongly accused many Americans of being Communists.

Plagiarizing: Intellectual stealing; quoting or paraphrasing words and phrases without identifying the source. During the 1987 presidential primaries, Senator Joseph Biden of Delaware was forced to withdraw from the race because he used phrases from the speeches of other politicians without giving them proper credit.

Providing False Information: Any argument that is inaccurate, false, taken out of context, or deliberately distorts information to mislead the audience. This practice is often called "the big lie." After Chinese Communists massacred protesters in the 1989 pro-democracy demonstrations, they used "the big lie" to tell Chinese citizens that the military had fired warning shots into the air and that no demonstrators had lost their lives.

Using Offensive Language: Language that is vulgar, obscene, or insulting; language that is offensive or injurious to any person or group. Any public speaker who uses obscenities for shock value violates the ethical standards of the community and causes most audience members to stop listening.

Card-stacking: Presenting arguments in a biased and unfair manner; arguments that unfairly stack the deck against an issue, deliberately ignoring opposite information. Here's an example of a "buy-American" sales pitch: "Americans buy more American cars than any other models; American cars cost less than foreign models; American cars have increased fuel efficiency over the past decade, and American cars have better overall performance than foreign makes." This ad ignores the fact that foreign sales have skyrocketed over the past fifteen years to more than 30 percent of the market. It also fails to mention that many foreign cars are still more fuel efficient and more reliable than their American counterparts.

Pathos: The Emotional Appeal

Pathos plays a very important part in persuasion. Speeches come alive when the speaker appeals to the heart as well as to the intellect of the listener. Without emotion, persuasive speeches would contain a lifeless collage of intellectual quotations and statistics. Speakers can touch listeners through examples expressing love, joy, despair, anger, sorrow, pride, hope, or tragedy.

IN A CONVINCING SPEECH, IT IS THE SPEAKER'S GOAL TO PERSUADE LISTENERS TO ACCEPT A SPECIFIC POINT OF VIEW.

© Michael Springer/
Gamma Liaison

A speaker's delivery determines the degree and intensity of emotion. Increased or decreased volume can communicate strength of feeling. Verbal emphasis, facial expression, movement, and gesture can reinforce important emotional segments. Dramatic pauses can allow time for emotional feelings to sink in. Effective delivery of emotions is crucial to a successful persuasive speech.

Appeals to emotion and logic are often used in combination. The following speaker joined logic and emotion to convey ideas:

> Of twenty-eight million children of alcoholics in this country, the odds are that there are two within this class. Now I'm not going to survey and try to prove or disprove the odds. I will tell you that there is definitely one. Like Suzanne Somers, I too am an adult child of an alcoholic. I am in the process of learning how to talk about it, how to trust, and how to feel and own all my emotions. Suzanne's story is incredible because her entire family recovered, including those who were alcoholic. In my family there were four children. I too, like Suzanne, escaped alcoholism. But two of my siblings did not. It is my hope that, one day, my entire family will recover.

The statistic, example, and personal testimony comprise the logical evidence. But the evidence becomes emotional when the speaker reveals personal experience. The emotion genuinely moved the audience because the speaker used effective facial expressions, vocal inflections, and eye contact to communicate strong personal feelings. As Aristotle said about pathos, "We give very different decisions under the sway of pain or joy, and liking or hatred."[3]

Strong emotion has advantages and disadvantages. Emotion is a powerful motivator, and audiences are often captivated when speakers employ passionate examples. Emotion can be inappropriate, however, if speakers use a long string of emotional examples without appealing to the listener's intellect. While emotion can arouse curiosity and maintain audience interest for awhile, strong emotion tends to fade, resulting in a shallow basis for persuasion. You will be more effective in your speeches if you use emotion judiciously, combined with logical appeals.

Charisma   Some speakers possess special magnetic qualities, called *charisma*, that attract audiences and inspire confidence. Franklin D. Roosevelt, John F. Kennedy, Martin Luther King, Jr., Ronald Reagan, and Jesse Jackson are leaders who were able to influence audiences because of these unique abilities.

No one expects you to have the charisma of these political leaders. But every speaker has a unique personal style that can be developed with speaking experience. Whether you use dramatic pausing, effective gestures, or vivid mental images, you can refine your personal style to communicate emotion successfully.

You can gain a better understanding of this quality by reading Jesse Jackson's speech "Common Ground and Common Sense" at the end of this book. Remember, however, that a silent reading of the speech does not do justice to the charismatic style of Jackson. You should view the videotape to experience the feelings Jackson conveyed through his gestures, vocal inflections, and facial expressions.

A Word of Caution While emotion and charisma can be constructive persuasive tools, they can also be dangerously exploitive. In Chapter 6 we discussed how a strong emotional appeal and a magnetic personality may often conceal *hidden agendas* of greed. Numerous charlatans have successfully contrived emotional appeals to religious feelings, humanitarian causes, or consumer needs to reap huge personal benefits. Be wary of the individual who uses only strong appeals to personal feelings. Remember that the effective persuader must appeal to ethics and logic, as well as to emotion.

Logos: The Appeal to Reason

Your ultimate goal in a persuasive speech is to influence the audience to consider and ultimately to accept your point of view through *logos*. Your task is similar to that of a trial attorney who builds a case based upon solid evidence and draws conclusions to persuade jurors of a defendant's guilt or innocence.

One way to achieve your persuasive objective is to follow a process called *reasoning,* in which you present logical arguments to your audience. We are familiar with arguments or disputes where we express our feelings and personal opinions about relationships, current events, movies, or fashion. Logical *arguments* in a persuasive speech, however, must be grounded in correct facts, complete evidence, and accurate reasoning. A common way for persuasive speakers to develop arguments is by presenting relevant supporting materials such as statistics, testimonies, and examples and by drawing conclusions from the data to back up a point of view.[4]

A speaker wanting to support a claim that a campus parking problem exists, could phrase an argument like this:

I'm sure many of you already know that we have a severe parking problem on our campus. Statistics from the Dean of Student's office indicate that there are 2,000 more commuter students than there are parking spaces. I did an informal survey of 50 students and asked them if they thought there were parking problems on campus. Thirty-nine of them said yes, six who used the bus said no, and five didn't have an opinion. The majority of the students in this survey—78 percent—felt that a parking problem exists. I also interviewed the Director of Student Activities who told me that [quote] "We have a campus parking crisis." And I want you all to know that I was ten minutes late for this class, and almost missed my speech today because I had to "hawk" a parking place way over on the other side of campus next to the stadium. You can see that the evidence indicates that we have a severe problem—a problem that we've got to solve.

The speaker has provided a list of supporting materials which includes two statistical cases, one testimony of authority, and a personal experience. The speaker cites a clear conclusion to summarize the data and to support the claim. The logical argument can be written in the form of a diagram:

Claim: There is a parking problem on campus.

Supporting evidence: A.   There are 2,000 more commuter students than parking spaces.

B.   Seventy-eight percent of students in an informal survey said there was a parking problem.

C.   Director of Student Activities says there is a parking "crisis."

D.   I was late for class because of parking problem.

Conclusion: Evidence suggests that there is a parking problem on campus.

When you construct arguments, be very careful how you draw conclusions from your data. Notice that this speaker states that evidence "indicates"—The speaker does not say they "prove" the conclusion. Evidence does not offer conclusive proof, but rather "points to" a conclusion. Your audience will be more open to persuasion if you use terms such as *imply, signify, suggest, indicate,* or *reveal,* and stay away from terms that express absolute statements of proof.

When you use a logical argument you must avoid fallacious reasoning. A *fallacy* occurs whenever a speaker uses incorrect facts, incomplete evidence, and/or erroneous reasoning.

Biased sampling is a fallacy where statistics or examples are not representative of the entire population. For instance, were students in the informal parking survey selected by random sample, or were they deliberately chosen because they already agreed with the speaker's point of view?

A *hasty generalization* is another fallacy that occurs when a speaker draws a faulty conclusion from extreme exceptions or from limited evidence. Are there other university officials who agree with the student activity director's viewpoint, or is the director the only exception? Were the parking difficulties experienced by the speaker a normal occurrence, or were they due to a special event such as a conference or a basketball game? We've all been guilty of making hasty generalizations. The victim whose home has been burglarized declares, "I came home and discovered I had been robbed. I called the 911 emergency number and it took 25 minutes for the police to respond. The cops are never around when you need them." While the victim is obviously frustrated, the one example could have been an isolated case. Much more statistical and testimonial evidence must be presented before a speaker should draw such a conclusion.

Some arguments are so frequently used that they have been classified and labeled. These arguments can help you apply general models of reasoning to your persuasive speeches. We will consider arguments based upon enumeration, analogy, and causation.[5]

Arguments Based upon Enumeration When you employ *enumeration* in a speech, you cite a series of specific cases to support a generalization. If you wanted to support a claim that most large cities have a drug problem, you could develop the following argument of enumeration:

Claim: Most large cities have a drug problem

Supporting evidence: A. Los Angeles, in the top twenty largest cities, has a drug problem.

B. New York, in the top twenty largest cities, has a drug problem.

C. Chicago, in the top twenty largest cities, has a drug problem.

D. Houston, in the top twenty largest cities, has a drug problem.

Conclusion: Most of the top twenty largest cities have drug problems.

In this argument, the speaker cites four different examples of large cities with drug problems, and states a conclusion which accurately reflects supporting evidence. The speaker uses the word "most" in the conclusion to indicate that "a great majority" of the largest cities have drug problems. The speaker could present a stronger argument by stating that "*All* of the twenty largest cities have a drug problem." The word "all" cannot be used, of course, unless each of the twenty largest cities has been researched and found to have these difficulties. The weakest arguments are those where the word(s) *some* or *a few* are used. If supporting evidence were to force a speaker to draw the conclusion that only "some cities have a drug problem," then the argument would lack strength and influence.

Determine the amount of evidence you need for a particular conclusion. If your conclusion is highly controversial, such as for or against nuclear power plants, surrogate parenthood, or the right to die, you will need many more statistics, examples, and testimonies to construct coherent arguments and draw logical conclusions.

Arguments Based upon Analogy When you reason from *analogy*, you are comparing two or more similar cases to show that, because of their similarity, what applies to one case, can also apply to the other.[6] For example:

Claim: Baltimore is similar to other cities with new stadiums

Supporting evidence: A.   Baltimore, the Twin Cities, Phoenix, and Indianapolis have populations of 500,000 or more.

B.   These cities have a similar sports tradition.

C.   The Twin Cities, Phoenix, and Indianapolis all have built and/or planned new stadiums.

D.   Further, we know that the Twin Cities, Phoenix, and Indianapolis have been successful in attracting new major league franchises.

Conclusion: Because Baltimore is similar in important ways to other cities that successfully attracted major league franchises, it is likely that Baltimore will be successful in attracting a major league football franchise.

In this analogy, the speaker has cited examples to illustrate the similarity of other cities to Baltimore. The conclusion then seeks to persuade listeners that because conditions in Baltimore are similar to conditions in other cities, Baltimore will obtain a similar result.

Arguments based on analogies can be effective if the examples being compared share a number of characteristics. *Faulty analogies* occur, however, when examples are dissimilar. A speaker in New Jersey who wants to raise the speed limit to 65 m.p.h. on state highways and compares New Jersey to Wyoming and Kansas is guilty of a faulty analogy. New Jersey is an urban state with high population density, while Wyoming and Kansas are not.

For an effective analogy, your examples must have a variety of similar principles or characteristics. Your audience will be persuaded if your analogy is valid in several areas.

Arguments Based upon Causation   When you use logical arguments based upon *causation*, you identify known causes to determine unknown effects (cause–to–effect reasoning), or you identify known effects to determine the unknown cause (effect–to–cause reasoning). Here is an example of cause–to–effect reasoning:

Claim: The current severe drought in the Midwest will contribute to higher food prices in the fall.

Supporting evidence: A.   People continue to buy food during droughts.

B.   Severe droughts contribute to food shortages.

C.   In the past, severe droughts have created higher food prices.

Conclusion: The current drought will create a shortage which will cause food prices to rise in the fall.

In this argument, the speaker has used the known cause—the current drought—as well as evidence of past droughts, to predict the unknown effect—that prices will rise in the fall. So the speaker's claim that food prices will rise during the harvest is persuasive because it is based upon good evidence and sound reasoning.

Fallacies, known as *faulty causes* or *faulty effects*, can sometimes occur in causative reasoning. Effects often have more than one cause. For instance, the food shortage could have other causes, such as fewer farms producing wheat due to the grain-subsidy program and/or massive government exports that depleted grain reserves.

Also, some causes are not capable of producing the assumed effects. For example, it has always been assumed, based upon testimonies from eyewitnesses, that the *Titanic* sank because of a collision with an iceberg. But explorers who have actually seen the *Titanic* on the ocean floor now argue that the jagged hole in the *Titanic*'s side points to other theories, such as an explosion from a previously unreported fire on board ship, or the use of inferior steel. The current reasoning suggests that an iceberg could not have caused the contour of the gaping hole.

Make certain that your evidence clearly supports a single cause of the effect, and that the cause is capable of producing the identified effect. Here is an example of reasoning based upon effect–to–cause:

Claim: High cholesterol contributed to Jack's heart attack.

Supporting evidence: A. Jack's doctor repeatedly warned Jack to lower his intake of cholesterol.

B. Diets containing high cholesterol can increase blockage of arteries, which according to the American Medical Association contributes to heart attacks.

C. Jack's cholesterol level was checked a week before his heart attack and found to be high.

Conclusion: Jack's diet of high cholesterol contributed to his heart attack.

In this example, the speaker has observed the known effect, Jack's heart attack, and drawn a speculative conclusion about the unknown cause from supporting data provided about Jack.

While it is highly probable that Jack's diet of high cholesterol contributed to his heart attack, there may be a faulty cause. Were there other possible causes of the heart attack such as Jack's weight, his lack of exercise, or his stressful lifestyle? Was his diet of high cholesterol merely a coincidental contributing factor? If Jack had lost weight, exercised, and reduced tension, would his diet have contributed to a heart attack?

Use caution when you reason from effect to cause. A woman with a black eye may not have been beaten by her husband, but might have been in a car accident. Concern about the economy may not have been the only cause of the deline in stocks; there could have been a variety of reasons, including computerized trading and a falling dollar.

Other Logical Fallacies   In the previous logical arguments, we have considered several fallacies—biased sampling, hasty generalizations, faulty analogies, and faulty causes or effects. Here is a chart listing some additional fallacies that you should avoid as you build your persuasive speeches.

Fallacy	Example	Explanation
Loaded Question	"Are you still using drugs?"	The question forms a no-win trap. Answering "yes" is an admission of guilt; responding "no" still admits to former drug use.
Either-Or Question	"We can continue the deficits and corruption of this administration, or we can elect a new, competent, honest government."	The "choice" presents two extremes: one evil, one good. Alternatives are seldom this simplistic.
Begging the Question	Mr. A: "The U.S must reduce defense commitment and spend more on social programs." Ms. B: "Why?" Mr. A: "Because it's imperative that our defense spending be reduced and our social programs be increased."	The reasoning is circular. Debater A "begs the question" by restating the issue and offering the claim as evidence. The claim remains unsubstantiated.
Complex Question	"America's strong defense program contributed to the decline and fall of the Soviet Union."	Several complicated issues are combined into one claim, making it difficult to sort through.
Irrelevant Evidence	"Joe Smith should be elected attorney general: He is a true American, a good	The information does not support the claim. To evaluate Joe, we need to know about his experience, his skill at handling cases, and

family man, a church attender, and a friend of the poor."	opinions of Joe from other attorneys. The "evidence" has little to do with the job of attorney general.

Developing Rebuttal Arguments Some persuasive issues are so controversial that audiences will listen with skepticism, raising doubts about the wisdom of the speaker's proposition. A speaker who ignores this resistance will not be taken seriously. To counteract such misgivings, the speaker develops *rebuttal arguments*, which help to diffuse possible disagreement by raising opposing viewpoints and providing evidence to indicate that they are flawed or inaccurate. For instance, in a speech advocating the construction of more nuclear power plants, a speaker could acknowledge the fears listeners have about nuclear energy, mentioning the disaster at Chernobyl and the incident at Three Mile Island. The speaker might then point out that these examples are well-publicized failures which do not fairly represent the more stringent policies and guidelines now regulating nuclear reactors.

The rebuttal argument helps the speaker to bring up the opposite point of view and face it openly. In a controversial issue such as nuclear power plants, the speaker must resolve listeners' fears with reasonable arguments demonstrating the speaker's understanding of the problems. To ignore the area of safety in such a speech would be persuasive suicide. Audience members would question the speaker's awareness of the facts, as well as the speaker's interest and concern about their welfare.

METHODS OF ORGANIZING PERSUASIVE SPEECHES

Because there are different goals in persuasion, there are different methods of structuring persuasive messages. In an actuating speech, for instance, the speaker must organize the message to identify a problem which requires solution and action. In a speech to convince, the speaker uses reasons to develop a positive case in support of the proposition. In order to build a successful persuasive speech, you need to understand and be able to apply the best methods of organization for your particular assignment. You can structure persuasive messages according to reasons, problem–solution, comparative advantages, and the motivated sequence.

Reasons

Using the method of citing *reasons* is a clear and straightforward organizational approach, especially in a speech to convince. With this method, a speaker uses the three or four convincing reasons as main headings in the body of the outline. If you use this technique, be certain that your reasons are the strongest possible, that they support the specific purpose or proposition, and that they themselves can be supported with concrete evidence.[7]

Speaker David Stesch wanted to convince his audience that the Twenty-second Amendment, limiting a president to two terms, should be repealed. After researching his proposition of policy, David found three strong reasons which he felt would persuade the audience to agree with him. Evaluate his reasons as well as their arrangement in the outline.

Specific purpose (proposition of policy):   to convince the audience that the Twenty–second Amendment, limiting a president to two terms, should be repealed

Thesis statement: The Twenty-second Amendment was rejected by the Founding Fathers, it is detrimental to the executive branch of government, and it is undemocratic.

Body

Reason 1	I. The concept was rejected by the Founding Fathers.
	A. Alexander Hamilton argued that a president should not be changed in time of national crisis.
	B. In the book *Decision in Philadelphia* historians write that the Founding Fathers felt a president should be judged by the people frequently.
Reason 2	II. It is detrimental to the executive branch.
	A. A fixed term creates a lame-duck presidency.
	B. A fixed term damages the president's ability to conduct foreign policy.
Reason 3	III. It is undemocratic.
	A. The amendment implies that people are ignorant.
	B. Many constitutional scholars say the amendment constrains the popular will.

The speaker was successful in choosing three equally strong reasons to support the proposition. Notice that he saved the strongest reason—that the amendment is undemocratic—until the last. Also notice that Dave supports reason 1 and 3 with testimonial evidence, and reason 2 with examples.

Students sometimes have difficulty coordinating their reasons smoothly with the proposition. To phrase each heading of the body more clearly, place a mental "because" in front of each reason. This method is an effective organizational tool for both speaker and listener. It helps a speaker to be logical and clear in supporting the proposition, and it enables the listener to follow the speaker's principal arguments.

Problem–Solution

The *problem–solution* method is also useful in structuring a speech to convince. This method reflects the problem-solving techniques developed many years ago by educator John Dewey in his book *How We Think*.[8] The problem–solution method is most often used for propositions of policy, and is easy to incorporate into a speech outline. In the following outline about the automotive repair industry, Karen Anderson made effective use of the problem–solution structure.

Specific purpose (proposition of policy):   to convince the audience that the auto repair industry should be strictly regulated

Thesis statement: Incompetent and unnecessary repairs must be corrected by strict regulations.

Body

Problem

I. Americans taken advantage of
   A. 40 % of consumer auto repair spending wasted on unnecessary repairs
   B. Sears scandal demonstrates company fraud
   C. "Gypsy" parts are purposely inferior
   D. Small, everyday scams rip off public
   E. Incompetent service affects consumer

Alternative solutions

II. Several means exist to rectify problem
   A. Voluntary certification
   B. Industry-wide control
   C. Consumer awareness

Selected solution

III. Regulation can help consumer: California model
   A. Mediate disputes
   B. Detect fraud
   C. Protect consumer

The body of the speech contains three main headings which identify the problem, explore alternative solutions, and present the desired solution. The speaker uses a combination of statistics and examples as evidence to support her three headings.

One variation of this method is *problem–cause–solution* in which the speaker includes a section identifying principal causes of, or reasons for, the problem. Here's how the preceding outline can be adapted to this method:

Thesis statement: Incompetent and unnecessary repairs, caused by lack of control, must be corrected by strict regulations.

Body

Problem	I. Americans taken advantage of
Cause of problem	II. Lack of control contributes to negligence
	A. Anyone can claim automotive expertise
	B. ASE sets only voluntary standards
	C. Consumers are uneducated
	D. Most states don't regulate
Alternative solutions	III. Several means exist to rectify problem
Selected solution	IV. Regulation can help consumer

In this outline, only one additional heading was needed to include the reason for the problem. You can see that the problem–solution method is adaptable to a variety of arrangements. You don't need to let any of these methods constrict your topic; adjust the approach to the unique demands of the topic, developing your speech in logical sequence.

Comparative Advantages

The *comparative advantages* method is helpful in organizing convincing speeches about problems with many solutions. A speaker compares the advantages of a proposed solution with the advantages and disadvantages of other solutions. Politicians who support the death penalty for drug dealers often use the comparative-advantages method to convince voters that capital punishment is more effective than other solutions.

Specific purpose (proposition of value):   to convince the audience that capital punishment presents the best alternative for dealing with drug kingpins

Thesis statement: The death penalty is a severe punishment, which has a greater chance of deterring drug kingpins.

Body

I. Capital punishment is the most severe of all penalties.
II. Capital punishment has a greater chance of deterring drug kingpins than lesser sentences.

Each main heading in the body presents a comparison of the proposed solution with alternatives. Numeral I compares the severity of various punishments, and II compares the merits of each penalty as an effective deterrent. The comparative advantages method is useful when you want to persuade your audience that your solution is superior to other approaches to the problem.

BUILDING THE PERSUASIVE SPEECH TO CONVINCE

We've discussed the nature, means, and organization of several persuasive speeches. Here is a list of guidelines to help you build your persuasive speech to convince.

1. Choose a controversial topic.
   a. Examine your attitudes and the opinions of others.
   b. Select a topic that is appropriate to listeners.
   c. Explore current events topics.
   d. Avoid overworked issues.
   e. Provide new insights into familiar topics.

2. Conduct extensive research.
   a. Examine library sources for testimonies, statistics, and examples to build your case.
   b. Be certain that sources are accurate and up-to-date.
   c. Interview experts on the topic.
   d. Research specialized institutions and organizations.
   e. Develop visual aids for variety.
   f. Be willing to change or modify the topic if evidence does not support your viewpoint.

3. Phrase a clear proposition.
   a. Know the difference among fact, value, and policy propositions.
   b. Make sure that the proposition is controversial.

4. Analyze the audience.
   a. Determine prior attitudes about a topic through interviews, surveys, or questionnaires.
      (1) Agreement implies the opportunity of using evidence as reinforcement of audience attitudes.
      (2) Neutrality indicates the necessity of employing strong evidence to influence listeners.
      (3) Opposition to the topic suggests the need to present extensive supporting evidence.
   b. Develop persuasive appeals linking your topic to audience interests and motivations.
   c. Make the audience the central focus of speech development.

5. Develop sound arguments and coherent organization.
   a. Present well-defined claims supported by good evidence and sound reasoning.
      (1) Use evidence in the context of its intended meaning.

      (2) Include materials which are relevant and up-to-date.
   b. Avoid subjective phrases such as "I think," or "in my opinion."
   c. Identify research sources to build credibility.
   d. Avoid unethical practices.
   e. Use a balance of logic and emotion.
   f. Choose an appropriate organizational method for the topic.
   g. Use external transitions to emphasize major arguments.

6. Construct a sophisticated introduction.
   a. Choose a strategy to generate curiosity and establish rapport.
   b. Present the proposition and thesis statements at the end of the introduction.
      (1) Avoid opinionated statements such as "I'm going to convince," or "prove," alienating the audience.
      (2) State the proposition in a straightforward manner.
      (3) State the thesis clearly, creating receptiveness among listeners.

7. Develop a forceful conclusion.
   a. Use a challenge in the convincing speech to stimulate thought or ask listeners to change their minds.
   b. Use the challenge in combination with most types of conclusions.
   c. Avoid summary conclusions in convincing speeches.

8. Build an effective delivery
   a. Maintain eye contact with listeners when conveying emotional examples.
   b. Report statistics accurately without stumbling.
   c. Use gestures to emphasize arguments and facial expressions to express emotion.
   d. Express feelings through enthusiasm, verbal emphasis, and vocal inflections.
   e. Practice the speech in order to project confidence in the topic.[9]

Motivated Sequence

The motivated sequence is an organizational method which is used in speeches to actuate. This strategy is composed of five steps: attention, need, satisfaction, visualization, and action. We present a detailed discussion of this important technique in Chapter 18.

This persuasive speech was developed by an advanced student who was a committed consumer advocate. Karen Anderson researched the topic extensively and found powerful supporting materials to appeal to listeners. Convincing speeches can be organized by using reasons or a problem-solution sequence. The body of this speech is arranged according to the reasons organizational sequence. An alternative body, arranged according to the problem–cause–solution structure, appears in the Appendix.[10]

LET'S STOP AUTO REPAIR RIP–OFFS!

Persuasive Speech to Convince

Karen Anderson

[1] The speaker arouses audience curiosity by starting with an example.

1 A man who worked the night shift got off work one morning and drove his Cadillac into a repair shop for servicing. He had a repair order written up, went back to his car and for some unknown reason crawled in the back seat and fell asleep. When he woke up, much to his surprise, he realized that it was now afternoon and no one had been out to service his car yet. He returned to the service desk and a cashier handed him a repair order which was completely filled out listing, in detail, all parts used and labor performed on the vehicle. The cashier then demanded full payment before the owner could get his car keys back. Does this story about auto repair fraud sound incredible or far–fetched? Well after you hear what I have to tell you today, you may not find an example like this hard to believe.

[2] The speaker states the proposition of policy followed by the thesis, which contains three reasons. The reasons represent the core of the speaker's persuasive argument and identify the three numerals of the body.

2 The auto repair industry should be strictly regulated because of unnecessary repairs, incompetent work, and because regulation will help to protect the consumer.

3 Americans are being ripped off by unnecessary repairs. Consumer advocate Ralph Nader writes about the U. S. Department of Transportation's study of the auto repair industry in the foreword of a book entitled *Auto Repair Shams and Scams*. The survey indicates that today approximately 40 billion dollars a year associated with auto repairs are unnecessary. The major reasons: "Unneeded repairs due to inadequate diagnosis; faulty repairs for which owners did not get their money back; unneeded repairs sold with possible fraudulent intent; accidents due to faulty repairs." Mr. Nader further comments that this sector of the auto industry has done little to reduce fraud and incompetence over the last ten years.

[3]Karen establishes support for the first reason by siting a statistic from U. S. Department of Transportation and using a quotation from Ralph Nader, a well–known consumer advocate.

4 Think it won't happen to you? An article in a June 1992 issue of *Business Week* reported in what is now a much publicized case, that Sears Auto Centers in California had "systematically ripped off customers." According to the article, Ruth Hernandez of Stockton, California, went to Sears for new tires. The auto technician who serviced Ms. Hernandez's Honda "insisted" the car also needed new struts with a hefty additional cost of $419.95. Ms. Hernandez went for a second opinion and was told the struts did not need replacing. Furthermore, according to the article, Sears consistently charged consumers an average of $235 for unnecessary repairs.

[4]The speaker poses a question to threaten listeners' safety and security. The example from a credible source is further support that consumers are being taken advantage of.

5 Here are two ways that consumers pay for unnecessary repairs. You can unknowingly purchase a so–called "gypsy part," that is, an inferior auto part such as a common oil filter, which is repackaged in a box with a well–known brand name, and passed off to you as a quality product. Here is an example. [Shows a slide which displays two oil filters, one is a "gypsy part" and the other is the legitimate filter.] One has less paper, which provides less filtering capability. The other contains more paper and will last longer. Upon close examination, the difference is obvious. Or what about the technician who deliberately sabotages your car for profit and whose favorite weapon is an ice pick? [Holds up an ice pick.] Now although these instances are rare, they happen to out–of–state motorists who set themselves up as easy targets by leaving their cars with attendants while they grab snacks or make necessary pit stops. Returning to the car, the unsuspecting motorists are informed by attendants that a leaking tire must be patched or, better yet, replaced with a brand new tire.

[5]The visual aids add interest and provide concrete examples of attempts to defraud consumers.

6 Then there is the blatant fraud. I conducted a telephone interview with Tom Hopkins, a lead investigator for the Bureau of Automotive Repair in California, who related the following despicable crime. An elderly California couple took their motor home in for repairs. The disabled wife remained in the motor home while the vehicle was raised on the lift in the repair shop. Employees removed the suspension system, brakes, and wheels. The disabled woman was literally held hostage in the air until her husband paid the demanded fee to get the wheels and other equipment put back on their vehicle.

[6]The speaker wisely uses this example as the last supporting element for reason one. The emotional incident is verified by a credible primary source. Notice the speaker uses concrete language—"despicable crime," "held hostage"—to elicit an emotional response from the audience.

[7]Although she is careful not to indict the entire auto repair industry, the speaker clearly indicates that listeners could be at risk.

[7] **These incidents** represent a minority, and I want to stress the majority of the auto repair industry is caring and reputable, but these cases are real and they could happen to you.

[8]The external transition connects reasons one and two (numerals I and II) of the body.

[8] Not only do Americans experience unnecessary repairs; we are also subjected to incompetence.

[9]A survey and quotation from a verifiable source present early supporting evidence for reason two.

[9] In his book *From Bumper to Bumper,* Bob Sikorsky did a remarkable survey of the auto repair business across America. Posing as an average driver, Mr. Sikorsky pulled into 225 repair shops with a simple problem: a loose spark–plug wire. He reported fair and competent repairs in only 28 percent of the stops, a satisfactory repair only 44 percent of the time, and in Sikorsky's own words, "I was victimized by incompetence, cheated, sold unnecessary parts... over-charged, and lied to."

[10]Another quotation and a detailed example provide further evidence that consumers are often victims of incompetence.

[10] Sal Fariello states alarming information regarding brake repairs from his twenty–year involvement with the automotive industry. Fariello explains that brake discs often require machining on a lathe to correct vibration or noise. But the likelihood of incompetent work is high. He advises that if a brake shop tells you that your brakes need to be machined, ask them to measure the final thickness. If they resist, it may be because they can't read a micrometer, which means they shouldn't be in the brake repair business. He concludes by saying: "I've seen some incredible butcher jobs come out of these places as far as brake work is concerned. For the sake of your own safety, make sure you are doing business with a competent brake mechanic."

[11] Incompetence is not always intentional. It is often a result of the sophisticated high–tech machines we all drive and the failure of some technicians to keep up with the technology. A service assistant may be able to change the oil in your car but lack the more advanced skills to diagnose a problem in the engine, emission system, or transmission.

[12]The computer–generated visual aid introduces humor, generates interest, and also makes the point that anyone can go into auto repair business.

[12] One important factor which contributes to incompetence is the lack of regulation. Let me explain. [Holds up sign reading "Karen's Car Center—Unlimited Major and Minor Repair Service —Major Credit Cards Accepted"] Pretty impressive, Huh? Listen, I'll even adjust your brakes for half–price, and I'll throw in a complete diagnostic muffler analysis for free—but I don't do windows! Trust me! Anyone with a computer and a graphics program can make a sign like this as I did, call themselves an auto technician, and open up a shop. Nothing stands in their way. How could I get away with this, you ask? Well,

there is no mandatory licensing or certification program. There is an organization called Automotive Service Excellence, or ASE, which, according to their newsletter, is designed to help consumers "to distinguish between competent and incompetent mechanics." ASE administers an excellent voluntary certification program through paper and pencil testing in conjunction with two years automotive repair experience. But the key word is "voluntary." Anyone can hang out a sign as long as they don't use the term "certified mechanic."

13 Since it is clear that incompetence occurs in the auto repair industry, let's consider how regulation will help to protect the consumer.

[13]The external transition links reason two with reason three of the body (numerals II and III).

14 California is one example of a governmental control program that benefits the consumer and the auto repair industry as well. Remember Ms. Hernandez from California, who didn't have confidence in what Sears was advising her to do? She had a place to file a complaint and was assured that a remedy would be found. This is an excellent example of mandated control through the California Bureau of Automotive Repair, or BAR. [Displays slide describing information about the BAR.] Kate McGuire, Public Information Officer for the BAR, provided me with information about this agency. It was established in 1971 to prevent abuses in the auto repair industry. With a staff of 600 working in 36 field offices, the BAR operates on an annual budget of $70 million, which is funded by the smog check program and a $200 registration fee paid by auto repair businesses. It provides consumers with mediation centers that handle over 40,000 formal complaints a year. This agency also sends representatives to assist and support consumers at hearings in small claims court. And money—some $4.6 million alone—was returned to consumers from auto repair shops in 1991–92.

[14]Karen uses an extended example to explain how regulation can protect the consumer. She returns to the Sears example stated earlier in the speech and describes how the California BAR is used to resolve complaints and abuses in the industry. The speaker uses a slide projector to display factual information which reinforces the narration. The speaker indicates that the information is verified by a source.

15 In addition, the Bureau conducts undercover sting operations to snare dishonest technicians or detect fraudulent repair shops. BAR investigator Hopkins said that they can't inspect all of the repair shops. But he explained: "We have sophisticated means of intelligence gathering. We have field offices, consumer complaints and field investigators—we know what's going on. We want to put the bad guys out of business. We want to revoke their licenses so that no one goes to them." Talk about protection!

[15]The quotation from a primary source is powerful support for reason three.

16 Now, there are many in the auto repair industry who feel that the government or state should not be involved in overseeing the industry. I interviewed Rick Glenn, an Auto Service Technology Professor at Catonsville Community College in Maryland, who commented that many technicians feel that government or state regulation would impose a cumbersome layer of bureaucracy which should only make matters worse. But investigator Tom Hopkins told me that, in California, the auto industry is not hostile to the Bureau. In fact, he said that honest auto repair businesses welcome the BAR because it helps to keep a level playing field and put the dishonest

[16]The speaker presents the principal argument of opponents to acknowledge objections to regulation. The argument is supported by a credible source.

Here the speaker refutes the opposition with a clear rebuttal argument which is also supported by a source.

shops out of business. So you can see that regulation does not need to be antagonistic to the repair industry.

¹⁷Karen returns to the Sears example to provide additional reinforcement for her rebuttal argument.

¹⁷ Had the BAR not existed, we may never have discovered the Sears scandal. It was the chief of the BAR who launched an investigation after noticing a pattern of consumer complaints against Sears Auto Centers. The Bureau conducted 38 undercover runs at 33 Sears shops statewide in California. The investigation exposed Sears' unethical practices, and forced the company to change its ways.

¹⁸To begin the conclusion, the speaker refers back to the example she used in the introduction.

Karen ends this convincing speech with a hard–hitting challenge to the audience.

¹⁸ Do you remember the man with the Cadillac I referred to in the opening of my speech? Well that true story was told to me by Dré Brungardt, an Automotive Consultant on a WTTR radio show in Westminster, Maryland. That example is known as a "wall job" in the auto repair industry, because when you return to the auto shop, you find your car parked next to the same wall, untouched, where you left it, but with a repair invoice attached. We don't have to take this type of behavior. We don't have to be at the mercy of fraudulent or incompetent auto repair companies. The vast majority of men and women in this business are decent and hardworking. But we need to ensure this same high standard of decency throughout the industry. Let's apply the brakes. Let's require strict ground rules.

SUMMARY

Persuasive speakers influence audiences by altering beliefs, reinforcing feelings, or generating action. Speakers phrase persuasive topics into arguable propositions of fact, value, or policy. To persuade an audience, a speaker must construct ethical appeals to build trust and confidence; emotional appeals to deepen feeling; and logical arguments based upon correct facts, complete evidence, and accurate reasoning. At the same time, a speaker must avoid unethical practices, extreme emotionalism, and fallacious reasoning. Persuasive speeches can be structured according to reasons, problem–solution, comparative advantages, and the motivated sequence.

EXERCISES

1. Choose a controversial topic for a persuasive speech. Phrase the topic into propositions of fact, value, and policy.
2. Using the Attitude Survey provided in Chapter 3, find out the strength and weakness of audience attitudes toward each proposition. Use the survey to help you decide what type of persuasive speech to present— convincing, stimulating, or actuating.

3. When you have selected your proposition and type of speech, develop three emotional and three logical appeals. Be careful to avoid fallacious reasoning.
4. Turn to the back of the book and analyze the speech delivered by Jesse Jackson at the Democratic National Convention in 1988. Identify specific examples of logical and emotional appeals. Does the speech contain any fallacies? Be specific in your answer. What was Jesse Jackson's reputation as a speaker? As a politician? Were there positive or negative ethical factors which helped or hurt Jackson's persuasive influence? What type(s) of persuasive speech did Jackson present? Consider your answer carefully.
5. For the following topics, write outlines for persuasive speeches using the reasons, problem–solution, and comparative advantages methods.

   Foreign trade restrictions
   Frivolous law suits
   Overcoming racism
   Rebuilding our inner cities
   Reducing the federal deficit
   Reforming the welfare system
   The significance of fraternities and sororities
   The campus parking problem
   The health care system
   The national speed limit

NOTES

[1] Lane Cooper, *The Rhetoric of Aristotle* (New York: Appleton–Century–Crofts, 1932), p. 8. [Brackets two and three ours.]

[2] Ibid., p. 9.

[3] Ibid. p. 9.

[4] Stephen W. Littlejohn and David M. Jabusch, *Persuasive Transactions* (Glenview, Illinois: Scott, Foresman, 1987), p. 54. I thank James L. Koury, professor of philosophy at Catonsville Community College, who gave me valuable help and advice in the logic section of this chapter.

[5] For the purposes of this section on the appeal to reason, I used a system of argumentation similar to Hugenberg and Yoder's section entitled: "Use Logical Proof: Appeal to Logic and Reason," pp. 188–191 in *Speaking in the Modern Organization*. However, I have made alterations in terminology, examples, and numbers of logical proofs. For a more traditional approach, see Ross and Ross, *Understanding Persuasion*, pp. 155–168.

[6] Lawrence W. Hugenberg and Donald D. Yoder, *Speaking in the Modern Organization* (Glenview, Illinois: Scott, Foresman, 1985), p. 190.

[7] The following speeches used in this chapter were presented in speech class, Catonsville Community College: a speech where the name was withheld to protect privacy; David Stesch, "The Twenty-Second Amendment Should Be Repealed," 1988. Used by permission.

[8] John Dewey, *How We Think* (Boston: D. C. Heath, 1933), pp. 102–118. Read Chapter 7 to

understand the five phases of "reflective thinking." You will discover that there is a great similarity to some of the problem–solution models presented in this persuasive speaking chapter.

[9] I thank the following students who provided topic ideas for this chapter: Candy Chancellor, Evan Feinberg, Colleen Hamilton, Deborah E. Hensley, Lisa Hilton, Ken Kuzo, Marie Miller, Jeff Ritter, Grover Sauter, David Stesch, Michelle M. Tawes, and Cheryl Zuretti.

[10] Karen Anderson, "Let's Stop Auto Repair Rip-offs!" persuasive speech to convince, Carroll Community College, Westminster, Maryland, 1993. Used by permission.

READINGS

Littlejohn, Stephen W., and Jabusch, David M. *Persuasive Transactions.* Glenview, Illinois: Scott, Foresman, 1987. Chapter 9 helps you to understand the methods of persuasive organization in relation to propositions of fact, value, and policy.

Ross, Raymond S., and Ross, Mark G. *Understanding Persuasion.* Englewood Cliffs: Prentice-Hall, 1981. This brief but well-written book contains a number of chapters which are extremely helpful to someone who wants more information about persuasion. Chapter 4 has some good material on the organization of persuasive speeches, and Chapter 5 includes sections on formal reasoning and fallacies. A good appendix contains ethical codes for public relations, journalism, and broadcasting.

Simons, Herbert W. *Persuasion: Understanding, Practice and Analysis,* 2d ed. New York: Random House, 1986. Simons provides an excellent analysis of the many aspects of persuasion. Chapter 8 examines audience analysis and contains a section on targeting. In Chapter 9, Simons explores propositions of fact, value, and policy. In addition to a good discussion of argument and evidence in Chapter 10, the author includes an interesting analysis of logical reasoning in the famous "Checkers Speech," where Richard Nixon presented an impassioned defense of his ethical conduct while a candidate for vice-president in 1952.

Chapter Eighteen

SPEAKING TO PERSUADE: MOTIVATING AUDIENCES

Chapter Outline

Key Terms and Names

Action
Alan Monroe
Attention
Hierarchy of needs
Long-term incentive
Motivated sequence
Need
Satisfaction
Short-term incentive
Visualization

© Shahn Kermani/
Gamma Liason

"Our nature is inseparable
from desires."
—THOMAS HOBBES

On her way to work, Jill passed a highway billboard. "Step up to a new cigarette—Step up to living," the caption read. "Sure," Jill muttered, "Step up to cancer!" A commercial was running on the FM station. "So hurry, the sale ends tonight. Prices are slashed on all TVs, VCRs, and stereos." Jill needed a new TV and she turned up the sound to hear the address of the store. The car phone rang and Jill's husband called from his office to ask her to buy some groceries on the way home. Jill told him that she didn't have time and suggested that they go out to dinner. He quickly agreed, and promised to meet her at 6:30 for pizza. Jill made a call to a real-estate client. "I've found the perfect home for you," she said. "It's spacious, located at the end of a dead-end street where your children can play, and is only ten minutes from schools. It's a lovely community, the mortgage is assumable, and I think the property has everything you're looking for." The client seemed interested and wanted to see the house as soon as possible. In less than five minutes, Jill had been an active participant in several persuasive messages, and whether she realized it or not, she had demonstrated considerable skill in evaluating and constructing these motivational presentations.

This chapter describes strategies for motivating audiences, presents Monroe's motivated sequence, and identifies guidelines for constructing the persuasive speech to actuate.

STRATEGIES FOR MOTIVATING LISTENERS

As a persuasive speaker, you can influence listeners to believe in your message, feel more deeply about an issue, or act upon a proposal. It is difficult to be effective, however, unless you find specific ways of motivating your audience. We suggest several strategies: appeal to needs; appeal to beliefs and values; provide incentives; and involve emotions.

Appeal to the Needs of the Audience

In Chapter 3 we discussed some of the basic needs that all human beings have in common and we briefly described how one psychologist, Abraham H. Maslow, organized these drives into five levels called a "hierarchy of needs." When you connect a topic to these drives, your persuasive speech will have more impact upon listeners. For example, if you wanted to persuade your audience to plant trees to improve the environment, you could conceivably develop persuasive appeals which progressed through each level of Maslow's hierarchy. Here are some examples:

Physical. Trees remove the carbon dioxide out of our air and give us oxygen. One acre of trees can keep 15 people breathing for one year. Unfortunately, we are losing this valuable resource at the rate of 3,000 acres per hour.

Safety and security. Trees keep us warm in the winter, and they cool us with their shade in summer. Trees hold large amounts of soil which help to control erosion and filter out nitrogen and phosphorous contained in run-off. When trees are cut down, a chain reaction is started which not only harms the ecology, but affects us as well. When too much nitrogen and phosphorous enter the water system, algae grows and shades aquatic grasses which are nurseries for fish. When aquatic grasses are shaded they die, and there is no food for fish. When the fish die, our food supply is depleted, the fishing industry is affected, and the economy is damaged.

Love. Trees provide wildlife with habitat, from the tiniest little microorganism, to the largest elk. Trees are the oldest living things: there's a bristlecone pine tree in California that is more than 4,600 years old.

Esteem. The governor has officially declared this month to be "Tree-mendous" month. So why don't we all pitch in and help plant a tree to make our community better? If you plant a tree, you can return this application to the agricultural department and you will receive a certificate identifying you as a "Tree-mendous Marylander."

Self-actualization. Teddy Roosevelt established the national park system in order to preserve the beauty and wonders of nature for future generations. Today, there are over 200 million acres of forests in these national parks for all of us to enjoy.

The speaker reminds listeners that trees provide the oxygen necessary to physical survival. She also describes how the lack of trees can lead to a chain reaction which is harmful to the safety and economic security of the audience. Next the speaker uses the elk and the bristlecone pine to appeal to her listeners' love of wildlife and respect for antiquity. She introduces esteem by referring to the governor's program and awarding certificates to those who plant trees. In a final appeal to self-actualization, the speaker asks listeners to "enjoy" and "preserve" the wonder and beauty of these forests.[1]

Not all persuasive topics can be linked so comprehensively to audience needs. But you will be more effective motivating your listeners if you can develop persuasive appeals which involve several of these basic drives.

Appeal to Listeners' Beliefs and Values

As you develop motivational appeals, it is important that you understand the specific beliefs and values of your audience. What beliefs do listeners have in common? What goals are important to audience members? What characteristics or qualities do your listeners most admire? You can influence listeners by explaining how your proposal is in harmony with their beliefs and value systems.

PERSUASIVE SPEAKERS MOVE AUDIENCES TO ACTION BY IDENTIFYING PROBLEMS AND PROPOSING WORKABLE SOLUTIONS.

© Michael Dwyer/
Stock Boston

Some of the most common examples of appeals to values and beliefs are found in media advertising campaigns.

AT&T used a creative strategy to promote its long distance service to businesses who value high productivity and efficiency. The company developed a black and white TV ad showing anxious office workers who had lost long distance telephone service from a competing company due to a malfunction. The use of jerky, amateur-looking video footage made the scene appear even more frantic and dysfunctional. The sales pitch attempted to frighten businesses into buying the "reliable" long-distance service of the advertised company to avoid such a calamity.[2]

In the 1980s, Coca-Cola discontinued its traditional soft drink and marketed a product known as "new Coke" which was poorly received by the public. People wanted their traditional, familiar product and resented any change to a new version. Capitalizing upon the controversy, Pepsi developed an attention-getting TV ad showing a space ship "beaming up" Coke and Pepsi vending machines from earth. The alien creatures rejected the new Coke, of course, and heartily embraced Pepsi. The slogan clinched the appeal at the end of the commercial:

"One has changed; one is chosen." The ad clearly linked Pepsi to consumers who valued stability, reliability, and tradition. Perhaps the unfavorable reactions to the new soft drink persuaded Coca-Cola to return Classic Coke to the market.[3]

Appeals to beliefs and values can also be successful in a negative sense. The R.J. Reynolds Tobacco Company created a magazine ad picturing a hip cartoon character named Joe Camel enjoying a cigarette. The ad attracted the attention of numerous children, who are fascinated by cartoons and caricatures. Armed with studies from the *Journal of the American Medical Association*, health groups protested the ad campaign and accused Camel of devising strategies that persuaded children as young as twelve to smoke cigarettes.[4] The tobacco company denied the allegations, and continued the ad campaign using the Joe Camel character.[5]

These strategies were effective because the advertisements connected products to the values of listeners. If you are interviewing for a job, you can sell yourself by linking your qualifications to the goals of your prospective employer. If you are presenting a classroom speech, you can relate many topics to the specific interests and values of your listeners. If you are required to promote your company's products at a trade convention, you can look for creative ways of appealing to the beliefs and values of prospective customers. Remember that it is the speaker's responsibility to analyze and understand the values of a specific audience in order to develop appeals which are successful.

Provide Listeners with Incentives

When you are presenting a persuasive speech, you need to be aware that listeners will silently ask themselves how they will benefit from your proposals. An effective persuasive speaker clearly communicates the advantages of a proposal by providing long- and short-term incentives for the audience. *Long-term incentives* are benefits which listeners gain over a period of time after agreeing to a speaker's proposal. One speaker advocated a tax deduction for responsible pet owners. She provided statistics showing that county governments are spending significant tax funds to maintain animal shelters for stray pets. The speaker provided two long-term incentives for those who agreed with her plan: 1. Deductions would provide financial assistance to individuals who adopted stray animals, and 2. Increased pet adoptions would save taxes by reducing the number of strays in animal shelters.[6] Another speaker who urged listeners to research their family genealogy identified these specific incentives: 1. Researching family history can help individuals discover genetic illness, 2. Understanding genealogy can encourage people to alter previous family lifestyles and prolong life, 3. Enlightenment can lead to actions that improve the health of future generations in families.[7]

In these examples speakers explained that listeners would benefit by saving money or improving their health. If audience members are told that a proposal will help them to look or feel better, protect their families, save money, improve their safety, be wiser consumers, or live more successfully, they will see the long-term advantages of supporting the plan.

Speakers can also include *short-term incentives* to motivate listeners and provide immediate reinforcement of ideas. A speaker who advocated courteous driving practices handed out buttons with the slogan "Please be patient: God isn't finished with me yet." [8] Another student who suggested that listeners improve their nutrition passed out carrot sticks at the end of a speech. A speaker who urged audience members to bring toys for tots at Christmas presented a carnation with a friendly reminder to each listener. Bumper stickers reading "I brake for animals" were given out to support a speech on animal rights. Speakers have used pamphlets, seeds, T shirts, pens, sugarless cookies, refrigerator magnets, and pins as short-term incentives to reinforce messages. Remember that these items should not detract from the speech, but should be handled in a manner which enhance the presentation.

Present listeners with long-and short-term incentives. Let members of your audience know how their lives will be improved by agreeing to your proposal, and provide immediate incentives to encourage them.

Involve the Audience Emotionally

A persuasive speaker cannot be completely successful unless listeners experience an emotional connection to the topic. Speakers make these connections by using colorful language, stirring examples, and an expressive delivery.

Pat Masimore, a speaker of Indian descent, believed that professional teams should not adopt Native American names because the practice is insulting and disrespectful. She described how sports fans who wear costumes made from chicken feathers unknowingly ridicule the Indian ceremonial headdress of eagle feathers. She used this quotation from an editorial in *Sports Illustrated*[9] to express her strong emotional feelings about Indians.

> An anthropologist was studying Indians in the mid-1800s when he came across an old, old tribal chief. He asked the chief what America was called before the white man came. The old Indian looked at him and said, "Ours."

The speaker used vocal emphasis and a dramatic pause to stress the emotion in the line containing the Indian's response. Audience members got the message.

Another speaker conveyed sympathy for the homeless by asking listeners to hold small plastic bags filled with ice cubes during a portion of a speech. When audience members became uncomfortable with the subfreezing temperatures, Becky Meyers asked listeners to briefly express how they felt. One listener commented: "My fingers were so numb that I could hardly concentrate on what you were saying." Another observed: "If I had difficulty holding ice cubes for two minutes, imagine how a homeless person feels, existing in these temperatures for an entire winter." Becky had succeeded in using emotion to link members of the audience to her topic.[10]

Ashley Pettis wanted listeners to volunteer for Movable Feast, an organization that distributes one meal a day to AIDS sufferers. At one point in the presentation, the speaker played a videotape of her interview with a patient who had benefited from the program. In simple but emotional words, the AIDS victim appealed to Ashley's audience: "I don't know what to say, but I know it's a great organization and I certainly couldn't have done without it. I didn't realize it existed until I needed it. They're beautiful people."[11]

These speakers understood the importance of relating their topics to the emotions of audience members. Similarly, you can employ emotional examples, vivid language, and expression in your persuasive speeches. Recognize that listeners will be more likely to accept your ideas if you touch their emotions.[12]

THE SPEECH TO ACTUATE

The persuasive speech to actuate is an excellent presentation to build if you want to motivate listeners to perform a specific action. This speech often incorporates an organizational method known as the *motivated sequence*, which was developed by Alan Monroe, a professor of speech at Purdue University in the 1930s. Monroe used this method successfully to train sales personnel by combining problem–solution techniques with motivational approaches.[13] The motivated sequence consists of five steps: *attention*, *need*, *satisfaction*, *visualization*, and *action*.

Attention Step

The attention step is the introductory phase of the speech which arouses the curiosity and stimulates the interest of the listener. Any of the types of introductions we discussed in Chapter 11 (shocking statement, quotation, narrative) would be appropriate techniques to get the attention of your audience in a speech to actuate.

Need Step

Next, a speaker must persuade the audience that there is a need or problem that remains unsolved. Issues such as "our oceans and beaches are being polluted," "our nation is going bankrupt," or "our educational system is at risk" can be appropriate choices for actuating speeches. When you identify a problem, use statistics, testimony, and examples that persuade the audience that there is a real problem, and that the problem affects them. For example, if you show pictures of polluted beaches and cite instances of ocean-dumping, you are providing supporting evidence for the problem. If you tell your audience about unpleasant vacations at the ocean, where hospital waste has washed ashore, your listeners will begin to see that the problem affects them directly.

Satisfaction Step

When you have identified and developed the problem, you must provide a solution. It is helpful if you have evidence which indicates that the solution has worked in similar situations, and that a number of authorities and experts have supported it. If you advocate that "Congress must adopt a strict law which regulates dumping in our oceans," you need to supply statistics, testimonies, and/or examples which persuade the audience that this solution is sensible and workable.

Visualization Step

In the visualization step, you must "picture" in vivid words and examples what will happen in the future if your listeners adopt your proposed solution and the negative results if they do not. A speaker tells the audience, "We can continue to watch as more used needles, syringes, and vials containing the AIDS virus wash up on our beaches, or we can support the bill in Congress imposing strict fines on ocean-dumping." While this statement must be supported with specific evidence, it is an effective visualization because it portrays both positive and negative results. Visualization is a crucial step in the actuating speech—Audience members learn how supporting the solution will benefit their future.

Action Step

The action step is the how, where, and when of the motivated sequence. The speaker tells audience members exactly what they are to do if they support the solution. The action should be as specific as possible—"Give blood next Wednesday"; "Register to vote"; "Sign a petition to support the bill outlawing ocean dumping"—so that listeners can take an active part. The action step is placed near the conclusion and can be combined with an appeal, personal testimony, or experience. If your action is clear and specific, your audience will be able to demonstrate their agreement with your solution by performing the action you advocate.

APPLYING THE MOTIVATED SEQUENCE

Here are five excerpts from a speech to actuate by Kara Jenkins entitled "Feeding the Hungry Here at Home."[14] Notice how the speaker develops each phase of the motivated sequence to reach her ultimate goal of action.

Specific purpose: to actuate the audience to bring cans of food for the hungry
Thesis statement: If the homeless are provided with nourishing food, hope can be restored to these deserving Americans.

Attention Step. In her introduction, Kara gets attention by combining her personal testimony with a series of brief examples. She uses repetition of the words "A place where I saw…" for emphasis and dramatic effect.

> Not long ago, my older brother took me to a place that I will never forget. A place where I saw people who were homeless and poor and hungry. A place where I saw old women who carried trash bags with everything they owned in them. A place where a man begged me for one more piece of bread. A place where I saw a mother sit down with her four tiny children. This place is not on TV or in the movies—this place is not in Ethiopia. This place is Our Daily Bread—a soup kitchen right here in Baltimore.

The examples were short but powerful. Kara conveyed strong emotion as she related her personal testimony. The "I was there" approach achieved the purpose of the introduction and aroused the attention of her audience.

Need Step. Kara uses testimony from two experts and her own observation to develop the problem.

> I talked to Mrs. Johnson, a food coordinator for Social Services, and she told me that there are about thirty-one soup kitchens in Baltimore. I also talked to one of the workers at the soup kitchen, Raleigh Lemon, who said that anywhere from 350 to 500 people eat at Our Daily Bread in one day. The center is run by Catholic Charities and serves one meal between 11 A.M. and 1 P.M. Since this center is a private, non-profit organization, it depends on volunteers and donations to keep it running. I remember when I was there they were having a shortage of rye bread, so we could only give one slice to each person. I remember one very shy old man whispering to me, "Please Hon, could you just get me one more slice of bread?" More food is needed so people don't have to beg for another slice of bread. We need to develop some solutions to this problem.

The speaker used statistics as a logical appeal to help listeners understand how many people must be fed at the soup kitchen every day. She then quoted the old man to appeal to each listener's emotions and to convey the human dimension of the problem. Kara's use of logic and emotion was successful; listeners were deeply touched as they heard about the tragic consequences of hunger in their city.

Satisfaction Step. The speaker tells the audience what other people are doing to help the homeless. The variety of solutions allows the audience to choose their degree of commitment to the issue.

> Let me tell you what others are doing to help. Sue Thompson, an assistant director of Our Daily Bread, said that business groups sponsor breakfasts on Monday, Wednesday, and Friday mornings. Church groups, private organizations, and concerned individuals sponsor one main meal a month for the 350 to 500 hungry people. If that is too much for a small organization, they can sponsor just the juice, salad, or dessert portion of the meal. There are also many volunteers who donate their time to serve the food and help with the cleanup afterwards. And some who can't donate a meal or their time donate canned goods, clothes, socks, or toothpaste—anything that a homeless person could use. So while we may not be able to take 500 people into our own warm homes, the least that we can do is make sure that these people have some nourishing food.

Even though she lists a variety of solutions, notice that the speaker's easiest alternative—"Some who can't donate their time can donate canned goods"—is the last in the list. It is this solution which will be the requested action. Notice that the testimony from the assistant director provides valid evidence that businesses, churches, and "concerned individuals" are an important part of the solution.

Visualization Step. The speaker provides both negative and positive visualization. She tells the audience what will happen if the audience "just sits and does nothing," and she explains how adopting her solution will answer the immediate need.

> We've all driven past a bum or a bag lady, and most of us feel sorry for them and wish that we could do something. Today, I'm giving you all a chance to make a difference in their lives. We can just sit back and do nothing and that bag lady will miss another meal and those children I mentioned earlier won't get a second helping to fill their stomachs. Or we can provide more food so that all of these people can have nourishing and fulfilling meals. We can tell our friends, relatives, and neighbors about the ongoing need for food and keep providing these lifesaving meals.

Notice how skillfully Kara connects the solution to her listeners' motivation or wish to help the hungry. Also notice the effective use of language ("filling their stomachs," and "fulfilling meals") to visualize the results of supporting or of not supporting the solution.

Action Step. In the conclusion, the speaker requests a clear, direct, easy-to-follow action.

> I hope that you all care about this problem and really want to help. I'm not going to ask for a big portion of your time or your money. All I want you to do is to reach into your pantry and pull out a couple cans of corn or green beans and bring them to class on Tuesday, May 17th, and I will take them down to Our Daily Bread. Remember when your mother said, "Eat all your food—there are starving people in Ethiopia"? I think she forgot that we don't need to go as far as Ethiopia—there are people starving right here in Baltimore. I know that the people who eat your canned food may not know your name or who you are, but they will know that there is a light at the end of the tunnel—There is someone out there who cares. Please, won't you take a few minutes of your time and be that light for these people?

In one brief sentence, the speaker has told audience members the *what*, *where*, and *when* of the action step—"Bring cans to class Tuesday, May 17th." She has also taken the familiar motherly admonition of "Eat your food because of the starving in Ethiopia," and related it to the solution and action she advocates. Kara ends the speech with an earnest appeal to "take a few minutes of your time."

Building the Persuasive Actuating Speech

We've described several strategies for motivating audiences and presented the organization of the speech to actuate. Here is a list of guidelines to help you build this important persuasive message.

1. **Choose a topic requiring audience commitment**.
   a. Examine your attitudes and the opinions of others.
   b. Explore topics from current events.
   c. Avoid overworked issues.
   d. Provide new insights into familiar topics.
   e. Choose a topic which allows listeners to perform a specific action.
   f. Be certain the topic is appropriate.

2. **Conduct extensive research.**
   a. Examine library sources for testimonies, statistics, and examples.
   b. Interview experts on the topic.
   c. Research specialized institutions and organizations.
   d. Be certain that sources are accurate and up to date.
   e. Select audiovisual aids for variety.
   f. Be willing to change or modify the topic if evidence does not support your viewpoint.

3. **Phrase a clear specific purpose and thesis.**
   a. The specific purpose contains the specified action, but is not stated in the introduction.
   b. The thesis includes the need, satisfaction, and visualization steps of the body and is stated at the end of the introduction

4. **Analyze the audience.**
   a. Make the audience central to speech development.
   b. Determine prior attitudes about a topic through interviews, surveys, or questionnaires.
   c. Develop persuasive appeals linking your topic to audience interests and motivations.
   d. Plan alternative strategies if the audience resists solutions or suggested actions.

5. **Develop sound arguments and coherent organization.**
   a. Present well-defined claims supported by good evidence and sound reasoning.
      (1.) Use evidence in the context of its intended meaning.
      (2.) Include materials which are relevant and up-to-date.
   b. Avoid subjective phrases such as "I think," or "in my opinion."
   c. Identify research sources to build credibility.
   d. Avoid unethical practices.
   e. Use a balance of logic and emotion.
   f. Be able to apply the five stages of the motivated sequence.
   g. Use external transitions to emphasize major arguments.

6. **Construct a sophisticated introduction.**
   a. Employ a creative strategy for gaining audience attention.
   b. State a clear thesis at the end of the introduction.
      (1) Avoid stating the specific purpose containing the specified action.
      (2) Avoid opinionated statements such as "I'm going to actuate," or "prove," alienating the audience.
      (3) State the thesis in a straightforward manner, creating receptiveness among listeners.

7. **Develop a forceful conclusion.**
   a. Employ an appeal in the actuating speech to seek a specific commitment from the audience.
      (1) State the action clearly.
      (2) Provide listeners with all necessary details of the action.
   b. Use the appeal in combination with most types of conclusions.
   c. Avoid summary conclusions in actuating speeches.

8. **Build an effective delivery.**
   a. Maintain eye contact with listeners when conveying emotional examples.
   b. Report statistics accurately without stumbling.
   c. Use gestures to emphasize arguments and facial expressions to express emotion.
   d. Express feelings through enthusiasm, verbal emphasis, and vocal inflections.
   e. Practice the speech in order to project confidence in the topic.

Outlining the Motivated Sequence

It is easy to incorporate the motivated sequence into the traditional speech out-line. This brief outline of the following speech on current events can help you structure the introduction, body, and conclusion of the speech to actuate.

Specific purpose: to actuate the audience to become better informed about current events by reading the newspaper

Thesis statement: Our lack of knowledge must be overcome by educating ourselves in order to avoid ignorance.

Introduction

Attention Step: I. "Let's take a little quiz."
                         II. Ask audience series of open-ended questions
                             A. How is Japan overcoming U.S. distrust
                             B. What nation won World Soccer Championship
                             C. Whose mother and aunt are suing *National Enquirer*
                             D. Which major university is losing athletic director
                             E. What are effects of human growth hormone on body

Body

Need Step: I. Americans grossly uninformed, according to survey
                             A. Under 30 ages read less than in prior decades
                             B. 18-29 ages less likely to follow news events
                             C. Newspaper readership in decline
                             D. 1980s compare poorly with 1960s statistics
                             E. Over 35 ages exhibit decline in news interest

Satisfaction Step: II. This problem is solvable
                             A. Listen to radio news
                             B. Watch TV news broadcasts
                             C. Read evening paper

Visualization Step: III. We can blindly follow, or gain knowledge
                             A. Ignorance creates easy target for manipulation
                             B. Being informed leads to knowledge and aware-ness of society

Conclusion

Action Step: I. "You never know what you can find in the newspaper."
                         II. An appeal.
                             A. Don't miss news such as ad in local paper

B. Use gift of quarter to buy paper
C. Don't contribute to knowledge decline
D. Read, learn, enjoy

The following speech was presented by a journalism student who was extremely concerned about the lack of awareness exhibited by many younger Americans regarding news and current events. The speaker makes effective use of the motivated sequence and builds creative motivational appeals into her presentation. Although some of the introductory facts are now dated, Jessica raises some important issues for us to consider and put into practice.[15]

IGNORANCE IS NOT BLISS

Persuasive Speech to Actuate

Jessica Gregg

1 Let's take a little quiz. If you know the answers to these questions, you can just call them out. What is the Japanese government doing to overcome what they feel is a sense of mistrust in this country towards their nation? Anyone know? The answer is that they are undertaking a 330 million dollar effort to make Americans more familiar with Japan's cultural and social life. Question number 2. Which nation won the world cup soccer championship? West Germany? Yes, you're correct. I knew we had a soccer fan. Whose mother and aunt are suing the *National Enquirer* for publishing unauthorized photographs of this model? The answer is Marla Maples. And the athletic director of which major university is leaving for a job at the University of Connecticut? The University of Maryland, correct. And the final question: What effects have scientists discovered a human growth hormone to have on the body? No one knows? Well scientists have discovered that a human growth hormone reverses the effects of aging. This has interesting implications for the future, doesn't it?

2 If you did not know the answers to these questions, you are not alone. Despite the fact that we have entered an information age, a majority of the public remains uninformed and uninvolved when it comes to current events.

3 Our lack of knowledge must be overcome by educating ourselves in order to avoid ignorance.

4 According to a new study, "The Age of Indifference," released two weeks ago by the Times Mirror Center for the People and the Press, the under 30 generation

[1] Jessica used a series of open ended questions about current events as her attention step. The audience participation stimulated curiosity, yet prepared the way for the topic.

[2] Many listeners did not know the answers to these questions. Jessica related this lack of knowledge to her topic.

[3] The thesis includes the three numerals of the body, but avoids identifying the action.

[4] The speaker uses statistics from a study and an article

from a newspaper as support for the need or problem.

knows less, cares less, and reads the newspapers less than any other generation in the past five decades. The survey also states that persons between the ages of 18 and 29 are 20 percent less likely to follow important news stories such as events in Eastern Europe and they are 40 percent less likely to identify newsmakers like West German Chancellor Helmut Kohl. There are two exceptions to this. People in this age group show a high interest in sports and in issues like abortion. According to an article in the *Baltimore Sun* entitled "If You're Under 30 You'll Likely Skip This," the survey's most dramatic revelation is the decline in newspaper readership. Only 30 percent of Americans under the age of 35 said they had read a newspaper the previous day. This contrasts with figures in 1965 when 67 percent under 35 said they had read the previous day's newspaper. What is surprising is that TV has not filled the gap. The percentage of people viewing television newscasts is down as well. This then is truly the tuned out generation.

[5] Jessica recognized that her audience included older as well as younger listeners. She developed appeals to both groups.

5 If you're over 35 and you're sitting there relieved that none of this seems to affect you, think again. According to the Times-Mirror survey, the percentage of all of those reading newspapers and watching TV newscasts has declined in general. In other words, Americans don't have the information they need to be good consumers, make good business decisions, vote, or understand the current issues of today.

[6] A transitional sentence introduces numeral II, the satisfaction step.

6 We don't have to stay this way, however; there are options.

[7] The speaker provides alternative solutions to satisfy the need.

Jessica refers to an interview with an expert to support a statistic.

7 For example, we can listen to radio news. Most radio stations have a news program every hour and some have them as often as every half hour. There are some good news programs around. WTTR–1470 AM has a good program and National Public Radio–88.5 FM has excellent news. You can also watch TV news. This is possibly one of the easiest and most accessible options for everyone. On the average weekday, there are 56 news programs on television, and this does not include cable channels, business programs, talk shows, or interview programs like *20/20* which do stories about current events. I interviewed Sherri Parks, a Professor of Radio, Television and Film at the University of Maryland who told me that 99 percent of American households have TVs. In other words, more people have television in their homes than have running water. So it shouldn't be too hard for someone to find a television to tune in to.

[8] The speaker presents her third solution in detail, which is later connected to the action.

8 But just in case television isn't possible, there is a third option. For twenty-five cents, which is less than the price of a candy bar, you can buy the weekday edition of *The Baltimore Sun* or even *The Washington Post*. Many people shy away from newspapers because they feel they're too time-consuming or boring. Well the secret to reading a news article is understanding how it is written. Most news reporters use what is called inverted pyramid style. That is, they place the

most important details or facts at the beginning of the article and work their way down to the least important. So in order to understand an article, you only need to read a short way to get the main idea. Sometimes this means you only have to read the headline. Other times you must read the entire article. Now the inverted pyramid style does not apply to features or sports. As you can see, reading the newspaper does not have to be a chore. None of these options are. They are easy as well as important.

Jessica educates the audience about the inverted pyramid style.

[9] You may wonder why this is so important. What does it matter if you choose not to be informed?

[9] A transitional phrase introduces numeral III, the visualization step.

[10] Well, according to the Times-Mirror Survey, the fact that the under 35 generation is so uninformed makes them an easy target of manipulation. We know of powerful speakers such as Martin Luther King, who used his influence for the common good to get people involved in the civil rights movement. And we also know of Adolf Hitler, one of history's worst manipulators, who was also a powerful speaker. Do we want to get caught in that trap of blind following? Ignorance is bliss; but then again, ignorance is still ignorance.

[10] The speaker visualizes the negative consequences of choosing not to be informed. She appeals to safety and security, telling listeners that ignorance can lead to exploitation and "blind following."

𝕮𝖆𝖗𝖗𝖔𝖑𝖑 𝕮𝖔𝖚𝖓𝖙𝖞 𝕿𝖎𝖒𝖊𝖘

FIGURE 18.1

Thursday, July 12, 1990

18 Gorsuch Rd. July 1. Childrens clothes, benches, records, ffed animals, dishes,

family yard sale. Fri, pm; Sat., July 14th, shine. 4033 Rineha Rd.).

'12 Old Westminster . 8 a.m. -?. Quality lies clothes, teaching ore.

19 Fairfield Ave., Fri. Sears cartop carrier, scooter, clothes, toys, tc.

'19 Gahle Rd. Multi-

great music- GREAT TIMES! Radio professionals with music variety for your occasion. 848-4596.

NEED A DISC JOCKEY for your next party, dance or celebration? For reasonable rates, call Scott Young, 848-6433 after 5 pm.

SPEECH 101

We made it through the semester!

YOUNG MAN, age 24, 6'5", happy, out-going good looking sincere type person. Loves to live life to the fullest. Would like to meet female of same for a happy relationship. Not into bar scene or smoking. Send photo and letter to: P.O. Box 1543, Westminster, MD. 21157.

BLACK LAB, 3 year o shots, neutered, exc needs room to run. Call 876-6613.

CAT, 4 year old, ne white. Good outdoor home, 876-6613.

DESPERATELY NEEI farm kittens: 4 black friendly, 8 week old k Please call 833-2107

FIREWOOD. Large Already down. You Easy access along har 756-4062.

FREE 3 CAR METAI firewood inside. Yo

[11]Here the speaker visualizes numerous positive results and long-term incentives if listeners educate themselves. There are appeals to love, esteem, and self-actualization.

[11] We can avoid being uninformed and ignorant by following one of the three options. For example, let's look at reading the newspaper. By reading the paper you can learn much more about world events. You can learn about national events, happenings within the state and county. You can read the sports, the weather, stock figures, the foreign report, and the classifieds. You can find out the opinions of your favorite columnist as well as those individuals from your community who have written letters to the editor. You can read stories about real people like you in the features section. Plus there's all the fun stuff like horoscopes, comics, and crossword puzzles.

[12]To begin the conclusion, Jessica used a creative motivational appeal. She placed an ad in the local county newspaper which no one in the audience had read. The paper was dramatic visual evidence that listeners needed to become more informed.

[12] You never know what you can find in the newspaper. For example, if you happened to have read today's classifieds in the *Carroll County Times,* you might have seen this message [Figure 18.1] that I left for our class. It says, "Speech 101. We made it through the semester!" So you see, newspapers are truly a fun and enjoyable way to learn what is going on in the world.

[13]The speaker used another creative motivator for the action step. She provided a short-term incentive by giving each listener a quarter to buy the evening paper. Jessica demonstrated her willingness to "invest" in the education of her audience.

[13] Since it's so important for us to learn about the world, I'm going to ask you to follow through with that last option and to read the paper this week. I'm going to give you all a quarter so you don't even have to go to the library and borrow a copy. Buy a newspaper. Read it, learn, and enjoy. We don't want to be a nation in trouble because of our lack of knowledge.

SUMMARY

A persuasive speaker must find ways of motivating audiences. Strategies of involving listeners include appealing to needs, values, and beliefs; providing incentives; and involving emotions. The persuasive speech to actuate is an excellent motivational presentation. It is organized using Monroe's motivated sequence, which includes five steps: attention, need, satisfaction, visualization, and action.

EXERCISES

1. Select a topic and develop an outline for a speech to actuate using the five steps of the motivated sequence.
2. Select five magazine or newspaper advertisements that appeal to different levels in Maslow's hierarchy. Identify the specific appeals, and state how they connect to audience needs.

3. Most TV commercials and magazine ads use the motivated sequence to sell products. Select two commercials and identify each step in the motivated sequence. Which commercial is more effective? Do the commercials clearly target specific audiences? Is the persuasive approach employed in the commercial effective? Are any unethical tactics used? Can you find any research that indicates what kind of marketing tactics are successful for particular groups?

4. Find an advertisement in a magazine or on television that uses strong appeals to emotion, and provides long- and short-term incentives to listeners. Identify the emotional appeals, and name the specific incentives which are presented.

5. Read the speech by Mary Fisher in the Appendix. Identify the various types of appeals the speaker develops to relate to members of the audience.

NOTES

[1] Examples used for the five stages of Maslow's hierarchy were taken from two speeches: Cecelia Broos, "Deforestation," and Kimberly Warhime, "Chesapeake Bay Pollution," persuasive speeches to actuate, Carroll Community College, Westminster, Maryland, 1991 and 1992. Used by permission.

[2] Bob Garfield, "AT&T Refines Fine Art of Selling Long-Distance," *Advertising Age*, May 27, 1991, p. 38.

[3] Katherine Schofield, vice-president, Division of Strategic Planning, W. B. Doner, Inc., interview, March 1, 1993.

[4] "Old Joe Must Go," *Advertising Age*, January 13, 1992, p. 16.

[5] Schofield, Ibid.

[6] Gina Alexander, "Pet Owners Should Receive a Tax Deduction," persuasive speech to convince, Carroll Community College, Westminster, Maryland, 1990. Used by permission.

[7] Karen Mundell, "Research Your Family Genealogy," persuasive speech to actuate, Carroll Community College, Westminter, Maryland, 1990. Used by permission.

[8] Cathy Manzer, "Highway Etiquette," persuasive speech to actuate, Carroll Community College, Westminster, Maryland, 1990. Used by permission.

[9] Rick Reilly, "Let's Bust Those Chops," *Sports Illustrated*, October 28, 1991, p. 110, as cited by Patricia Masimore, "Sports Teams and Racism," persuasive speech to convince, Carroll Community College, Westminster, Maryland, 1991. Used by permission.

[10] Becky Meyers, "People in Need in Carroll County," persuasive speech to actuate, Carroll Community College, Westminster, Maryland, 1990. Used by permission.

[11] Ashley V. Pettis, "Have a Moving Experience," persuasive speech to actuate, Catonsville Community College, Catonsville, Maryland, 1992. Used by permission.

[12] Suggestions for incentives and appeals to emotions are based upon Rudolph F. Verderber, *Essentials of Persuasive Speaking* (Belmont: Wadsworth Publishing Co., 1991), pp. 114, 116–119.

[13] Bruce E. Gronbeck, Douglas Ehninger, and Alan H. Monroe, *Principles of Speech Communication*, 10th ed. (Glenview, Illinois: Scott, Foresman, © 1988), pp. 272–285. Reprinted by permission of Scott, Foresman and Company.

14 Kara Jenkins, "Feeding the Hungry Here at Home," persuasive speech to actuate, Catonsville Community College, Catonsville, Maryland, 1988. Used by permission.

15 Jessica Gregg, "Ignorance Is Not Bliss," persuasive speech to actuate, Carroll Community College, Westminter, Maryland, 1990. Used by permission.

READINGS

Gronbeck, Bruce E., Ehninger, Douglas, and Monroe, Alan H. *Principles of Speech Communication*, 10th ed. Glenview, Illinois: Scott, Foresman, 1988. Chapter 12 presents the classic motivated sequence, developed by the original author of the text, Alan Monroe. This important chapter helps you to understand each step of the motivated sequence in detail.

Chapter Nineteen

Speaking for Special Occasions

Chapter Outline

Key Terms

Eulogy
Keynote speech
Testimonial

© UPI Bettman News
Photos

"Ceremony keeps up all things."
—JOHN SELDEN

*O*n October 2, 1988, Americans returned to space, more than two-and-one-half years after the *Challenger* disaster. To commemorate the occasion, Commander Rick Hauck and Mission Specialist "Pinky" Nelson read this moving tribute from the space shuttle *Discovery:*

> At this moment our place in the heavens makes us feel closer to them than ever before. They were our fellow sojourners, they were our friends. Today, up here where the blue sky turns to black, we can say at long last to Dick, Mike, Judy, to Ron and Al, and to Kristen and Greg:
>
> > Dear friends, we have resumed the journey that we promised
> >   to continue for you.
> > Dear friends, your loss has meant that we could confidently begin anew.
> > Dear friends, your spirit and your dream are still alive in our hearts.[1]

The speech was simple and brief, yet it expressed the feelings of many Americans toward the seven astronauts who lost their lives in the explosion on January 28, 1986.

The tribute is one of many speeches prepared for special occasions which this chapter considers.

During your lifetime, you will probably be called upon to deliver speeches for a variety of special events or social occasions. A friend may ask you to propose a toast at a birthday party; your employer might request that you present an award or certificate to a deserving employee; your civic or social group might want you to introduce an important community leader.

While these presentations may appear uncomplicated, effective speeches for special occasions require careful planning and a clear understanding of the speech setting. You need to know the purpose of the occasion as well as the mood of the audience. If you deliver a eulogy, for instance, you need to include material that is appropriate to an audience experiencing grief; if you present a commencement speech, you need to know that listeners in a celebrating mood will not listen to a lengthy, intellectual discourse.

This chapter helps you to build speeches appropriate to a variety of occasions. We include the following types: tribute, presentation, acceptance, and dedication speeches; speeches of welcome and introduction; keynote, nomination, farewell, and commencement speeches; the after-dinner speech and the toast.

TYPES OF SPECIAL OCCASION SPEECHES

The Speech of Tribute

Speeches of tribute recognize distinguished careers and contributions of either the living or dead. The tribute may be a *testimonial* presented at a retirement or other going-away ceremony, or a *eulogy* delivered at a memorial service or funeral. The speech of tribute seeks to stimulate and reinforce feelings people share about a person (or group) admired within a community. In this presentation, the speaker's goals are to acquaint the audience with the individual's life, remind listeners of the person's significant contributions and virtues, and leave people feeling positive and hopeful for the future.

Construct a Brief Biographical Sketch Clearly identify the individual who is the subject of your tribute. Conduct accurate research to collect interesting anecdotes and incidents amplifying the individual's character and personality. Present a biography or life-sketch providing insights into the individual's family background, role models, education, and occupation. Be brief: include information that promotes understanding, and avoid insignificant details that interrupt the flow of the speech. Be sensitive to the setting of the presentation. If you are delivering a eulogy, recognize that your audience will be grieving at the loss of a family member, friend, or business associate; choose examples and quotations which contribute to the healing process. If your speech celebrates the current life of a distinguished person, you may have greater latitude in the use of supporting materials such as colorful vignettes and humorous anecdotes. In both cases, however, choose materials honoring individuals, and avoid negative incidents or hostile satire revealing unsavory qualities. Construct a positive and hopeful tribute celebrating a unique personality.

Acknowledge Significant Achievements and Virtues Speeches of tribute focus upon achievements and virtues. Speakers recount examples of heroism in battle, contributions in science, religion, or sports, or charitable service to humanity. These examples often identify and praise high moral values—qualities that serve as models for others. Speakers presenting tributes frequently include comments such as "She was the best athlete in her category," "He worked tirelessly in the cause of equality," or "He kept going in spite of extreme adversity." The intention is to remind the audience of the qualities that contributed to the significance or greatness of the individual.[2]

Convey Hope and Encouragement Effective tributes link past virtues and achievements to present times by encouraging listeners to continue similar struggles or to embrace the values of those they admire. Audiences experiencing separation from loved ones as a result of retirement, relocation, or death should not be left with a sense of despair or futility. It is appropriate to use Biblical quotations, citations of individuals being honored, or testimonies from others to reinforce feelings and to inspire listeners to grow from difficult experiences.

In a tribute presented at the funeral of Robert F. Kennedy in 1968, Edward M. Kennedy praised his brother's values and quoted one of his brother's speeches to encourage listeners to "shape" America with reason and principle.[3]

> "Our future may lie beyond our vision, but it is not completely beyond our control. It is the shaping impulse of America that neither faith, nor nature, nor the irresistible tides of history, but the work of our own hands, matched to reason and principle, will determine our destiny."
>
> There is pride in that, even arrogance, but there is also experience and truth, and, in any event, it is the only way we can live. That is the way he lived. That is what he leaves us.
>
> My brother need not be idealized or enlarged in death beyond what he was in life. He should be remembered simply as a good and decent man who saw wrong and tried to right it, saw suffering and tried to heal it, saw war and tried to stop it.
>
> Those of us who loved him and who take him to his rest today pray that what he was to us, and what he wished for others, will some day come to pass for all the world. . . .
>
> As he said many times, in many parts of this nation, to those he touched and who sought to touch him:
>
> "Some men see things as they are and say why. I dream things that never were and say, why not."

The Presentation Speech

Speeches of presentation are given to honor specific achievements of individuals in institutions, occupations, or in community organizations. The president awards the Medal of Freedom to distinguished Americans; the Pro Football Hall of Fame inducts sports personalities into membership; the Academy of Motion Picture Arts and Sciences annually selects a best actor, actress, director, and best picture; public school systems award certificates to outstanding teachers, and universities award scholarships to deserving students; businesses give away trips and prizes to employees with distinguished service records.

Since these speeches often take place in public ceremonies, they must be carefully crafted. The speech of presentation must be brief, accurate, and clear. It should identify the nature or type of award, provide brief information about the recipient's life or career, and acquaint the audience with the individual's specific achievement or service. The speech often includes adjectives like *most*, *best*, *first*, *last*, and *greatest*, to describe the individual's merits and accomplishments. The speaker usually ends the speech by formally presenting the award to the recipient.

The speech of presentation should exhibit polish and show evidence of rehearsal. The speaker must know how to pronounce the recipient's name correctly and deliver phrases smoothly. During the presentation, the speaker should avoid embarrassing actions such as dropping framed certificates, or handing out plaques upside down. The award should be presented carefully, without unnecessary fumbling. A speaker will often follow the presentation with a handshake or hug (if appropriate), and then step aside to allow the recipient to deliver the acceptance speech.

During the July 3, 1986 celebration marking the one-hundredth anniversary of the Statue of Liberty, President Reagan awarded the Medal of Liberty to twelve distinguished American immigrants—among them, comedian Bob Hope and songwriter Irving Berlin. ABC newsman Ted Koppel narrated the televised ceremony and made the twelve speeches of presentation. Here are two of these speeches—one honoring educator Hannah Holborn Gray, and another saluting author Elie Wiesel.[4] Because of the number of awards, each presentation had to be brief, yet each speech effectively acquainted listeners with the recipient, describing the individual's contribution to American life.

> When Hannah Holborn Gray was four years old, her father was dismissed from his teaching position in Heidelberg for opposing the Nazi party. He moved to New Haven, Connecticut, where Hannah pursued her education, becoming the first female provost at Yale University and eventually being chosen in 1979 to be the first woman president of the University of Chicago. The Medal of Liberty is awarded to this outstanding educator, Hannah Holborn Gray.

> Elie Wiesel was born in Rumania, and as a boy he lost both parents and a sister in the concentration camps. When the Americans liberated Buchenwald in 1945, they found the fourteen-year-old boy who had cheated death. He vowed to dedicate himself to bearing witness to what had happened during the Holocaust in the hope of preventing that dark history from ever being repeated. He has become, through his writings and teachings, the foremost voice of warning and remembrance. The Medal of Liberty is awarded to Elie Wiesel.

The Acceptance Speech

The acceptance speech is the response to the presentation. The recipient gratefully acknowledges an award, gives proper credit to those who have assisted in or been part of the achievement, and states personal values and convictions which led to the accomplishment.

The speech should be well prepared. In many ceremonies, individuals know in advance if they will receive awards; in others, individuals may know only that they have been nominated. In either case, potential recipients should have acceptance speeches prepared to deliver if called upon.

The speech should be brief. The recipient should thank the presenter and organization for the honor and identify colleagues who have contributed to the achievement, as well as personal friends or associates who have given emotional support. The speaker should exercise care, however, with the number of acknowledgments given. If you've ever watched the televised Academy Awards ceremony, you have seen embarrassing speeches where winners have thanked everyone from the obstetrician to the usher opening the theatre door. Such problems can occur when recipients attempt to deliver impromptu speeches or ramble on without considering the needs of their audiences.

The recipient should exhibit poise in delivery. The speaker should receive the award graciously, possibly holding up the plaque, statue, or certificate to allow the audience to see it easily. The speaker can then place the award on the lectern (if available) to allow freedom of gesture and movement. The recipient should try to avoid distractions such as wiping the forehead or clearing the throat. While agitated mannerisms or brief references to human feelings ("I'm really nervous tonight") might generate some empathy from the audience, listeners expect a speaker to show competence and demonstrate the qualities being honored.[5]

Dr. Benjamin Carson, Director of Pediatric Neurosurgery at Johns Hopkins Hospital, was honored at the Tenth Annual American Black Achievement Awards for his accomplishments in neurosurgery and for his success in the separation of West German Siamese twins joined at the head. Dr. Carson's remarks, accepting the Award in Business and the Professions, conveyed humility and gratitude, acknowledged emotional and spiritual support, and demonstrated the values that led to the achievement.

> I'd like to take this opportunity first of all to say that I'm tremendously honored. I don't feel, particularly after listening to the accomplishments of the other nominees, that I should be the one to receive this award. I'd also like to say how much I appreciate, as the representative of the business and professionals, the fact that Hollywood is recognizing that, in the Black community, achievements in intellectual fields are important.
>
> I'd like to thank my wife; and I'd like to thank my mother who, when I was in last place in my fifth-grade class, turned off the television set (believe it or not), said I had to read two books a week, and made the big difference in my life when I learned to appreciate learning; and lastly to my Father, who is the Owner of the universe, and anyone who knows my story, knows that I'm talking about my Father above. Thank you all very much.[6]

The Speech of Dedication

The speech of dedication is presented to commemorate the completion of a project such as a national monument, a museum, church, ship, or hospital. The speaker refers to the sacrifice and service of individuals who fostered the project and moved it to completion. Effective dedication speeches acknowledge the symbolism of the venture and convey its meaning to the community. Speakers often remind listeners of their values and emphasize the way the finished project will meet individual or collective needs. Dedication speeches usually include phrases revealing the purpose of the project: "This is a place where families can receive help," or "This building will be a house of culture and creative thought." Dedication speeches can bring the members of a community together by reacquainting listeners with their shared interests and common goals.[7]

On November 11, 1984, the Vietnam Veterans Memorial was presented to the United States government in a special dedication ceremony in Washington, D.C. One of the principal speakers at the event was Jan C. Scruggs, a Vietnam veteran whose commitment to the memory of his colleagues moved him to raise the $8 million needed for the monument. In his dedication speech, Mr. Scruggs acknowledged the bitter dissension caused by the war. But he also described the memorial as a symbol of national reconciliation: a "sacred" site where the sacrifices of young soldiers could be remembered, and where national healing could take place.

> But before we give the Vietnam Memorial away to the government, I have a few things to say. At age eighteen I was among the thousands who volunteered for combat in Vietnam. We returned home scorned as the nation was too divided over that war to honor those who served and only wanted to forget those who died. In 1979 I decided to remind America of our patriotic service and to make certain that the names of the 58,000 who died would never be forgotten.
>
> So today the memorial is to be given to the United States Government. Vietnam veterans are giving this beautiful statue and the wall of names to America. It seems ironic. Indeed, it seems that rather than Vietnam veterans building a memorial for the government, that the government should have built the memorial for the veterans. But Vietnam was that kind of war.
>
> My fellow veterans, because of this memorial, we now have our recognition. And we can now say that we have honored our dead. All of this has been a long time in coming, and is a time for America to be proud again.
>
> Yet this Memorial has given America far more than that. Out of the bitter divisiveness of Vietnam has come a symbol of national unity. This is a memorial to heal the wounds of the veterans and to heal the wounds of a nation.
>
> People will always debate that war—and let them. But this site is sacred ground where Americans have shown their honor and their respect for the sacrifices made by a generation of young soldiers who answered the call to duty...
>
> Today we also thank those who gave the funds for the memorial: locals from the AFL–CIO, school children, veterans' posts, anti-war protestors, conservative businessmen, retired people. From across America, compassionate people responded to the need for funds. Thank you America.[8]

The Speech of Welcome

Welcoming speeches extend greetings to new or returning members of organizations. University officials welcome incoming students, company representatives say hello to new employees, religious leaders greet new converts, and convention organizers extend warm regards to delegates. The speaker giving the welcome should express pleasure at seeing new as well as familiar faces, mention the goals of the group or organization, briefly identify problems to be solved, and convey best wishes to the audience members for success. The speech of welcome should be concise, communicate warmth in its tone and message, build trust and support, and establish common ground.

This welcome, presented to a group of public-speaking students on the first day of class, uses questions to build a sense of community, identifies general course goals, and emphasizes positive achievement.

> I want to give all of you a special welcome to this class. First, I'd like to ask a couple of questions. How many of you have ever had any type of speech or communications course before, either in high school or in some other college class? A few of you—Fine. Now for another question. How many of you have ever participated in a theatrical production or in a debate, given a report in a class, or been asked to deliver a talk in church or at your job? Well that's almost all of you. You can see that almost every one of you has had some experience with public speaking in your lifetime. And certainly all of you had to present a series of mini-speeches as you went through the registration line to sign up officially for the course.
>
> No matter what your background, your experience, or your knowledge, this course will help you. You'll get to know people you've never met before, you'll be confronted with a variety of ideas—some unfamiliar, some unconventional—and you'll participate in a number of learning situations that will contribute to your growth. If you're willing to work, listen, and participate, you should succeed.

The Speech of Introduction

The speech of introduction acquaints the audience with a speaker or lecturer. The introduction should help to establish speaker credibility by relating the speaker's occupation, experience, and expertise regarding the topic. The introduction might include descriptions of personal qualities—"He is a family man," or "She is an avid gardener"—and brief anecdotes providing insights into the speaker's personal life. The speech of introduction also describes values the speaker has in common with the audience.

The introduction should be concise and well organized. Lengthy or flowery introductions can exhaust audiences and defeat speakers before they are able to establish credibility on their own. The goal of the introductory speech is to enlighten the audience about a speaker and to prepare them positively for the speaker's remarks.

Dr. Paul Hardin, president of Drew University, gave the following introduction of actor Alan Alda, who delivered the commencement address at this small Methodist-affiliated institution in Madison, New Jersey. The university had originally invited Jesse Jackson to be the commencement speaker, but because of illness he was replaced by Mr. Alda. This excerpt from Dr. Hardin's speech demonstrates an effective verbal transition from Jackson to Alda, conveys familiar as well as unknown information about the speaker, and describes some of Alda's important qualities and virtues.

We are, of course, very sorry that Mr. Jackson became ill and most regretful that he cannot be with us today. We wish him a speedy recovery. I would have been proud indeed to present him to you.

I am equally proud, I assure you, to present to you the man who on just thirty-six hours notice, gracefully and unselfishly agreed to rescue us from a terrible predicament, and to speak from this platform today. Oh, I might say, Hawkeye to the rescue!

MASH is an acronym. MASH stands for Mobile Army Surgical Hospital. It also is the title of what has been called the most literate comedy series in the history of television. Probably everyone in this audience knows the series and loves its leading character, Captain Benjamin Franklin Pierce, better known as "Hawkeye." Hawkeye and his fellows are constantly fighting the insanity of war, even as they fight to save the wounded victims of war. They instruct as they entertain.

The talented actor who plays Hawkeye was a hard-working and much traveled and successful veteran of stage, screen and television, long before he made the role famous. This distinguished actor is the son of another distinguished actor, Robert Alda, who taught him much of what he knows. He is also a graduate of Fordham, an army veteran, a writer, producer, at times a television critic, an impassioned supporter of good causes, including the Equal Rights Amendment; and our speaker is justly respected as one of our nation's foremost family men. Happily for Drew on this occasion, our speaker, his wife Arlene, and their three daughters, love their small town in New Jersey.

Will you please give a very generous welcome to Hawkeye, to the very distinguished and humane actor and writer, Mr. Alan Alda![9]

The Keynote Speech

Keynote speeches are presentations given at the beginning of major conferences or conventions. Democrats and Republicans invite nationally known speakers to address their conventions every four years. Teachers, lawyers, physicians, auto makers, and chefs are among the many groups who ask experts to focus on specific issues at regional or national conferences.

Keynote speeches can be lengthy, sometimes as long as forty-five minutes to an hour. Keynote speakers highlight challenges and obstacles to goals such as divisiveness, inferior working conditions, unknown cures, or inequality. To help members face these challenges together, speakers remind listeners of unifying principles and values within party platforms, bylaws, or creeds. Portions of keynote speeches identify solutions the group must accomplish—overturning Supreme Court decisions, defeating opposing candidates, or building better cars. Keynote speeches should convey emotion, reinforce feelings about organizational values, and inspire commitment to group goals.

On July 12, 1976, Barbara Jordan became the first black woman to deliver a keynote addresss to the Democratic National Convention. In her remarks, the Congresswoman from Texas called for strong ethics in government, asked party faithful to provide America with a "vision for the future," and appealed for a sense of community and participation. As this excerpt reveals, Ms. Jordan's ideas are as applicable today as they were in the 1970s.

> And now, what are those of us who are elected public officials supposed to do? We call ourselves public servants but I'll tell you this: we as public servants must set an example for the rest of the nation. It is hypocritical for the public official to admonish and exhort the people to uphold the common good if we are derelict in upholding the common good. More is required of public officials than slogans and handshakes and press releases. More is required. We must hold ourselves strictly accountable. We must provide the people with a vision of the future.
>
> Now, I began this speech by commenting to you on the uniqueness of a Barbara Jordan making the keynote address. Well I am going to close my speech by quoting a Republican president and I ask you that as you listen to these words of Abraham Lincoln, relate them to the concept of a national community in which every last one of us participates: "As I would not be a slave, so I would not be a master. This expresses my idea of democracy. Whatever differs from this, to the extent of the difference, is no democracy."[10]

The Nominating Speech

Nominating speeches present the names of individuals for consideration to elective office before a group. The nomination should identify the qualifications necessary for the job, state the values and achievements of the nominee, and discuss how the group will succeed under the nominee's leadership.[11]

An effective nominating speech is accurate, brief, and optimistic. The speaker should have carefully researched the nominee's background to avoid embarrassing misstatements or factual errors. The speaker should mention the nominee's experience and qualifications, but eliminate biographical details having little significance to the position sought. A nominating speech should be short: a lengthy speech can affect listeners negatively, even damaging the nominee's chances of election. The nomination can include statements of the individual's virtues, quotations from speeches, or brief anecdotes and testimonials. The speech should end positively, conveying inspiration and promise.

In this speech nominating Bill Clinton for the presidency at the 1992 Democratic National Convention, Governor Mario Cuomo of New York cited examples of the nominee's competence as governor, referred to bipartisan acknowledgment of his skills, and described personal strengths which would make him an effective president.

> He was born and raised with all the personal attributes needed for leadership: God-given intelligence; vitality. And an extraordinary quality of character that allowed him to survive the buffeting and the trauma of a difficult youth.
>
> He was born poor in Hope, Arkansas. Now, the accents were different, even the colors may have been a tint different, but the feelings were the same feelings that many of us experience on the asphalt streets of some of the nation's great cities: the same pain; the same anguish; the same hopes.
>
> He has lived through years of hard challenges since that difficult youth. With each new challenge, he has grown wiser and stronger, as he demonstrated with his remarkable resiliency in the recent bruising Democratic primaries. In a world of fragile and thin-skinned politicians, he was an admirable aberration.
>
> Bill Clinton has always been driven by the desire to lift himself above his own immediate concerns: to give himself to something larger than himself.
>
> His entire life has been devoted to helping others through public service. And for 11 years now, he has been the governor of his beloved state, protecting Arkansas from a federal government that has been depriving the states and cities for over a decade; balancing 11 budgets in a row, doing the things that governors and presidents are supposed to do; enforcing the laws; providing educational opportunities for children and young adults; expanding health care; attracting new jobs; and reaching out to heal wounds caused by 300 years of unfairness and oppression.
>
> He has done it so well that the nation's other governors, both Democratic and Republican, have repeatedly acknowledged him to be a national leader.
>
> That's why we need Bill Clinton: because Bill Clinton still remembers. Because he is equipped to break the awful gridlock in Washington and to deliver effective government. Because he will remind this nation that we are too good to make war our most successsful enterprise.[12]

The Farewell Speech

Farewell speeches are given on the occasion of retirements, resignations, or some other change in status and position. The speaker thanks listeners for their association and friendship, conveys appreciation for their help and/or support, and expresses hope and best wishes for the future. These speeches are often emotional and moving, especially if speakers are saying goodby after many years of association with listeners.

Some of the most celebrated farewells in history were presented by leaders such as George Washington, who advised the new nation to "steer clear of permanent alliances with any portion of the foreign world"; General Douglas MacArthur, who identified himself with "old soldiers [who] never die; they just fade away"; and Abraham Lincoln, who told friends in Springfield, Illinois that he owed them "everything."[13]

In Lincoln's brief Farewell Address at Springfield in 1861, he acknowledged his friends and family origins, invoked God's blessing, and expressed almost prophetic uncertainty about the future:

> No one, not in my situation, can appreciate my feeling of sadness at this parting. To this place, and the kindness of these people, I owe everything. Here I have lived a quarter of a century, and have passed from a young to an old man. Here my children have been born, and one is buried. I now leave, not knowing when or whether ever I may return, with a task before me greater than that which rested upon Washington. Without the assistance of the Divine Being who ever attended him, I cannot succeed. With that assistance, I cannot fail. Trusting in Him who can go with me, and remain with you, and be everywhere for good, let us confidently hope that all will yet be well. To His care commending you, as I hope in your prayers you will commend me, I bid you an affectionate farewell.[14]

The Commencement Speech

Commencement speeches are given to honor the graduates of an institution, seminar, or field of study. Speakers congratulate listeners for their achievements, identify problems they will encounter throughout life, and refer to values which should guide their thinking.[15] Too often, when well-intentioned speakers become too self-absorbed, or try too hard to sound eloquent and intellectual, graduation speeches become tiresome affairs proclaiming platitudes having little meaning or interest to graduates.

Since the circumstances require the announcement of hundreds, and sometimes thousands of graduates, successful commencement speeches should be brief. The speaker should remember that the focus of the ceremony is the awarding of diplomas—not the speech. A graduation speech should contain clear ideas and meaningful examples. The "down-to-earth" speaker will often be received more favorably than the individual who attempts to create

A CEREMONIAL SPEAKER
MUST RESEARCH THE
NATURE AND PURPOSE OF
THE OCCASION IN ORDER
TO BUILD A SPEECH THAT
IS APPROPRIATE TO
THE SETTING.

© Frank Siteman/
Jeroboam, Inc.

high-sounding phrases. For an example of an effective commencement address, read cartoonist Garry Trudeau's "The Impertinent Questions" at the end of this book.

The After-Dinner Speech

The after-dinner speech is usually a light, humorous presentation designed to entertain or amuse an audience. There are numerous occasions where this type of speech would be appropriate: an "over-the-hill" party satirizing a friend's fortieth birthday; a football victory celebration poking good-natured fun at the coach; a business luncheon "roasting" the boss; a graduation party lampooning teachers; or an end-of-speech-class party reviewing the memorable blunders and bloopers of the semester.

While the objective of the after-dinner speech is usually to entertain, it should not consist of a series of unconnected jokes and disjointed stories. After-dinner speakers should observe the same principles of development needed for any other speech occasion.

An after-dinner speech requires a unifying theme—a topic that generates interest and captures the imagination of the audience. Topics such as

"Mind-expanding Courses to Get You Through College," "Doing Spain on One Foreign Word a Day," or "Renaming Vegetables" could be developed into successful, entertaining speeches. After-dinner speeches can be light-hearted, satiric, or subtly serious.

While research for entertaining speeches often involves exploring your own imagination and creativity, these presentations require specific supporting materials such as quotations and examples to clarify ideas. The introduction should generate curiosity and include a clear thesis statement identifying the main points of the speech. The body should contain proper transitions and references to sources where necessary. The speech should conclude with a suitable quote, reference to the introduction, or interesting narrative.

One way after-dinner speeches differ from other types is in the use of humor. While your speech may deal with a light topic designed to amuse an audience, you should not try to become a stand-up comic or a professional entertainer. Develop your own natural and spontaneous style. It is more important to elicit a few genuine smiles from the audience than to force raucous laughter. Humor depends upon timing and smooth delivery. If you've ever heard a comedian stumble over a punch line, you know how verbal blunders can destroy humor. Practice the after-dinner presentation as you would any other speech. Deliver anecdotes and punch lines clearly, and wait for laughter to subside before you continue. If you feel uncomfortable with humor, evaluate some of your strengths to determine what to include in the speech. Are you a good mimic? Can you tell a good story? Are you good at facial expressions or bizarre voices? Can you write clever rhymes or catchy poems?

Toasts

Toasts are presented to honor individuals at ceremonial occasions such as birthdays, bar mitzvahs, weddings, graduations, or the conclusion of negotiated agreements and business transactions. An effective toast acknowledges past relationships, salutes the events surrounding the present ceremony, and expresses best wishes and hope for the future.

Depending on the occasion, toasts can be serious or humorous. A U.S. president welcoming a foreign head of state will often use a toast to define areas of unity or disagreement between countries, demonstrate commitment to continuing association, and convey interest in solving problems. At a birthday or wedding party, a speaker can be more humorous. The toast can relate colorful incidents from past relationships to enliven the speech and to entertain the audience. The speaker usually concludes the toast by expressing sincere wishes for the happiness and future success of the individuals being saluted.

In the following wedding toast, the speaker summarizes listeners' mutual feelings, relates one humorous incident, and wishes the couple success and happiness for the future.

IN A WEDDING TOAST,
A SPEAKER MAY
ACKNOWLEDGE PAST
RELATIONSHIPS, RELATE
A HUMOROUS INCIDENT,
AND EXPRESS BEST
WISHES FOR THE
FUTURE.

© Mike Rizza/ Picture Cube

Good friends, I'd like to propose this toast to Mike and Diane—the reason
we're all here today. I remember when Mike came over to our house after
proposing to Diane, he said, "She didn't say yes, and she didn't say no," and
he asked me, "What should I do?" Now I don't usually give advice in these
situations, but I said to Mike, "Why don't you just wait and call her tomorrow.
Maybe Diane is testing you and she'll give you an answer in a day or two."
Well, the "test" lasted for about six weeks (you can see why I don't give
advice). But we're all glad that you both came to terms and decided to make
the arrangement official.

Will you all raise your glasses with me in wishing the best possible for
Mike and Diane—happiness in life's joys, mutual comfort in life's sorrows,
and most important, a lifelong respect and love for each other. Here's to the
bride and groom.

 SUMMARY

This chapter has considered speeches for special occasions. The tribute
recognizes distinguished careers and contributions of people either living
or dead. Speeches of presentation honor the accomplishments of individuals, and acceptance speeches are given by individuals who receive honors
and awards.

Dedication speeches memorialize the completion of national or community projects, welcoming speeches extend greetings to new or returning members of organizations, and speeches of introduction acquaint audiences with speakers or lecturers.

Keynote speeches are thematic presentations given at the beginning of major conferences or conventions; nominating speeches present the names of individuals for possible election to an office; farewell speeches are given on the occasion of retirements, resignations, or other changes in status and position; and commencement speeches honor candidates for attaining degrees.

The after-dinner speech is designed to entertain, while toasts are presented to honor individuals at ceremonial occasions.

EXERCISES

1. Choose someone you know or admire, such as a friend, family member, professor, or celebrity, and develop a two- to three-minute speech of tribute. Build the speech using the guidelines discussed in this chapter.
2. Using the brainstorming technique, compile a list of topics that could be developed into entertaining speeches. Choose one topic from this list and construct a four- to six-minute after-dinner speech. Use your creativity and imagination.
3. Choose one of the following ideas for a one- to two - minute classroom speech:
   a. Propose a toast to a friend or classmate.
   b. Present a welcome to a group of freshmen, or greetings to new employees at your job.
   c. Nominate a friend or classmate to a student government office.
   d. Introduce a well-known personality in sports, in entertainment, or in politics.
   e. Dedicate a memorial in your community or state.
   f. Present a farewell to your public speaking class.
4. Divide the class into equal groups. Have each group create an award for every member in the opposite group. Each group member should develop a one-minute speech of presentation, and each recipient should be prepared with a one-minute speech of acceptance.

NOTES

[1] ABC, *World News Tonight*, October 2, 1988.

[2] Richard L. Johannesen, R. R. Allen, and Wil A. Linkugel, *Contemporary American Speeches*, 7th ed. (Dubuque, Iowa: Kendall/Hunt Publishing, 1992), pp. 397–398.

[3] Edward M. Kennedy, "A Tribute To His Brother," *Vital Speeches of the Day*, July 1, 1968, p. 547.

[4] ABC, "Liberty Weekend," July 3, 1986.

[5] Richard L. Johannesen et al., *Contemporary American Speeches*, p. 343.

[6] This acceptance speech appears courtesy of Dr. Benjamin Carson, who gave permission for its use.

[7] Richard L. Johannesen et al., *Contemporary American Speeches*, p. 342.

[8] This excerpt was supplied courtesy of Jan C. Scruggs, who gave permission for its use.

[9] Speech by Paul Hardin, former president of Drew University, delivered at the 111th commencement of Drew University, May 19, 1979. Used by permission of Paul Hardin, Chancellor, University of North Carolina.

[10] Barbara Jordan, "Keynote Address," *Vital Speeches of the Day*, 1976 , p. 646.

[11] Richard L. Johannesen et al., *Contemporary American Speeches*, p. 343.

[12] Mario Cuomo, "Nominating Speech," *Vital Speeches of the Day*, October 1, 1992, p. 767.

[13] Andrew Bauer, ed., *A Treasury of Great American Speeches* (New York: Hawthorn Books, 1970), pp. 47, 296.

[14] Roy P. Basler, ed., *Abraham Lincoln: His Speeches and Writings* (New York: Grosset and Dunlap, 1962), p. 568.

[15] Richard L. Johannesen et al., *Contemporary American Speeches*, p. 342.

READINGS

Jamieson, Kathleen M. *Critical Anthology of Public Speeches.* Chicago: Science Research Associates, 1978. While the speech examples are somewhat dated, this pamphlet gives helpful information on a number of speeches for special occasions, including the toast, the eulogy, the speech of introduction, and the farewell.

Johannesen, Richard L., R. R. Allen, and Wil A. Linkugel. *Contemporary American Speeches*, 7th ed. Dubuque, Iowa: Kendall/Hunt, 1992. An excellent source for a large variety of speeches for special occasions. The authors provide interesting commentary on the examples, and include descriptions and guidelines of many of the types presented in this chapter.

Vital Speeches of the Day. City News Publishing Co., 389 Highway 17 By-Pass, Box 1247, Mount Pleasant, S. C. 29464. Published twice a month, this journal contains many special occasion speeches presented by individuals in government, business, education, science, and industry. It is an excellent source for researching all types of speeches on topics of current interest.

Chapter Twenty

SPEAKING IN GROUPS

Chapter Outline

Key Terms

Agenda
Autocratic
Buzz group
Cohesiveness
Democratic
Discussion question
Encounter group
Forum
Laissez-faire
Panel
Role-playing
Social group
Symposium
Task group
Trait

© David Strickler/
Image Works

"We have to face the fact that either all of us are
going to die together or we are going to learn to
live together, and if we are to live together we
have to talk."
—ELEANOR ROOSEVELT

*I*n 1924 Eugene A. Anderson started a band saw business with his father in the garage of their home in Atlanta, Georgia. Using business sense and organizational skills that he combined with optimism and a sense of humor, Mr. Anderson transformed this tiny enterprise into Southern Saw Service, Inc., a multi-million-dollar corporation with over two hundred employees. He has received numerous citations and awards including the Excellence in Exporting Award presented by President Reagan in 1987, and a proclamation from the Atlanta City Council declaring June 5, 1989 as "Eugene Alfred Anderson Day in the City of Atlanta."

We asked this international businessman, humanitarian, and public speaker what skills were necessary for effective membership in group situations.

> An effective group member is one who has developed the skill of wide-awake listening. He searches the words spoken to discover the intended message. He has a sense of empathy for the feelings of others. He has a keen sense of timing on when, what, and how to speak to the group.
>
> An effective group member is one who can make his or her personal contribution to the discussion, and then accept the decision of the group. His basic interest is the success of the team. While he continues to guard his "turf," he wholeheartedly directs his powers to promoting and maintaining the organizational structure.
>
> On the one hand, he accepts the need of stability and repetitiveness in the structure and in maintaining the continuing sameness of customer perception. He also recognizes the desirability of progressive change when the opportunity is available and the timing is right.
>
> He weighs the long-range effect on the organization, the people involved, and his personal goals.
>
> His general attitude, both present and long-range, is balance.[1]

This chapter applies many of Mr. Anderson's helpful suggestions to group discussions. It describes characteristics of small groups, types of discussion questions, and ways to solve problems. It includes guidelines for successful group participation and leadership.

Information concerning special discussion formats is also provided. We, too, want your participation in group discussions to be "balanced."

CHARACTERISTICS OF SMALL GROUPS

Think of the number of small groups to which you belong. You may be a participant in a campus club or association, a leader of an advertising committee at work, or a member of a bowling league. You may have joined these diverse groups for different reasons: to develop friendships, to get a job accomplished quickly, or simply to relax. While the groups may differ, they have several similar characteristics: each has a shared goal, group interactions, a number of members meeting over a specified period of time, and a leader.[2]

Shared Goals

Groups have goals which bring individuals together. Researchers refer to this quality as *cohesiveness*—that is, the unifying element, common purpose, or mutual feelings of members. Individuals belonging to a church have similar beliefs; employees in an assembly plant share production quotas. Small groups can be classified into types based upon general goals.[3]

    Task groups place emphasis on the completion of objectives or implementation of solutions. Employers form search committees to review applicants, conduct interviews, and recommend candidates for positions. Baseball teams develop athletes to play specialized positions in the effort to win games. Civic groups

IN A SUCCESSFUL GROUP, MEMBERS SHARE TASKS, MAINTAIN DYNAMIC INTERACTIONS, AND WORK TOGETHER TO ACHIEVE COMMON GOALS.

© Hal Rummel Photography

organize membership, nominating, entertainment, or fund-raising committees, each with a different objective. As a member of a college class, you have the task of completing certain specific course requirements for a number of credit hours.

Encounter groups contribute to interpersonal learning and to insight. Couples go away for weekend encounters to develop greater sensitivity and to improve communication. Companies sponsor retreats for employees, managers, or executives to increase self-understanding and awareness of others. Support and therapy groups such as Parents Without Partners, Victims of Child Abuse, or Alcoholics Anonymous provide a caring environment for individuals with similar experiences. Colleges and universities sponsor retreats for student leaders to identify leadership strengths and weaknesses.

Social groups help members to establish friendships and personal relationships. If you go to the park for a picnic with a few friends or invite a roommate to a party, you are participating in a group to fulfill social needs. A social group can be an informal gathering like the "lunch bunch" at work or a more structured arrangement like the Tuesday night bridge club.

Group Interaction

Groups usually require interaction among members to accomplish goals. Imagine construction workers trying to complete a building without speaking or a football team attempting a touchdown without signals or physical contact. Communication in groups is dynamic: it is continually active, steadily growing, and constantly changing. To maintain the dynamic energy of a group, members need personal contact with one another.

Size

A small group consists of from two to fifteen members. Six to eight individuals often makes an effective discussion—there are enough members for lively interaction, yet communication does not require limitation because of too many participants. Large groups are frequently divided into smaller work units of five or more members so that business can be conducted more easily and efficiently. The 535-member United States Congress, for example, conducts most of its business in small committees and subcommittees.

Time Period

To make progress towards an objective, a group must meet over a period of time. A schedule allows a group to develop cohesiveness and to explore issues in a systematic manner. Intervals between meetings are sometimes as valuable as the meetings themselves. Members have time to process ideas and to bring fresh insights to the next discussion. An education committee, for example, would need to schedule a variety of meetings in order to design a new computer graphics curriculum. Members would come together to share preliminary ideas and to assign tasks; the group would then schedule future meetings to assess data, to formulate alternatives, and finally to write the curriculum.

Leadership

Small groups usually require leaders to manage or to regulate discussion. In business, industry, or government, formal leaders with specific responsibilities are appointed or elected by organization members. A building foreman, a school principal, a club president, or a union negotiator are good examples of officially appointed or elected formal leaders. In groups without designated leaders, individuals with strong personality characteristics or competent management skills often become informal leaders. Leaderless gatherings such as protests, support groups, ad hoc committees, or social groups are often influenced by powerful individuals who gradually emerge as leaders during the course of group discussions.

SOLVING PROBLEMS IN GROUPS

Questions for Discussion

Issues for group discussions are usually phrased as questions. Open-ended questions tend to promote better discussions than yes-no alternatives. For example, the issue—"Should we increase tuition to solve financial problems at the university?"—limits discussion because it offers only two alternatives. The question does not give members the freedom to analyze the complexities of the problem or to explore a wide range of solutions. A more effective question would be "What can be done to solve the financial problems at the university?"

Discussion issues can be phrased as questions of fact, value, or policy.

Questions of *fact* explore issues where information is either unknown or disputed. For instance, when President John F. Kennedy was assassinated, the Warren Commission was established to search for answers to the question, "Who was responsible for the assassination of the President?" During the investigation of the Iran-*contra* arms scandal in the Reagan administration, the Senate Iran-*contra* Committee attempted to find answers to the question "What was the President's involvement in the arms-for-hostages deal?" Questions of fact require group members to research and analyze evidence in the effort to draw conclusions.

Questions of *value* require discussion members to use personal judgments or feelings to evaluate issues. Words such as "effective," "fair," "harmful," or "beneficial" are often used in the phrasing of value questions. A group might discuss "How has the women's movement improved American life?" or "Would pass–fail grading be more equitable than the current system?" The difficulty with these issues is that they are often more dependent upon personal opinions than upon evidence and research. While questions of value may be useful topics for encounter groups where personal feelings are important, these issues often have no real solution and simply generate circular discussions of members' views. Groups who want to gather facts to form conclusions or develop specific solutions to problems should avoid questions of value.

Questions of *policy* stimulate discussion about solutions or future actions. Issues such as "How should America meet its defense needs in view of the decline of world communism?" or "What should be done to reduce the possibility of oil spills?" would be effective problems for policy discussions. Questions of policy require research, analysis of facts, and discussion of possible solutions for implementation. The word *should* is frequently included in the phrasing of policy issues.

Developing a Problem-Solving Agenda

In order to discuss a problem, a group must have an *agenda*, or an orderly list of topics the meeting will cover. One of the most effective ways to organize an agenda is to use a process known as "reflective thinking" developed in 1910 by educator John Dewey in *How We Think*.[4] Through the years several researchers have adapted Dewey's ideas more comprehensively to the discussion process.[5] To develop a systematic approach in a group discussion, we suggest an eight-point problem-solving plan similar to that described by Larry L. Barker and others in *Groups in Process*.[6]

Define the Problem Groups should clearly understand all elements of an issue under consideration. Members may need to define ambiguous terms and provide explanations of key phrases found in the discussion question. For example, in the policy issue, "How should America meet its defense needs in view of the decline of world communism?" "defense needs" could be interpreted as the total defense budget, future expenditures, or new weapons systems. "Decline of world communism" might refer to the collapse of the Soviet Union and former Soviet satellites, or the decline of current communist regimes such as Cuba and China.

Narrow the Problem As is the case with speech topics, problems for discussion must be sufficiently limited. In narrowing topics, members should consider the needs of the group as well as the length of time available for discussion. The topic "What should be done to reduce the possibility of oil spills?" is a broad area which might require discussion for a period of several months or years. The issue might also include areas such as "government inspections" or "cleanup costs" which may be irrelevant to group objectives. One way to limit the problem would be to develop sub-categories that could be managed more efficiently:

A. New technologies for building tankers
B. Laws regulating shipping
C. Establishment of early detection systems
D. Prohibition of tankers in fragile ecological areas

The group could select the subtopics which were most important to its analysis, and gauge its discussion according to time limitations. In a one-time class discussion of fifty minutes, a group might be able to handle only two areas. A governmental group meeting over several weeks, however, might be able to handle ten or more categories.

Analyze the Issue   The next step in problem solving is to research and analyze the issue. If the group were to consider the question "What can be done to solve financial problems at the university?" members could divide up research responsibilities according to expertise or personal interest. An administrator could interview the Dean of Business Administration; an archivist could investigate the history of the financial dilemma; a faculty chair could contact other academic coordinators; a student could circulate questionnaires to fellow classmates; and a mathematician could do a statistical analysis of current fiscal difficulties. If members conduct thorough research into the problem, they will have the tools necessary to discuss the complexities of the issue and to develop workable solutions.

Set Up Criteria   Once the problem has been analyzed, the group should develop criteria or guidelines for a workable solution. This phase of problem solving keeps a discussion on track and helps a group to focus on successful results. A committee analyzing the question, "What kind of uniforms should we select for the marching band?" might set up the following criteria:

1. Uniforms should incorporate school colors.
2. Uniforms should be weather resistant.
3. Uniforms should be within budget constraints.
4. Uniforms should be eye-catching.
5. Uniforms should be comfortable and lightweight.

Suggest Solutions   Next, the group develops a variety of potential solutions from individual research, through spontaneous discussion, and/or as a result of brainstorming techniques. Group members discussing band uniforms might have obtained bids from several companies estimating the costs of the uniforms. Some members might have contributed new suggestions during the discussion process or thought of different alternatives as members jotted down ideas that came to mind.

Apply Criteria to Solutions   Once a group has selected alternatives, members can apply the predetermined criteria to identify the most desirable solution.

	Alternative Solutions	**Application of Criteria**
Company A	Colors for uniforms come in only three combinations— beige/red, black/gold, green/blue	Violates # 1 (School colors are maroon and white.)
Company B	Uniforms come in two fabric choices—wool, and cotton	Violates # 2 and # 5
Company C	Uniforms are inexpensive, but the company has only two standard styles	Violates # 4
Company D	One-of-a-kind, designer uniforms. Prices start at $300 per uniform	Violates # 3 (Budget ceiling is $125 per uniform.)
Company E	Company carries uniforms in maroon and white; has variety of styles in lightweight weather-resistant materials. Basic costs start at $85 plus accessories.	Solution meets all criteria

This step in problem-solving enables a group to eliminate solutions that are not workable. Notice how the above criteria can be applied to select a company to manufacture uniforms for the marching band.

Implement the Selected Solution When group members make a final choice, their job is not complete until they actually implement the solution. In well-organized groups, members develop a plan of action and divide up responsibilities. To implement the plan for uniforms, for instance, some group participants might contact the company to sign contracts, others might take clothing measurements from band members, and some could form another group to raise funds.

Monitor the Success of the Solution A solution needs to be monitored to determine its degree of success. Is the solution working as intended? Are there problems with any aspect of the plan? Does the group need to modify the solution or re-evaluate its decision in view of new information? A group might need to conduct interviews or circulate questionnaires to examine how well the solution is working. After initial observations, for example, group members might discover that the band uniforms were poorly manufactured. The group could withhold payment until satisfactory modifications were made or reject the contract entirely and choose another company. Group members might also decide to evaluate the decision by circulating a survey asking band members about the comfort, quality, and durability of the clothing.

A Sample Agenda Here is a sample agenda to demonstrate how problem-solving is applied in a group meeting. Notice that the agenda clearly identifies the time, date, and place of the meeting as well as the supporting documents included.

Meeting of the Search Committee

Tuesday, May 7, 1994
Room 201 (2nd Floor Conference Room)
2:00-4:00 P.M.

Topic: Which applicant(s) should be recommended for the position of Director of Public Relations?

   I. Introduction of new members

  II. Approval of minutes of 4/23/94

 III. Introduction of topic
    A. Discussion of decision-making process
    B. Scope of the committee responsibility
    C. Concerns of committee members

 IV. Qualifications required for P.R. position

  V. Review and evaluation of applications

 VI. Committee decision and recommendations
    A. Eliminate unqualified candidates
    B. Narrow choice to two to four qualified candidates

VII. Group assignments
    A. Conduct further research
      1. Contact previous employers
      2. Interview co-workers
      3. Collect samples of applicants' work
      4. Request educational transcripts
    B. Make appointments with applicants for interviews

VIII. Schedule next meeting

Documents Enclosed

1. Agenda
2. Minutes of 4/23/94
3. Fifteen Applications for Director of Public Relations

    Keep in mind that the committee discussions are an ongoing process: group members have made a preliminary decision to select two to four qualified applicants at the present meeting. But the committee needs to conduct further research and to meet again in order to make a final decision. The committee cannot monitor a solution at this stage, since a final choice has not yet been made.

PARTICIPATING IN GROUPS

Effective participation is vitally important to the success of a discussion and to the efficient completion of a task. Group members sometimes believe that they possess little power within an organization and that most of the authority remains with the leader. Such a view is usually mistaken. While leaders can exercise influence, success within a group is often determined by the skill and expertise of participants. One individual can exert a powerful influence to move a group towards the completion of a task, or to inhibit the decision-making process.

Self-Centered Behavior

Behavior that inhibits discussion in a group is often self-centered. A *self-centered* member uses the group to achieve personal goals and demonstrates a lack of interest in group needs or objectives. Self-centered conduct reroutes discussion and often stops problem-solving. In 1948, Kenneth D. Benne and Paul Sheats studied groups extensively to determine some of the positive and negative characteristics members exhibit within small groups. Here is a list of eight negative group behaviors based on Benne and Sheats' research:[7]

	Negative Self-Centered Behaviors	Example
Attacking	Displaying aggressive behavior towards group members by making hostile comments (telling nasty jokes or putting down individuals), showing envy, or expressing disapproval.	"You're dead wrong— You're DEAD wrong. Where did you go to school anyway?"
Blocking	Behavior that delays the decision-making process such as being unreasonable or negative, taking positions in opposition to the group (bringing up issues already decided or postponing issues members want to discuss), or generally failing to cooperate.	"I think we should table the motion— We've got a lot more important things to do than to spend our time talking about trivia like this."
Boasting	Attempts to impress group members and to maintain a central position in the group by bragging about professional expertise, personal qualifications, or past accomplishments.	"The company president always calls upon me when he needs a creative idea...In fact, I had lunch with him yesterday and he thought my proposal was an excellent solution."

Clowning	Exhibiting a lack of involvement in the group by telling inappropriate jokes, expressing cynicism, advocating recreational objectives, or simply "goofing off."	"Why don't we have our next meeting in a bar?"
Confessing	Using a group as an encounter or therapy session to fulfill personal needs by relating irrelevant stories, inappropriate personal examples, or boring anecdotes.	"That reminds me of the time my husband and I were having communication problems and we tried to work them out but..."
Dominating	Attempts to display self-importance and superiority by monopolizing or manipulating group discussions.	"This problem should be no surprise to anyone who has listened carefully to my past statements—I have repeatedly predicted this situation."
Pleading	Efforts to gain constant sympathy for help—or support from group members by expressing insecurity or inadequacy.	"I've never been in charge of a subcommittee before—It seems almost overwhelming. Why don't you ask Sharon—She's more experienced."
Promoting Special Interests	Behavior which seeks to manipulate a group based upon the needs, prejudices, or interests of one.	"I never function before 11 A.M. and I can't meet after 2:30 because of a dentist appointment. Could we plan a lunch meeting instead?"

Group-Centered Behavior

Groups cannot afford to waste time reacting to interpersonal problems caused by negative behaviors. An effective discussion requires group-centered behavior: Members need to cooperate with each other and share responsibility to help the group work efficiently towards solution. Here are six group-centered behaviors that can contribute to positive decision-making.[8]

Be an Active Observer An effective participant carefully observes a group by listening attentively and watching intently. When you are in a group situation, observe how members approach problems, how frequently they contribute to the discussion, or how effectively they perform tasks. Ask yourself these questions: Is there a difference between what members say and do? Is the group analyzing all aspects of the problem? Is the group making progress towards stated goals? Are there any contributions I can make which can move the group more effectively towards solutions? Active observation can help you to sense the right moment to make an appropriate contribution. For example, if you were to see a heated conflict developing between two group members, you might cool the argument with the suggestion. "We can't solve all these problems at once." When discussion is deadlocked, you might recommend that members return to the issue later, or introduce a new idea to rekindle discussion. If you have listened actively, you might have the opportunity to remind participants of previous decisions which have been forgotten.

Support Group Procedure   Discussion groups usually have a wide variety of tasks for members to perform. As an active participant, you should be willing to take on your fair share of assignments. You might be asked to chair a subcommittee; you might be placed in charge of duplicating and circulating committee pamphlets, questionnaires, or supporting materials; the group leader might even request your assistance in preparing the agenda or contacting fellow members. One job participants frequently dislike is recording minutes of committee conversations and decisions. Keeping accurate records is important, however, especially in formal organizations where documentation of past committee actions is required. If a group has no assigned secretary, it is helpful to rotate this important responsibility among group members. As a participant, you should view tasks as opportunities to help the group complete its goals.

Be Reliable   If groups are to function smoothly, members must perform tasks efficiently and on time. Groups are easily sabotaged by irresponsible members who are chronically late, who fail to complete assigned tasks, or who manage assignments carelessly. As a group member, take your responsibilities seriously. Be on time for group meetings and complete duties conscientiously. Take care of any arrangements that may be required for your portion of a meeting: do necessary research, notify invited guests of the time and place of the meeting, and have all handouts or other paperwork ready for circulation. Recognize that irresponsibility wastes everyone's time and energy within a group.

Be Willing to Compromise   Group participation is not a game of winners and losers; an effective group experience should exhibit a healthy give-and-take among members. When you are a part of a discussion, you must be willing to hear other points of view and accept changes to some of your ideas and proposals. While you are not expected to compromise your personal beliefs or values, you should be able to alter your thinking if other suggestions prove to be more workable. Compromising is often viewed as watered-down or weak-willed decision-making. But if a group is open to all the facts and genuinely seeks the best alternative, group members will often need to make compromises and modifications before coming to final decisions.

Be Courteous and Respectful Groups cannot function effectively when members are at odds. Participants who constantly interrupt each other, launch personal attacks, or exhibit insensitivity are engaging in disrespectful behavior which could eventually lead to the destruction of the group. While members don't need to like each other in order to accomplish group objectives, they must demonstrate respect and common courtesy. When another member is talking, give your full attention. Wait until the individual is finished before you contribute an idea or make a suggestion. Respect the background and expertise of others. Avoid tactics such as personal attacks or name-calling which can stimulate anger. Don't ridicule the ideas of members or jump to conclusions about their decision-making abilities. Be patient with irrelevancies or inappropriate remarks. Know when to exercise silence and let the leader handle difficulties.

Encourage and Energize Members Groups must work together to solve problems. If an outfielder drops a fly ball, the second baseman doesn't laugh at the error; the player tries to help the team by making a face-saving play. When members must complete difficult tasks, give assistance or make helpful suggestions. Show encouragement to participants who perform competently. Compliment a member by saying, "Your idea is a good one—Maybe we can use it as a basis for the solution." This type of support builds group cohesiveness and cooperation, and helps to energize members to complete assignments. Participation is not a contest of wills: individuals must be able to subordinate personal egos for the overall benefit of the group.

GROUP LEADERSHIP

Leadership Theories

There are many theories concerning group leadership. Some researchers believe that leaders possess certain powerful *traits* such as physical appearance, speaking ability, or behavior which determine leadership.[9] The trait approach suggests that leaders do not learn or acquire these skills but are born with natural abilities. It can be argued, for example, that Abraham Lincoln, Winston Churchill, Franklin Roosevelt, and Martin Luther King all possessed natural leadership abilities.

Another theory suggests that *power* and *authority* are significant factors in leadership.[10] Members of a group will respond to a leader's position, expertise, or job title—"chief executive officer," "lieutenant," "heart specialist," "committee chair," "florist," "builder," or "tax accountant." According to this theory, members opposing a decision might be persuaded to comply with an argument such as, "You may not agree, but this proposal is what the president wants."

In the 1930s, Kurt Lewin, Ronald Lippitt, and Ralph K. White studied the reactions of ten-year-old boys to three different leadership behaviors over a three-month period. This research, now classic in the field, identified three leadership styles: *autocratic, democratic,* and *laissez-faire.*[11] The autocratic leader acted as the chief decision-maker of the group, giving orders and commands to group members. Democratic leaders functioned more as coordinators, promoting discussion and stimulating group decision-making. The laissez-faire style was a leaderless group where members themselves took care of managerial or administrative responsibilities. In this study, researchers found that members of democratic groups experienced the greatest degree of satisfaction with leaders and group outcomes, while autocratic group members were least satisfied with leadership and group achievements. Members of leaderless groups were pleased with mutual associations and friendships acquired within groups, but participants felt that little was accomplished.

Research updating the Lewin study combines leadership style and personality. Investigators suggest that authoritarian personalities are more "object-oriented" while democratic personalities tend to be more "people-oriented."[12]

Today, some researchers view effective leadership in terms of adaptability. Arbitrary leadership styles or predetermined traits may not be appropriate in many group situations. Leaders may need to adopt a variety of approaches to meet group needs and to help members accomplish organizational tasks.[13]

Positive Leadership Behaviors

Most of us will be leaders at some time in our lives, either by choice or necessity. Whether you are a PTA president, a manager, a self-employed professional, or a committee chair, you need to know some of the skills that contribute to effective leadership. In this section, we examine four positive leadership behaviors which are necessary for successful group management.

Be Prepared A leader cannot simply appear and improvise an agenda for a group meeting; effective leadership requires careful advance planning. A leader must choose an appropriate location, prepare an agenda, and anticipate potential problems.

Choose an Appropriate Location. Know the size of the meeting area; don't try to fit a large group into a tiny cubicle, or a small group into a huge auditorium.

Understand the characteristics of the room and ask yourself these questions: Are there tables for discussion, are there enough chairs for participants, and can all members see each other easily? Will participants need small tables, blackboards, or screens for visual aids? Do invited guests have any special room requirements? Is the meeting located near noisy traffic areas, or can the room be closed for privacy? Is the area flexible enough to accommodate any rearrangement which may be necessary during the meeting? Is a telephone accessible for messages, and is a tape recorder available to document committee discussions and actions? Make any arrangements required for scheduling the room. Be sure that the room will be unlocked and set up for the discussion on the day of the meeting.

Circulate an Agenda. As a leader you will need to prepare an agenda of the major topics to be covered during a meeting. Contact group participants to determine topics included in their presentations, and remind invited experts of their meeting obligations. Have the agenda and all supporting documents duplicated and circulated to the group well in advance of the meeting so that participants are prepared for the discussion and can notify you if changes are necessary. Be certain that the agenda clearly identifies the date, time, and place of the meeting. If any guests may be unfamiliar with the location, include clear directions to the meeting place.

Anticipate Potential Problems. If you have smokers as well as non-smokers, establish a general policy to alleviate conflicts. In order to stimulate a positive discussion, it may be helpful to place shy members near more talkative participants, or to separate members who constantly argue. Members with disabilities or special difficulties may require assistance with wheel chairs, interpreters, or readers. You may also need to handle potentially disruptive members by assigning specific tasks to keep them occupied. As a leader, you should be in contact with members a day or two before the meeting to determine if there are significant problems that could affect discussion and alter planning: members with schedule conflicts might need to arrive late or leave early; members having complicated group assignments may need extended deadlines; members discovering additional information may request further group discussion. A knowledge of potential problems and an awareness of special circumstances can help you manage a discussion smoothly.

Keep to Time Limits Meetings should start and end on schedule. Tardiness not only wastes everyone's time, but it also conveys disorganization, and contributes to member hostility. Individuals who are angry because a meeting began 25 minutes late will not be in a constructive mood for decision-making. Leaders should be prompt and expect members to be on time. If a meeting is scheduled to end at a specific time, the leader should do everything possible to close off discussion. When a meeting drags beyond the closing time members convey negative feedback by stacking papers into neat piles, watching the clock, or squirming uncomfortably. A leader should be sensitive enough to realize that little will be accomplished by keeping participants overtime. Keeping to schedules can increase the satisfaction of group members and contribute to efficient problem-solving.

Be Organized Begin the meeting by announcing any changes in the published agenda. Remember that agendas are not fixed in stone: they contain topic outlines designed to serve group needs. A leader who is willing to be flexible and make a few changes builds cohesiveness and improves the climate for decision-making. A brief procedural comment can convey sensitivity to individuals: "We'll consider item 3 on the agenda first—Julie is here from the day care center. Because she has to leave to supervise the children, it would help her if we could deal with day-care issues first. Do you have any objections?"

Guide group members skillfully through the agenda. If the agenda is long, set time limits for specific items so that the group will cover all topics efficiently. If issues remain unresolved, establish additional subcommittees or work units to complete analysis and problem-solving.

Help members seek information and analyze problems. Promote decision-making by asking questions or interjecting thoughts such as "Has that problem occurred before?" or "Maybe we need to distribute a questionnaire." Move members towards solution of issues by asking for alternatives and requesting data verifying solutions—"Has this solution been successful in other places?" Work for consensus on issues. Groups don't need to vote on everything; constant hand-raising or balloting can disrupt the flow of discussion. Reserve formal votes for final decisions or solutions.

Communicate effectively when you manage a discussion. Identify agenda topics clearly. Refer to exhibits, page numbers, or supporting documents distinctly so that members can easily follow what is being discussed. Be open to procedural questions or comments from members: Let participants know that you want them to move forward toward solutions.

At the end of the meeting, clarify group tasks, summarize individual goals, and define future objectives. Set the time and place of the next meeting. Make sure the group feels a sense of accomplishment with the discussion, commitment to goals, and awareness of future responsibilities.

Know When to Intervene No theory or rule can tell you the exact moment you should do or say something as a leader of a group. It often takes many leadership experiences for an individual to develop a group "sense" or intuition regarding appropriate leadership behavior. There are, however, several ways a leader can intervene constructively during a group discussion. A good leader can resolve conflicts, provide emotional support, clarify and summarize, and demonstrate flexibility.

Resolve Conflicts. Conflicts are inevitable when group members are involved in the decision-making process. Participants can become fixed in their attitudes or take positions they feel the group must adopt. While disagreement can stimulate debate among participants, serious conflict can damage the survival and success of a group. The leader must handle major conflicts carefully to allow the group to complete its objectives. If a serious argument develops between two members or opposing forces, the leader should identify areas of common ground. If none exist, the leader can then restate each argument, identifying its relative strengths and weaknesses. When reviewing the conflicting positions, a leader should give equal time to each argument and avoid taking sides. Being fair will strengthen the leader's position; showing partiality will compromise and undermine the leader's effectiveness. If no agreement can be reached, the leader should define areas of progress, honestly acknowledge unresolved conflict, and move the discussion to other topics. Disputes can often be settled at a later time when emotions have cooled. [14]

Provide Emotional Support. There are occasions in a discussion when a leader must provide members with emotional support in order to maintain a positive climate for decision-making. Group members may experience hurt feelings after engaging in disputes, suffer humiliation after losing arguments, or need encouragement when not participating. A comment such as "That's an excellent idea—but it may work better in a different situation" might help a member to save face in a discussion, or a statement like "That's a great idea—Why don't you expand on it?" might encourage a member to participate more actively.

Clarify and Summarize. A good discussion is dynamic—There is a great deal of give-and-take. While dynamism is a positive force in a discussion, a leader must occasionally summarize the comments of group members who relate incomplete information, make disjointed remarks, or draw vague conclusions. Summaries help members follow the discussion easily, keep the discussion from backtracking, and clarify group decisions. A good summary is brief and clear, providing an accurate synopsis of a participant's contribution or a group's decision. A leader who comments, "Bill, I think you're asking us to compare the data, is that right?" is diplomatically summing up Bill's remarks, while at the same time checking the accuracy of the comment with the member.

Demonstrate Flexibility. A flexible and observant leader knows when to intervene and when to be silent. If a conversation gets off track, the leader should step in to check the irrelevancies. When a participant monopolizes the conversation, the leader should guide the discussion to other members. The leader needs to quiet the group clown who constantly engages in inappropriate humor or to gently reprimand the member who frequently interrupts others. Uncomfortable group silence may require the leader to activate discussion, while a hostile exchange may necessitate leader mediation. Not all situations, however, require intervention by the leader. A participant raising a point that seems irrelevant may, if allowed to continue, contribute important insights into an issue. A spontaneous joke related at the right moment can reduce tension and move an immobile conversation forward. Group silences can be necessary to help members think through ideas. A lively argument can be a productive force in solving a problem.

The style a leader adopts is often determined by the needs of the group as well as the requirements of the moment. Well-motivated participants who are experienced at discussion may require less intervention by the leader, while inexperienced members may require more guidance. A discussion which is moving along effectively may actually be impeded by an autocratic leader who tries to interject ideas or impose solutions. At the same time, members who are floundering may be frustrated with a democratic leader who provides little direction. During the life of a group, a combination of democratic, autocratic, and *laissez-faire* leadership styles may be necessary.

SPECIAL DISCUSSION FORMATS

There are a variety of groups with different formats: the forum, panel, and symposium as well as buzz groups and role-playing groups.[15]

The Symposium

The *symposium* is a highly structured group in which two to six experts reveal their views and perspectives on some aspect of a problem. Participants deliver

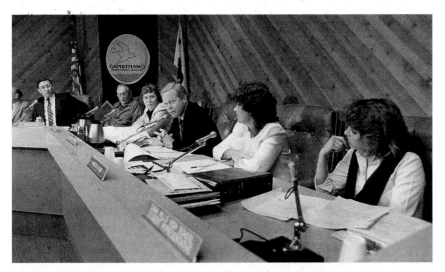

IN A PANEL DISCUSSION, PARTICIPANTS EXCHANGE IDEAS, ANALYZE ISSUES, AND EXPLORE SOLUTIONS TO PROBLEMS WITH THE GUIDANCE OF A LEADER OR MODERATOR.

© Spencer Grant/
Picture Cube

prepared speeches to an audience but do not discuss issues informally. A chairperson usually identifies the question, introduces each member, and explains how the meeting will proceed. Participants are usually seated at a table facing the audience while one member speaks from a lectern. An example of a symposium would be a convention program in which three renowned scientists reported differing results from similar fusion experiments.

The Panel

A *panel* is an informal discussion with three to six individuals in front of an audience. One person acts as moderator, regulating participation and guiding the discussion through the problem-solving sequence. Panel members are often experts who speak from their own experience and knowledge. Participants do not deliver prepared speeches in a panel discussion; members make one point at a time, frequently interrupting each other, and commenting upon ideas presented by other individuals. Panelists are often seated in a semicircle or in another arrangement so that members can see each other during the discussion. Panels present issues and examine problems to inform and educate the audience. An example of a panel would be the nation's four chief law-enforcement officers considering America's drug policy.

The Forum

A *forum* is a public discussion in which all members of an audience have the opportunity to ask questions, make statements, or deliver speeches about issues. Because so many individuals are involved, a leader is needed to set the ground rules for the discussion and to regulate participation. The seating should be arranged so that all audience members can see everyone easily. The U.S. Senate and House of Representatives function as forums. In legislative forums, participation is guided by a speaker or president who operates according to strict rules of parliamentary procedure. In more informal town meetings or council hearings, moderators might allocate specific time limits for individual contributions. Forums are often used in combination with other formats such as symposium–forums or panel–forums. When panelists have completed discussion, or symposium participants have presented speeches, the audience becomes involved in the discussion.

Buzz Groups

Buzz groups are often used in large organizations to involve many people in the decision-making process. Individuals are divided into small units or "buzz groups" of three to eight members. These smaller groups are then given specific tasks to accomplish or issues to examine within a time limit. Groups then report the results of their discussions to the larger organization through elected or appointed leaders. For example, a company could ask its 200 employees to discuss the topic, "What can be done to improve productivity?" and divide into twenty-five groups of eight individuals each. Using this method, a large number of ideas could be generated by many people in a brief period of time.

Role-Playing Groups

In *role-playing*, group members assume characters or personalities to portray relationships and interactions among individuals. Members act out conflicts between parents and children, criminals and victims, or supervisors and employees to reveal dilemmas and to portray inner turmoil. Role-playing experiences are used effectively in encounter groups to stimulate discussion and to help members with decision making and problem solving.

SUMMARY

Small groups are characterized by shared goals, several individuals engaged in face-to-face interactions over a period of time, and a leader. Types of groups include task, encounter, and social groups. Issues for discussion are phrased as questions of fact, value, or policy. Problem solving involves choosing a systematic agenda based upon John Dewey's method of "reflective thinking." When involved in group discussions, members should adopt group-centered behavior and avoid negative self-centered conduct. Although there are many leadership theories, recent research emphasizes the need for leaders to demonstrate flexibility in managing a group. Special discussion formats include the panel, symposium, forum, buzz groups, and role-playing groups.

EXERCISES

1. The instructor will divide your class into several small groups. When you are assigned to a group, help fellow members select a leader to manage the discussion. Choose several issues for discussion, and write at least one fact and one policy question. With the advice of your instructor and the opinions of other group members, choose one question for analysis and presentation to the class. Schedule group meetings to make assignments, conduct research, and develop an agenda. Present the issue in a twenty-five to forty minute class discussion.

Here are some possible discussion topics.
   a. What should be done to reform Congress?
   b. What can the United States government do to encourage the development and use of synthetic fuels?
   c. What can be done to eliminate acid rain?
   d. Who is responsible for juvenile crimes?
   e. How does the Palestinian issue affect Americans?
   f. What are the causes and effects of illiteracy?
   g. What are the characteristics of prison work-release programs?
2. As you participate in the discussion process, keep a journal of your reactions to the group. Write down any problems or frustrations occurring in your group such as unreliability, difficulty in keeping to the task, ineffective participation or leadership. Try to use the journal to help members overcome difficulties and to make progress towards group tasks.
3. Observe a "professional" committee or group in operation. You might watch the televised hearings of a congressional committee, a task group at your work, or a committee of volunteers in a church or social organization. Analyze the group carefully and write an evaluation of the following factors:
   a. the discussion issue
   b. the process used for decision-making
   c. the nature of participation by group members
   d. the quality and effectiveness of leadership
   e. the success of the group in analyzing and in solving problems

---

NOTES

[1] Eugene A. Anderson, personal letter, September 8, 1989.

[2] Compare the definition and characteristics of a group discussion found in Larry L. Barker et al., *Groups in Process*, 4th ed. (Englewood Cliffs: Prentice-Hall, 1991), pp. 7–10, with descriptions provided by Ernest G. Bormann, *Discussion and Group Methods* (New York: Harper and Row, 1969), pp. 3–6.

[3] Compare John F. Cragan and David W. Wright, *Communication in Small Group Discussions* (New York: West Publishing Company, 1980), pp. 46–48, with H. Lloyd Goodall, Jr., *Small Group Communication in Organizations* (Dubuque, Iowa: Wm. C. Brown Publishers, 1985), p. 94. Cragan and Wright list three "generic" types of groups: task, encounter, and consciousness-raising groups, while Goodall uses Julia Wood's typology of task, social, and dually oriented groups (a combination of task and social groups). Since we believe that encounter and consciousness-raising groups can be combined into one category, we have used the labels *task, encounter,* and *social* as the classifications for our study.

[4] John Dewey, *How We Think* (Boston: D. C. Heath and Company, 1933), pp. 102–118.

[5] See James H. McBurney and Kenneth G. Hance, *Discussion in Human Affairs* (New York: Harper and Brothers, 1950), pp. 3–15.

[6] Barker et al., *Groups in Process*, pp. 110–116.

[7] Kenneth D. Benne and Paul Sheats, "Functional Roles of Group Members," *Journal of Social Issues* 4 (Spring 1948): 45–46. Also see Cragan and Wright, *Participating in Small Group Discussions*, pp. 116–117, and Barker, *Groups in Process*, pp. 46–47.

[8] For this discussion we have combined recommendations appearing in Cragan and Wright, *Participating in Small Groups*, pp. 114–116, as well as Benne and Sheats, "Functional Roles of Group Members," pp. 44–45, with some of our own suggestions.

[9] H. Lloyd Goodall, Jr., *Small Group Communication in Organizations* (Dubuque, Iowa: Wm. C. Brown Publishers, 1985), p. 122.

[10] Cragan and Wright, *Communication in Small Group Discussions*, pp. 75–76.

[11] Kurt Lewin, Ronald Lippitt, and Ralph K. White, "Patterns of Aggressive Behavior in Experimentally Created 'Social Climates,'" *The Journal of Social Psychology* 10 (1939): 271–299.

[12] Lawrence B. Rosenfeld and Timothy G. Plax, "Personality Determinants of Autocratic and Democratic Leadership," *Speech Monographs* 42 (August 1975): 203–208.

[13] Julia T. Wood, "Leading in Purposive Discussions: A Study of Adaptive Behavior," *Communication Monographs* 44 (June 1977): 152–165.

[14] Goodall, *Small Group Communication in Organizations*, p. 145.

[15] Barker et al., *Groups in Process*, pp. 193–219.

READINGS

Barker, Larry L.; Wahlers, Kathy J.; Watson, Kittie W.; and Kibler, Robert J. *Groups in Process*, 4th ed. Englewood Cliffs: Prentice–Hall, 1991. A well-written, easy to read, yet comprehensive text on group discussion. The authors introduce each chapter with a list of study questions and identify important principles at the end of major headings. Projects and activities as well as ideas for discussion are suggested at the conclusion of each chapter.

Brilhart, John K., and Galanes, Gloria J. *Effective Group Discussion*. Dubuque, Iowa: Wm. C. Brown Publishers, 1989. An outstanding book for both the group leader and participant. The text is well organized, with a glossary of important terms introducing each chapter. In Chapter 6, "The Language of Discussion," the authors provide helpful examples of group agendas and discussion minutes.

Cragan, John F., and Wright, David W. *Communication in Small Group Discussions*. New York: West Publishing Company, 1980. This text is theoretical in its explanation of discussion concepts. The authors include interesting case studies with thought-provoking questions that help the reader to apply the ideas presented in chapters. Chapter 5, "Participating in Small Group Discussions," is extremely helpful to the potential member of a group. The authors describe positive and negative group behaviors in detail and provide excellent suggestions for successful group participation.

Annotated Speeches by Mary Fisher, Garry Trudeau, Jesse Jackson, and Karen Anderson

INTRODUCTION TO REMARKS BY MARY FISHER

Mary Fisher does not conform to the profile of the typical AIDS sufferer. She is the daughter of a Detroit banker and real-estate millionaire, a Republican political activist, and the mother of two children. She enjoys strong emotional support from her family. Mary Fisher contracted the HIV virus from her husband, who had been an intravenous drug user before their marriage. After learning that she had tested positive for HIV in July of 1991, Fisher's life changed dramatically. She decided to tell her story to the public and to the privileged circles of which she had been a part for most of her life. She became an advocate for AIDS patients, served as a consultant to the National Commission on AIDS, and created the Family AIDS Network to provide support systems for HIV–infected people. In the following address to the 1992 Republican National Convention, she explains that one of her goals has been to "lift the shroud of silence" about AIDS. Delegates listened intently, and many wept as Fisher delivered her emotional, yet enlightening, remarks.[1]

REMARKS TO THE 1992 REPUBLICAN NATIONAL CONVENTION

(Persuasive Speech)

Mary Fisher

[1] Less than three months ago, at [Republican party] platform hearings in Salt Lake City, I asked the Republican party to lift the shroud of silence which has been draped over the issue of HIV and AIDS. I have come tonight to bring our silence to an end.

[1] Mary Fisher reveals her purpose.

²I bear a message of challenge, not self-congratulations. I want your attention, not your applause. I would never have asked to be HIV–positive. But I believe that in all things there is a purpose, and I stand before you, and before the nation, gladly.

³The speaker cites statistics to demonstrate the devastation of AIDS.

³The reality of AIDS is brutally clear. Two hundred thousand Americans are dead or dying; a million more are infected. Worldwide, forty million, sixty million, or a hundred million infections will be counted in the coming few years. But despite science and research, White House meetings and congressional hearings, despite good intentions and bold initiatives, campaign slogans and hopeful promises—it is, despite it all, the epidemic which is winning tonight.

⁴The speaker appeals to her Republican audience to think beyond politics regarding the AIDS epidemic.

⁴In the context of an election year, I ask you, here, in this great hall, or listening in the quiet of your home, to recognize that the AIDS virus is not a political creature. It does not care whether you are Democrat or Republican. It does not ask whether you are black or white, male or female, gay or straight, young or old.

⁵She establishes common ground with all people infected with the HIV virus.

⁵Tonight, I represent an AIDS community whose members have been reluctantly drafted from every segment of American society. Though I am white, and a mother, I am one with a black infant struggling with tubes in a Philadelphia hospital. Though I am female, and contracted this disease in marriage, and enjoy the warm support of my family, I am one with the lonely gay man sheltering a flickering candle form the cold wind of his family's rejection.

⁶The speaker motivates listeners by using several appeals to fear.

⁶This is not a distant threat; it is a present danger. The rate of infection is increasing fastest among women and children. Largely unknown a decade ago, AIDS is the third-leading killer of young-adult Americans today. But it won't be third for long, because, unlike other diseases, this one travels. Adolescents don't give each other cancer or heart disease because they believe they are in love. But HIV is different.

⁷The speaker acts as a conscience for her party and for many Americans by attacking the prejudice against AIDS sufferers. The rhetorical question contains an ironic meaning.

⁷And we have helped it along. We have killed each other—with our ignorance, our prejudice, and our silence. We may take refuge in stereotypes, but we cannot hide there long. Because HIV asks only one thing of those it attacks: Are you human? And this is the right question: Are you human?

⁸She appeals for love and compassion for those whom "God made," and asks listeners to withhold judgment.

⁸Because people with HIV have not entered some alien state of being. They are human. They have not earned cruelty and they do not deserve meanness. They don't benefit from being isolated or treated as outcasts. Each of them is exactly what God made: a person. Not evil, deserving of our judgment; not victims, longing for our pity. People. Ready for support, and worthy of compassion.

⁹ My call to you, my party, is to take a public stand no less compassionate than that of the President and of Mrs. Bush. They have embraced me and my family in memorable ways. In place of judgment, they have shown affection. In difficult moments, they have raised our spirits. In the darkest hours, I have seen them reaching not only to me, but also to my parents, armed with that stunning grief and special grace that comes only to parents who have themselves leaned too long over the bedside of a dying child.

⁹She uses President and Mrs. Bush's compassion toward her as a model for her listeners to follow, citing the death of one of their children by leukemia as an analogy.

¹⁰ With the President's leadership, much good has been done. Much of the good has been unheralded. As the President has insisted, "Much remains to be done." But we do the President's cause no good if we praise the American family but ignore a virus that destroys it. We must be consistent if we are to be believed. We cannot love justice and ignore prejudice, love our children and fear to teach them. Whatever our role, as parent or policy maker, we must act as eloquently as we speak, else we have no integrity.

¹⁰Again, Mary Fisher acts as a conscience for her party, pointing out what she sees as inconsistencies in thought and behavior.

¹¹ My call to the nation is a plea for awareness. If you believe your are safe, you are in danger. Because I was not hemophiliac, I was not at risk. Because I was not gay, I was not at risk. Because I did not inject drugs, I was not at risk. My father has devoted much of his lifetime to guarding against another Holocaust. He is part of the generation who heard Pastor Niemoller come out of the Nazi death camps to say:

¹¹⁻¹²In this analogy, the speaker compares those who did not protest the Holocaust with those who feel safe from the AIDS virus.

¹² "They came after the Jews, and I was not a Jew, so I did not protest. They came after the trade unionists, and I was not a trade unionist, so I did not protest. Then they came after the Roman Catholics, and I was not Roman Catholic, so I did not protest. Then they came after me, and there was no one left to protest."

¹³ The lesson history teaches is this: If you believe you are safe, you are at risk. If you do not see this killer stalking your children, look again. There is no family or community, no race or religion, no place left in America that is safe. Until we genuinely embrace this message, we are a nation at risk.

¹³The speaker employs another appeal to fear and physical survival.

¹⁴ Tonight, HIV marches resolutely toward AIDS in more than a million American homes, littering its pathway with the bodies of the young. Young men. Young women. Young parents. And young children. One of the families is mine. If it is true that HIV inevitably turns to AIDS, then my children will inevitably turn to orphans.

¹⁵ My family has been a rock of support. My eighty-four-year-old father, who has pursued the healing of nations, will not accept the premise that he cannot heal his daughter. My mother refuses to be broken. She still calls at midnight to tell wonderful jokes that make me laugh. Sister and friends, and my brother Phillip (whose birthday is today), all have helped carry me over the hardest places. I am blessed, richly and deeply blessed, to have such a family.

¹⁵⁻¹⁶In a strong emotional appeal, Mary Fisher contrasts the love and support she receives from her family with the situation of AIDS victims who "grieve alone."

[18]The speaker asks her audience to "act wisely" and engage in courageous leadership.

[16] But not all of you have been so blessed. You are HIV–positive but dare not say it. You have lost loved ones, but you dared not whisper the word "AIDS." You weep silently. You grieve alone.

[17] I have a message for you. It is not you who should feel shame, it is we. We who tolerate ignorance and practice prejudice, we who have taught you to fear. We must lift our shroud of silence, making it safe for you to reach out for compassion. It is our task to seek safety for our children, not in quiet denial but in effective action. Someday our children will be grown. My son Max, now four, will take the measure of his mother. My son Zachary, now two, will sort through his memories. I may not be here to hear their judgments, but I know already what I hope they are.

[18] I want my children to know that their mother was not a victim. She was a messenger. I do not want them to think, as I once did, that courage is the absence of fear. I want them to know that courage is the strength to act wisely when we are most afraid. I want them to have the courage to step forward when called by their nation, or their party, and give leadership, no matter what the personal cost. I ask no more of you than I ask of myself or of my children.

[19-21]In her conclusion, Fisher uses strong emotion by speaking directly to her children, calling for her listeners to learn "the lessons of history," and appealing for actions that will lead to a better future.

[19] To my children, then, I make this pledge: I will not give in, Zachary, because I draw my courage from you. Your silly giggle gives me hope. Your gentle prayers give me strength. And you, my child, give me the reason to say to America, "You are at risk." And I will not rest, Max, until I have done all I can to make your world safe. I will seek a place where intimacy is not the prelude to suffering.

[20] I will not hurry to leave you, my children. But when I go, I pray that you will not suffer shame on my account. To all within the sound of my voice, I appeal: Learn with me the lessons of history and of grace, so my children will not be afraid to say the word "AIDS" when I am gone. Then their children, and yours, may not need to whisper it at all.

[21] God bless the children. God bless us all. Good night.

INTRODUCTION TO COMMENCEMENT ADDRESS BY GARRY TRUDEAU

Satiric cartoonist Garry Trudeau (creator of the "Doonesbury" comic strip) delivered this commencement address at Wake Forest University on May 19, 1986. Its political content may be viewed by some as dated or debatable; some economic experts trace the Soviet Union's 1991 collapse in part to the USSR's failed attempt to compete with America's SDI program. However, this speech indicates that wit and satire can convey serious underlying themes, regardless of the era. Trudeau escapes the bounds of mundane graduation speeches by mixing humor with supporting materials to challenge his listeners to become, in his words, "self-aware," "open," and "seeing."[2]

"THE IMPERTINENT QUESTIONS"

Commencement (Special Occasion) Address

Garry Trudeau

[1]Ladies and gentlemen of Wake Forest: My wife [TV personality Jane Pauley], who works in television, told me recently that a typical interview on her show used to run ten minutes. It now runs only five minutes, which is still triple the length of the average television news story. The average pop recording these days lasts around three minutes, or about the time it takes to ready a story in *People* magazine. The stories in *USA Today* take so little time to read that they're known in the business as "News McNuggets."

[1]In his introduction, Trudeau relaxes the audience with humor.

[2]Now, the average comic strip takes only about ten seconds to digest, but if you read every strip published in the *Washington Post,* as the President of the United States claims to, it takes roughly eight minutes a day, which means, a quick computation reveals, that the Leader of the Free World has spent a total of eleven days, three hours, and forty minutes of his presidency reading the comics. This fact, along with nuclear meltdown, are easily two of the most frightening thoughts of our time.

[2]To make a serious as well as humorous point, the speaker calculates the number of days that then-president Ronald Reagan has reportedly spent reading newspaper comic strips.

[3]There's one exception to this relentless compression of time in modern life. That's right—the graduation speech. When it comes to graduation speeches, it is generally conceded that time—a generous dollop of time—is of the essence.

[4]This is because the chief function of the graduation speaker has always been to prevent graduating seniors from being released into the real world before they've been properly sedated.

[4-5]Trudeau pokes fun at graduation speeches, referring to them as "anesthetics."

[5]Like as anesthetics, graduation speeches take time to kick in, so I'm going to ask you to bear with me for about a quarter of an hour. It will go faster if you think of it as the equivalent of four videos. (If you put up with Jimmy Carter for four years, you can put up with me for fifteen minutes.)

[6]I want to speak to you today about questions. About pertinent questions and impertinent questions. And where you might expect them to lead you.

[6]The speaker states his specific purpose and thesis.

7 I first learned about pertinent questions from my father, a retired physician who used to practice medicine in the Adirondacks. Like all parents racing against the clock to civilize their children, my father sought to instruct me in the ways of separating wheat from chaff, of asking sensible questions designed to yield useful answers. That is the way a diagnostician thinks. Fortunately for me, his own practical experience frequently contradicted his worthiest intentions.

[8]Trudeau relates an anecdote from personal experience.

8 Here's a case in point: A man once turned up in my father's office complaining of an ulcer. My father asked the pertinent question: Was there some undue stress, he inquired, that might be causing the man to digest his stomach? The patient, who was married, thought about it for a moment and then allowed that he had a girlfriend in Syracuse, and that twice a week he'd been driving an old pickup down to see her. Since the pickup frequently broke down, he was often late in getting home, and he had to devise fabulous stories to tell his wife. My father, compassionately but sternly, told the man he had to make a hard decision about his personal priorities if he was ever to get well.

[9–10]The speaker effectively sets up and delivers the punchline of his story.

9 The patient nodded and went away, and six months later came back completely cured, a new man. My father congratulated him and then delicately inquired if he'd made some change in his life.

10 The man replied, "Yup. Got me a new pickup."

11 So the pertinent question sometimes yields the impertinent answer. In spite of himself, my father ended up teaching me that an unexpected or inconvenient truth is often the price of honest inquiry. Of course, you presumably wouldn't be here if you didn't know that already. I'm confident that your education has been fairly studded with pertinent questions yielding impertinent answers.

[12]The speaker employs a transitional question to relate the anecdote to his specific purpose.

12 But how many of you have learned to turn that around—to ask the impertinent question to get at that which is pertinent?

[13–16]Trudeau presents an enumerative argument by listing a series of cases to support his generalization that "the impertinent question is the glory and the engine of human inquiry."

13 The impertinent question is the glory and the engine of human inquiry. Copernicus asked it and shook the foundations of Renaissance Europe. Darwin asked it and is repudiated to this day. Thomas Jefferson asked it and was so invigorated by it that he declared it an inalienable right.

14 Daniel Defoe asked it and invented the novel. James Joyce asked it and reinvented the novel, which was promptly banned.

15 Nietzsche asked it and inspired Picasso, who restated it and inspired a revolution in aesthetics.

[16] The Wright brothers asked it, and their achievement was ignored for five years. Steven Jobs asked it and was ignored for five minutes, which was long enough for him to make $200 million.

[17] Whether revered or reviled in their lifetimes, history's movers framed their questions in ways that were entirely disrespectful of conventional wisdom. Civilization has always advanced in the shimmering wake of its discontents. As the writer Tristan Vox put it, "Doubt is precisely what makes a culture grow. How many of what we call our classics were conceived as the breaking of laws, exercises in subversion, as the expression of doubts about the self and society that could no longer be contained?"

[18] The value of the impertinent question should be self-evident to Americans, for at no time in human history has it been asked more persistently and to greater effect than during the course of the American experiment. It is at the very core of our political and cultural character as a people, and we owe our vitality to its constant renewal.

[19] Today, the need for that spirit of renewal has never seemed more pressing. There is a persistent feeling in the country that many of our institutions have not measured up, that with all our recourses and technology and good intentions, we as a nation are still a long way from fulfilling our own expectations. The social programs that have failed to eliminate poverty, an educational system which has seen its effectiveness seriously eroded, the chemical breakthroughs that now threaten man's environment, the exploding booster rockets, malfunctioning nuclear power plants—these are but some of the images that have shaken our confidence. According to a recent poll, the only American institution that still enjoys the trust of a majority of college students is medicine; only forty-four percent of those polled trust educational institutions, twenty-nine percent trust the White House, twenty-three percent trust the press, and only twenty-one percent say they trust religion.

[20] It's difficult to think of an institution in this country that has not had to re-examine its agenda, to ask impertinent questions about its purpose and the means of its missions. Society's leaders, whose number you join today, face a wall of public cynicism. As professionals, they have to speak more clearly about what they can do. As citizens, they have to speak clearly about what they should do.

[21] Nowhere is the need for accountability more urgent that in what is shaping up to be the largest coordinated undertaking of your generation—the Strategic Defense Initiative. It may well become the most fiercely contested issue of your times. Already 6,500 college[-affiliated] scientists, including a majority of professors in 109 university physics and engineering departments, have declared their opposition to SDI, and have signed a "pledge of non-participation" in a

[17] The speaker also uses a quote to support his argument.

[19] In another argument of enumeration, the speaker relates a series of cases to support his claim that the nation is "a long way from fulfilling [its] expectations." While he does not state a source, the speaker presents the findings of an opinion poll, which reveals many people's lack of confidence in American institutions.

[21] Here Trudeau introduces an argument against the SDI program. He cites statistics involving scientists and professors as his support.

project they have called "ill-conceived and dangerous." This group, including fifteen Nobel Prize-winners, maintains that the weapons system is inherently destabilizing, and that further pursuit of its development is likely to initiate a massive new arms competition.

22 The actions of these scientists constitute an extraordinary repudiation of the amorality of indiscriminate weapons research. Science, since it leads to knowledge, has all too frequently led its practitioners to believe that it is inherently self-justifying; that there is nothing dangerous about splitting atoms in a moral vacuum. These attitudes are held in abundance by some of the brightest people of your generation, who are already hard at work on what nearly all of them concede is a dangerous fantasy.

23 Listen to these comments from the young Star Warriors, still in their twenties, working on particle beams and brain bombs at Lawrence Livermore National Laboratory.

[24]The speaker uses testimony from young scientists working on SDI to support his contention that SDI is a "dangerous fantasy."

24 This from the inventor of the atomic-powered x-ray laser: "Until 1980 or so, I didn't want to have anything to do with nuclear anything. Back in those days I thought there was something fundamentally evil about weapons. Now I see it as an interesting physics problem."

25 His co-worker, another brilliant young physicist, says he has doubts about the wisdom of SDI, but concurs that "the science is very interesting."

26 A third member of the team had this to say: "I think that the great majority of the lab's technical people view the President's [SDI] speech as somewhat off the wall and the program being proposed as being, in the end, intrinsically rather foolish. But, obviously, the lab is benefiting right now and will continue to benefit, and everybody's happy with the marvelous new work."

[27]Trudeau cynically cites the conclusion to his argument.

27 Marvelous new work, indeed.

[28]Does the speaker draw a hasty generalization?

28 No one in the defense industry seriously believes in a "peace shield"; in fact they're betting against it. If an American SDI is big business, then the hardware needed to overcome the anticipated Soviet response is even bigger business. The industry is further encouraged by the mindless momentum of the program, as evidenced by the recent admission of Reagan's undersecretary of defense that he pulled the $26 billion price tag out of the air.

[29]The speaker uses a quote from an unnamed Pentagon official as evidence of what he considers "the mindless momentum of the program."

29 Said the official, "I tried to figure out what the hell we're talking about. Congress wanted a number and kept on insisting on having a number. Okay. [The] first year was $2.4 billion, and I figure, okay, [the] best we could handle is maybe a twenty percent—twenty-five percent—growth."

30 It should not surprise us that so many in the scientific establishment find this obscene. Said computer scientists David Parnas, who recently quit an SDI advisory panel, "Most of the money spent will be wasted; we wouldn't trust the system even if we did build it. It is our duty... to reply that we have no technological magic [that will make nuclear weapons obsolete]. The President and the public should know that."

30Another quote, from a former SDI advisory panel member, is used to support the speaker's view that money spent on SDI is "obscene."

31 The impertinent question. We need it now more than ever.

32 And yet, sadly, healthy skepticism is at odds with the prevailing sentiment of our times. As Tristan Vox sees it, "Arguments abound to the effect that a nation does not grow great by doubting itself; indeed, that self-criticism was the trap that American democracy had laid for American greatness."

33 We've been here before. It was called the [nineteen-] fifties. This supposedly conservative doctrine holds that the very qualities from which this country has traditionally drawn its strength—idealism, openness, freedom of expression—are naive and dangerous in a Cold War struggle. It maintains that America's raucous squabbles, our noisy dissent—in short, its very heritage—have weakened us as a nation and caused it to lose its unchallenged supremacy.

33Trudeau compares his view of the 1980s to that of the 1950s.

34 As the *New Republic* [magazine]'s Mike Kinsley put it: "Talk about blaming America first."

35 In such an atmosphere, the impertinent question comes with risks. Ask the two engineers at Morton Thiokol who protested the launch of the doomed *Challenger* space shuttle. Ask any Pentagon procurement whistle-blower. Ask David Stockman. The mere fact of this president's widespread popularity casts suspicion on the motives of even the loyalest [*sic*] of oppositions. There is, of course, no question that this president seems to have fulfilled a deep yearning in many Americans to feel positively about their country. And yet the Reagan presidency often reminds me of a remark made by a woman to sportscaster Heywood Broun following the victories of the great racehorse Secretariat in the Triple Crown. After the trauma of Vietnam and Watergate, she told Broun, Secretariat had "restored her faith in mankind."

35Trudeau presents yet another list of examples to support his claim that many who asked "impertinent questions" were either ignored or psychologically threatened.

36 I would submit to you that Ronald Reagan is the Secretariat of the eighties. He has restored our faith in ourselves, and for that, we are all in his debt. It does not, however, exempt his administration from criticism from concerned citizens who love their nation as much as he does. One of the things that has always distinguished this country from most others is that we've always challenged ourselves to do better. As a satirist, I can't foresee any administration, Republican or Democratic, under which the basic message wouldn't be the same—that it's possible to do better.

36Trudeau uses an anecdote to make a derisive analogy involving President Ronald Reagan.

37Trudeau refers disparagingly to the 1984 Summer Olympic Games, held in Los Angeles; the metaphor of the "Caribbean golf course" refers to the island of Grenada, where, in October 1983, U.S. armed forces met, defeated, and ousted Cuban troops in combat following a Marxist coup there.

37 This is the true glory of America. This hope is what stirs me as a patriot—not a winning medal count at the Olympics, not the ability to drop nine thousand servicemen on a Caribbean golf course, not jingoistic commercials that tell me that "the pride is back, America," when for many of us the pride never left—and certainly not by the fantasy of a thousand laser rays crisscrossing the heavens in software-orchestrated precision, obliterating a swarm of supersonic projectiles.

38The speaker again uses humor to lighten his return to the topic of SDI.

38 Skeptical? You bet. You're looking at a man who has attended sixteen graduations, at four of which, including one technical college, the microphone failed.

39The speaker uses a quotation to relate his specific purpose to each listener. Trudeau is saying, "Examine your own thought processes; ask yourself impertinent questions."

39 The impertinent question. The means by which we reaffirm our noblest impulses as a people. But what about the impertinent question as it pertains to us as individuals? [The physicist Jacob] Bronowski had an addendum to his comments on the subject. "Ask the same kind of question," he charged [interviewer] Studs Terkel, "not about the outside, but the inside world; not about facts, but about the self."

40Trudeau cites (without source) a figure pointing to political corruption as "the new prevailing ethic."

40 This is impertinence of the gravest sort. The inner life finds very little currency in this, the age of hustle. David Stockman has written of a leadership circle which is intellectually inert, obsessed by television, bored by introspection and ideas of substance. Meanwhile, all across town, the sad stories of sleaze abound, one hundred and ten to date, all pointing to the new prevailing ethic of corner-cutting and self-advancement, whose only caveat is the admonition not to get caught.

41Trudeau describes the need to think critically and "to see and feel . . . the connectedness among things."

41 It can seem a pretty grim picture. Indeed, as you look around you, you see very little to distract you from this narrow path. And yet that is exactly what your liberal education—with its emphasis on ideas, on inquiry, on humanist values— sought to do. As the president of my *alma mater* [Yale University] once observed, "The whole point of your education has been to urge you to see and feel about the connectedness among things and how that connectedness must be fostered so that civilization is sustained."

42Trudeau presents himself as taking a strong position and as unafraid of being negatively received.

42 This won't please you, but let me share a little of what one of the more astute voice of your generation, twenty-four-year-old David Leavitt, has written about his peers: "Mine is a generation perfectly willing to admit its contemptible qualities. But our contempt is self-congratulatory. The buzz in the background, every minute of our lives, is that detached, ironic voice telling us: *At least you're not faking it, as they did. It's okay to be selfish as long as you're up-front about it.*"

43 This is a pretty bleak portrait of the values of a generation, and my guess is that I'm staring at hundreds of exceptions. My further guess is that the yearning for moral commitment is as intense as it always was, but that the generation with no rules—the generation that grew up in the rubble of smashed idealism, fallen heroes, and broken marriages—is deeply suspicious.

[43]He then softens his stance by complimenting his listeners as including "hundreds of exceptions."

44 Columnist Ellen Goodman has speculated that this is why apartheid and the soup kitchen have emerged as the causes of choice; they offer that stark unambiguous clarity that World War II offered their [sic] grandparents, that sense that there is no good news about the other side of the argument. But Goodman, being incorrigibly of her era, also believes that micro evolves into macro; that to be involved inevitably leads to decisions between imperfect options; that many of you will take risks, make mistakes, and become citizens in spite of yourselves.

[44]Trudeau paraphrases fellow media personality Ellen Goodman, a newspaper columnist.

45 I'm afraid there's simply no other way. If ours becomes a society intolerant of failure and uncompassionate in the face of suffering, then surely we are lost. With the uncertainties of the future hedging in on you, you need to assess your commonalities. You need to say how you would treat other people, and how you would have them treat you back.

[45]In conclusion, the speaker asks listeners to apply his speech to themselves, loosely paraphrasing the Golden Rule.

46 The best your college education can do for you is to remind you that it's one thing to be self-absorbed, and quite another to be self-aware. It comes down to a matter of being open, of seeing. It comes down to a matter of remaining intrigued enough by life to welcome its constant renewal. In short, it comes down to the impertinent question.

[46]Trudeau returns to his stated theme, and challenges listeners to become "self-aware" rather than "self-absorbed."

47 From those of us out here in the real world, to those of you preparing to enter it, may I just say, Welcome. We need you.

48 Thank you and good luck.

[47-48]Presenting himself as a representative of the "real world," Trudeau offers warm words of encouragement and "welcome."

INTRODUCTION TO PERSUASIVE SPEECH BY JESSE JACKSON

The following is an abridged version of the keynote speech Jesse Jackson delivered to the Democratic National Convention in Atlanta, Georgia, on July 20, 1988. At the time, the Reverend Mr. Jackson had just concluded his second bid for the Democratic nomination for the presidency. While the speech contains traditional appeals for party unity, it is organized—and was delivered—in Jackson's own inimitable style.[3]

"COMMON GROUND AND COMMON SENSE"

(Persuasive Speech)

Jesse Jackson

[1-2]In his introduction, Jackson acknowledges spiritual support, and refers (paraphrasing a hymn) to the ethnic diversity that his campaign termed "The Rainbow Coalition." He also pays tribute to individuals who advanced the cause of civil rights, and to members of his own family who supported his political aspirations.

1 Tonight we pause and give praise and honor to God for being good enough to allow us to be at this place at this time. When I look out at this convention, I see the face of America—red, yellow, brown, black, and white—we're all precious in God's sight—the real Rainbow Coalition. All of us, all of us who are here and think that we are seated. But we're really standing on someone's shoulders, ladies and gentlemen. Mrs. Rosa Parks, the mother of the civil-rights movement.

2 I want to express my deep love and appreciation for the support my family has given me over these past months. They have endured pain, anxiety, threat, and fear. But they have been strengthened and made secure by a faith in God, in America, and in you.

[3]Jackson briefly introduces his topic in a statement of contrast.

3 We meet tonight at a crossroads, a point of decision. Shall we expand, be inclusive, find unity and power; or suffer division and impotence?

[4]The speaker refers to the location of his speech and provides brief examples signifying historic change.

4 We come to Atlanta, the cradle of the Old South, the crucible of the New South. Tonight there is a sense of celebration because we are moved, fundamentally moved, from racial battlegrounds by law, to economic common ground; tomorrow we will challenge to move to higher ground.

5 Common ground! Tonight in Atlanta, for the first time in this century, we convene in the South. A state where governors once stood in schoolhouse doors. Where Julian Bond was denied his seat in the state legislature because of his conscientious objection to the Vietnam War. A city that, through its five black universities, had graduated more black students than any city in the world. Atlanta, now a modern intersection of the New South. Common ground!

[6]Jackson presents the specific purpose of his speech.

6 Tonight we choose interdependency in our capacity to act and unite for the greater good. The common good is finding commitment to new priorities, to expansion and inclusion. A commitment to expanded participation in the Democratic party at every level. A commitment to a shared national strategy and involvement at every level. A commitment to new priorities that ensure that hope will be kept alive.

[7]Throughout his speech, Jackson repeats the words "common ground" for emphasis and for transitional purposes.

7 Common ground. Easier said than done. Where do you find common ground at the point of challenge? This campaign has shown that politics need not be marketed by politicians, packaged by pollsters and pundits. Politics can be a marvelous arena where people come together, define common ground.

8 We find common ground at the plant gate that closes on workers without notice. We find common ground at the farm auction where a good farmer loses his or her land to bad loans or diminishing markets. Common ground at the schoolyard where teachers cannot get adequate pay, and students cannot get a scholarship and can't make a loan. Common ground, at the hospital admitting room where somebody is dying tonight because they cannot afford to go upstairs to a bed that's empty, waiting for someone with insurance to get sick. We are a better nation than that. We must do better.

9 Common ground. What is leadership if not present help in a time of crisis? And so I met you at the point of challenge in Jay, Maine, where paper workers were striking for fair wages; in Greenfield, Iowa, where family farmers struggle for a fair price; in Cleveland, Ohio, where working women seek comparable worth; in McFarland, California, where the children of Hispanic farm workers may be dying from poison land, dying in clusters with cancer; in the AIDS hospice in Houston, Texas, where the sick support one another. twelve are rejected by their own parents and friends.

10 Common ground. America's not a blanket woven from one thread, one color, one cloth. When I was a child growing up in Greenville, South Carolina, and grandmother could not afford a blanket, she didn't complain, and we did not freeze. Instead, she took pieces of old cloth—patches, wool, silk, gabardine, croakersack on the patches—barely good enough to wipe off your shoes with.

11 But they didn't stay that way very long. With sturdy hands and a strong cord, she sewed them together into a quilt, a thing of beauty and power and culture.

12 Now, Democrats, we must build such a quilt. Farmers, you seek fair prices and you are right, but you cannot stand alone. Your patch is not big enough. Workers, you fight for fair wages. You are right. But your patch is not big enough. Women, you seek comparable worth and pay equity. You are right. But your patch is not big enough. Women, mothers, who seek Head Start and day care and prenatal care on the front side of life, rather than jail care and welfare on the back side of life, you're right, but your patch is not big enough.

13 Students, you seek scholarships. You are right. But your patch is not big enough. Blacks and Hispanics, when we fight for civil rights, we are right, but our patch is not big enough. Gays and lesbians, when you fight against discrimination and [for] a cure for AIDS, you are right, but your patch is not big enough. Conservatives and progressives, when you fight for what you believe—right-wing, left-wing, hawk, dove—you are right, from your point of view, but your point of view is not enough.

14 But don't despair. Be as wise as my grandmama. Pool the patches and pieces together, bound by a common thread. When we form a great quilt of unity and

8 Jackson speaks metaphorically of the "plant gate," "farm auction," "schoolyard," and "hospital admitting room" as brief examples of social issues.

9 This series of brief examples is supported by personal observation, enhancing the speaker's credibility.

10 The speaker begins an analogy by referring to personal experience.

12–13 In the analogy, Jackson relates his grandmother's quilt to the various "patches" of economic and social groups in the country.

14 The speaker draws the conclusion that the different

social and economic "patches" will bring "hope to our nation" if joined by the "common thread" of "unity and common ground."

common ground, we'll have the power to bring about health care and housing and jobs and education and hope to our nation.

[15]The speaker uses statistics and examples to bolster his view that America's economic priorities should be changed.

15 I just want to take common sense to high places. We're spending $150 billion a year defending Europe and Japan forty-three years after the war [World War II] is over. We have more troops in Europe tonight than we had seven years ago, yet [*sic*] the threat of war is ever more remote. Germany and Japan are now creditor nations—that means they've got a surplus. We are a debtor nation —it means we are in debt.

[16]The speaker uses repetition of a phrase to introduce different examples.

16 Let them share more of the burden of their own defense—use some of that money to build decent housing! Use some of the money to educate our children! Use some of that money for long-term health care! Use some of that money to wipe out these slums and put America back to work!

[17]Jackson compares the investment required to "bail out" Europe and the Chrysler Corporation with one he believes is needed to support American farmers.

17 I just want to take common sense to high places. If we can bail out Europe and Japan, if we can bail out Continental Bank and Chrysler—and Mr. [Lee] Iacocca [of Chrysler Motors] makes $8,000 an hour—we can bail out the family farmer.

18 I just want to make common sense. It does not make sense to close down 650,000 family farms in this country while importing food from abroad subsidized by the U. S. government.

19 Leadership must meet the moral challenge of its day. What's the moral challenge of our day? We have public accommodations. We have the right to vote. We have open housing.

20 What's the fundamental challenge of our day? It is to end economic violence. Plants closing without notice, economic violence. Even the greedy do not profit long from greed. Economic violence. Most poor people are not lazy. They're not black. They're not brown. They're mostly white, and female, and young.

[21]The speaker describes the plight of the poor in extended, emotional statements.

21 But whether white, black, or brown, the hungry baby's belly turned inside out is the same color. Call it pain. Call it hurt. Call it agony. Most poor people are not on welfare.

22 Some of them are illiterate and can't read the want-ad sections. And when they can, they can't find a job that matches their address. They work hard every day, I know. I live amongst them. I'm one of them.

[23]Jackson refers to his own eyewitness observations to establish his credibility.

23 I know they work. I'm a witness. They catch the early bus. They work every day. They raise other people's children. They work every day. They clean the streets. They work every day. They drive vans with cabs [*sic*]. They work every

day. They change the beds you slept in, in these hotels last night, and can't get a union contract. They work every day.

24 No more. They're not lazy. Someone must defend them because it's right, and they cannot speak for themselves. They work in hospitals. I know they do. They wipe the bodies of those who are sick with fever and pain. They empty their bed-pans. They clean out their commodes. No job is beneath them, and yet when they get sick, they cannot lie in the bed they made up every day. America, that is not right. We are a better nation than that. We are a better nation than that.

[24]Here the speaker uses an ironic example—those who care for the sick but are themselves not "cared for."

25 Leadership. What difference will we make? Leadership cannot just go along to get along. We must do more than change presidents. We must change direction. Leadership must face the moral challenge of our day. The nuclear war build-up is irrational. Strong leadership cannot desire to look tough and let that stand in the way of the pursuit of peace. Leadership must reverse the arms race.

[25]The speaker repeats one word for emphasis and as an introduction to the next section.

26 Leadership—we now have this marvelous opportunity to have a breakthrough with the Soviets. Last year, two hundred thousand Americans visited the Soviet Union. There's a chance for joint ventures into space, not Star Wars and the war-arms escalation, but a space defense initiative. Let's build in space together, and demilitarize the heavens. There's a way out.

27 America, let us expand. When Mr. Reagan and Mr. Gorbachev met, there was a big meeting. They represented together one-eighth of the human race. Seven-eighths of the human race was locked out of that room. Most people in the world tonight—half are Asian, one-half of *them* are Chinese. There are twenty-two nations in the Middle East. There's Europe, forty million Latin Americans next door to us, the Caribbean, Africa's half-billion people. Most people in the world today are yellow or brown or black, non-Christian, poor, female, young, and don't speak English—in the real world.

[27]The speaker uses statistics to support his view that seven-eighths are not represented by what were then the two superpowers.

28 I'm often asked, "Jesse, why do you take on these tough issues?" . . . . A poem by an unknown author went something like this: *We mastered the air, we've conquered the sea, and annihilated distance and prolonged life, we were not wise enough to live on this earth without war and without hate.*

[28–29]Jackson uses a poem to express his feelings.

29 As for Jesse Jackson:

"I'm tired of sailing my little boat

"Far inside the harbor bar.

"I want to go out where the big ships float,

"Out on the deep where the great ones are.

"And should my frail craft prove too slight

"The waves seep those billows o'er,

"I'd rather go down in a stirring fight

"Than drown to death in the sheltered shore."

[30]The speaker issues an emotional challenge to motivate listeners to "dream" and "hope" to "rise above the pain." Jackson then paraphrases a line—written by playwright George Bernard Shaw—that was often quoted by Senator Robert Kennedy ("You see things; and you say, 'Why?' But I dream of things that never were; and I say, 'Why not?'").

30 Wherever you are tonight, I challenge you to hope and to dream. Don't submerge your dreams. Exercise above all else [*sic*]—Even on drugs, dream of the day you're drug-free. Even in the gutter, dream of the day that you'll be up on your feet again. You must never stop dreaming. Face reality, yes. But don't stop with the ways things are; dream of things as they ought to be. Dream. Face pain, but love, hope, faith, and dreams will help you rise above the pain.

[31]Jackson continues his emotional challenge with several figures of speech: repetition, rhyme, and alliteration.

31 Dream of teachers who teach for life and not for [a] living. Dream of doctors who are concerned more about public health than private wealth. Dream of lawyers more concerned above justice than a judgeship. Dream of preachers who are concerned more about prophecy than profiteering. Dream on the high road of sound values.

32 And in America, as we go forth to September, October, and November, and then beyond, America must never surrender to a high moral challenge.

33 Do not surrender to drugs. The best drug policy is no first use. Don't surrender with needles and cynicism. Let's have no first use on the one hand, or clinics on the other. Never surrender, young America.

34 Don't surrender and don't give up. Why can I challenge you this way?

[35]The speaker concludes with a narrative drawn from his own experience.

35 I have a story. I wasn't always on television. Writers were not always outside my door. When I was born late one morning, October eighth, in Greenville, South Carolina, no writers asked my mother her name. Nobody chose to write down our address, My mama was not supposed to make it. You see, I was born to a teen-age mother who was born to a teen-age mother.

36 I understand. I know abandonment and people being mean to you, and saying you're nothing and nobody, and can never be anything. Jesse Jackson is my third name. I'm adopted. When I had no name, my grandmother gave me her name. My name was Jesse Burns until I was twelve. So I wouldn't have a blank space, she gave me a name to hold me over. I understand when nobody knows your name. I understand when you have no name. I understand.

37 I wasn't born in the hospital. Mama didn't have insurance. I was born in the bed at home. I really do understand. Born in a three-room house, bathroom in the backyard, slop jar by the bed, no hot and cold running water. I understand. Wallpaper used for decoration? No, for a windbreaker. I understand. I'm a working person's person; that's why I understand you whether you're black or white.

38 I was born in the slum, but the slum was not born in me. And it wasn't born in you, and you can make it. Wherever you are tonight, you can make it. Hold your head high, stick your chest out. You can make it. It gets dark sometimes, but the morning comes. Don't you surrender. Suffering breeds character. Character breeds faith. In the end, faith will not disappoint.

39 You must not surrender. You may or may not get there, but just know that you're qualified and you hold on and hold out. We must never surrender. America will get better and better. Keep hope alive. Keep hope alive. Keep hope alive. On tomorrow night and beyond, keep hope alive.

39–40This final emotional challenge reveals Jackson's energy, enthusiasm, and warm, charismatic style.

40 I love you very much. I love you very much.

INTRODUCTION TO PERSUASIVE SPEECH BY KAREN ANDERSON

Convincing speeches can be organized by using reasons or by problem–solution sequences. Karen Anderson developed the following alternative version of the speech presented in Chapter 17 to demonstrate how the body of that speech could instead be arranged according to the problem–cause–solution organizational structure. The following speech is introduced and concluded by strategies different from the speech reproduced in Chapter 17. It is also followed here by alternate opening and closing sections.[4]

LET'S STOP AUTO REPAIR RIP-OFFS!

Persuasive Speech to Convince

(Problem-Cause-Solution Organizational Sequence)

Karen Anderson

1 I'd like each of you to hand over $1,500 right now! Come on, $1,500. I'll take a check, credit card, cash, or money order. What's the problem? You don't have it? I don't care if it's your car insurance, house payment, or hospital bill. Let me

[1]In the introduction, the speaker uses a strategy that shocks listeners.

put it to you this way. You are driving to work and your transmission feels, you know, "funny"—it slips out of gear. Fearing for your safety more than a reprimand from your supervisor for being late, you go directly to the nearest auto repair shop. Luckily, the technician on duty has time to look at your car and determine that a faulty transmission needs, in his opinion, to be overhauled or replaced, to the tune of $1,500. Or does $25 seem a little easier to manage? Because in many cases that "slipping out of gear" problem may have been solved by a relatively simple and cheap twenty-five dollar adjustment. Because of situations like the one I just described, we are at the mercy of automotive repair shops.

[2] The thesis identifies the main points of the body and clearly presents the proposition of policy.

[2] Unnecessary, incompetent repairs, caused by lack of control, should be corrected by strict regulations.

[3] Karen cites a study and an example, supported by credible references, to begin her explanation of the problem. Notice that the speaker connects to listeners by asking a question.

[3] Americans are being ripped off. As reported by Sal Fariello in his book *Mugged by Mr. Badwrench,* a study done by the United States Department of Transportation indicates that as much as forty percent of the money American consumers spend on auto repairs is wasted due to fraud and incompetence. Think it won't happen to you? An article in a June 1992 issue of *Business Week* reported, in what is now a much-publicized case, that Sears Auto Centers in California had "systematically ripped off customers." According to the article, Ruth Hernandez, of Stockton, went to Sears for new tires. The auto technician who serviced Ms. Hernandez's Honda "insisted" the car also needed new struts with a hefty additional cost of $419.95. Ms. Hernandez went for a second opinion, and was told the struts did not need replacing. Furthermore, according to the article, Sears consistently charged consumers an average of $235 for unnecessary repairs.

[4] Karen uses the words "Now listen to this" to maintain audience interest and to set up this credible survey and quotation.

[4] Now listen to this. In his book *From Bumper to Bumper,* Bob Sikorsky posed as an average driver and did a remarkable survey of the auto repair business across America. Mr. Sikorsky pulled into 225 repair shops with a simple problem: a loose spark-plug wire. He reported fair and competent repairs in only twenty-eight percent of the stops, a satisfactory repair only forty-four percent of the time, and, in Sikorsky's own words, "I was victimized by incompetence, cheated, sold unnecessary parts, overcharged, and lied to."

[5] The speaker employs two visual aids to explain how listeners can be harmed by unscrupulous auto repair businesses.

[5] Here are two ways that consumers pay for unnecessary repairs. You can unknowingly purchase so-called "gypsy parts"—that is, an inferior auto part, such as a common oil filter, which has been repackaged in a box with a well-known brand name and passed off to you as a quality product. Here is an example. [*Shows slide comparing two oil filters.*] One oil filter has less paper, which provides less filtering capability, clogging sooner. The other contains more paper, is of higher quality, and will last longer. Upon close examination,

the difference is evident. Or what about the technician who deliberately sabotages your car for profit, and whose favorite weapon is an ice pick? [*Holds up ice pick.*] Now, although these instances are rare, they happen to out-of-state motorists who set themselves up as easy targets by leaving their cars with the attendants while they grab snacks or make necessary pit-stops. Returning to the car, the unsuspecting motorists are informed by attendants that a leaking tire must be patched, or better yet, replaced with a brand new tire.

6 I conducted a telephone interview with Tom Hopkins, a lead investigator for the Bureau of Automotive Repair in California, who related the following despicable crime. An elderly California couple took their motor home in for repairs. The disabled wife remained in the motor home while the vehicle was raised on the lift in the repair shop. Employees removed the suspension system, brakes, and wheels. The disabled woman was literally held hostage in the air until her husband paid the demanded fee to get the wheels and other equipment put back on their vehicle.

> [6]The speaker cites an interview with a credible primary source to validate this strong emotional example. Language such as "despicable" and "held hostage" are designed to evoke powerful feelings in listeners.

7 These incidents represent a small minority, and I want to stress that the majority of the auto repair industry is caring and reputable, but these cases are real and they could happen to you.

> [7]The speaker continues to connect to listeners by indicating that these incidents "could happen to you."

8 The issue is apparent and many of you, I'm sure have experienced auto repair rip-offs. So let's shift gears, and talk about the causes.

> [8]Karen uses creative metaphors ("Let's shift gears") as a transition from the problem to the cause of auto repair rip-offs.

9 One factor that contributes to incompetence is the lack of control. Let me demonstrate. [*Holds up sign reading, "Karen's Car Center—Unlimited Major and Minor Repair Service--Major Credit Cards Accepted."*] Pretty impressive, huh? Listen, I'll even adjust your brakes for half-price, and I'll throw in a complete diagnostic muffler analysis for free—but I don't do windows! Do you trust me? If you have a computer and a graphics program you can make a sign like this (as I did), call yourself an auto technician, and open up a shop. Nothing stands in your way.

> [9]The speaker uses a creative visual aid to add interest and demonstrate one cause of the problem.

10 Nancy Tian, the communications coordinator of the Automotive Service Excellence program, made it clear that there are no federally mandated regulations. Think of a person opening up a medical practice without prior education, internship, testing or experience. Would you let such a person perform intricate open-heart surgery on you or a loved one without first checking their credentials? There's an adage in the automotive profession: Doctors bury their mistakes, auto technicians just keep having theirs return.

> [10]Karen makes a comparison to the medical profession and asks a question that connects to listeners.

[11] She employs another automotive metaphor for her transition from causes to alternative solutions.

[11] Another cause of auto repair incompetence is our own ignorance. Admit it. We expect to be ripped off, we expect repairs to be expensive, yet we put up with it. There are several routes we can take to solve this nationwide problem.

[12] Throughout her discussion of alternative solutions, the speaker briefly identifies the possible solution, and then explains why it is unworkable.

[12] I mentioned the National Institute for Automotive Service Excellence, or ASE, which was established in 1972 to improve auto repair service by testing and certifying auto repair technicians. They develop exams in automotive specialties, such as transmission, brake and wheel, and emission repair. They offer tests twice a year. It is an excellent idea, and it is the only nationwide certification program. But there are several problems. One: A technician who is certified in one area, such as suspension and steering, may not be certified in another area, such as electrical systems. Two: Certification does not necessarily mean competence. And, three: This certification program is only voluntary—and again, there is no nationwide, mandatory licensing of the auto repair industry. Remember my business sign? The only thing I could not advertise was an earned certification. This program is a start, but voluntary certification doesn't go far enough.

[13] I interviewed Richard Glenn, an associate professor of Automotive Service Technology at Catonsville Community College, near Baltimore, Maryland, who suggested industry-wide regulation as the solution. This would be similar to the medical profession's self-regulation through the AMA. Licensed technicians and experienced automotive-board specialists would take matters into their own hands by assessing fees and fines to enforce regulations. But according to Mr. Glenn, the majority of technicians prefer to go with the status quo, and it has been difficult to rally enough interest or enthusiasm from auto technicians to support self-regulation.

[14] The automotive metaphor is used for the final transition from alternative choices to the speaker's selected solution.

[14] But there is one route we can take to help us out of the auto repair roadblock.

[15] Through documented examples, statistics, and a credible interview with an expert, the speaker has constructed a persuasive case for the effectiveness of her selected solution.

[15] California is one example of a governmental control program that not only benefits the consumer but the auto repair industry as well. Remember Ms. Hernandez from California, who did not have confidence in what Sears was advising her to do? She had a place to file a complaint, and was assured that a remedy would be found. This is an excellent example of mandated control through the California Bureau of Automotive Repair, or BAR. [*Turns on slide projector showing summary of information about the BAR.*] Kate McGuire, Public Information Officer for the BAR, provided me with information about this agency. As you can see from this slide, it was established in 1971 to prevent abuses in the auto repair industry. With a staff of six hundred, working in thirty-six field offices, the BAR operates on an annual budget of $70 million, which is funded by the smog check program and a $200 registration fee paid

by auto repair businesses. It provides consumers with mediation centers that handle over forty thousand formal complaints a year. This agency also sends representatives to assist and support consumers at hearings in small claims court. The bureau also conducts undercover sting operations to snare dishonest technicians or detect fraudulent repair shops. And money—some $4.6 million alone—was returned to consumers from auto repair shops in 1991–92.

16 Now there are many in the auto repair industry who feel that the government or state should not be involved in overseeing the industry. Rick Glenn, the Auto Service Technology professor I interviewed, commented that many technicians feel that government or state regulation would impose a cumbersome layer of bureaucracy which could only make matters worse. But BAR investigator Tom Hopkins told me that in California the auto industry is not hostile to the bureau. In fact, he said that honest auto repair businesses welcome the BAR because it helps to keep a level playing-field and put the dishonest shops out of business. Mr. Hopkins also said that some of the best technicians leave the auto repair industry and work for the bureau. So you can see that regulation does not need to be antagonistic to the repair industry.

16Here the speaker presents the opposition and rebuttal arguments. Information from an interview is used to raise a major argument against governmental regulation of the auto repair industry. Then the speaker uses another interview to refute the opposition argument.

17 Had the BAR not existed, we might never have discovered the Sears scandal. It was the chief of the BAR who launched an investigation after noticing a pattern of consumer complaints against Sears Auto Centers. The Bureau conducted thirty-eight undercover runs at thirty-three Sears shops statewide in California. The investigation exposed Sears' unethical practices, and forced the company to change its ways.

17The speaker returns to the Sears example to provide listeners with concrete support for the recommended solution.

18 We don't have to be at the mercy of fraudulent auto repair companies. The vast majority of men and women in this business are decent and hard-working. But we need to ensure this same high standard of decency throughout the industry. Let's put the brakes on incompetence and unnecessary repairs by requiring strict ground rules. I think California Consumer Affairs Director Jim Conran spoke for all of us when he said: "We are here today to send this message to the entire automotive repair industry: If you are ripping off the consumers of the State of California, we are after you. We have zero tolerance for abuse of the public trust."

18In the conclusion, the speaker uses a hard-hitting challenge, combined with a powerful quotation, to motivate listeners.

ALTERNATIVE INTRODUCTION AND CONCLUSION

Here are an alternative introduction and conclusion to Karen Anderson's speech, which demonstrate additional strategies for opening and closing a speech. The introduction ties into the thesis in Paragraph 2 of the problem–cause–solution and reasons organizational sequences. The conclusion is inserted after Paragraph 17 in the problem–cause–solution and reasons sequences.

Alternate Introduction: Personal Reference with Statistic

The speaker makes a personal reference, and describes a stereotype relating to women and automobile repair. Karen destroys this myth with a study which indicates that in the auto repair industry "there is no sex discrimination."

What I know about automobiles would fit into a thimble. But don't think for a second it's because I'm a woman. In the past, females have taken a bad rap when it comes to car knowledge—like all we know is where the key goes. Of course, we are made out to be totally helpless when it comes to changing a flat tire, too. And forget any kind of repair work. We're so automobile illiterate that we will believe anything the repair person tells us. If a fan belt, carburetor, or dipstick needs replacing and we're told it'll cost $50, we have the reputation of saying, "Sure, whatever it costs, just get it done fast because I'm headed to the mall." Well, I'll clue you: When it comes to auto repairs, there is no sex discrimination—we are all at risk. According to a study done by the U.S. Department of Transportation, as much as forty percent of our money is wasted as a result of fraudulent or incompetent repairs. Well, it's time for us to stop being so vulnerable.

Alternate Conclusion: Challenge, Statistic, and End Questions

Karen uses a challenge and a statistic to ignite listeners in this conclusion. Notice that the speaker poses questions in the final lines to get audience members to think about her persuasive proposals.

We no longer have to be targets of irresponsible behavior in the auto repair industry. The vast majority of men and women in this business are honest, decent, and hardworking. But we need to ensure this same high standard of decency throughout the industry. Do we really want to continue paying almost forty percent of our hard-earned dollars on unnecessary or incompetent repairs? Isn't it about time to put the brakes on this behavior by requiring strict ground rules to protect everyone?

NOTES

[1]See Elizabeth Gleick and Don Sider, "An Heiress Fights AIDS," *People*, August 17, 1992, pp. 54–56. Mary Fisher is a nationally acclaimed artist and the founder of the Family AIDS Network, Inc. Copyright © 1992, Family AIDS Network. Used by permission.

[2]Garry Trudeau, "The Impertinent Questions," is used by permission of *Vital Speeches of the Day*, LIX, no. 21.

[3]Jesse Jackson, "Common Ground and Common Sense," is used by permission of *Vital Speeches of the Day*, LIX, no. 20.

[4]Karen Anderson, "Let's Stop Auto Repair Rip-Offs!" Persuasive speech to convince, Carroll Community College, Westminster, Maryland, 1993. Used by permission.

COMPLETE BIBLIOGRAPHY FOR

"THE COMPUTER VIRUS: DISEASE OF THE COMPUTER AGE"

Dewdney, A. K. "Computer Recreations of Worms, Viruses, and Core War." *Scientific American*, March 1989, pp. 110–113.

Elmer–DeWitt, Phillip. "Invasion of the Data Snatchers!" *Time*, September 26, 1988, pp. 62–67.

———."The Kid Put Us Out of Action." *Time*, November 14, 1988, p. 76.

Henderson, Bruce W. and Nordwall, Bruce D. "Rapid Spread of Virus Confirms Fears About Danger to Computers." *Aviation Week and Space Technology*, November 14, 1988, p. 44.

Honan, Patrick. "Avoiding Virus Hysteria." *Personal Computing*, May 1989, pp. 85–87, 89, and 91–92.

Markoff, John. "How Need for Challenge Seduced Computer Expert." *New York Times*, November 6, 1988, Sec. A, pp. 1 and 30.

———."Computer Experts Say Virus Carried No Hidden Danger." *New York Times*, November 9, 1988, Sec. A, p. 18.

Marshall, Eliot. "The Scourge of Computer Viruses." *Science*, April 8, 1988, pp. 133–134.

———."Worm Invades Computer Network." *Science*, November 11, 1988, pp. 855–856.

"The Worm's Aftermath." *Science*, November 25, 1988, pp. 1121–1122.

Peterzell, Jay. "Spying and Sabotage by Computer." *Time*, March 20, 1989, pp. 25–26.

Schendler, Brenton R. "Computer Security Firms Suggest Ways to Stop Viruses." *Wall Street Journal*, November 7, 1988, Sec. B, p. 4.

U. S. Congress. Office of Technology Assessment. *Defending Secrets, Sharing Data: New Locks and Keys for Electronic Information*, 1987, pp. 3–6.

U.S. Department of Justice. "Student Who Released Computer Virus Indicted," Official press release #89–231, July 26, 1989.

Vogel, Shawna. "1988 Disease of the Year: Illness as Glitch." *Discover*, January 1989, pp. 64–66.

Wines, Michael. "FBI Begins Investigation of Computer Virus Case." *New York Times*, November 8, 1988, Sec. A, p. 16.

Appendix B

Suggested Topic Areas

The following lists contain suggested topics for speeches. Some issues are general and include a wide range of ideas, while others are more specific. Topic areas can be altered easily to fit the interests of a speaker, the needs of an audience, or the requirements of an occasion. We include these suggestions to stimulate creative thinking and productive investigation.

ART, CRAFTS, AND HUMANITIES

Classic movies

Collecting: *airplanes, art glass, baseball cards, bottles, buttons, cars, Civil War memorabilia, clocks, coins, comic books, dolls, fossils, guns, hats, minerals, model trains, phonograph records, porcelain, stamps, teddy bears*

Creating: *batik, designer cowboy boots, Greek moussaka, ice sculptures, perfect diamonds, stained-glass art*

Designing: *a home, clothing, flower arrangements, a landscaped garden, a mall, a wedding cake, a high-rise condominium, a city*

Famous *composers, musicians, painters, sculptors, actors, actresses, dancers*

Famous *Broadway theaters, cathedrals, jewels, lighthouses, museums, opera houses, palaces, prisons, ships*

Fashion design and the consumer

Government funding of controversial art projects

Learning to make clay pottery

Life in a symphony orchestra

Looking for treasures at antique stores and flea markets

Major contemporary architectural styles

Manufacturing musical instruments

Re-enacting battles from the War of Independence or the Civil War

The costs of maintaining museums

The science of restoring artworks

Understanding ethnic food, music, or dance

Understanding Japanese Origami

BUSINESS AND INDUSTRY

Analyzing employee-owned companies

Bar owners' responsibilities to their intoxicated customers

Cleaning up industrial pollution from major waterways

Change in the United States from an industrial to a service economy

Creative packaging for increased sales

Enforcing food-industry health standards

Making U.S. products more competitive with foreign goods

Maintaining business and industrial health and safety standards

Overcoming the groupthink mentality in large corporations

Positive and negative impact of labor unions on U.S. business

Rating airlines' service and safety

Regulating the U.S. auto industry

Regulating savings & loan institutions

CONTEMPORARY ISSUES

Banning cigarette sales

Effective prison rehabilitation programs

Eliminating street gangs

Endangered species

Government-supported day-care centers

Regulating insurance rates

Mandating energy-efficient appliances and lighting

National health-care insurance

Police roadblocks as a deterrent to drunk driving

Reliability of child witnesses in sexual-abuse trials

Preventing crime in public schools

Solutions to prison overcrowding

Stopping frivolous lawsuits

Destructive nature of "designer drugs"

Most wanted criminals in the United States

Legality of car radar detectors

Solutions to homelessness

CURRENT EVENTS

Detecting auto-sales fraud

Eliminating nuclear weapons

Gay soldiers in the military

Government effectiveness in responding to disasters

Illegal tampering with foods and medicines

Solving serial murders

Repairing the interstate highway system

Raising taxes vs. cutting spending to reduce the federal deficit

Supreme Court decisions regarding *search and seizure, freedom of the press, freedom of expression, surrogate parenting, executive privilege, separation of church and state*

Declining role of the United States in European affairs

Relevance or irrelevance of the vice-presidency

Success or failure of the president's economic program

U.S. effectiveness in dealing with foreign enemies

U.S. foreign policy (pro and con): *aid to Russia or China, the United States as "the world's policeman," accepting immigrants from third-world countries, building U.S. factories in other countries for cheap labor, responsibility in feeding the world's hungry, free trade agreements*

EDUCATION

Creative financing for a college education

Decline of the U.S. educational system

Eliminating the factory model of education

Defining and eliminating illiteracy

Public schools issues (pro and con): *mainstreaming students with special needs, mandating the learning of a foreign language, mandating year-around education, requiring high-schoolers to perform community service*

Performance stress among pre-schoolers

Prescriptive vs. non-prescriptive approaches to general education requirements for college

Reforming America's public schools

Differences between U.S. and Japanese educational systems
Future of fraternity and sorority systems
Impact of magnet schools on school districts
Television as a positive or negative force in education
Understanding learning disabilities

FAMILY ISSUES

Adoption: *alternative methods, adopting foreign children, bureaucratic difficulties, foster care, adoption scams*
Children divorcing parents
Coping with the sudden death of a family member
Famous and infamous families
Helping a family member with special needs
Making a will
No-fault divorce
Nursing homes for the elderly
Parents without partners
Positive and negative effects of a permissive upbringing
Family problems: *abuse, incest, alcoholism, dysfunctional family members, sibling rivalry, in-laws, parent-child jealousy*
pre-nuptial agreements
Preparing for a: *wedding, baby, formal dinner party, funeral, bar mitzvah*
Prison marriages
Effects of touch deprivation
Psychological bonding of twins
"Tough-love" programs
Unusual wedding ceremonies
Donating the organs or tissues of deceased babies for transplants

HEALTH

Advances in artificial-limb technology
Cross-species organ transplants
Curing: *infertility, cancer, diabetes, AIDS, multiple sclerosis*
Doctors who make house calls

Doctors' perspectives on national health insurance

Effectiveness of transplant procedures

Family therapy as a treatment for abuse or other problems

Health insurance for pets

In-home hospice care

Pro or con: Regulating caps on doctor and hospital fees

Limiting financial awards for malpractice

Low-cholesterol cooking

New treatments for mental illness

Tips for choosing a veterinarian

Advantages and disadvantages of cosmetic surgery

National crisis of nurse shortages

Comparative quality of health care in the United States

Transsexual surgery

Treatments for sexual dysfunctions

OCCUPATIONS

Working as a park warden in Hawaii's Volcano National Park

Coaching a football team

Creating cartoons

Constructing neon signs

Jobs generated by the high-technology revolution

Making movies

Managing stocks and bonds

Protecting the Alaskan wilderness

The history of: *skywriting, pro bowling, chimney sweeping, jousting, polo, wind-surfing, the Olympics, bungee-jumping, tennis*

Unusual occupations for women and men

Weather-forecasting

PERSONAL EXPERIENCE

Becoming a(n): *chef, skydiver, gymnast, cruise director, clogger, bagpiper, para-sailing expert, actress, ballet dancer, explorer of sunken ships, mountain climber, circus-animal trainer, woman priest, zookeeper*

Forgettable and unforgettable characters

Surviving: *isolation, loneliness, death of a loved one, illness, hunger, poverty, children, parents, addiction, crime, divorce, the military, stress, mothers-in-law, the family vacation, college*

Traveling to unusual places

SCIENCE AND TECHNOLOGY

Laser technology in medical science

How radio telescopes help astronomers

Hydroponic gardening as a solution to world hunger

New computer technologies

Availability of alternative low-cost fuels

Potential benefits from superconductor technology

Carbon-dating

Development of space-exploration plans

Impact of fiber-optic technology on the consumer

High-definition television

Positive and negative impacts of robotics

Possibility of developing "designer" genes

Status of research into fusion

Undersea exploration and colonization

Understanding the patterns of individual biorhythms

Index

Permissions and Acknowledgments

The poem "To Santa Claus, and little sisters" (page 221) is reproduced from *A Cry for Help*, by Mary Griffin, M. D., and Carol Felsenthal. Copyright © 1983 by Mary Griffin, M. D., and Carol Felsenthal. Used by permission of Doubleday, a division of Bantam Doubleday Dell Publishing Group, Inc.

The table "Negative Self-Centered Behaviors" (pages 433–434) is reproduced from Kenneth D. Benne and Paul Sheats, "Functional Roles of Group Members," *Journal of Social Issues*, Volume 4, Number 2, pp. 41–49.

Acknowledgments for, and permissions data on, speeches and articles reproduced within the text are given in the "Notes" section at the close of their respective chapters.

Line Art and Cartoons

The illustrations that open each of the five units of this book are reproduced from Stephen Calloway, general editor, *The Elements of Style: A Practical Encyclopedia of Interior Architectural Details from 1485 to the Present* (New York: Simon & Schuster, 1991). Copyright © 1991 by Mitchell Beazley Publishers. Illustrations copyright © 1991 by Mitchell Beazley Publishers. Reprinted by permission of Simon & Schuster, Inc.

Figure 1–1 (page 10) from Claude Shannon and Warren Weaver, *The Mathematical Theory of Communication*, © 1949 by the University of Illinois Press. Used by permission. "Doonesbury" cartoon (page 33) © 1988 by G. B. Trudeau. Reprinted with permission of Universal Press Syndicate. All rights reserved. Figure 4–1 (page 66) based upon copyrighted material of Dr. Lyman K. Steil, president, Communication Development, Inc., St. Paul, Minnesota, for the Sperry Corporation. Reprinted with permission of Dr. Steil and Sperry Corporation (now Unisys). "Gumdrop" cartoon (page 72) reprinted by permission of UFS, Inc. "Marvin" cartoon by Tom Armstrong (page 90) reprinted with special permission of North American Syndicate, Inc. Figure 12–3 (page 253) reprinted by permission of *The Wall Street Journal*, © Dow Jones & Company, Inc. All rights reserved worldwide. Figure 12–4 (page 254) copyright 1985 Time, Inc. Reprinted by permission. Figure 18–1 (page 401) used with permission of the *Carroll County Times*.

Photographs

Chapter 1: Opening photo (page 4) © Janice Fullman Photography/Picture Cube. Photo 1–1 (page 6) © Frank Siteman/Stock Boston. **Chapter 2:** Opening photo (page 24) © Walter Silver/Picture Cube. Photo 2–2 (page 31)